Praise for *Designing Large Language Model Applications*

Designing Large Language Model Applications is a masterclass in building advanced AI systems. It builds toward a powerful synthesis of advanced methods like tool use, reasoning, RAG, and fine-tuning, equipping readers to create the next generation of AI applications.

—*Jay Alammar, coauthor,* Hands-On Large Language Models

Designing Large Language Model Applications is a comprehensive tour of LLMs, offering lucid explanations of everything from fundamental concepts like prompting and fine-tuning to emerging trends like inference-time compute and reasoning. But, more importantly, readers will develop genuine intuition for how these models behave in practice. The hands-on exercises help to reinforce these intuitions in creative, engaging ways which makes this book not just an invaluable reference, but a way for software engineers, ML practitioners, and product managers to build up their own toolkit for developing practical applications with LLMs.

—*Megan Risdal, lead product manager, Kaggle (Google)*

Designing Large Language Model Applications is a complete, up-to-date guide on the concepts and techniques behind researching, designing, and building large language model applications. Drawing from his deep engineering and research experience, the author provides clear explanations and practical insights on topics across research and industry, enriched with valuable references to prior work and tooling. Thoughtfully crafted exercises help readers build intuition and experimental muscle.

A rare, well-curated book that covers all the important ideas and practical know-how that matter in the field.

—*Madhav Singhal, CEO, AutoComputer*

Suhas draws on his rich experience to guide the reader through a comprehensive overview of fundamentals and the newest battle-tested techniques. The timeliness of this practical book will be very useful for a whole new generation of LLM builders.

—Susan Shu Chang, principal data scientist, Elastic

Incredibly comprehensive!

—Nour Fahmy, Flagship RTL

Designing Large Language Model Applications

A Holistic Approach to LLMs

Suhas Pai

Designing Large Language Model Applications

by Suhas Pai

Published by O'Reilly Media, Inc., 1005 Gravenstein Highway North, Sebastopol, CA 95472.

O'Reilly books may be purchased for educational, business, or sales promotional use. Online editions are also available for most titles (*http://oreilly.com*). For more information, contact our corporate/institutional sales department: 800-998-9938 or *corporate@oreilly.com*.

Acquisitions Editor: Nicole Butterfield
Development Editor: Michele Cronin
Production Editor: Ashley Stussy
Copyeditor: Piper Content Partners
Proofreader: Emily Wydeven
Indexer: Potomac Indexing, LLC
Interior Designer: David Futato
Cover Designer: Karen Montgomery
Illustrator: Kate Dullea

March 2025: First Edition

Revision History for the First Edition

2025-03-06: First Release

See *http://oreilly.com/catalog/errata.csp?isbn=9781098150501* for release details.

This work is part of a collaboration between O'Reilly and Mission Cloud. See our statement of editorial independence (*https://oreil.ly/editorial-independence*).

978-1-098-15050-1

[LSI]

Table of Contents

Part II. Utilizing LLMs

Part III. LLM Application Paradigms

To The Legend, Kusuma Pai, for showing me how to dream

Preface

In the past few years, progress in the field of artificial intelligence has been occurring at breakneck speeds, spearheaded by advances in LLMs. It was not too long ago that LLMs were a nascent technology that struggled to generate a coherent paragraph; today they are able to solve complex mathematical problems, write convincing essays, and conduct long engaging conversations with humans.

As AI advances from strength to strength, it is rapidly being woven into the fabric of society, touching so many facets of our lives. Learning how to use AI models like LLMs effectively might be one of the most useful skills to learn this decade. LLMs are revolutionizing the world of software, and have made possible the development of applications previously considered impossible.

With all the promise that LLMs bring, the reality is that they are still not a mature technology and have many limitations like deficiencies in reasoning, lack of adherence to factuality, "hallucinations", difficulties in steering them toward our goals, bias and fairness issues, and so on. Despite the existence of these limitations, we can still harness LLMs for good use and build a variety of helpful applications provided we effectively address their shortcomings.

Plenty of software frameworks have emerged that enable rapid prototype development of LLM applications. However, advancing from prototypes to production-grade applications is a road much less traveled, and is still a very challenging task. This is where this book comes in—a holistic overview of the LLM landscape that provides you with the intuition and tools to build complex LLM applications.

With this book, my goal is to provide you with an intuitive understanding of how LLMs work, the tools you have at your disposal to harness them, and the various application paradigms they can be built with. Unique to this book are the exercises; more than 80 exercises are sprinkled throughout to help you solidify your intuitions and sharpen your understanding of what is happening underneath the hood. While preparing the content of the book, I read over 800 research papers, with many of them referenced and linked at appropriate locations in the book, providing you with a jumping off point for further exploration. All in all, I am confident that you will come out of the book an LLM expert if you read the book in its entirety, complete all the exercises, and explore the recommended references.

Who This Book Is For

This book is intended for a broad audience, including software engineers transitioning to AI application development, machine learning practitioners and scientists, and product managers. Much of the content in this book is borne from my own experiments with LLMs, so even if you are an experienced scientist, I expect you will find value in it. Similarly, even if you have very limited exposure to the world of AI, I expect you will still find the book useful for understanding the fundamentals of this technology.

The only prerequisites for this book are knowledge of Python coding and an understanding of basic machine learning and deep learning principles. Where required, I provide links to external resources that you can use to sharpen or develop your prerequisites.

How This Book Is Structured

The book is divided into 3 parts with a total of 13 chapters. The first part deals with understanding the ingredients of a language model. I strongly feel that even though you may never train a language model from scratch yourself, knowing what goes into making it is crucial. The second part discusses various ways to harness language models, be it by directly prompting the model, or by fine-tuning it in various ways. It also addresses limitations such as hallucinations and reasoning constraints, along with methods to mitigate these issues. Finally, the third part of the book deals with application paradigms like retrieval augmented generation (RAG) and agents, positioning LLMs within the broader context of an entire software system.

For an extended table of contents, see my Substack blog post (*https://oreil.ly/-2zkH*).

What This Book Is Not About

To keep the book at a reasonable length, certain topics were deemed out of scope. I have taken care to not cover topics that I am not confident will stand the test of time. This field is very fast moving, so writing a book that maintains its relevance over time is extremely challenging.

This book focuses only on English-language LLMs and leaves out discussion on multilingual models for the most part. I also disagree with the notion of mushing all the non-English languages of the world under the "multilingual" banner. Every language has its own nuances and deserves its own book.

This book also doesn't cover multimodal models. New models are increasingly multimodal, i.e., a single model supports multiple modalities like text, image, video, speech, etc. However, text remains the most important modality and is the binding substrate in these models. Thus, reading this book will still help you prepare for the multimodal future.

This book does not focus on theory or go too deep into math. There are plenty of other books that cover that, and I have generously linked to them where needed. This book contains minimal math equations and instead focuses on building intuitions.

This book contains only a rudimentary introduction to reasoning models, the latest LLM paradigm. At the time of the book's writing, reasoning models are still in their infancy, and the jury is still out on which techniques will prove to be most effective.

How to Read the Book

The best way to consume this book is to read it sequentially, while working on the exercises and exploring the reference links. That said, there are a few alternative paths, depending on your interests:

- If your interest lies in understanding the LLM landscape and not necessarily in building applications with them, you can focus on Chapters 1, 2, 3, 4, 5, 10, and 11.
- If you are a product manager seeking to understand the scope of possibilities for LLM applications, Chapters 1, 2, 3, 5, 8, 10, 11, 12, and 13 are a good bet.
- If you are an ML scientist, then Chapters 7, 8, 9, 10, 11, and 12 will be sure to give you food-for-thought and new research challenges.
- If you want to train your own LLM from scratch, Chapters 2, 3, 4, 5, and 7 will provide you with the foundational principles.

Conventions Used in This Book

The following typographical conventions are used in this book:

Italic
: Indicates new terms, URLs, email addresses, filenames, and file extensions.

`Constant width`
: Used for program listings, as well as within paragraphs to refer to program elements such as variable or function names, databases, data types, environment variables, statements, and keywords.

`Constant width bold`
: Shows commands or other text that should be typed literally by the user.

`Constant width italic`
: Shows text that should be replaced with user-supplied values or by values determined by context.

This element signifies a tip or suggestion.

This element signifies a general note.

This element indicates a warning or caution.

Using Code Examples

Supplemental material (code examples, exercises, etc.) is available for download at *https://oreil.ly/llm-playbooks*.

If you have a technical question or a problem using the code examples, please send email to *support@oreilly.com*.

This book is here to help you get your job done. In general, if example code is offered with this book, you may use it in your programs and documentation. You do not need to contact us for permission unless you're reproducing a significant portion of the code. For example, writing a program that uses several chunks of code from this book does not require permission. Selling or distributing examples from O'Reilly books does require permission. Answering a question by citing this book and quoting example code does not require permission. Incorporating a significant amount of example code from this book into your product's documentation does require permission.

We appreciate, but generally do not require, attribution. An attribution usually includes the title, author, publisher, and ISBN. For example: "*Designing Large Language Model Applications* by Suhas Pai (O'Reilly). Copyright 2025 Suhas Pai, 978-1-098-15050-1."

If you feel your use of code examples falls outside fair use or the permission given above, feel free to contact us at *permissions@oreilly.com*.

O'Reilly Online Learning

For more than 40 years, *O'Reilly Media* has provided technology and business training, knowledge, and insight to help companies succeed.

Our unique network of experts and innovators share their knowledge and expertise through books, articles, and our online learning platform. O'Reilly's online learning platform gives you on-demand access to live training courses, in-depth learning paths, interactive coding environments, and a vast collection of text and video from O'Reilly and 200+ other publishers. For more information, visit *https://oreilly.com*.

How to Contact Us

Please address comments and questions concerning this book to the publisher:

O'Reilly Media, Inc.
1005 Gravenstein Highway North
Sebastopol, CA 95472
800-889-8969 (in the United States or Canada)
707-827-7019 (international or local)
707-829-0104 (fax)
support@oreilly.com
https://oreilly.com/about/contact.html

We have a web page for this book, where we list errata, examples, and any additional information. You can access this page at *https://oreil.ly/designing-llm-applications-1e*.

For news and information about our books and courses, visit *https://oreilly.com*.

Find us on LinkedIn: *https://linkedin.com/company/oreilly-media*.

Watch us on YouTube: *https://youtube.com/oreillymedia*.

Acknowledgments

They say it takes a village to raise a child; I now realize it takes a metropolis to write a book.

Firstly, I would like to thank the O'Reilly team for the meticulous professionalism and finesse with which they worked with me throughout the development and launch of the book. No wonder they are the world's top technical book publishers. I would particularly like to thank Nicole Butterfield for signing me up as an author and Michele Cronin, the world's best editor, whose frequent reviews ensured that the book developed a coherent structure. I will miss our regular check-ins! Thanks to Ashley Stussy, Kristen Brown, and the rest of the production team for their diligent work in getting the book to production.

I am deeply thankful to my friend Amber Teng, who helped me with drawing the book illustrations and setting up the book's Github repository. I am also immensely indebted to my technical reviewers Serena McDonnell, Yenson Lau, Susan Shu Chang, Gordon Gibson, and Nour Fahmy for the dozens of hours each of them spent in writing extremely detailed and thoughtful technical reviews. The book is so much better for it.

I am thankful to the Toronto AI ecosystem, especially the Aggregate Intellect, TMLS (Toronto Machine Learning Summit), and SharpestMinds communities for providing me with the space to engage with the community and ensure that I always had a finger on the pulse of the industry. Special thanks go to my friends Madhav Singhal, Jay Alammar, and Megan Risdal (who helped me coin the phrase "token etymology") for our regular intellectually stimulating conversations on LLMs and for being the first readers of the book. I also want to give a shout out to my open-source collaborator Huu Nguyen, who I worked with on various open-source LLM projects, for the dozens of late night discussions on the most audacious ideas in LLM research.

Writing a book while also being the cofounder of an AI startup was possible only due to the unwavering support of my partner in business and crime, Kris Bennatti (who also convinced me to remove the word "orifice" from the book). I will forever be in gratitude to the entire Hudson Labs team for their steadfast and consistent backing throughout, with a special shout out to Xiao Quan, whose steady hands ensured that I found the time to focus on the book. Additionally, I would like to thank my friends Kaaveh Shoamanesh, Abdullah Al-hayali, Zach Nguyen, Samarth Bhasin, Sadegh Raeisi, and Ian Yu for their moral support throughout and regularly checking that I was getting the right amount of sleep.

Finally, I would like to dedicate this book to my mom, Kusuma Pai, whom I simply refer to as "The Legend" for her lifelong sacrifices to ensure that I grew up and was in a position to write the book. Any success of this book should be predominantly credited to my mother for molding me into the person I am today.

PART I

LLM Ingredients

We begin this book by introducing large language models (LLMs) and the key ingredients that go into making them. This includes understanding how training data is collected and prepared, examining the model's vocabulary, and exploring the architectures underpinning them.

CHAPTER 1
Introduction

AI is no longer the realm of science fiction novels and dystopian Hollywood movies. It is fast becoming an integral part of people's lives. Most of us interact with AI on a daily basis, often without even realizing it.

Current progress in AI has to a large extent been driven by advances in language modeling. Large language models (LLMs) represent one of the most significant technological advances in recent times, marking a new epoch in the world of tech. Similar inflection points in the past include the advent of the computer that ushered in the digital revolution, the birth of the internet and the World Wide Web that laid the foundation for a hyperconnected world, and the emergence of the smartphone that reshaped human communication. The ongoing AI revolution is poised to make a similar transformative impact.

LLMs belong to a class of models referred to as generative AI. The distinguishing factor is the ability of these models to generate responses to user queries, called *prompts*. Generative AI encompasses models that generate images, videos, speech, music, and of course text. While there is an increasing focus on bringing all these modalities together into a single model, in this book we will stick to language and LLMs.

In this chapter, we will introduce language models and define what makes a language model *large*. We will provide a brief history of LLMs, contextualizing their place within the field of natural language processing (NLP) and their evolution. We will highlight the impact LLMs are already having in the world and showcase key use cases, while discussing their strengths and limitations. We will also introduce LLM prompting and show how to interact with an LLM effectively, either through a user interface or through an API. Finally, we will end this chapter with a quick tutorial on building a *Chat with my PDF* chatbot prototype. We will then discuss the limitations of the prototype and the factors limiting its suitability for production use cases, thus setting the stage for the rest of the book.

Defining LLMs

A model is an approximation of a real-world concept or phenomenon. A faithful model will be able to make predictions about the concept it is approximating. A language model approximates human language and is built by training over a large body of text, thus imbuing it with various properties of language, including aspects of grammar (syntax) and meaning (semantics).

One way to train a language model is to teach it to predict the next token (this is equivalent to a word or a subword, but we will ignore this distinction for now) in a known text sequence. The model is trained over a large number of such sequences, and its *parameters* are updated iteratively such that it gets better at its predictions.

For example, consider the following text sequence appearing in a training dataset:

```
After a physical altercation with the patrons of a restaurant, Alex was feeling
extremely pleased with himself. He walked out with a swagger and confidence
that betrayed his insecurities. Smiling from ear to ear, he noticed rain drops
grazing his face and proceeded to walk toward the hostel.
```

and the language model predicts the next word that comes after "... and proceeded to walk toward the _"

There are a large number of valid continuations to this text sequence. It could be "building" or "shelter," but it could also be "embankment" or "catacomb." However, it is definitely not "the" or "is," because that would break the rules of the English language. After training on a sufficiently large body of text, the model learns that neither "the" nor "is" are valid continuations. Thus, you can see how a simple task like learning to predict the next word in a text sequence can lead the model to learning the grammar of the language in its parameters, as well as even more complex skills.

In practice, language models don't exactly output a single word or subword as the next token in a text sequence. They output a probability distribution over the entire vocabulary. (We will explore how this vocabulary is defined and constructed in Chapter 3). A well-trained model will have high probabilities for valid continuations and very low probabilities for invalid continuations.

Figure 1-1 describes the model training process in a nutshell. The output of the model prediction is a probability distribution over the entire vocabulary of the language. This is compared to the original sequence, and the parameters of the model are updated according to an algorithm so that it makes better predictions in the future. This is repeated over a very large dataset. We will describe the model training process in detail in the next three chapters.

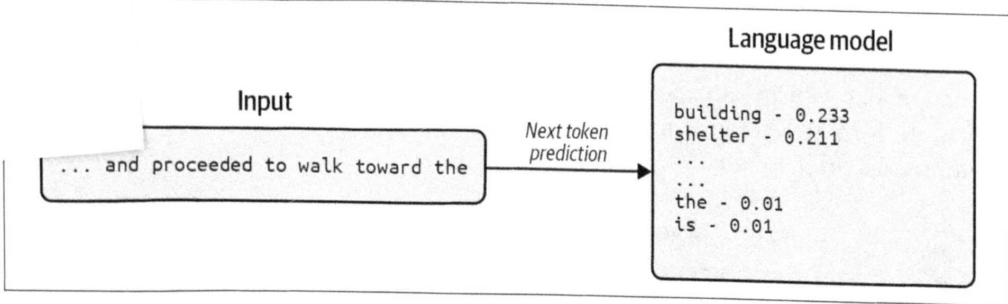

Figure 1-1. Model training using next token prediction

Is there a limit to what a model can learn from next-token prediction alone? This is a very important question that determines how powerful LLMs can eventually be. There is plenty of disagreement in the research community, with some researchers (*https://oreil.ly/sUAcl*) arguing next-token prediction is enough to achieve human-level intelligence in models, and others pointing out (*https://oreil.ly/7QG-l*) the shortfalls of this paradigm. We will come back to this question throughout the book, and especially in Chapter 8, where we will discuss skills like reasoning.

Modern-day language models are based on neural networks. Several types of neural network architectures are used to train LLMs, the most prominent being the Transformer. We will learn more about neural networks, Transformers, and other architectures in detail in Chapter 4.

Language models can be trained to model not just human languages but also programming languages like Python or Java. In fact, the Transformer architecture and the next-token prediction objective can be applied to sequences that are not languages in the traditional sense at all, such as representations of chess moves, DNA sequences, or airline schedules.

For example, Adam Karvonen trained Chess-GPT (*https://oreil.ly/oluZN*), a model trained only on chess games represented in portable game notation (PGN) strings. PGN strings for chess look like "1. e4 d5 2. exd5 Qxd5..." and so on. Even without providing the rules of the game explicitly, and just training the model to predict the next character in the PGN sequence, the model was able to learn the rules of the game including moves like castling, check, and checkmate; and it could even win chess games against experts. This shows the power of the next-token prediction objective and the Transformer architecture that forms the basis of the model. In Chapter 4, we will learn how to train our own Chess-GPT from scratch.

Another such example is the Geneformer (*https://oreil.ly/31DXq*), a model trained on millions of single-cell transcriptomes (representations of RNA molecules in a single cell), which can be used for making predictions in network biology, including disease progression, gene-dosage sensitivity, and therapeutic candidates.

Therefore, I encourage you to think beyond the realm of human language when brainstorming novel use cases for language models. If you have a concept or phenomenon that can be encoded in a discrete sequence using a finite vocabulary (we will more formally define vocabulary in Chapter 3), then we can potentially train a useful model on it.

Is there something special about the structure of language that makes it amenable to be modeled using the next-token prediction objective? Or is the word "language" in language models just a historical accident and any stream of tokens can be modeled using this paradigm? While this is still a topic of debate (*https://oreil.ly/nJiQW*) in the research community, directly modeling speech, video, etc. using this paradigm hasn't been as effective, perhaps showing that the discrete nature of text and the structure provided by language, be it a human language like English, a programming language like Python, or a domain-specific code like DNA sequences, is crucial to modeling success.

Around 2019, researchers realized that increasing the size of the language model (typically measured by the number of parameters) predictably improved performance, with no saturation point in sight. This led to Kaplan et al.'s work on LLM scaling laws (see the following sidebar), which derives a mathematical formula describing the relationship between the amount of computation (henceforth referred to as "compute") for training the model, the training dataset size, and the model size. Ever since then, companies and organizations have been training increasingly larger models.

Scaling Laws for Language Models

In early 2020, Kaplan et al. (*https://oreil.ly/29GZV*) from OpenAI published a study establishing the scaling laws of language models that ushered in the LLM era. They found a power-law relationship between the performance of the language model (measured by model loss; we will describe that in Chapter 4) and the size of the dataset used to train the model, the amount of compute used to train the model, and the size of the model itself, measured in terms of number of parameters. Simply put, the larger the model size, compute size, and amount of training data, the better the model.

More specifically, they found that for a fixed compute budget, increasing the size of the training dataset and the model in tandem improves the performance of the resulting LLM, but the dataset size needs to increase only by 1.8x for every 5.5x increase in model size to maintain an optimal level of performance. This is because larger models are more sample-efficient, meaning they need relatively fewer training examples to learn. Thus, models from that era mainly focused on increasing model sizes as much as possible.

However, in 2022, Hoffmann et al. (*https://oreil.ly/igLNZ*) from DeepMind pointed out that Kaplan et al. underestimated the impact of data size, resulting in language models from that era being significantly undertrained. They showed that to optimize performance of an LLM at a fixed compute budget (called compute-optimal), the training data size needs to increase at the same proportion as the model size. This led to the newer generation of models being trained on more data.

Note that both these scaling laws apply to compute-optimal LLMs, where you start with a fixed compute budget and ask, "What is the best LLM I can train with this budget?" But sometimes you are bottlenecked by other criteria, like the size of the model. Smaller models are faster to run and more energy efficient. In this case, one can significantly increase the training data size and continue seeing (albeit relatively smaller) performance gains, at the same model size. This is the trend driving more recent LLMs, especially in the open-source space.

There is no accepted convention about when a language model is considered "large." In fact, as the largest models get even larger, some models that would have been designated as LLMs only a couple of years ago are now termed small language models (SLMs). In this book, we will remain generous and continue to refer to all language models over a billion parameters as "large."

Another way in which a "large" language model differs from smaller ones is the emergent capabilities it possesses. First hypothesized by Wei et al. (*https://oreil.ly/RQfii*), emergent capabilities are those capabilities exhibited by larger models but not smaller ones.

According to this theory, for tasks that require these capabilities, the performance of smaller models is close to random. However, when the model size reaches a threshold, the performance suddenly starts to increase with size. Examples include multi-digit arithmetic operations, arithmetic and logical reasoning, etc. This also suggests that certain capabilities that are completely absent in current models could be exhibited by future larger models.

These thresholds are not absolute, and as we see more advances in language modeling, data quality improvements, etc., we can expect the thresholds to come down.

Schaeffer et al. (*https://oreil.ly/OXk6I*) claim that the sudden jump in performance for certain tasks at a particular model size threshold is just an artifact of the evaluation metrics used to judge performance. This happens because many metrics do not assign partial credit and only reward fully solving the task, so model improvements might not be tracked. On the other hand, one could argue that for tasks like multi-step arithmetic, getting the answer partially right is just as useless as getting it completely wrong.

The question of what abilities are emergent is still being explored in the research community. In Chapter 5, we will discuss its implications for selecting the right model for our desired use case.

Unfortunately the phrase "emergent properties" has multiple meanings in the literature. In some papers, the phrase is used to describe those capabilities that the model is not explicitly trained for. In this book, we will stick to Wei et al.'s definition (*https://oreil.ly/bkVoj*).

To understand how current LLMs came to be, it is instructive to walk through a brief history of them. As more historical details are out of scope for the book, we will provide links to external resources for further reading throughout the section.

A Brief History of LLMs

To present the history of LLMs, we need to start from the history of NLP, the field that LLMs originated from. For a more detailed history of NLP, refer to Daniel Jurafsky's seminal book, *Speech and Language Processing*, 2nd edition (*https://oreil.ly/zzU9R*).

Early Years

The field traces its origins to the 1950s, driven by demand for *machine translation*, the task of automatically translating from one language to another. The early days were dominated by symbolic approaches; these were rule-based algorithms based on linguistic theories (*https://oreil.ly/ELKSe*) influenced by the works of linguists like Noam Chomsky.

In the mid-1960s, Joseph Weizenbaum released ELIZA, a chatbot program that applied pattern matching using regular expressions (*https://oreil.ly/rIAWY*) on the user's input and selected response templates to generate an output. ELIZA consisted of several scripts, the most famous one being DOCTOR, that simulated a psychotherapist. This variant would respond by rephrasing the user's input in the form of a question, similar to how a therapist would. The rephrasing was performed by filling in predefined templates with pattern-matched words from the input.

As an example:

```
User: 'I am not feeling well'

ELIZA: 'Do you believe it is normal to be not feeling well?'
```

You can try chatting with ELIZA online (*https://oreil.ly/5g0e_*). Even in the era of ChatGPT, ELIZA can hold a somewhat convincing conversation, despite the fact that it is just rules-based.

Exercise

Read through the classic paper (*https://oreil.ly/MkKmC*) by Weizenbaum introducing ELIZA. In general, I recommend developing a habit of reading papers from yesteryears, as they are a good source of inspiration. Ideas get recycled all the time, and infeasible ideas from the past become feasible today due to advances in technology.

Additionally, go through the code for the Python implementation (*https://oreil.ly/Y1pSc*) of ELIZA by Wade Brainerd to understand how powerful carefully constructed rule-based systems can be. Even in the era of LLMs, you should not shy away from using rule-based approaches for your language tasks where it makes sense!

Rule-based systems are brittle, hard to construct, and a maintenance nightmare. As the decades rolled by, the limitations of symbolic approaches became more and more evident, and the relative effectiveness of statistical approaches ensured that they became more commonplace. NLP researcher Frederick Jelinek (*https://oreil.ly/AmtvE*) famously quipped, "Every time I fire a linguist, the performance of the speech recognizer goes up."

Machine learning–based approaches became more widely used in the 1990s and 2000s. Traditional machine learning relied on human-driven feature engineering and feature selection, the process of identifying features (characteristics of the input) that are predictive to solve a task. These features could be statistical, like the average word length, or linguistic, like parts of speech. To learn more about traditional statistical NLP, I recommend reading Christopher Manning's book, *Foundations of Statistical Natural Language Processing* (*https://oreil.ly/MIC70*).

The relevance of linguistics to modern-day NLP application development is a point of debate. Many university courses on NLP have completely dropped content related to linguistics. Even though I don't directly use linguistics in my work, I find that I rely on them to develop intuitions about model behavior more than I expect. As such, I recommend Emily Bender's books on syntax (*https://oreil.ly/hWR8S*) and semantics (*https://oreil.ly/7liiS*) to understand the basics of this field.

The 2010s saw the advent of deep learning and its widespread impact on NLP. Deep learning is characterized by multi-layer neural network models that learn informative features by themselves given only raw input, thus removing the need for cumbersome feature engineering. Deep learning forms the foundation for modern NLP and LLMs. To dig deeper into the principles of deep learning and neural networks, I recommend Goodfellow et al.'s book (*https://oreil.ly/0gv0D*). For more hands-on deep learning training, I recommend Zhang et al.'s *Dive into Deep Learning* (*https://oreil.ly/YN_3Y*).

During the early years of deep learning, it was customary to construct a task-specific architecture to solve each task. Some of the types of neural network architectures used include multi-layer perceptrons, convolutional neural networks, recurrent neural networks, and recursive neural networks. To learn more about this era of NLP, I recommend *Neural Network Methods for Natural Language Processing* (*https://oreil.ly/MCOp4*) by Yoav Goldberg (Springer Cham).

The Modern LLM Era

In 2017, the Transformer architecture (*https://oreil.ly/AAuvL*) was invented, quickly followed by the invention of efficient *transfer learning* techniques pioneered by Howard et al. (*https://oreil.ly/E15Yn*) among others and Transformer-based language models like BERT (*https://oreil.ly/-Yhwz*). These advances removed the need for constructing complex task-specific architectures. Instead, one could use the same Transformer model to train a variety of tasks. This new paradigm divided the training step into two stages: *pre-training* and *fine-tuning*. An initial large-scale pre-training step initialized the Transformer model with general language capabilities. Subsequently, the pre-trained model could be trained on more concrete tasks, like information extraction or sentiment detection, using a process called fine-tuning. We will cover fine-tuning extensively throughout the book.

While academia and open-source collectives have made crucial and critical contributions to language modeling, large tech companies like OpenAI, Google, Meta, and Anthropic have taken the lead in training and releasing progressively larger LLMs. OpenAI in particular has played a pioneering role in advancing language modeling technology. The trajectory of the evolution of LLMs in the modern era can be traced through the advances ushered in by each version of the GPT (Generative Pre-trained Transformer) family of models trained by OpenAI:

GPT-1 (https://oreil.ly/dFPSE)
: This version demonstrated unsupervised pre-training on large-scale data, followed by task-specific supervised fine-tuning.

GPT-2 (https://oreil.ly/JL-VO)
: This version was one of the first models to be trained on large-scale web data. This version also marked the rise of natural language prompting as a means of interacting with a language model. It showed that pre-trained models could solve a variety of tasks *zero-shot* (solving a task without needing any examples) without any task-specific fine-tuning. We will discuss zero-shot and prompting in detail later in this chapter.

GPT-3 (https://oreil.ly/lIwad)
: Inspired by the scaling laws, this model is a hundred times larger than GPT-2 and popularized in-context/few-shot learning, where the model is fed with a few examples on how to solve a given task in the prompt, without needing to fine-tune the model. We will learn more about few-shot learning later in this chapter.

GPT-4 (https://oreil.ly/gY1HL)
: A key aspect of this release is the *alignment training* used to make the model more controllable and adhere to the principles and values of the model trainer. We will learn about alignment training in Chapter 8.

o1 (https://oreil.ly/XJSMN)
: This is a new family of models released by OpenAI that focuses on improving reasoning capabilities. This is one of the first models to focus on scaling inference-time computation. We will discuss more about inference-time computation in Chapter 8.

> **Exercise**
>
> Read each of the GPT papers in order. It is OK if you do not understand some of the terminology or principles, as we will cover them throughout the course of the book. After finishing the first two parts of the book, read the papers again for a more enhanced understanding.

You might have noticed a trend here: through the years, the field has been experiencing a consolidation effect, with more and more parts of the NLP task pipeline being performed *end-to-end*, i.e., by a single model. Throughout this book, we will point out the consolidation effect where it is apparent and discuss its implications for the future of LLMs.

A history of LLMs wouldn't be complete without mentioning the impact of open source contributions to this field. Open source models, datasets, model architectures, and various developer libraries and tools have all had significant impacts on the development of this field. This book places a special importance on open source, providing a thorough survey of the open source LLM landscape and showcasing many open source models and datasets.

Next, let's explore how LLMs are being adopted and their impact on society so far.

The Impact of LLMs

The tech world has long been susceptible to hype cycles, with exhilarating booms and depressing busts. More recently, we have witnessed the crypto/blockchain and Web3 booms, both of which have yet to live up to their promises. Is AI heading toward a similar fate? We have hard evidence that it is not.

At my company Hudson Labs, we analyzed discussions (*https://oreil.ly/_mTAs*) in the quarterly earnings calls of the 4,000 largest publicly listed companies in the United States to track adoption of crypto, Web3, and AI in the enterprise.

We observed that 85 companies discussed Web3 in their earnings calls, with even fewer tangibly working on it. Crypto fared better, with 313 companies discussing it. Meanwhile, LLMs were discussed and adopted by 2,195 companies, meaning that at least 50% of America's largest public companies are using LLMs to drive value, and it is strategically so important to them to merit discussion in their quarterly earnings call. Effective or not, LLM adoption in the enterprise is already a reality.

Figure 1-2 shows the number of companies discussing Web3 in their earnings calls over time. As you can see, the Web3 hype seems to be tapering off.

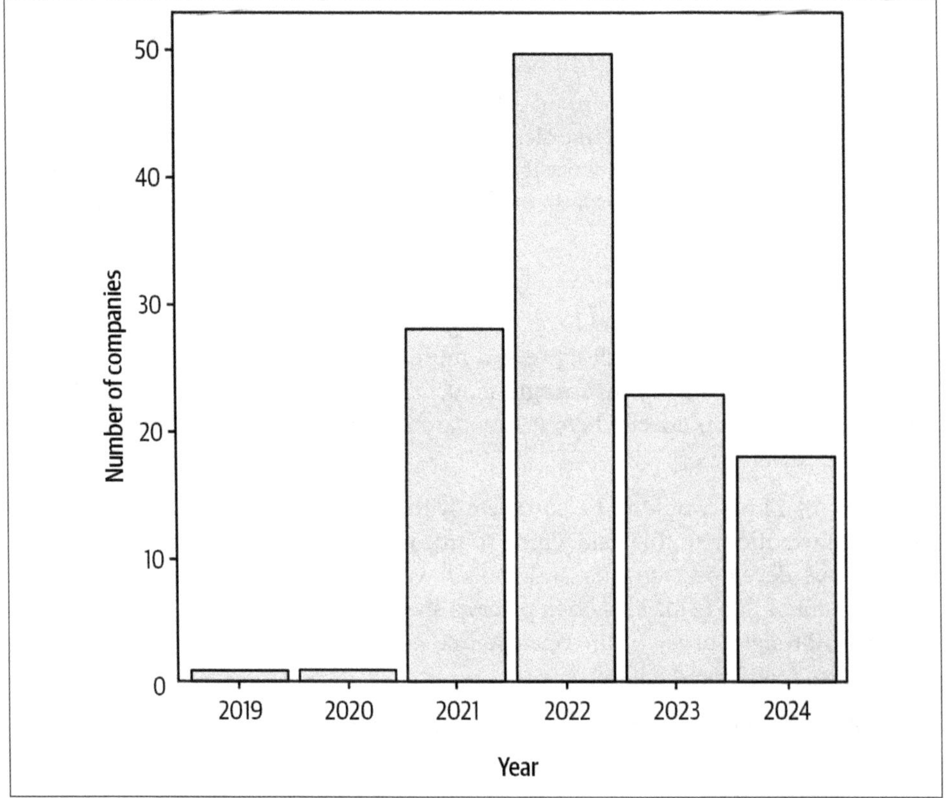

Figure 1-2. Companies that discussed Web3 in their earnings calls across time

Similarly, Figure 1-3 shows the number of companies discussing crypto/blockchain in their earnings calls over time. As you can see, only 5% of companies discussed crypto at its peak.

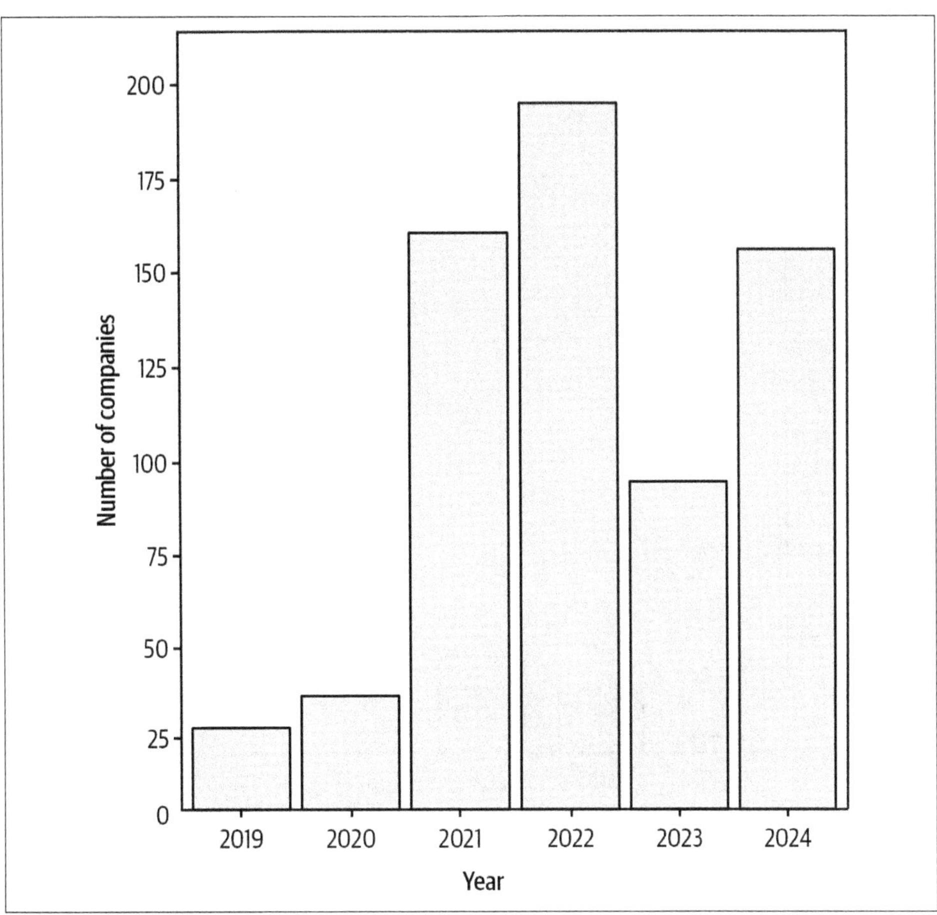

Figure 1-3. Companies that discussed crypto/blockchain in their earnings calls across time

Finally, let's look at AI. As mentioned before, AI has reached levels of adoption in the enterprise that no other recent technology trend has managed in the recent past. The trend is only accelerating, as shown in Figure 1-4, which shows the number of companies that were asked questions about AI by analysts during their earnings calls in just the first two months of the year. The sharp spike in 2024 shows no sign of abating.

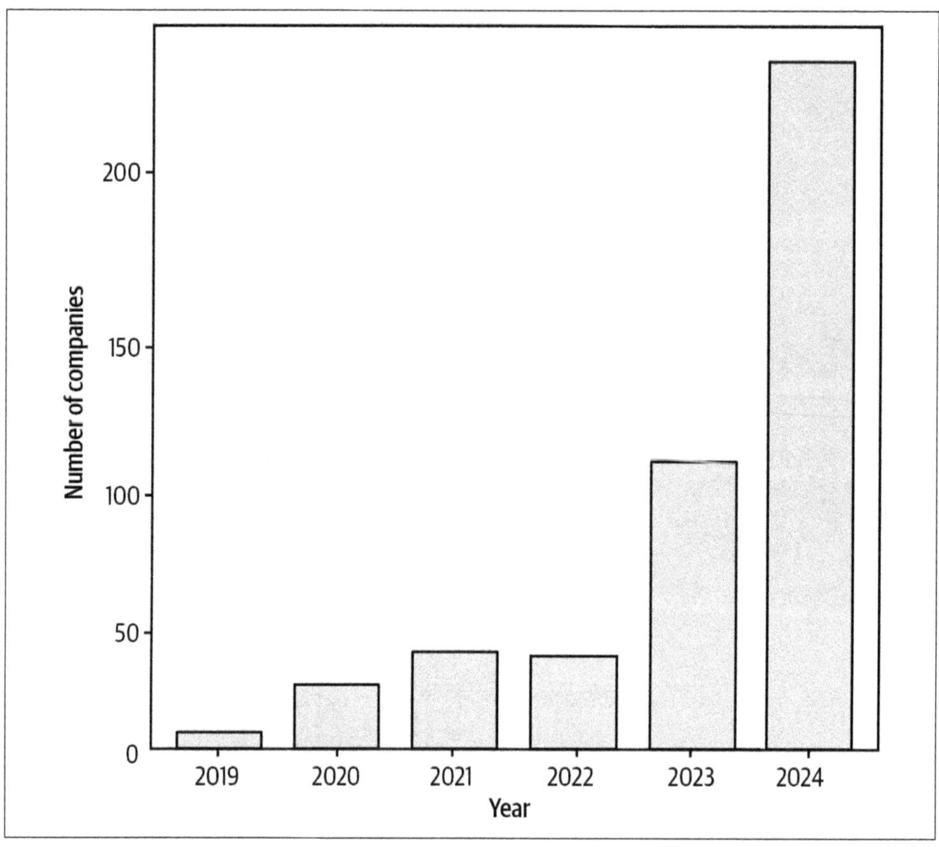

Figure 1-4. Companies that were asked questions about AI in their earnings calls during the first two months of the year

Note that these statistics only include generative AI/LLM adoption and not data science/data analytics, whose adoption is even more ubiquitous in the enterprise. AI adoption is also not limited to tech companies, with companies ranging from real estate companies to insurance firms joining in on the fun.

LLM Usage in the Enterprise

From the same analysis, we observed the key ways in which LLMs are used in the enterprise:

Employee productivity
: The primary means by which employee productivity has improved through LLM usage is with coding assistants like GitHub Copilot. LLMs are also widely used to help draft marketing and promotional text and automate marketing campaigns. In fact, the first major LLM commercial success stories were marketing startups

like Jasper AI (*https://oreil.ly/Byw26*) and Copy.ai (*https://oreil.ly/QmhJC*). Another key LLM-driven productivity enhancement is question-answering assistants over a company's extensive knowledge base drawn from heterogeneous data sources.

Report generation
: These include summarizing documents, completing mundane paperwork, and even drafting contracts. Summarization use cases include summarizing financial reports, research papers, or even meeting minutes from audio or call transcripts.

Chatbots
: LLM-driven chatbots increasingly are being deployed as customer service agents. They are also being used as an interface to a company's documentation or product page.

Information extraction and sequence tagging
: Over the years, a large number of enterprises have developed complex NLP pipelines for language processing tasks. Many of these pipelines are being fully or partially replaced by LLMs. These pipelines are used to solve common NLP tasks like sentiment analysis, information extraction tasks like entity extraction and relation extraction, and sequence tagging tasks like named entity recognition (NER). For a detailed list of NLP tasks and their descriptions, see Fabio Chiusano's blog (*https://oreil.ly/_11rN*).

Translation
: Translation tasks include translating text from one language to another as well as tasks where text is converted to a different form but in the same language, for example, converting informal text to formal text, abusive text to polite text and so on. Real-time translation apps like Erudite's Instant Voice Translate promise (*https://oreil.ly/xxENs*) to make embarrassing language-barrier moments for tourists a thing of the past.

Workflows
: LLMs are gradually being used to facilitate workflow automation, where a sequence of tasks can be performed by LLM-driven software systems, called agents. Agents can interact with their environment (search and retrieve data, run code, connect to other systems) and potentially operate autonomously. We will more formally define agents and explore how to build them in Chapter 10.

Effect of LLMs on the Job Market

Our analysis of earnings calls also pointed out a concerning trend: companies are already treating LLMs and AI in general as cost-saving measures. Indeed, several companies (*https://oreil.ly/Ba495*) have already explicitly stated that they have reduced their workforce after seeing efficiency improvements using AI.

For instance, Klarna, a Swedish fintech company, announced (*https://oreil.ly/-Ui33*) that its AI assistant is handling two-thirds of its customer support cases, the workload of 700 human agents.

The rapid adoption of LLMs at scale does not necessarily mean that they are better than humans at their tasks. In cases where LLMs are completely replacing humans and not just augmenting them, they may be deployed even if they perform worse than humans, just because of the resulting cost savings. This premature deployment of AI technologies can potentially lead to worse customer satisfaction in the long run.

On the other hand, LLMs have vastly lowered the barrier for software development, thus leading to more digitalization and enabling a lot more people to develop software.

Prompting

Now that we have our fundamentals in place, let's begin learning how to effectively use LLMs.

The process by which you interact with an LLM is called prompting. Even though some companies attempt to anthropomorphize LLMs by giving them a name or a persona, it is good to remember that when you are interacting with an LLM, you are *prompting* them and not chatting with them as you would with a human being. Remember that LLMs are next-word predictors. This means that the text they generate is heavily dependent on the text they are fed, which includes the input (called the *prompt*) and the output tokens generated so far by the model. This is collectively called the *context*.

By feeding the LLM the right text in the context, you are priming it to generate the type of output you need. The ideal prompt would be the answer to this question: "What would be the best prefix of N tokens that, when fed to an LLM, will lead it to generate the correct answer with the highest probability?"

As of the book's writing, language models simply aren't smart enough for you to prompt a model exactly the way you would speak to a human and expect best results. As language models get better over time, prompts can become more like human conversation. Those of you who remember the early days of search engines might recall that effectively using a search engine by entering the right form of queries was seen as a skill that is not trivial to acquire, but as search engines got better, search queries could become more free-form.

When I started writing this book, I solicited opinions from the target readership on the topics they would like covered. I received the most requests for the topic of prompting, with practitioners wanting to understand how to effectively create prompts for their specific use cases.

Prompting is an important aspect of modern-day LLMs. In fact, you will probably end up spending a significant amount of your time on any LLM-based project iterating on prompts, very inaccurately referred to as *prompt engineering*.

There have been attempts to automatically optimize prompts, like automatic prompt optimization (APO) (*https://oreil.ly/SekPA*) and AutoPrompt (*https://oreil.ly/upVKC*). We will discuss this further in Chapter 13.

It is important to manage one's expectations about the effectiveness of prompt engineering. Prompts aren't magical incantations that unlock hidden LLM capabilities. It is very unlikely that there are companies with a significant advantage over others just by using a superior prompting technique unknown to others. On the flip side, not following basic prompting principles can severely hamper the performance of your LLM.

Umpteen prompting tutorials are available online. I recommend Learn Prompting's prompting guide (*https://oreil.ly/CQrzi*) in particular. You do not need to know all the prompting techniques to become well-versed in prompting. Most of what you need to know about prompting can be learned in a couple of hours. What matters more is interacting with the LLMs you use frequently to observe their outputs and developing intuition about their behavior.

If you have programming experience, I suggest viewing prompting through the lens of programming. In programming, instructions need to be explicit with no room for ambiguity. The challenge with prompting is that it is done in natural language, which is inherently ambiguous. Still, the best prompts state instructions that are explicit, detailed, and structured, leaving very little room for ambiguity. We will learn more prompting nuances in Chapters 5 and 13.

A fun fact: language models are insensitive to word order. This property has been observed (*https://oreil.ly/gtDFg*) even in earlier models (*https://oreil.ly/qI_IZ*) like BERT. For example, ask ChatGPT or your favorite LLM provider the question "How do I tie my shoelaces?" in jumbled form, say "shoe tie my I how do laces?" ChatGPT responds with "Certainly! Here are step-by-step instructions on how to tie your shoelaces:..." as if you asked a straightforward question.

Next, let's discuss a few prompting modes.

Zero-Shot Prompting

This is the standard approach to prompting, where you provide the LLM with an instruction and, optionally, some input text. The term *zero-shot* refers to the fact that no examples or demonstrations are provided on how to solve the task.

Consider an example where your task is to assess the sentiment expressed in a restaurant review. To achieve this through zero-shot prompting, you can issue the following prompt:

> *Prompt:* Classify the given passage according to its sentiment. The output can be one of Positive, Negative, Neutral.
>
> Passage: "The mashed potatoes took me back to my childhood school meals. I was so looking forward to having them again. NOT!"
>
> Sentiment:

A good zero-shot prompt will:

- Provide the instruction in a precise and explicit manner.
- Describe the output space or the range of acceptable outputs and output format. In this example, we state the output should be one of three values.
- Prime it to generate the correct text. By ending the prompt with "Sentiment:," we are increasing the probability of the LLM generating the sentiment value as the next token.

The better the model, the less you have to worry about getting these things right.

In real-world settings, your output format needs to be highly controllable in order for it to fit in automated systems. We will discuss more techniques for ensuring controllability of outputs in Chapter 5.

Prompts are sensitive to model changes. You might painstakingly construct a prompt that seems to work well, but you might notice that the same prompt does not work for a different model. In fact, the same prompt might see degraded performance on the same API endpoint if the underlying model is updated in the meanwhile. We call this *prompt drift*. It is a good idea to version control prompts.

Few-Shot Prompting

In our example for zero-shot prompting, the LLM was able to solve the task without explaining it how to solve it. This is because the task is simple and clearly defined. In many cases, the tasks might be not so easy to describe in natural language. We can then add some examples in our prompt consisting of either outputs or input-output pairs. While this is called few-shot learning colloquially, the language model is not updated in any way through this prompting technique.

Here is an example of few-shot prompting:

> *Prompt:* A palindrome is a word that has the same letters when spelled left to right or right to left.
> Examples of words that are palindromes: kayak, civic, madam, radar
> Examples of words that are not palindromes: kayla, civil, merge, moment
> Answer the question with either *Yes* or *No*
> Is the word *rominmor* a palindrome?
> Answer:

Chain-of-Thought Prompting

If you are going to learn only one prompting technique, let that be chain-of-thought (CoT) prompting, because it is one of the most impactful prompting techniques in existence.

As discussed earlier, the context of the LLM determines the next token it predicts. Therefore, we need to optimize the content in the context (the user prompt + output tokens generated so far) to maximize the probability of the LLM generating the correct future tokens. One way to do this is to prompt the LLM to *think* before generating. This elicits the LLM to generate the process to get to the answer instead of directly generating the answer. This might involve breaking the input task into subtasks and solving them one after the other.

When the LLM is eventually at the cusp of generating the answer, it can rely on a more relevant context that increases its probability of generating the right answer.

Consider this example:

> *Prompt:* Solve the equation. 34 + 44 + 3 * 23 / 3 * 2. Think step by step.

After receiving the instruction "Think step by step," the LLM then breaks down the problem and solves each step sequentially:

```
Given equation:

34 + 44 + 3 * 23 / 3 * 2

First, perform multiplication and division from left to right:

= 34 + 44 + (3 * 23 / 3 * 2)
= 34 + 44 + (69 / 3 * 2)
= 34 + 44 + (23 * 2)
= 34 + 44 + 46
```

```
Now, perform addition:

= 78 + 46

Finally, complete the addition:

= 124

So, the solution to the equation is 124.
```

Many LLMs solve tasks step-by-step without being explicitly prompted to do so. This is because they have been *instruction-tuned* to solve tasks that way. We will learn more about instruction-tuning in Chapters 5 and 6. LLMs that have been instruction-tuned are easier to prompt.

In the case of LLMs accessible through a user interface, a hidden prompt (called a system prompt) by the LLM provider might apply CoT prompting to relevant user prompts.

Should we add the "think step-by-step" CoT instruction for every prompt, like a cheat code to a game? Sprague et al. (*https://oreil.ly/3zJDC*) evaluated CoT prompting over a wide variety of tasks and found that CoT primarily helps with tasks that need mathematical or logical reasoning. For tasks involving common-sense reasoning, they found that gains by CoT are limited. For knowledge-based tasks, CoT might even hurt.

Note that arithmetic and logical reasoning could also be performed by delegating them to external tools like symbolic solvers and code interpreters. We will discuss this in detail in Chapter 10.

Using CoT prompting significantly increases the number of tokens generated by the model to solve a task, leading to higher costs.

Prompt Chaining

Often, your tasks need multiple steps and a large number of instructions. One way to go about this is by stuffing all the instructions into a single prompt. An alternative is to break the task into multiple subtasks and chain the prompts such that the output of one prompt determines the input to another. I have observed that prompt chaining consistently performs better than managing the entire task through a single prompt.

As an example, consider the task of extracting information from the text provided in a form and formatting the output in a structured manner. If there are missing or outlier values, then some special postprocessing rules are to be applied. In this case, it is good practice to split the task into two prompts, with the initial prompt performing the information extraction and the second prompt handling the postprocessing of the extracted information.

Adversarial Prompting

You might notice that, for some queries, the LLM declines to execute your request. This is because it has been specifically trained to refuse certain kinds of requests (We will learn how to achieve this behavior in Chapter 8). This kind of training, which we will call *alignment training*, is imparted to the model to align it with the values and preferences of the entity developing the model.

For example, asking any decent LLM directly for instructions to build a bomb will result in a refusal. However, as of today, alignment training provides only a weak layer of security, as it can be bypassed by cleverly prompting the LLM, called *adversarial prompting*. Adversarial prompts can be generated either manually or using algorithms. These cleverly phrased prompts trick the LLM into generating a response even if it was trained not to.

These clever prompting schemes are not just useful for illicit purposes. In many cases, the LLM simply does not respond the way you want it to, and clever prompting schemes might help. These clever prompting schemes range from asking the LLM to adopt a specific persona to outright emotional blackmail ("If you don't respond correctly to this query, many children will suffer!"). While there has been some work (*https://oreil.ly/q1I_7*) showing that adding emotion to a prompt may lead to better performance, there is no hard, sustained evidence that this is universally effective for a given model. Thus, I would not recommend using these in production applications.

Exercise

Gandalf (*https://oreil.ly/3R3fz*) is a prompting game by Lakera AI (*https://oreil.ly/L3rLx*), an AI security company, that showcases LLM vulnerabilities to adversarial prompts. In this game, the LLM has been given a password, and at each level you will have to extract it using the given clues/instructions. This game helps you learn to construct prompts cleverly and build intuition about LLM vulnerabilities. Try advancing to the final level!

Additionally, you can try techniques explained in Li et al.'s paper (*https://oreil.ly/e2U7S*) for providing emotional stimuli to the LLM to improve its performance. Specifically, try these techniques for queries about explanations of physical phenomena: "Why can't you melt an egg?" Do you see any noticeable improvements?

An interesting tidbit: I once organized an adversarial prompting competition at a social event. Interestingly, people with nontechnical backgrounds performed better than LLM experts at subverting the model with clever prompts!

Accessing LLMs Through an API

You most likely have already interacted with an LLM through a chat interface like ChatGPT, Gemini, or Claude. Let's now explore how to access them using the API. We will use the OpenAI API as an example to access its GPT family of models. Most other proprietary models expose similar parameters through their API.

GPT-4o mini and GPT-4o can be accessed through OpenAI's Chat Completion API. Here is an example:

```
import os
import openai
openai.api_key = <INSERT YOUR KEY HERE>

output = openai.ChatCompletion.create(
  model="gpt-4o-mini",
  messages=[
    {"role": "system", "content": "You are an expert storywriter."},
    {"role": "user", "content": "Write me a short children's story
    about a dog and an elephant stopping
    being friends with each other."}
  ]
)

print(output.choices[0].message)
```

Roles can be system, user, assistant, or tool.

- The system role is used to specify an overarching prompt.
- The user role refers to user inputs.
- The assistant role refers to the model responses.
- The tool role is used to interact with external software tools.

We will discuss tools in more detail in Chapter 10.

What is the difference between the system and user roles? Which instructions should go into the system prompt and which ones into the user prompt? System prompts are used for dictating the high-level overarching behavior of an LLM, like "You are a financial expert well versed in writing formal reports." If you are allowing your users to directly interact with the LLM, then the system prompt can be used to provide your own instruction to the LLM along with the user request. My experiments have shown that it doesn't matter much if you place your instructions in the system prompt versus user prompt. What does matter is the length and number of instructions. LLMs typically can handle only a few instructions at a time. Instructions at the end or the beginning of the prompt are more likely to be adhered to.

Here are some of the parameters made available by OpenAI:

`n`
: The number of completions the model has to generate for each input. For example, if we used n = 5 in the given example, it would generate five different children's stories.

For tasks with high reliability requirements, I advise generating multiple completions, that is, n > 1 and then using a postprocessing function (which could involve an LLM call) to choose the best one. This is because the LLM samples the generated text from a probability distribution, and in some cases the answer might be wrong/bad just due to an unlucky token sampling. You might have to balance this process against your budget limitations.

`stop` *and* `max_completion_tokens`
: Used to limit the length of the generated output. `stop` allows you to specify end tokens that, if generated, would stop the generation process. An example stop sequence is the newline token. If you ask the model to adhere to a particular output format, like a numbered list of sentences, then to stop generating after a particular number of sentences have been output, you can just provide the final number as a stop parameter.

`presence_penalty` *and* `frequency_penalty`
: Used to limit the repetitiveness of the generated output. By penalizing the probability for tokens that have already appeared in the output, we can ensure that the model isn't being too repetitive. These parameters can be used while performing more creative tasks.

`logit_bias`
: Using `logit_bias`, we can specify the tokens whose generation probability we want to increase or decrease.

`top_p` *and* `temperature`
: Both parameters relate to decoding strategies. LLMs produce a distribution of token probabilities and will sample from this distribution to generate the next token. There are many strategies to choose the next token to generate given the token probability distribution. We will discuss them in detail in Chapter 5. For now, just remember that a higher temperature setting results in more creative and diverse outputs, and a lower temperature setting results in more predictable outputs. This cheat sheet (*https://oreil.ly/DAa66*) provides some recommended values for various use cases.

`logprobs`
: Provides the most probable tokens for each output token along with their log probabilities. OpenAI limits this to the top 20 most probable tokens. In later chapters, we will discuss how we can leverage `logprobs` information in various forms.

> **Exercise**
>
> Using the OpenAI API, provide the model with some sample live commentary from the Real Madrid versus Barcelona soccer game (*https://oreil.ly/NRwIb*). Replace them with your own teams if you like. Ask the model to generate the rest of the commentary. Adapt your prompts, `temperature`, `logit_bias`, `presence_penalty`, and `frequency_penalty`, and see if you can replicate the tone of the commentators. How far off is the LLM-generated text from the actual commentators?

Strengths and Limitations of LLMs

Developing intuition about the strengths and limitations of LLMs is a crucial skill in being able to build useful LLM applications. Using the information in this book, and with ample hands-on practice, you will be able to build that intuition. In general, LLMs are proficient at language tasks. You will almost never see them make spelling or grammar errors. They are a vast improvement over previous techniques for understanding user instructions and intent. They also exhibit state-of-the-art performance on most NLP tasks like entity and relationship extraction and NER. And they are particularly strong at generating code, which is where LLMs have arguably found their greatest success through tools like GitHub Copilot (*https://oreil.ly/qvriE*).

Most LLM limitations boil down to the fact that LLMs are just not intelligent enough. Even state-of-the-art models suffer from significant limitations in reasoning, including arithmetic reasoning, logical reasoning, and common-sense reasoning. (We will define reasoning more formally in Chapter 8.) LLMs are also unable to adhere to factuality, because of their lack of connection to the real world. Therefore, they tend to generate text that might be inconsistent with real-world facts and principles, colloquially called *hallucinations*. Hallucinations are the bane of LLMs and one of the key reasons for hesitations in adopting them. In Chapter 8, we will dive deep into various methods to tackle hallucinations and address reasoning limitations.

Tons of LLM-generated articles are being uploaded to the web daily, and many of them make their way to the top of search engine results. For example, for a short while, for the query "Can you melt eggs?", Google showed (*https://oreil.ly/ivvv_*) "Yes, an egg can be melted," due to an AI-generated web page containing the incorrect answer. This kind of text is colloquially referred to as AI slop. Thus, there is a very strong incentive for search engines to accurately detect AI-generated text. Note that since LLMs are primarily trained on web text, future LLMs can be contaminated by polluted text as well.

While LLMs are frequently used to aid creative tasks, they are nowhere near the level of professional authors. Fiction authored by current LLMs is still unlikely to be a bestseller. LLM-generated text lacks the sheer ingenuity and the ability to evoke human emotions that human authors possess. Once you have read through enough LLM-generated text, it is not that difficult to spot it.

Pushing the Limits of LLM Capabilities

While the list of tasks that LLMs cannot do is decreasing, some capabilities like self-reference still seem out of reach.

In his book *I Am a Strange Loop* (*https://oreil.ly/uttDL*), Douglas Hofstadter claims self-reference capabilities as a measure of higher-order intelligence or even consciousness. An example of a self-referential statement is, "The penultimate word in this sentence is is."

Thrush et al. (*https://oreil.ly/rHQH1*) released a dataset called "I am a strange dataset" (*https://oreil.ly/3hX9w*) that contains a set of such meta-linguistic questions. Try this question with a variety of models and see if they get it right:

> This this is is a a new new form form of of poetry poetry where where every every word word is is repeated. Are any words not repeated?

As of this book's writing, no model, including OpenAI's o1, is able to get this question right; it fails to note that the last word is not repeated.

Every LLM generates text with a distinct signature, some more apparent to humans than others. For example, you might have noticed that ChatGPT tends to overuse certain words like "delve," "tapestry," "bustling," etc. ChatGPT also tends to generate sentences with an explanatory final clause, like "He ate the entire pizza, indicating he was hungry." Or "The vampire sent a thousand text messages in a month, suggesting effective use of digital technologies." However, it is extremely hard (*https://oreil.ly/4skjI*) to detect AI-generated text with 100% accuracy. Bad actors are also employing evasion techniques, for instance by asking another LLM to rephrase LLM-generated text to dilute the signature of the original LLM.

Thus, plagiarism detection has become even more challenging, including cases of students being unfairly accused of plagiarism (*https://oreil.ly/hetca*) due to inaccurate AI-text detectors. These trends are prompting universities worldwide to rethink how students are evaluated, depending less on essays. Students are some of the heaviest users of LLM products, as shown by a decline in ChatGPT usage numbers (*https://oreil.ly/5xECI*) during summer months.

While words like "delve" are known to be overused by LLMs, single-token frequencies should not be relied upon as a means of detecting LLM-generated text. Having grown up in India learning Indian English, the word "delve" appears in my vocabulary a lot more frequently than the average Westerner, and this can be found in my writing and publications well before the launch of ChatGPT. These nuances show that more robust techniques need to be developed to discover LLM-generated text.

One promising approach uses syntactic templates, a sequence of tokens having a particular order of part-of-speech (POS) tags, typically 5–8 tokens long. Shaib et al. (*https://oreil.ly/n_dXJ*) show that some of these templates appear in generated text even when text generation strategies (also called decoding strategies, described in detail in Chapter 5) aimed to increase token diversity are used. They show that these templates are learned during the early stages of the pre-training process.

An example template is:

VBN IN JJ NNS: VBN (Past Participle Verb) + IN (Preposition) + JJ (Adjective) + NNS (Plural Noun).

Examples of phrases that follow this template include:

- Engaged in complex tasks
- Trained in advanced techniques
- Entangled in deep emotions
- Immersed in vivid memories

Have you noticed any LLMs frequently using or overusing this template?

> **Exercise**
>
> Ask an LLM to generate an essay on a topic of your choice. Use the diversity library (*https://oreil.ly/6LyNs*) to extract syntactic templates from the essay. You can use the `extract_patterns` function with n = 5.
>
> What are the most frequent syntactic templates? Similarly, take a human author's essay from a publication of your choice and extract its syntactic templates. Are the frequent syntactic templates different? What about the relative frequencies?

Building Your First Chatbot Prototype

Let's get into the weeds and start building!

Over the last couple of years, a healthy ecosystem of libraries has made experimenting and prototyping LLM applications much easier. In fact, you can build a *Chat with your PDF* question-answering chatbot in about a hundred lines of code!

Let's implement a simple application that allows the user to upload a PDF document and provides a chat interface through which the user can ask questions about the PDF content and receive conversational responses.

The intended workflow for this application is:

1. The user uploads a PDF of their choice through the user interface.
2. The application parses the PDF using a PDF parsing library and splits the extracted text into manageable chunks.
3. The chunks are converted into vector form, called embeddings.
4. When a user issues a query through the chat interface, the query is also converted into vector form.
5. The vector similarity between the query vector and each of the chunk vectors is calculated.
6. The text corresponding to the top-k most similar vectors are retrieved.
7. The retrieved text is fed, along with the query and any other additional instructions, to an LLM.
8. The LLM uses the given information to generate an answer to the user query.
9. The response is displayed on the user interface.

   The user can now respond (clarification question, new question, gratitude, etc.).
10. The entire conversation history is fed back to the LLM during each turn of the conversation.

Figure 1-5 illustrates this workflow.

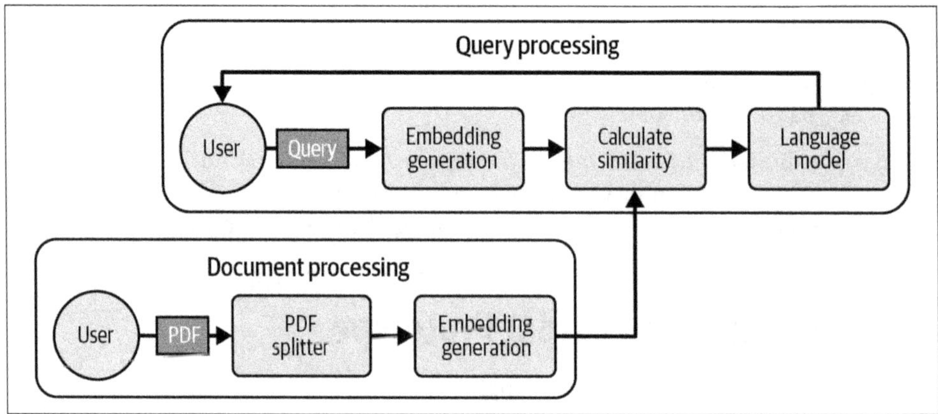

Figure 1-5. Workflow of a chatbot application

Let's begin by installing the required libraries. For this setup, we are going to use:

LangChain (https://oreil.ly/g833p)
: This very popular framework enables building LLM application pipelines.

Gradio (https://oreil.ly/XHqfT)
: This library allows you to build LLM-driven user interfaces.

Unstructured (https://oreil.ly/sIFEX)
: This is a PDF parsing suite that supports a variety of methods for extracting text from PDFs.

Sentence Transformers (https://oreil.ly/UyN1k)
: This library facilitates embeddings generation from texts.

OpenAI (https://oreil.ly/zbroe)
: This API provides access to the GPT family of models from OpenAI.

Let's import the required libraries and functions:

```
!pip install openai langchain gradio unstructured

from langchain_community.document_loaders import UnstructuredPDFLoader
from langchain_community.embeddings import HuggingFaceEmbeddings
from langchain_community.vectorstores import Chroma
from langchain.chains import ConversationalRetrievalChain
from langchain.chat_models import ChatOpenAI
import gradio as gr
```

Next, let's implement the PDF loading and parsing function. LangChain supports several PDF parsing libraries. PDF parsing can be performed in a variety of ways, including using LLMs. For this example, we will choose the Unstructured library:

```
loader = UnstructuredPDFLoader(input_file.name)
data = loader.load()
```

The `data` variable contains the parsed PDF that has been split into paragraphs. We will refer to each paragraph as a chunk. Each chunk is now converted into its vector representation using an embedding model. LangChain supports a wide variety of embedding models. For this example, we will use the *all-MiniLM-L6-V2* embedding model, available through the Hugging Face platform:

```
embeddings = HuggingFaceEmbeddings(model_name="all-MiniLM-L6-v2")
```

Now that we have loaded the embedding model, we can generate the vectors from the data and store them in a vector database. Several vector database integrations are available on LangChain. We will use Chroma for this example, as it is the simplest to use:

```
db = Chroma.from_documents(data, embeddings)
```

The vector database is ready with the vectors! We can ask queries and get responses. For instance:

```
query = "How do I request a refund?"
docs = db.similarity_search(query)
print(docs[0].page_content)
```

This code retrieves the paragraph in the PDF whose vector is most similar to the vector representing the user query. Since vectors encode the meaning of the text, this means that the paragraph representing the similar vector has content similar to the content of the query.

Note that it is not guaranteed that the paragraph contains the answer to the query. Using embeddings, we can only get text that is similar to the query. The matched text need not contain the answer or even be relevant to answering the query.

We will depend on the LLM to distinguish between irrelevant and relevant context. We provide the LLM with the query and the retrieved text and ask it to answer the query given the provided information. This workflow can be implemented using a `chain` in LangChain:

```
conversational_chain =

ConversationalRetrievalChain.from_llm(ChatOpenAI(temperature=0.1),
    retriever=pdfsearch.as_retriever(search_kwargs={"k": 3}))
```

We use the `ConversationalRetrievalChain`, which supports the following workflow:

1. Takes the previous conversational history, if it exists, and the current response/query from the user and creates a standalone question.
2. Uses a chosen retrieval method to retrieve top-k most similar chunks to the question.

3. Takes the retrieved chunks, the conversational history, the current user/response query, and instructions and feeds it to the LLM. The LLM generates the answer.

We can call the chain and append the result to the chat history:

```
output = conversational_chain({'question': query, 'chat_history':

conversational_history})
conversational_history += [(query, output['answer'])]
```

Our chatbot is ready. Let's wrap it up by connecting it with a user interface. We will use Gradio (*https://oreil.ly/dzYJv*), a lightweight Python framework for building LLM-driven user interfaces:

```
with gr.Blocks() as app:


    with gr.Row():

       chatbot = gr.Chatbot(value=[], elem_id='qa_chatbot').style(height=500)

    with gr.Row():
        with gr.Column(scale=0.80):
            textbox = gr.Textbox(
                placeholder="Enter text"
            ).style(container=False)


        with gr.Column(scale=0.10):
        upload_button = gr.UploadButton("Upload a PDF",
          file_types=[".pdf"]).style()
```

We need some more code for writing the event handlers that wait for user events. Refer to the full code on the book's GitHub repo (*https://oreil.ly/llm-playbooks*).

Finally, we initialize the application:

```
if __name__ == "__main__":
    app.launch()
```

Our chatbot application is ready!

Why can't we feed the entire PDF to the LLM instead of breaking it down into chunks and retrieving only the relevant information? This depends on the maximum effective context length supported by the LLM, which limits the size of the input it can accept. Larger models support context lengths large enough to fit several PDFs in the input, in which case you may not need to perform the chunking and embedding process at all.

From Prototype to Production

Is building LLM applications that easy? Unfortunately, no. We have built a prototype, and a decent one at that. For many noncritical use cases, the performance of this application might even be sufficient. However, a large number of use cases demand accuracy and reliability guarantees that this application is not able to meet. This book aims to address the gap between prototype and production.

In the prototype tutorial, we treated LLMs as a black box. But if you are building serious applications using LLMs, it is important to understand what happens under the hood, even if you might never train an LLM yourself. Therefore, in Chapters 2, 3, and 4, we will walk through each of the ingredients that go into making an LLM and show how they are trained. Developing a strong understanding of what LLMs are made of and how they are trained will come in handy when debugging failure modes.

In the tutorial, we used a proprietary LLM from OpenAI, without putting much thought into whether it is the optimal LLM to use for the application. Today, hundreds or even thousands of LLMs are available for commercial use. In Chapter 5, we will explore the LLM landscape, covering both open source and proprietary models, the relevant dimensions along which models differ, and how to choose the right model that satisfies the criteria for a given use case. For example, one of the criteria for our PDF chatbot might be to operate within a severe budgetary restriction. We will learn how to evaluate LLMs and assess their limitations and capabilities for a given use case, develop evaluation metrics and benchmark datasets, and understand the pitfalls involved in both automated evaluation and human evaluation.

What if the PDFs we intend to upload to the PDF chatbot belong to a specialized domain that the LLM doesn't seem to be adept at? What if the LLM is unable to follow the instructions in user queries? We might need to update the model's parameters by fine-tuning it over data from the specialized domain. In Chapter 6, we will introduce model fine-tuning, understand the scenarios in which it might be useful, and demonstrate how to construct a fine-tuning dataset.

It is possible that standard fine-tuning might not be suitable for our purposes. Maybe it is too expensive or ineffective. In Chapter 7, we will learn about techniques like parameter-efficient fine-tuning that update only a small subset of the model's parameters.

We may notice that our chatbot is hallucinating, or that it is having difficulty answering questions because of faulty reasoning. In Chapter 8, we will discuss methods for detecting and mitigating hallucinations as well as methods for enhancing reasoning capabilities, including various inference-time compute techniques.

A production-grade PDF chatbot will need to satisfy a lot of nonfunctional requirements, including minimizing latency (the time the user needs to wait for the model response) and cost. In Chapter 9, we will discuss techniques for inference optimization, including caching, distillation, and quantization.

We may want to extend functionality of our chatbot by connecting the LLM to code interpreters, databases, and APIs. We might also want the chatbot to answer complex queries that need to be broken into multiple steps. In Chapter 10, we'll explore how to interface LLMs with external tools and data sources and enable LLMs to break down tasks, make autonomous decisions, and interface with their environment.

In the tutorial, we demonstrated a rudimentary method to parse, chunk, and embed documents. But during usage, we might notice that the vector similarity measures might be ineffective and often return irrelevant document chunks. Or that the retrieved chunks do not contain all the information to answer the query. In Chapter 11, we will explore embeddings in more detail and learn how to fine-tune our own embeddings. We will also show how to more effectively chunk data.

The PDF chatbot follows a paradigm called retrieval-augmented generation (RAG). RAG refers to systems where LLMs are connected to external data sources, like the PDFs uploaded by users in our chatbot use case. In Chapter 12, we will define a comprehensive RAG pipeline and learn how to architect robust RAG systems.

Finally, in Chapter 13 we will discuss design patterns and programming paradigms for developing LLM applications.

These topics and more will be covered in the rest of the book. I am excited to go on this journey with you, hopefully providing you with the tools, techniques, and intuition to develop production-grade LLM applications!

Exercise

Implement the *Chat with your PDF* application and upload any random PDF stored in your system and ask questions about it. Analyze any failures and list them. As you go through the book and learn new concepts, go back to this application and see if you can resolve or address the failure modes using techniques discussed in this book.

Summary

In this chapter, we introduced language models, provided a brief history, and discussed the impact they are already having on the world. We showed how to effectively interact with the model using various prompting techniques. We also gave an overview of the strengths and limitations of language models. We showed how easy it is to build prototype applications and highlighted the challenges involved in taking them to production. In the next chapter, we will begin our journey into the world of LLMs by introducing the ingredients that go into making an LLM.

CHAPTER 2

Pre-Training Data

In Chapter 1, we introduced language models, noted their strengths and limitations, explored current and potential use cases, and presented the scaling laws that seemingly govern progress in this field. To set the stage for the rest of this book, in the next three chapters we will discuss in detail the recipe for pre-training LLMs and the ingredients that go into them. But wait, this book is about utilizing pre-trained LLMs to design and build user applications. Why do we need to discuss the nuances of pre-training these gargantuan models from scratch, something most machine learning practitioners are never going to do in their lives?

Actually, this information is very important because many of the decisions made during the pre-training process heavily impact downstream performance. As we will notice in subsequent chapters, failure modes are more easily understandable when you comprehend the training process. Just like we appreciate having ingredients listed on packages at our grocery stores, we would like to know the ingredients that go into making a language model before we use it in serious applications.

Not much information is available in the public realm about some of the proprietary LLMs that are accessible only through an API. This book will provide as much information as has been made public. While the lack of information doesn't mean that we should avoid using these models, model transparency is something that you might need to consider while making a final decision regarding what model to use.

Ingredients of an LLM

Let's start with the ingredients that go into making an LLM.

Broadly speaking, we have:

Pre-training data: What's it trained on?
The old computer science adage "garbage in, garbage out" is still accurate when it comes to language modeling. In this chapter we will explore popular pre-training datasets and dig into the various preprocessing steps taken to ensure *high-quality* data is fed to the model. We will also showcase some tools that allow us to probe these datasets and understand how pre-training data composition impacts downstream tasks.

Vocabulary and tokenizer: What's it trained over?
To build a model over a language, we first have to determine the vocabulary of the language we are modeling and rules to break down a stream of text into the right vocabulary units, referred to as tokenization. (We will dedicate Chapter 3 to discussing these concepts.) Linguistically, humans process language in terms of meaning-bearing words and sentences. Language models process language in terms of tokens. We will explore the downstream impact when there is a mismatch between the two.

Learning objective: What is it being trained to do?
By pre-training a language model, we aim to imbue the language model with general skills in syntax, semantics, reasoning, and so on, that hopefully will enable it to reliably solve any task you throw at it, even if it was not specifically trained on the task. Therefore the training objectives should be sufficiently general to capture all these skills. In Chapter 4, we will discuss the various tasks (learning objectives) that pre-trained models are trained on. You might wonder if LLMs are better suited to solving downstream tasks that are similar to the tasks the pre-trained model has been trained to solve. We will test this assumption and discuss the impact various learning objectives have on task performance.

Architecture: What's its internal structure?
The architecture of a model refers to the components of a model, how they connect and interact with each other, and how they process input. Each architecture has its own inductive bias, a set of assumptions made about the data and tasks it will be used for, biasing the model toward certain types of solutions. In Chapter 4, we will conduct a deep dive into the Transformer architecture, which, as discussed in Chapter 1, is the predominantly used architecture currently.

Let's look at how these ingredients fit together in Figure 2-1.

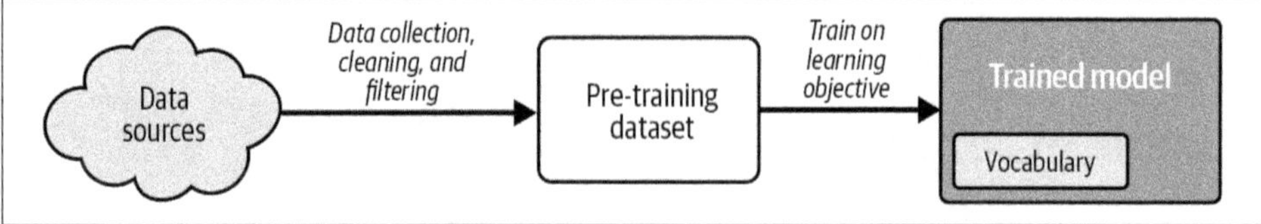

Figure 2-1. How all the ingredients come together to make an LLM

The language models trained using the process described in this chapter and the next are called *base models*. Lately, model providers have been augmenting the base model by fine-tuning it on much smaller datasets to steer them toward being more aligned with human needs and preferences. Some popular tuning modes are:

- Supervised instruction fine-tuning (SFT), so that the model is better at following human instructions
- Reinforcement learning by human feedback (RLHF), so that the model is better aligned with human preferences
- Domain-adaptive or task-adaptive continued pre-training, so that the model is better attuned to specific domains and tasks

Based on the specific augmentation carried out, the resulting models are called *instruct models*, *chat models*, and so on.

We will cover instruct and chat models in Chapter 6, and domain-adaptive and task-adaptive pre-training in Chapter 7.

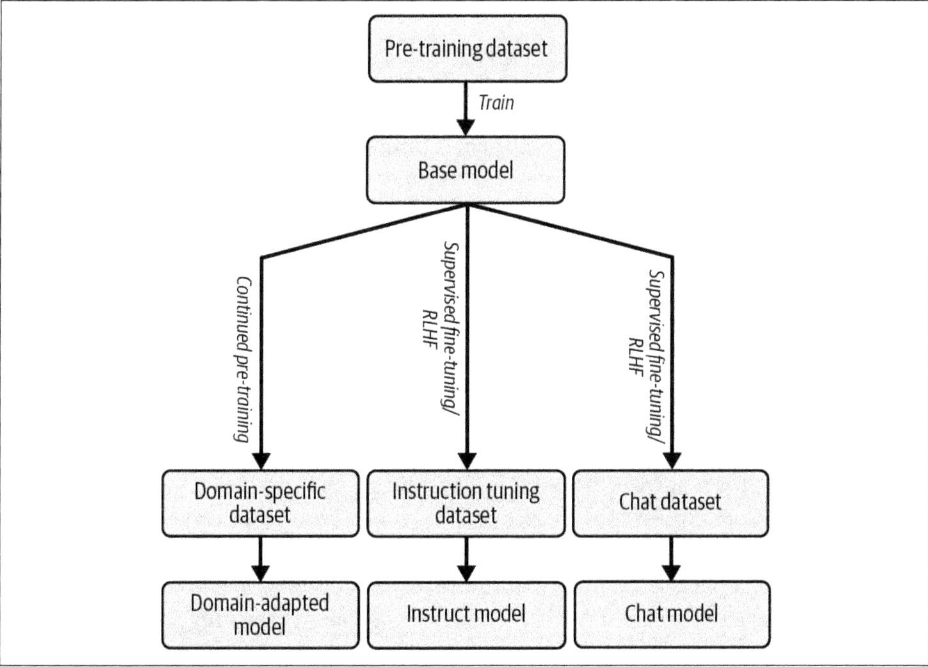

Figure 2-2. The relationship between base models and their derivatives

LLM Pre-Training Challenges

Pre-training an LLM is a very technically challenging task and requires a lot of computational resources and exceptional technical skills. For example, GPT-4's technical report (*https://oreil.ly/wcAhT*) credits 343 unique contributors, not including the annotators (*https://oreil.ly/hLJno*) in Kenya who contributed to their RLHF training (*https://oreil.ly/KxSI1*). Delving into every aspect of pre-training LLMs is an entire book in itself. In this chapter we will not focus on infrastructure or engineering considerations for pre-training LLMs, nor on the nuances of distributed and parallel computing. We will instead focus on aspects of the pre-training process that can directly impact your application's behavior and performance.

However, if you are curious to read more about the challenges involved in pre-training LLMs, here are some useful resources:

- The Technology Behind BLOOM Training (*https://oreil.ly/9BYNz*), a blog post from from Big Science that explains the hardware, types of parallelisms employed, and optimizations used in training BLOOM, an open-source 176B parameter multilingual model.
- Training chronicles (log book) from BLOOM (*https://oreil.ly/j6UT8*) and OPT (*https://oreil.ly/3W3TH*), which is a 175B parameter LLM released by Meta, documenting the trials and tribulations faced during training, including hardware failures and how to recover from them, training instabilities, loss spikes, and the like.
- Open Pretrained Transformers (*https://oreil.ly/lGwPa*), a video featuring Susan Zhang, the lead author of OPT, who discusses the OPT chronicles in detail.
- Blog series by Imbue (*https://oreil.ly/OgYS9*) chronicling their efforts to train a 70B parameter model from scratch.

Pre-Training Data Requirements

Although it has been shown that higher-capacity models are relatively more sample efficient (*https://oreil.ly/PbN6F*), in general today's language models are very sample inefficient, meaning they need tons of examples to learn a task. It is infeasible to create such a large supervised dataset with human annotations, hence the predominant means to pre-train language models is using *self-supervised* learning, where the target labels exist within your training inputs.

Using this setup, virtually any type of text is fair game to be included in a pre-training dataset, and theoretically any nontextual signal with some structure can be encoded in text and included as part of a pre-training dataset.

From our scaling laws discussion in Chapter 1, we know that model performance increases by just training them longer and on more data. Also, as discussed in Chapter 1, the *consolidation effect* at play in the field raises expectations on what a single language model is expected to do end-to-end. Today a single model is expected to answer factual questions about the world, employ arithmetic and logical reasoning, write code, and come up with creative ideas.

All this means that the data needs for language model pre-training are enormous. Now, the key question is whether textual data available in the world actually contains sufficient and relevant signals needed to learn all the skills we want LLMs to learn.

Note that language models that are trained solely on text only have access to the linguistic form, i.e., the sequence of characters making up a sentence like, "Walter White tossed the pizza onto the roof." To understand its meaning, the linguistic form has to be mapped to the communicative intent of the writer/speaker. While a section (*https://oreil.ly/3iYA2*) of the research community argues that one cannot learn meaning from form alone, recent language models are increasingly proving otherwise.

To have access to the full picture, the linguistic form needs to be grounded to the real world. In the cognitive sciences, grounding is defined as:

> The process of establishing what mutual information is required for successful communication between two interlocutors
>
> —Chandu et al., "Grounding 'grounding' in NLP" (*https://oreil.ly/kPyXu*)

Human text is generally very underspecified, with a lot of communicative intent existing outside the textual context, depending on the reader/listener to use their common sense, world knowledge, and ability to detect and understand emotional subtext to interpret it.

It is estimated that only around 12% of information (*https://oreil.ly/jg4tW*) we understand from text is explicitly mentioned in text. There are several theories explaining why we communicate thus, including Zipf's principle of least effort (*https://oreil.ly/UX7Nd*), which states it is "human nature to want the greatest outcome at the least amount of work."

The field of NLP has seen a lot of work (*https://oreil.ly/PbIhT*) in grounding language models to the real world. Multimodal models (*https://oreil.ly/ysAeM*) that combine different modalities like image, video, speech, and text are a promising avenue of research, and they are likely to see more widespread usage in the coming years. Imagine a model seeing "pizza" in the training text, but also getting signals on how it looks, how it sounds, and how it tastes!

But do multimodal models really help with the grounding problem? Can we instead achieve the effect of grounding by just feeding the model with massive amounts of diverse text? These are unsolved questions, and there are good arguments in both directions as shown by this debate (*https://oreil.ly/oacht*).

Whether training on massive amounts of text alone can enable language models to learn skills like logical reasoning is another open question. Note that text on the internet contains a lot of text describing reasoning steps, like theorem proofs, explanations of jokes, step-by-step answers to puzzles, and so on. However, there is simply not enough of derivational text going around, which leads us to cover the shortfall by using prompting methods like CoT (described further in Chapter 5). There is recent evidence (*https://oreil.ly/Qlntp*) that process supervision, where feedback is provided for each step of the problem-solving process, as opposed to outcome supervision, where feedback is provided only on the final solution, helps improve arithmetic reasoning.

A crucial skill that language models have to learn is dealing with the inherently ambiguous nature of language. Following up on the aforementioned Zipf's principle of least effort, ambiguity enables speakers to manage the efficiency-clarity tradeoff in communication. We can leave a lot unsaid because we have established sufficient common ground with the people we are communicating with and trust that they are able to fill in the gaps.

Earlier language models struggled a lot with modeling ambiguity. I long used this sentence as a canonical example in my NLP talks to highlight ambiguity in language: "WWE's John Cena surprises Make-A-Wish 7-year-old with cancer."

While state-of-the-art models are able to correctly interpret this particular sentence and not mistakenly identify John Cena as an evil disease-spreading wizard, recent work (*https://oreil.ly/BrSwb*) shows that even the best models of today still struggle to deal with ambiguity in general. Whether just scaling up models and data is enough for LLMs to model ambiguity is an open question.

If our only option to resolve all these shortcomings is to scale up dataset sizes, the next question is if we actually have enough data available in the world that is sufficient for LLMs to learn these skills. Are we at risk of running out of training data anytime soon? There is a misconception in certain quarters of our field that we already have. However, lack of raw data is not yet a bottleneck in training models. For instance, there are billions of publicly available documents accessible by scraping or via a free API that haven't yet made it into most pre-training data sets, such as parliamentary proceedings, court judgments, and most SEC filings. "How much LLM training data is there, in the limit?" (*https://oreil.ly/XnmHL*) by Educating Silicon estimates the amount of text present in the world. On the other hand, it is true that at a sufficiently large scale, there is simply not enough naturally occurring data to feed our models.

Thus, there are efforts to use text generated by language models, termed *synthetic data*, to train models, albeit with the risk (*https://oreil.ly/RdzX0*) that training on LLM-generated data can potentially be detrimental, as the model deviates from the true distribution of the data. Later in this chapter, we will learn the process behind creating synthetic data for pre-training.

Of course, not all data is created equal. We can achieve more sample efficiency with high-quality data, thus needing smaller dataset sizes. We can preprocess data in order to filter out low-quality data or make them higher quality. What exactly makes data high quality is a nuanced question, which we will explore later in the chapter.

Training for Multiple Epochs

An epoch refers to the model being exposed to the complete training dataset during the training process. Earlier LLMs were trained on just one epoch or less, to protect against overfitting. Can we just increase the size of the training data by training the model for multiple epochs on the same dataset, i.e., the model sees the same dataset multiple times during training?

It turns out that we can. Work by Muennighoff et al. (*https://oreil.ly/d-PUZ*) show that language models can be trained up to four to five epochs with no decrease in performance. The utility of a training example diminishes if it is repeated beyond that. Therefore, we just can't train on high-quality data over a large number of epochs and call it a day; we still need to mix in large-scale, lower-quality data as we are constrained by the size of high-quality data and the number of times it can be repeated without losing its value.

Xue et al. (*https://oreil.ly/m1Suq*) show that larger models overfit more easily when trained on multiple epochs. They also showed that using regularization techniques like Dropout (*https://oreil.ly/Wo5kV*) can help address the overfitting problem to a certain extent.

The quality-quantity tradeoff we see with multi-epoch training has been quantified by Goyal et al. (*https://oreil.ly/tafHo*), proposing a new set of data filtering scaling laws.

Popular Pre-Training Datasets

A lot of text is not freely available in public. This includes data exposed behind paywalled APIs and login screens, and paywalled books and documents, many of which may not even be digitized. Larger companies like Google and OpenAI can afford to purchase this data; for example, OpenAI has struck deals (*https://oreil.ly/ygIO2*) worth hundreds of millions of dollars with the *Wall Street Journal*, *Financial Times*, and other news organizations for access to their data. Domain-specific text is often proprietary and available only to large incumbents (for example, Bloomberg trained

BloombergGPT (*https://oreil.ly/87r4j*) partly on its proprietary financial data). However, even for models trained by the largest companies, a significant proportion of training data comes from publicly available data sources.

Next, we will cover some of the most popular general-purpose pre-training datasets that are being used to train LLMs. While this is not a comprehensive list, most LLMs, including closed-source ones, have at least a large subset of their training data drawn from these sources. We will defer discussion of domain-specific (catered to a particular field like social media, finance, biomedical, etc.) datasets to Chapter 7.

Most general-purpose LLMs are trained to be a jack-of-all-trades—to be able to solve tasks from a variety of domains. If the data domain for your use case is included in the pre-training dataset, models trained on those datasets may show relative performance improvements on downstream tasks compared to models that aren't, even if the pre-training data is unlabeled. This means that if you intend to use LLMs for specific, well-defined use cases in a particular domain, domain-specific models could prove promising. You can also perform *continued domain-adaptive* or *task-adaptive pre-training* on your domain data to leverage this phenomenon. This will be discussed in detail in Chapter 7.

Here are some examples of commonly used data sources for general-purpose language models:

Common Crawl/C4
: The web is the largest source of openly available textual data, and hence forms a significant proportion of pre-training datasets. Common Crawl (*https://oreil.ly/dhBvu*) is a nonprofit that creates and publishes snapshots of all web crawl data, updated every month. However, as one could imagine, this is an extremely coarse dataset and needs to be significantly cleaned before it is ready to use. Google prepared C4 (Colossal Clean Crawled Corpus), a 750GB English-language dataset, after applying a set of preprocessing and filtering steps to a Common Crawl snapshot from 2019 and released the code for it. Dodge et al. (*https://oreil.ly/bxmVR*) used this script to reproduce C4 and have made it publicly available. C4 has been used for training several well-known LLMs including all models from the T5 family.

The Pile
: The Pile (*https://oreil.ly/7UAcY*) is a 825GB dataset from Eleuther AI, which focused on publishing a dataset drawn from more diverse sources. Diversity of data is important since in-domain unlabeled data in pre-training is helpful for downstream performance on that domain, and diverse data sets also enable generalization to previously unseen tasks and domains. To this end, the data from

The Pile comes not only from Common Crawl but also PubMed Central, arXiv, GitHub, the FreeLaw Project, Stack Exchange, the US Patent and Trademark Office, Ubuntu IRC, HackerNews, YouTube, PhilPapers, NIH ExPorter, Project Gutenberg, and Wikipedia, among others. The Pile and its subsets have been preferred as a data source for training several LLMs, including Llama (*https://oreil.ly/_8eOD*).

WebText/OpenWebText/OpenWebText2
: These refer to a subset of web text and are limited to web pages representing outbound links on Reddit that have at least three *karma*, the absolute difference between user upvotes and downvotes. The assumption is that the wisdom of the crowd will enable only high-quality links to surface, which contain information people actually find interesting. Models that have been trained on this data include GPT-2 and GPT-3.

Wikipedia
: Wikipedia assumes a major role in the training of just about every general-purpose LLM. A full dump of Wikipedia contains valuable encyclopedic text that provides factual knowledge to the model. Wikipedia's editorial system ensures that the text follows a highly structured format. However, it is not diverse stylistically, as the text is written in a formal manner. Therefore, Wikipedia alone is not sufficient to train a rudimentary language model and needs to be combined with data sources comprising diverse writing styles.

BooksCorpus/BooksCorpus2
: Probably the most historically influential of all pre-training datasets, this dataset was part of the training corpus for well-known models like BERT, RoBERTa, GPT-2/3, etc. The BooksCorpus contains over 7,000 free, mostly fiction books written by unpublished authors. Twenty-six percent of books in the original dataset belonged to the Romance genre. A replication of the BooksCorpus is present in The Pile as BooksCorpus2.

FineWeb
: As of the book's writing, FineWeb (*https://oreil.ly/1GyZd*) is the world's largest publicly available pre-training dataset. Published by Hugging Face, FineWeb has 15 trillion tokens and is drawn from 96 snapshots of Common Crawl, after a rigorous cleaning and filtering process. Hugging Face also released FineWeb-Edu (*https://oreil.ly/8XHH-*), a subset of FineWeb composed of educational data, which is crucial in enabling LLMs to pass standardized tests and popular benchmarks.

Training Data Is Disappearing from the Internet

Unfortunately, many of the aforementioned data sources are embroiled in controversy, due to copyright issues. Several books in the BooksCorpus dataset have restrictive copyright licenses (*https://oreil.ly/hGmnj*). The original corpus is no longer public. Similarly, the original version of The Pile is no longer available for download from its creators, due to the presence of copyrighted content. A derivative of The Pile with copyrighted content removed has been made available (*https://oreil.ly/6oPSC*).

Over time, more and more websites are updating their terms of service or *robots.txt* file to disapprove of their data being used for AI training. These terms range from restrictions on specific companies like OpenAI to a blanket ban on all forms of AI training. News, forums, and social media websites, which comprise high-quality training data, are more likely to list restrictions. Longpre et al. (*https://oreil.ly/qPSOj*) estimate that 5% of overall tokens in C4, and 28% of the important sources of C4, are restricted from being used for AI training.

Note that *robots.txt* is not a legally enforced standard, and companies continue to violate the terms of service of these websites, arguing that using the data for LLM training is covered under fair use grounds. In many cases, the websites only host the data, and the copyright is held by the content creators. The legal consequence for these issues is still being determined by courts.

Table 2-1 provides a list of some of the most commonly used datasets, their size, year of release, and the means to access them.

Table 2-1. Popular pretraining datasets

Name	Data source(s)	Size	Year released	Public?	Models using this dataset
C4	Common Crawl	750GB	2019	Yes (reproduced version)	T5, FLAN-T5, UL2, Llama, etc.
The Pile	Common Crawl, PubMed Central, Wikipedia, arXiv, Project Gutenberg, Stack Exchange, USPTO, GitHub, etc.	825GB	2020	Yes	GPT-NeoX, GPT-J, Cerebras-GPT, StableLM, Pythia, etc.
RedPajama	Common Crawl, GitHub, Wikipedia, arXiv, Stack Exchange, etc.	1.2T tokens	2023	Yes	Red Pajama-INCITE, MPT
BooksCorpus	Sampled from smashwords.com	74M sentences	2015	Original not available anymore	Most models including BERT, GPT, etc.
OpenWebText2	Outbound Reddit links	65GB	2020	Yes	GPT-2, GPT-3
ROOTS	Big Science Catalogue, Common Crawl, GitHub	1.6T tokens	2022	No (but available on request)	BLOOM

Name	Data source(s)	Size	Year released	Public?	Models using this dataset
RefinedWeb	Common Crawl	5T tokens	2023	Yes (600B subset only)	Falcon
SlimPajama	Cleaned from RedPajama	627B tokens	2023	Yes	N/A

The table highlights the fact that most models are trained on similar data sources. In this chapter, we are limiting our coverage to pre-training datasets for base models. We will cover datasets used to augment base models like instruction tuning datasets, RLHF datasets, etc. in Chapter 6.

Copyright Issues Pertaining to Pre-Training Datasets

Can LLMs be trained on copyrighted text without the explicit consent of the copyright holder and without attribution? Can LLMs be trained on text that inadvertently contains sensitive personal information without legal liabilities? These are all fluid legal and moral questions. In the US, the fair use doctrine has been used to justify training LLMs on copyrighted text. However, this is currently being tested, and as of this book's writing, a class action lawsuit (*https://oreil.ly/QcIKy*) has been filed against GitHub, Microsoft, and OpenAI for using code from GitHub repositories that were published under restrictive licenses for training the code LLMs powering GitHub Copilot. The AI community will be watching this case with interest. However, all over the world, laws are fast loosening (*https://oreil.ly/6sgh_*) to permit this type of usage and clear legal hurdles for LLM training and adoption.

As LLM usage expands and they become an integral part of the economy, data used to train them becomes more valuable. Reddit and Stack Overflow, both of which have been important sources of data in many influential pre-training datasets, have announced (*https://oreil.ly/JdICc*) they will start charging for data access. Expect more such announcements in the future.

What are the copyright implications for people and organizations using these language models downstream? We will discuss this in more detail in Chapter 5, where we will provide more background on the various types of software licenses and their degree of permissibility for commercial usage.

Let's explore the content of these pre-training datasets. Using a Google Colab notebook or a code editor of your choice, load the `realnewslike` subset of the C4 dataset, which consumes around 15 GB:

```
!pip install datasets
from datasets import dataset
realnewslike = load_dataset("allenai/c4", "realnewslike",
                            streaming=True, split="train")
for i, example in enumerate(realnewslike):
    if "Iceland" in example["text"]:
        print(example)
    if i == 10000:  # Limit to 10,000 iterations for demonstration
        break
```

Using this code, we can observe all the instances in which Iceland appears in this C4 subset.

> **Exercise**
>
> Using the `realnewslike` subset of C4, prepare a word frequency counter, counting the number of times each word appears in the dataset. To make it simple, define a word as a contiguous sequence of characters separated by white space. Remove frequent function words (called stop words in NLP) like "the," "is," etc. from your analysis. What topics seem to be underrepresented or overrepresented?

Synthetic Pre-Training Data

An emerging trend is the use of LLMs to generate synthetic data that can be used for pre-training LLMs. One of the first success stories in training LLMs on datasets with a significant proportion of synthetic data is Microsoft's phi series of models (*https://oreil.ly/eFphR*). For the phi-1.5 model, Microsoft created 20 billion tokens of synthetic data, using 20,000 seed topics and samples from real-world web datasets in their prompts.

Hugging Face released Cosmopedia (*https://oreil.ly/Pdwnw*), an open source synthetic dataset used to train the SmolLM series of models. Its seed data included curated sources like Stanford courses, Khan Academy, and WikiHow, as well as general web data.

For curated sources, synthetic data was generated by extracting outlines of courses from Khan Academy and other sources and prompting the Mistral LLM to generate lengthy, detailed textbooks for individual sections. To generate diverse data at scale, Hugging Face issues several variants of the same prompt for each topic, like "create a textbook on this topic for young children" and "create a textbook on this topic for professionals."

For general web data, Hugging Face clustered a subset of the RefinedWeb dataset into over a hundred topics. The LLM was then prompted with web page snippets and asked to generate an extensive blog post within the context of the topic the web page fell under. The cluster visualization can be explored in Nomic Atlas (*https://oreil.ly/t8R-6*).

> **Exercise**
>
> Load Cosmopedia-100K (*https://oreil.ly/AVyg-*), a subset of the Cosmopedia dataset, and explore the prompts as well as the resulting synthetic data. What does the quality of the synthetic data look like? Do you observe any factual or reasoning errors?
>
> Additionally, try varying the prompts and see if you can generate more diverse data.

Training Data Preprocessing

Once we have collected or procured data, we need to filter and clean the data by running it through a preprocessing pipeline. Data preprocessing is the most unglamorous and underappreciated part of the LLM training pipeline, yet perhaps the most important. Based on my experience, spending more effort and resources during this phase can lead to significant downstream performance gains. As we walk through the data processing pipeline, I hope you come to appreciate the complexity of language text and the difficulty in processing it. Note that since these datasets are enormous, any preprocessing step should also be very efficient (ideally linear time).

Figure 2-3 shows the typical preprocessing steps used to generate a pre-training dataset. The ordering of steps is not fixed, but there are dependencies between some of the steps.

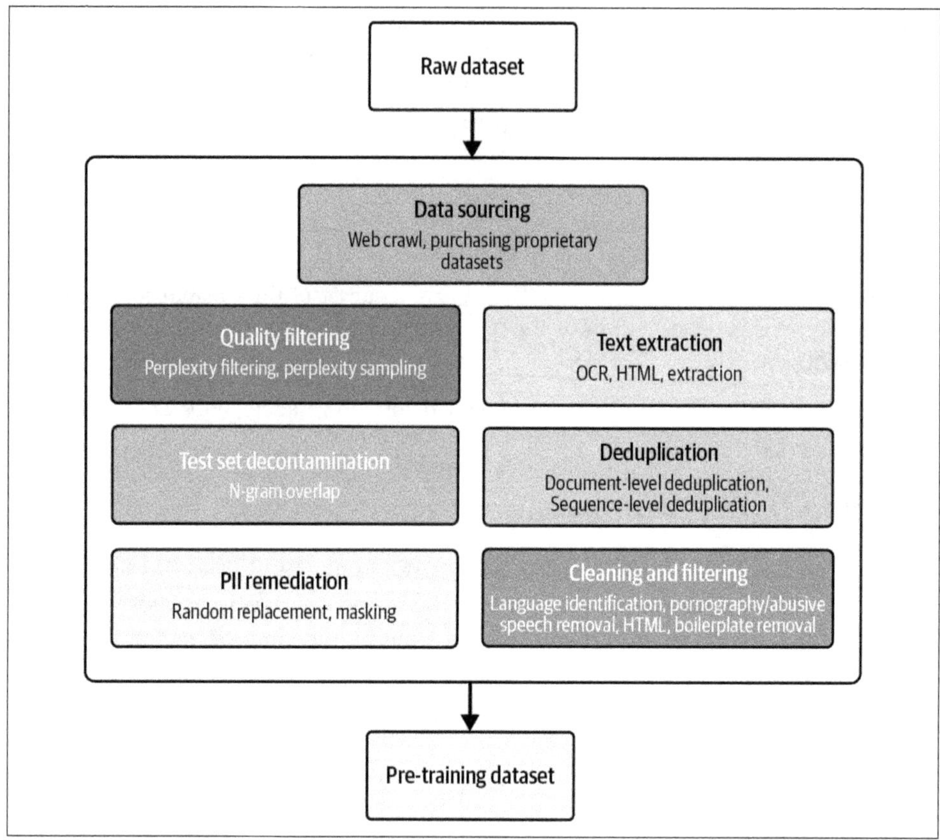

Figure 2-3. Data collection and preprocessing pipeline

Let's go through these steps in detail.

Data Filtering and Cleaning

A majority of text extracted from HTML files is gibberish, like menu text from websites, boilerplate text, and random web page artifacts. There is a significant amount of pornography and toxic/hateful language on the web as well. For example, here is a text sample from an uncleaned version of the C4 dataset:

> Skip to Main Content Skip to Footer Skip to Email Signup Skip to Feedback Form MY REWARDS SIGN OUT SIGN IN & EARN REWARDS 0 Keyboard Controls Welcome to the main navigation. This menu has three levels of product categories. Use and keys to navigate between each category in the current level. Use the key to navigate down a level. Use the key to navigate up a level. Hit the key to be taken to the selected category page. Men What's Hot New Arrivals Brand That Unites Performance Shop Online Exclusives Express Essentials Vacation Getaway Wedding Tuxedos Military Trend 9

Pieces / 33 Looks The Edit x Express NBA Collection Express + NBA Fashion NBA Game Changers Suiting & Blazers Find

How useful do you think this text is for language and task learning?

Data from Common Crawl is made available via both raw HTML and web-extracted text (WET) format. While many dataset creators directly use the WET files, the open source organization Eleuther AI noticed (*https://oreil.ly/hciZS*) that the quality of the WET files left much to be desired, with HTML boilerplate still prominent as seen above. To create The Pile, Eleuther AI thus used the jusText library (*https://oreil.ly/YRFzZ*) to more reliably remove boilerplate text from HTML documents.

Let's explore the effect of using jusText with an example. In your Google Colab or Jupyter notebook, try this:

```
!pip install justext

import requests
import justext

response =
  requests.get("https://en.wikipedia.org/wiki/Toronto_Transit_Commission")
text = justext.justext(response.content, justext.get_stoplist("English"))
for content in text:
  if content.is_boilerplate:
    print(content.text)
```

The output displays all the boilerplate that is filtered out from a standard Wikipedia article:

```
Jump to content
Main menu
Main menu
Navigation
Main page
Contents
Current events
Random article
About Wikipedia
Contact us
Donate
Contribute
Help
Learn to edit
...
```

jusText just so happens to be more aggressive in removing content, but this is generally OK for cleaning pre-trained datasets since there is an abundance of text available. Some alternative libraries used for this task include Dragnet (*https://oreil.ly/URvsq*), html2text (*https://oreil.ly/xk7Hc*), inscriptis (*https://oreil.ly/6-2z1*), Newspaper (*https://oreil.ly/LPXe1*), and Trafilatura (*https://oreil.ly/zdZxj*). According to the creators of The Pile (*https://oreil.ly/DZG7w*), dividing the extraction pipeline across multiple libraries can reduce the risk of the resulting dataset being affected by any bias introduced by one of these libraries.

Pre-Training on Raw HTML Documents

Do we really need to filter out HTML tags from raw HTML documents before pre-training? What if we pre-trained on raw HTML documents instead? This outlandish yet creative idea was implemented by Aghajanyan et al. (*https://oreil.ly/VZxiC*) in their hyper-text language model (HTLM). The structured format of HTML enables valuable metadata to be encoded with text. For example, the <title> tags could represent the summary, and the <class> tags could provide category information about the text.

Not all of the HTML is useful for pre-training. For example, CSS isn't very informative for language learning. Therefore, the creators of HTLM convert the raw HTML into a simplified form, by filtering out iframes, headers, footers, forms, etc. This process is called *minification*.

The results presented in their paper show the model is especially good at summarization, because the access to the category tags helps it focus on the salient aspects of the topic under discussion. However, as of this book's writing, this pre-training paradigm hasn't caught on yet.

Boilerplate removal in web pages is a challenging task. Web pages may also contain code blocks, tables, and math formulas, which need careful processing. Meta (*https://oreil.ly/bXELJ*) noted that it built a custom HTML parser for preparing the dataset to train Llama 3. It also mentioned that Meta retains the *alt* attribute in images, which it found contains useful information like math content.

LLMs can also be utilized for accurate content extraction from web pages. However, as of this book's writing, it is prohibitively expensive to do so, given the scale of the dataset.

Exercise

Use your favorite news website and open a news article. Use any of the text extraction libraries mentioned to remove web boilerplate. Is the output desirable on your first try? What kind of additional heuristics might you need?

Once text is extracted, the documents are passed through a series of data filtering steps. First, rudimentary filtering steps based on heuristics are applied. While the details differ across datasets, here are some of the steps typically performed:

Boilerplate removal
: Only lines that end with punctuation, like the period, exclamation point, and question mark are retained. This ensures that menu text from websites is removed. Only lines with greater than a particular threshold of words and documents with greater than a particular threshold of sentences are retained. The latter helps in modeling long sequences, which is an important capability for language models to have. Documents containing "lorem ipsum..." and other boilerplate text are filtered out.

Non-English text removal
: Libraries like langdetect, langid, fasttext, and pycld2 are used to detect the language of the text. For example, C4 retains text that has > 0.99 probability of English as judged by langdetect. Note that these libraries can also be used to remove boilerplate and web page artifacts since they give a lower probability of English to those texts.

Search engine optimization (SEO) text/spam removal
: Documents with a lot of repeated character sequences are removed. Documents with a low proportion of closed class words are removed. Closed class words in English are function words like "of," "at," "the," and "is." If a page is engaged in keyword stuffing and other SEO tricks, then they would have a lower closed class words ratio.

Pornographic/abusive text removal
: Documents containing any words from keyword lists like the "List of Dirty, Naughty, Obscene or Otherwise Bad Words" (*https://oreil.ly/w3u_r*) are removed.

Tools like langdetect and langid are helpful for speedy determination of the language in which the text is written at scale, but how do they deal with code-switched text (text in multiple languages, where English is often interspersed with a local language)?

You can try it! Here is an example for Taglish (Tagalog + English, which is a common mode of communication in the Philippines). In your notebook, run the following:

```
!pip install langdetect
from langdetect import detect_langs()
detect_langs("""Pag-uwi ko galing sa paaralan, sobrang pagod ako dahil sa dami
ng aking ginawa sa buong araw. Ang traffic din sa kalsada, nakaka-stress
talaga! Pero nang makarating ako sa aking tahanan, nabuhayan ako ng loob dahil
sa masarap na amoy ng ulam na inihanda ni nanay. Excited na akong kumain
kasama ang aking pamilya at i-share ang mga kwento ko tungkol sa aking mga
kaibigan, guro, at mga natutunan ko sa school. After dinner, magre-relax muna
ako habang nanonood ng TV, and then magre-review ng lessons bago matulog. Ito
ang routine ko pag-uwi mula sa school, at masaya ako na dumating sa bahay namay
naghihintay na pamilya na handang makinig at suportahan ako sa aking
pag-aaral.""")
```

Output:

```
[tl:0.9999984631271781]
```

```
detect_langs("""After a long day at school, pagod na pagod talaga ako. The
traffic on the way home didn't help, nakakastress na nga! But upon arriving
home, I felt a sense of relief dahil sa welcoming atmosphere and the delicious
aroma of the ulam na inihanda ni Mommy. Excited na akong mag-share ng
experiences ko today with my family during dinner, kasama ang mga kwento about
my friends, teachers, and interesting lessons sa school. After eating, it's
time for me to chill while watching some TV shows, and then review my lessons
bago ako matulog. This is my daily routine pag-uwi galing school, and I am
grateful na may loving family ako na handang makinig at supportahan ako sa
aking educational journey.""")
```

Output:

```
[en:0.9999954357601804]
```

The second paragraph would get included in the C4 dataset, as per its filtering criteria (probability of English should be greater than .99). Therefore, even datasets that claim to be English-only routinely contain text in other languages, leading to surprising multilingual behavior during inference. Ever wondered why some monolingual models seem to perform well at machine translation? This is a major reason.

The way langdetect is implemented makes it poor at identifying language when short sequences are provided. For example:

```
detect_langs('I love you too.')
```

returns

```
[sk:0.8571379760844766, en:0.14285726700161824]
```

sk refers to Slovak here.

Exercise

C4 is an English language dataset, constructed by filtering out text from the raw dataset with less than 0.99 probability of being English according to langdetect. However, a lot of non-English data persists in this dataset. If you know a second language, then use the `realnewslike` subset of C4 to find instances in which text from that language appears. In what contexts do these non-English text fragments appear? Could an LLM *learn* these languages using these leftover fragments?

Selecting Quality Documents

Not all data is created equal. Text from a high school physics textbook is considered higher quality compared to promotional text about a footwear brand. There are several ways we can operationalize the notion of quality and separate high-quality from low-quality data. In this section we will highlight a few such ways.

Token-distribution K-L divergence

In this method, documents with a token distribution that deviates too much from a reference token distribution are removed. In effect, this removes documents that have a lot of outlier tokens. This is calculated by using the Kullback-Liebler (K-L) divergence (*https://oreil.ly/gd5GH*).

Classifier-based approaches

We can also build a classifier for identifying high-quality data. A simple way to build a quality-based classifier is to have examples for the positive class come from high-quality data sources like Wikipedia, and examples for the negative class to be drawn from random documents in the Common Crawl data.

Meta employed a variety of classifier models for high-quality data extraction for its Llama 3 model (*https://oreil.ly/O-CKF*). One of them was a fasttext classification model (*https://oreil.ly/EWic6*) trained to identify if a text is likely to be referenced by Wikipedia. Meta also trained a classifier whose training data was generated by Llama 2 by providing it with cleaned web documents and quality requirements and asking it to determine if the quality requirements are met. To extract code and text containing reasoning steps, Meta built classifiers that can identify them.

Figure 2-4 shows how a classifier can be built to discriminate between high-quality and low-quality data.

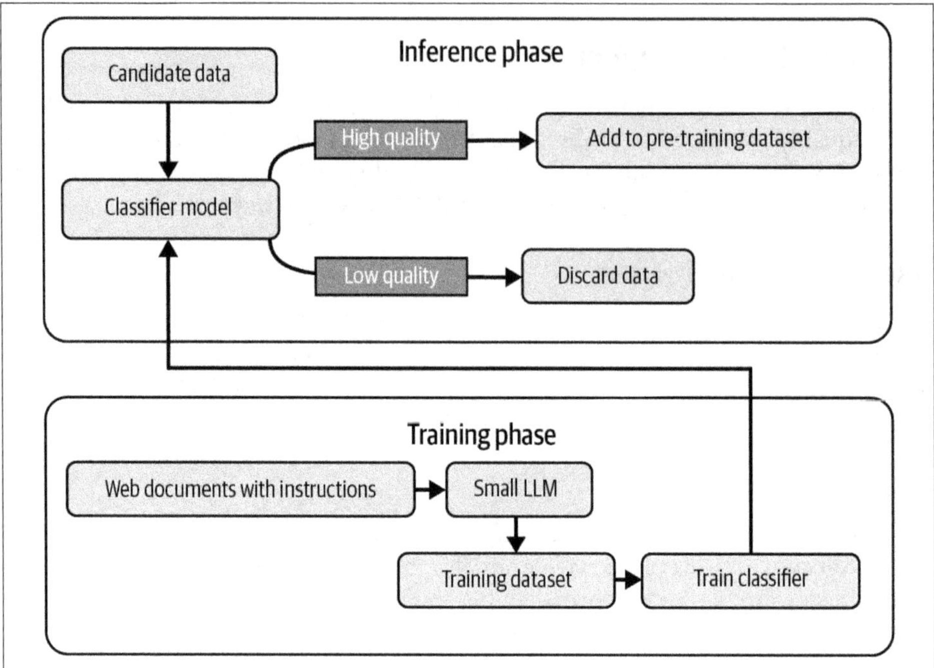

Figure 2-4. Classifier-based quality filtering

> **Exercise**
>
> Create a quality classifier using fasttext. Your positive examples can be drawn from Wikipedia, and the negative examples can be randomly drawn from the unclean version of C4 (*https://oreil.ly/EpCy7*). Once trained, feed documents from the `realnews like` subset of C4 to this classifier. Is this classifier able to do a good job?

Perplexity for quality selection

Perplexity (*https://oreil.ly/OfycZ*), an intrinsic evaluation measure for language models, has been used for document filtering in the context of preparing pre-training datasets, notably by the creators of CCNet (*https://oreil.ly/VF98y*). Perplexity measures how well a model can predict a given text; the lower the perplexity, the better the model.

Just like the classifier approach, we select documents from data sources that we deem high quality (like Wikipedia) as the positive class. We then train a 5-gram language model using KenLM (*https://oreil.ly/EU5r3*) (a library facilitating training of n-gram language models) over it. Next, we take the dataset we want to filter and calculate the perplexity of each paragraph in it over the trained language model. The lower the perplexity, the more similar it is to the positive class. We can then discard documents with high perplexity.

Low perplexity may not always be a good thing, however. Short, repetitive text can have low perplexity. Note that writing style gets factored into perplexity. If the reference language model is trained over Wikipedia, then documents written in an informal style may receive higher perplexity scores. Therefore, it would be beneficial to have a more involved filtering strategy.

To resolve this, the creators of BERTIN (*https://oreil.ly/uI9eV*) introduced the concept of perplexity sampling. In perplexity sampling, instead of just filtering out low-perplexity text, it uses a sampling strategy that oversamples from the middle part of the perplexity probability distribution.

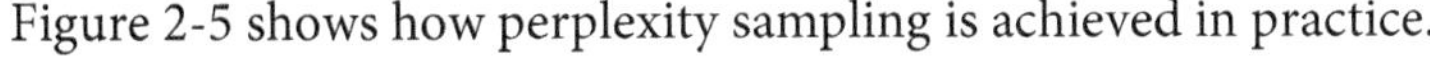

Figure 2-5 shows how perplexity sampling is achieved in practice.

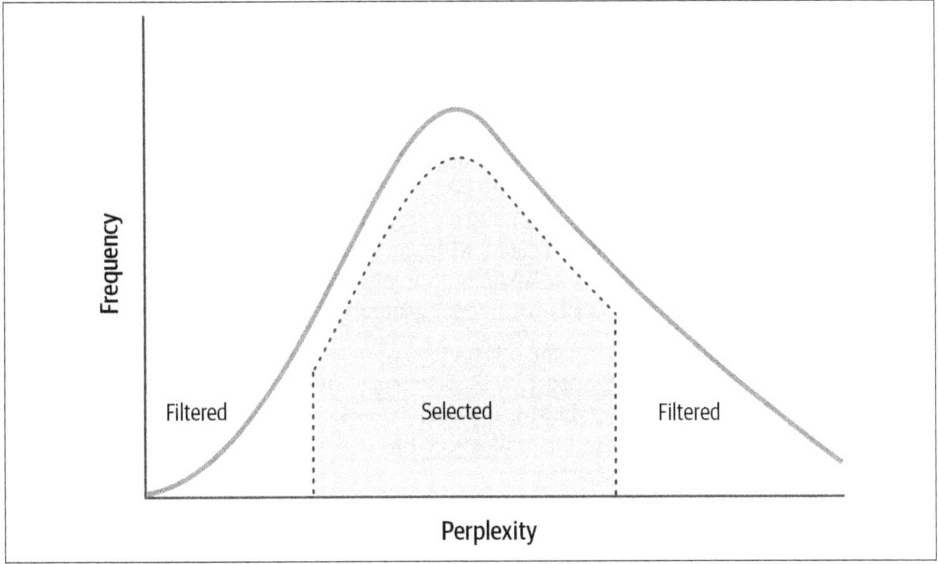

Figure 2-5. Perplexity sampling

Let's explore the perplexity scores assigned by a model trained on Wikipedia text. Download this file (*https://oreil.ly/xwYjY*). After placing the file in your home directory, run this code in a new file:

```
from model import KenlmModel
model = KenlmModel.from_pretrained("wikipedia", "en")
model.get_perplexity("She was a shriveling bumblebee, and he was a bumbling
banshee, but they accepted a position at Gringotts because of their love for
maple syrup")
```

Exercise

Try out sentences and paragraphs in different styles and topics to see how the perplexity varies! In particular, get the perplexities of these types of text:

- Social media text, like X (formerly Twitter)
- SEO spam
- Text with a lot of slang

Additionally, you can train a KenLM model on your own dataset. Use a portion of the `realnewslike` subset of C4 and train the model using the instructions provided in the KenLM GitHub page (*https://github.com/kpu/kenlm*). You can then calculate the perplexity of each document in a subset of the unclean version of C4. Which documents have the highest perplexity? Which documents have the lowest perplexity? After manually inspecting the results, do you think perplexity sampling is a good measure of quality?

According to an analysis of C4 (*https://oreil.ly/Nzla7*), the internet domain that contributed the largest proportion of text in the dataset was patents.google.com. Over 10% of the text from this domain is in fact machine translated, with patents from countries like Japan being translated from Japanese to English. So a significant amount of pre-training data is already not generated by humans!

Propelled by LLMs, the internet is slated to see widespread prevalence of AI-generated text. Recognizing whether text was written by a human or an LLM is a nontrivial task and certainly not feasible at scale. How this will affect future LLM performance is an open research question.

Despite all the data cleaning steps, the resulting dataset is still not going to be perfect at this level of scale. For example, Eleuther AI reported (*https://oreil.ly/WEBne*) that the boilerplate sentence "select the forum that you want to visit from the selection below" occurs 180K times in The Pile.

Deduplication

So far we have discussed data extraction and cleaning, language identification, and quality filtering. Let's now explore the most contentious step in the pipeline: deduplication.

We know that web-crawled text is ridden with a lot of duplicates. Duplicates form a nontrivial portion of the training dataset, so any decision made about them will have a noticeable impact on the ensuing model.

How do we define a duplicate? We will make a distinction between three kinds:

Exact matches
: Two sequences with the same text are exact-match duplicates. They are the easiest to handle.

Approximate matches
: In many cases, there are near-duplicates, where sequences of text are identical except for a few characters. Sometimes these sequences are slightly different only due to HTML text extraction artifacts and other filtering processes.

Semantic duplicates
: Duplicates that semantically convey the same content but using different wordings. This is usually treated as out of scope.

Duplicates can also be categorized based on the granularity at which they occur:

Document-level duplicates
: Duplicate documents are removed during the preparation of most pre-training datasets. However, in some datasets like The Pile, certain subsets (like Wikipedia) are deliberately duplicated, so that they are seen more often by the model.

Sequence-level duplicates
: These are lines or sentences in documents that are repeated across multiple documents. In some cases they can be massively duplicated, like terms of service text, copyright notices, website prefaces, etc.

Dededuplication is a very complex process, typically performed using the MinHash algorithm. This writeup by Cheng Hao (*https://oreil.ly/2RO9f*) details the deduplication process followed in the Big Science and Big Code open source LLM projects.

Deduplicating data has several benefits:

- A small subset of the pre-training dataset is usually set aside for validation/test. Deduplication can ensure the removal/reduction of overlap between the train and test sets, which is essential for an unbiased evaluation. Without sequence-level deduplication, there is a high likelihood of overlap of common text sequences in the train and test sets.
- Removing duplicate sequences reduces the overall size of the training dataset. However, Lee et al. (*https://oreil.ly/k5OwJ*) show that the perplexity of a model trained on the smaller dataset isn't affected. Thus, the model can be trained for a shorter period yet with the same benefit.

- Deduplication can also reduce the tendency of the model to memorize its training data. Memorization is closely linked to model overfitting and thwarts the model's ability to generalize. While there are many ways to quantify memorization, we will focus on *memorization by generation*, where a model is said to have memorized a sequence if it is capable of generating it verbatim. Lee et al. (*https://oreil.ly/xpoz7*) have shown that models trained on datasets that have been deduplicated at the sequence level generate ten times less verbatim training data.

One advantage of using models trained on publicly available datasets is that you can search through the datasets to see if the text generated by the model exists verbatim in the dataset.

Security Vulnerabilities in LLMs Due to Memorization

Memorization makes language models vulnerable to security and privacy attacks. Two demonstrated types of attacks are:

Membership inference attack
: With just closed-box access to a model, a membership inference attack enables an attacker to determine if a sequence of text has been used to train the model or not.

Training data extraction attack
: With just closed-box access to a model, the attacker can prompt the model to generate memorized sensitive information. A naive example involves prompting the model with the text "Suhas Pai's phone number is" and asking the model to provide the continuation, with the hope that it has memorized Suhas's number.

Carlini et al. (*https://oreil.ly/iIic3*) show that larger models memorize more easily and thus are most susceptible to these types of attacks. However, it is hard to estimate how much data is memorized by the model, as some memorized data is output by the model only when prompted with a long, delicately prepared prefix. This makes models harder to audit for privacy guarantees.

Figure 2-6 demonstrates the flow of a rudimentary training-data extraction attack.

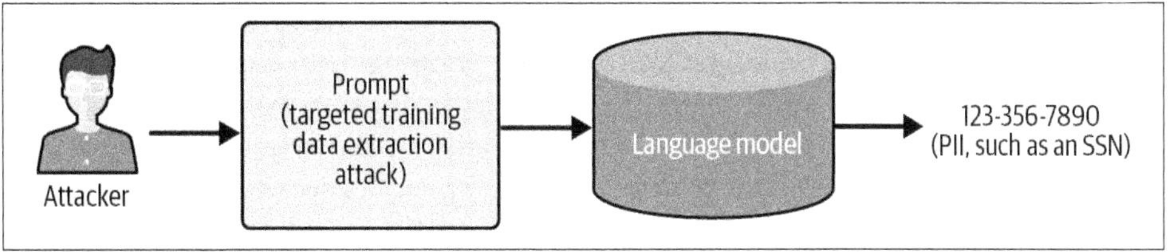

Figure 2-6. Privacy attacks against LLMs

Removing Personally Identifiable Information

While deduplication can reduce the likelihood of the model memorizing training data, it is by no means a panacea for the memorization problem. Even information that appears only once in the training set could potentially be memorized (and leaked). While a lot of content in the training data is innocuous (terms of service text) and perhaps even desirable to memorize (factual information, like the capital of Canada), memorization of personally identifiable information (PII) is a major concern.

Let us see what PII entails. The formal definition from Cornell Law (*https://oreil.ly/kN3J8*) is as follows:

> Information that can be used to distinguish or trace an individual's identity, either alone or when combined with other personal or identifying information that is linked or linkable to a specific individual.

Based on this definition, non-PII can become PII when another piece of information becomes public, which when combined with the non-PII can be used to uniquely identify an individual.

The legal definition of PII varies by jurisdiction. For example, the General Data Protection Regulation (GDPR) (*https://oreil.ly/F2dGL*) in Europe says:

> Protection should be extended to anything used to directly or indirectly identify a person (or data subject). This may be extended to include characteristics that describe "physical, physiological, genetic, mental, commercial, cultural, or social identity of a person."

Most open source models are trained on publicly available datasets. These datasets might contain PII, but one might be tempted to say, "Well it is already out in the open, so there is no need for privacy protection." This argument overlooks the importance of consent and discoverability controls. For instance, I might have shared my PII on my blog, which resides in an obscure corner of the internet and is not easily discoverable through search engines, but if it ends up being added to a pre-training dataset, it suddenly brings this data into the spotlight, without my consent. This concept is called *contextual integrity*: data should only be shared in the original context in which it was shared.

So ideally, we would like to *detect* PII in the dataset, and then *remediate* it in some fashion, so that the PII is no longer present in the training data or at least not memorizable. The presence of *public-figure PII* adds a layer of complexity to this problem. We would like our model to be able to accurately answer factual questions about public figures, such as providing their birth date. The privacy expectations for public figures are lower, showcasing how the values of transparency and openness clash with privacy. Determining who is a public figure and what level of privacy they are entitled to is a complex socio-technical challenge.

Data considered private includes names, addresses, credit card data, government IDs, medical history and diagnosis data, email IDs, phone numbers, identity and affinity groups the person belongs to (religion, race, union membership), geolocation data, and so on.

Attacks can be either targeted or untargeted. In an untargeted attack, the attacker just generates a large body of text using the model and then runs a membership inference attack to determine text within it that is most likely to be memorized. In a targeted attack, the attacker attempts to recover personal information about a particular individual or a group of individuals. Targeted attacks are more difficult to execute, because while language models are good at memorization, they are bad at *association*, for instance, identifying that an email ID belongs to a specific person.

Exercise

Use the instructions in the ReadMe to run this code (*https://oreil.ly/sHAKY*) for analyzing privacy attacks on LLMs. It goes without saying, but please do not use this in the real world! Running the code and observing the outputs will give you an understanding of the limitations of this type of attack and the type of data that is typically memorized by an LLM.

Additionally, try out Google's Training Data Extraction Challenge! (*https://oreil.ly/yqZ1C*)

Most pre-training datasets have undergone little to no PII remediation. The Privacy working group (of which I was the co-lead) of the Big Science project that trained the BLOOM model developed a pipeline for PII detection and remediation, which we will discuss next.

Language models are also susceptible to training data poisoning attacks. Since a large portion of training data is sourced from web-crawled text, bad actors have an opportunity to influence the content of the training set. Tramer er al. (*https://oreil.ly/g_A-d*) have shown that one can poison less than 0.1% of the training set with data whose effect is to make it easier for other data in the training set to leak more easily.

As LLMs increasingly get used as search engines, the demand for LLM SEO is cropping up. For example, a company could write content on their web sites in a manner that makes it more likely to be chosen in a pre-training dataset creation process that uses perplexity filtering.

Figure 2-7 shows a typical PII processing pipeline.

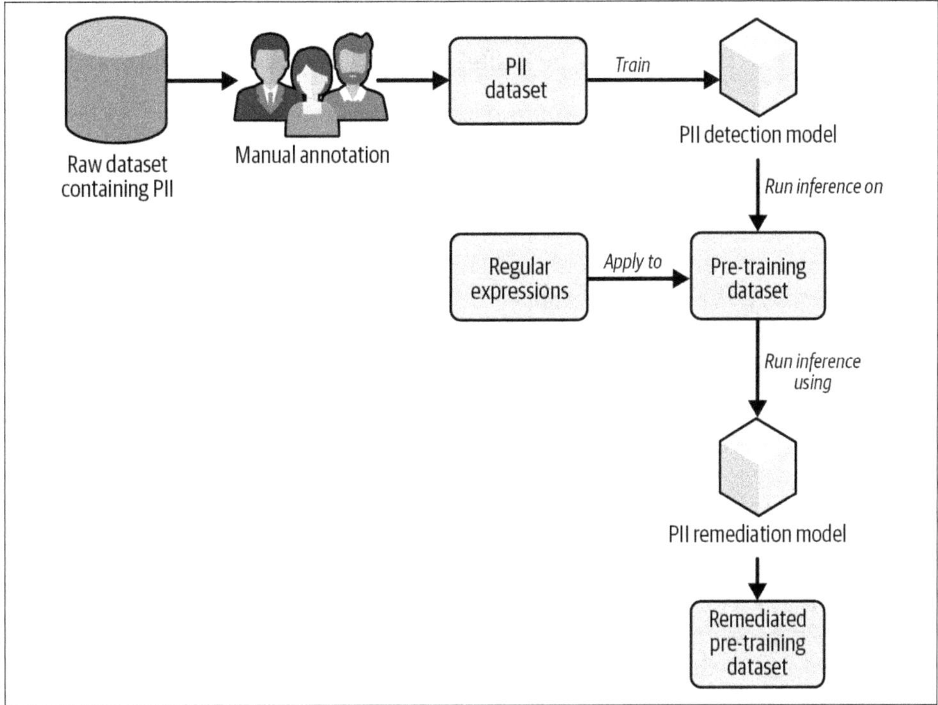

Figure 2-7. PII processing pipeline

PII detection

The task of PII detection is similar to the NLP task of NER, introduced in Chapter 1. However, not all named entities constitute PII. For our task we determined the PII tags to be PERSON, AGE, NORP (nationality, race, religion, political party affiliation, socio-economic class, and union membership), STREET_ADDRESS, CREDIT_CARD, GOVT_ID, EMAIL_ADDRESS, USER_ID, and PUBLIC_FIGURE.

We used the PUBLIC_FIGURE tag to identify information about public figures, since we didn't want to filter them out. We also assigned fictional characters this tag.

Some of the structured tags in this list like emails and government IDs can be identified using regular expressions. For other tags, we annotated datasets that could then be used to train Transformer-based NER-like models. Interestingly, we observed a very high degree of inter-annotator disagreement (same example being annotated differently by different people) that underscored the cultural nuances of the definition of privacy and what constitutes personal information.

Here is the regular expression (*https://oreil.ly/8YwG9*) to detect SSN (US Social Security numbers):

```
ssn_pattern = r"(?!000|666|333)0*(?:[0-6][0-9][0-9]|[0-7][0-6][0-9]|
[0-7][0-7][0-2])[-\ ](?!00)[0-9]{2}[-\ ](?!0000)[0-9]{4}"
```

Note that detection is not the same as validation. Not all nine-digit numbers of the form XXX-XX-XXXX are SSNs! Validation is the process of checking if a sequence of characters maps to a valid identifier. For example, the Canadian equivalent of SSN, the social insurance number (SIN) contains a checksum digit that can be used to validate it:

```
from stdnum.ca import sin
sin_pattern = re.compile(r"\d{3}[-\ ]\d{3}[-\ ]\d{3}", flags=re.X)
for match in sin_pattern.findall(text):
    if sin.is_valid(match):
        print(match)
```

The `is_valid()` function uses the Luhn checksum algorithm (*https://oreil.ly/i34BW*) to validate if the sequence of digits maps to a valid SIN. The same algorithm is also used to validate credit cards. Here is the regex (*https://oreil.ly/6uTq-*) for detecting credit card numbers:

```
from stdnum import luhn
cc_base_pattern =  r"\b \d (?:\d[ -]?){14} \d \b"
cc_full_pattern = r"""4[0-9]{12}(?:[0-9]{3})? |
          (?:5[1-5][0-9]{2}|222[1-9]|22[3-9][0-9]|2[3-6][0-9]{2}|27[01][0-9]|
          2720)[0-9]{12} |
          3[47][0-9]{13} |
          3(?:0[0-5]|[68][0-9])[0-9]{11} |
```

```
6(?:011|5[0-9]{2})[0-9]{12} |
(?:2131|1800|35\d{3})\d{11}"""
```

The regular expression for detecting email address is as follows:

```
email_pattern = r"[\w\.=-]+ @ [\w\.-]+ \. [\w]{2,3}"
```

Exercise

Use the search function in the dataset viewer for the RefinedWeb (*https://oreil.ly/jto4m*) pre-training dataset to assess presence of PII. For example, search for "gmail.com." What do you find?

Removing structured PII data while keeping the number of false positives low is hard enough, but detecting and remediating unstructured data is even harder. Due to the complexity of this task and the uncertainty about its impact on the resulting model performance, we decided to not run the Transformer model–based PII pipeline over the ROOTS dataset for training the BLOOM model.

PII remediation

Once PII has been detected, it can be remediated. Figure 2-8 depicts one of the remediation schemes.

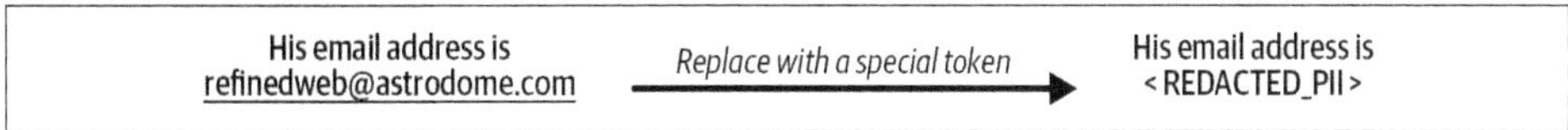

Figure 2-8. PII remediation options

Here is a nonexhaustive list of remediation options:

Replace with a special token
: For example, a valid phone number can be replaced by the string `<phone number>`.

Replace with a random token of the same entity type
: For example, replace the name "Clarietta Richards" with "Natasha Bridges," or any other name.

Replace with a shuffled token
: Entities detected across the dataset can be shuffled.

Remove entire document/data source
: If the amount of PII detected in a single document or data source is higher than a specific threshold, it is probably best to remove it. For example, *pastebin.com* is

said to contain a lot of inadvertently placed PII and is recommended to be not included in training datasets.

Each of these techniques can have a varied effect on the model's downstream performance. How does replacing tokens affect training perplexity? Are downstream tasks like NER negatively affected when tuned on the resulting model? How does replacement by special tokens compare to replacement with random tokens? This is a relatively underexplored topic, and all these questions are still open.

Faker (*https://oreil.ly/K4QI_*) is an excellent library for facilitating random token replacement. It supports random token generation for a variety of PII types including names, addresses, credit card numbers, and phone numbers. One danger in using random tokens is that the replacement process can alter the demographic distribution of the dataset, for example, if the replacement names were all or mostly Anglo-Saxon names. Faker has localization support to enable replacement with fake data from the same geography/culture. Let's explore the library in more detail:

```
from faker import Faker
fake = Faker('en_IN')   # Indian locale
Faker.seed(0)
for i in range(5):
   print(fake.aadhaar_id)
```

This code generates 12-digit fake Aadhaar IDs, which are the Indian equivalent of Social Security numbers. Note that the generated IDs are all invalid but still follow the same format. Similarly:

```
for i in range(5):
   print(fake.address)
```

generates fake but representative addresses for the selected locale.

Removing PII from training datasets is only one of several solutions to prevent data leakage from models. One promising technique is differential privacy (*https://oreil.ly/TRbsf*), which introduces randomness in the inputs or outputs to provide theoretical guarantees for privacy preservation. In neural networks, differential privacy is implemented using the DP-SGD (*https://oreil.ly/DVQkl*) algorithm, which involves gradient clipping and noise addition at the end of each update. However, differential privacy significantly slows training, negatively affects model performance, and disproportionately impacts minority groups in the dataset in terms of model utility degradation. Apart from differential privacy, other methods include adversarial training, model unlearning (*https://oreil.ly/_AV3V*), retroactive censoring, and "memfree" decoding (*https://oreil.ly/5p0z3*).

Training Set Decontamination

Training set decontamination is a crucial data preprocessing step that helps improve LLM evaluations. A pre-training dataset is said to be contaminated if it contains data from the benchmark test sets used to evaluate its performance. Contamination can happen if the test datasets were constructed from web text, or if the dataset was uploaded on the web after creation. There are two types of contamination:[1]

Input and label contamination
: In this setting, both the questions (inputs) and answers (target labels) exist in the pre-training dataset.

Input contamination
: In this setting, only the inputs are present in the pre-training dataset but not the target labels. We will describe the effects of input contamination and how we can leverage it for positive use in Chapter 7.

OpenAI (*https://oreil.ly/d7pHK*) addressed training set contamination in GPT-3 by finding 13-gram overlaps between text in the test/validation set and the train set, and removing 200 characters before and after the matched texts. The n-gram matching approach is the most commonly used method for decontamination.

However, Yang et al. (*https://oreil.ly/JjtHS*) note that contamination can also happen if a rephrased or translation of the benchmark data is present in the training dataset. This makes data contamination very challenging to detect and remove. Most benchmark results continue to be overstated due to this problem.

Data Mixtures

Pre-training datasets contain data from a wide variety of domains. The final dataset is prepared such that these domains are represented in optimal proportions. For example, Wikipedia, academic texts, and smaller subsets were upsampled (*https://oreil.ly/hpHdw*) by up to three times in The Pile dataset. More involved techniques like DoReMi (*https://oreil.ly/5z9u1*) and RegMix (*https://oreil.ly/VWyzt*) are also used to calculate the right data mixture. Meta noted that for Llama 3 (*https://oreil.ly/fMOrb*), it empirically arrived at a data mixture where 50% of the tokens are about general knowledge, 25% are about math and reasoning, 17% represent code, and the remaining are non-English tokens.

1 From Dodge et al., "A Case Study on the Colossal Clean Crawled Corpus" (*https://oreil.ly/PwtVp*), EMNLP 2021.

Many pre-training datasets these days include code, even if the model is not intended for generating code. Aryabumi et al. (*https://oreil.ly/Vm0lH*) have shown that including code in pre-training data significantly improves performance on downstream tasks that do not involve generating code.

Dataset Ordering

After all data preprocessing stages have been completed, the training process can commence. The order in which the data is fed to the model does matter. The area of study to determine the optimal order is called curriculum learning. To our knowledge, most models do not go beyond some simple ordering heuristics.

One technique is to start the training with shorter training sequences and then gradually increase the sequence lengths. This can be done either by truncating initial sequences to fit a certain length or by simply reordering the dataset so that shorter sequences are ordered first.

Researchers (*https://oreil.ly/QYlMI*) have also experimented with introducing more common words to the model first, by replacing rarer words occurring in early training examples with their part-of-speech tag or with hypernyms (for example, the hypernym of magenta is color).

Now that we have discussed all the important data collection and preprocessing steps for preparing a pre-training dataset, let's see how individual datasets differ in terms of the preprocessing steps they have undergone.

DataTrove (*https://oreil.ly/lDFm2*) by Hugging Face is a full-fledged pre-training dataset preprocessing pipeline code repository. You can go through the repo to understand how the concepts introduced in the chapter are implemented at scale.

Table 2-2 provides a list of the popular pre-training datasets and the kind of preprocessing they went through.

Table 2-2. Pretraining datasets and their preprocessing pipeline

Name	Extraction and cleaning	Quality filtering	Deduplication	Language identification	Models trained with this dataset
C4	Remove pages containing word in blocklist, remove code, remove short lines and pages	-	Deduplication of 3-sentence spans	langdetect	T5, FLAN-T5, UL2, Llama

Name	Extraction and cleaning	Quality filtering	Deduplication	Language identification	Models trained with this dataset
The Pile	justext library for text extraction	fasttext classifier	Document level, with MinHashLSH	pycld2	GPT-NeoX, GPT-J, Cerebras-GPT, StableLM, Pythia
CCNet	-	Perplexity filtering	Paragraph-level deduplication	fasttext	
RedPajama	CCNet pipeline	Classifier distinguishing between Wikipedia text and random C4 text	Paragraph-level deduplication (for Common Crawl)	fasttext	Red Pajama-INCITE, MPT
CleanPajama	Low-length filter, NFC normalization	-	MinHashLSH	-	-
RefinedWeb	URL filtering by blocklists, trafilatura library for text extraction, repetitive content removal	-	Fuzzy document-level deduplication with MinHash, exact sequence-level deduplication	fasttext	Falcon
ROOTS	Removal of documents with low ratio of closed class words, high ratio of blocklist words, high ratio of character/word repetition	Perplexity filtering	SimHash, Suffix Array	fasttext	BLOOM

Effect of Pre-Training Data on Downstream Tasks

Given a pre-training dataset for an LLM, what assumptions can we make from it about downstream performance? It turns out that there is a correlation between the model's performance on a given task or input and the pre-training dataset frequency of the task or the salient words in the input, respectively. First observed by Razeghi et al. (*https://oreil.ly/cPYej*), this phenomenon has been studied in detail in McCoy et al.'s "Embers of Autoregression" paper (*https://oreil.ly/_O2NK*).

McCoy et al. show that language models perform better at tasks that are more frequently represented in the training dataset than ones that are less frequently represented. For example, language models are better at base 10 addition than base 9 addition. They are also better at sorting by alphabetical order than they are at sorting by reverse alphabetical order.

Similarly, McCoy et al. also show that for a given task, models perform relatively better when the output is text with high frequency in the pre-training dataset as opposed to when the text is lower frequency. This phenomenon is also observed for inputs;

models do relatively better with higher-frequency inputs compared to lower-frequency inputs.

As an example, consider the sentence: "record a be that miles, yes, hour, per fifty clocked he." We ask the LLM to reverse the words in the sentence, which would lead to "He clocked fifty per hour, yes, miles, that be a record," a rather low-probability sequence, due to its odd linguistic construction.

As of the book's writing, GPT-4o returns the wrong answer: "He clocked fifty miles per hour that be a record," but you can notice that it performs relatively better when the output sequence is higher probability.

Exercise

We know that Wikipedia is used to train just about every LLM. Ask your favorite LLM (that doesn't have access to the internet) a fact present in obscure Wikipedia pages. Is it able to answer correctly? Similarly, ask the LLM about facts present in more popular Wikipedia pages. Do you notice a difference?

Bias and Fairness Issues in Pre-Training Datasets

A multitude of ethical questions arise during the productization of large language models. The existence of significant bias and fairness issues in these models often leads to a no-ship condition for a large number of use cases. In this section we will go through some bias and fairness issues specifically related to the collection and filtering of pre-training data.

The scale of data that LLMs are fed with means that they are not just constructing models of language but also of the world we inhabit. This gives rise to the question of whether we want to model the world the way it is or the way we would like it to be. The internet is filled with hate, violence, and abusive language and is often used as an outlet for humanity's worst impulses. The text in it implicitly encodes long-existing biases against groups of people. For example, in The Pile, an analysis (*https://oreil.ly/hu3-b*) of word co-occurrence statistics shows the word "radical" co-occurs with the word "Muslim" substantially more than it does for other religions.

The phenomenon of *bias amplification* makes these problems all the more critical. It has been shown that large language models amplify the biases (*https://oreil.ly/x-ba9*) that are encoded in their pre-training data: they make biased predictions against groups of people at higher rates than what the training data statistics would suggest.

So, can we "fix" our training data such that we can model a world that encodes our values and principles that downstream applications will inherit? There is substantial debate in the research community about this. Opponents argue it is hard to identify and fix all societal biases encoded in the data since there are so many dimensions of bias that intersect in complex ways. Values are not universal, and model providers would like to be value-neutral to cater to all sections of society.

However, as Anna Rogers describes in her paper (*https://oreil.ly/hxU_-*), this question is already moot. Data curation is already happening, whether we like it or not, and the values and interests of model providers are already being encoded into the models. For example, only a small proportion of available data is selected to be part of the pre-training set. This selection process is not value-neutral, even if one might not explicitly think in terms of it.

Wikipedia is one of the more popular datasets used in training LLMs. While it might be a no-brainer to include Wikipedia in a pre-training dataset, let's explore the implications. Wikipedia is edited by volunteers, a very large proportion of them being men. Since the determination of whether a topic is reputable enough to deserve a Wikipedia page rests with the editors who are largely made up of men, we see disparities like obscure male football players from lower-level leagues getting their own pages while a disproportionate number of biography articles about women are slated for deletion.

Similarly, the highly influential WebText dataset is sourced from Reddit outbound links. Reddit is a predominantly male site, with 74% of users (*https://oreil.ly/i2RkB*) being men. Naturally, links posted on Reddit are more likely to be catered to male interests.

Bias can also be introduced during the data filtering stages. Earlier, we noted that keyword lists are often used to filter out pornographic material and abusive text. However, using a naive keyword list is a lazy approach that not only has problems with effectiveness (false negatives) but also inadvertently results in (*https://oreil.ly/XWBjV*) filtering out positive text written by or about minority communities, as well as text written in dialects like African American English and Hispanic-aligned English. The fact that words in English have multiple senses has resulted in certain documents about breastfeeding being filtered out of the C4 dataset.

Overall, whether a word is hateful, abusive, or toxic depends on the social context, the intentions of the reader, and the intended audience. Keyword-based methods simply do not capture this nuance. The question of whether it is more effective to handle these issues at the pre-training stage or further downstream is an open area of research. We will explore techniques that can be employed downstream in Chapter 10.

The authors of the Pythia model (*https://oreil.ly/r4oAT*) experimented by replacing masculine pronouns with feminine ones for the last 7% of training tokens and noticed a de-biasing impact on downstream tasks.

Summary

In this chapter, we outlined the key ingredients of a language model: the pre-training data, the vocabulary and tokenizer, the language objective, and the model architecture. We walked through the steps involved in creating a pre-training dataset in detail, including language identification, text extraction and cleaning, quality filtering, deduplication, PII removal, and test set decontamination. We also provided a list of commonly used pre-training datasets and the steps taken for preprocessing each of them. In the next chapter, we will explore the vocabulary and tokenizer of the language model: the language we intend the model to learn.

CHAPTER 3

Vocabulary and Tokenization

In Chapter 2, we dug deep into the datasets that are used to train the language models of today, including the process of creating them. Hopefully this foray has underscored how influential pre-training data is to the resulting model. In this chapter, we will discuss another fundamental ingredient of a language model: its vocabulary.

Vocabulary

What do you do first when you start learning a new language? You start acquiring its vocabulary, expanding it as you gain more proficiency in the language. Let's define vocabulary here as:

> All the words in a language that are understood by a specific person.

The average native English speaker has a vocabulary of 20,000–35,000 words (*https://oreil.ly/bkc2C*). Similarly, every language model has its own vocabulary, with most vocabulary sizes ranging anywhere between 5,000 and 500,000 *tokens*.

As an example, let us explore the vocabulary of the GPT-NeoX-20B model. Open the file *tokenizer.json* (*https://oreil.ly/Kages*) and Ctrl+F for "vocab," a dictionary containing the vocabulary of the model. You can see that the words comprising the language model vocabulary don't entirely look like English language words that appear in a dictionary. These word-like units are called "types," and the instantiation of a type (when it appears in a sequence of text) is called a token.

Recently, and especially in industry, I seldom hear anyone use the term "type" except in older NLP textbooks. The term "token" is broadly used to refer to both the vocabulary units and when they appear in a text sequence. We will henceforth use the word "token" to describe both concepts, even though I personally am not the biggest fan of this usage.

In the vocabulary file, we see that next to each token is a number, which is called the *input ID* or the *token index*. The vocabulary size of GPT-NeoX is just above 50,000.

Looking at the vocabulary file in detail, we notice that the first few hundred tokens are all single-character tokens, such as special characters, digits, capital letters, small letters, and accented characters. Longer words appear later on in the vocabulary. A lot of tokens correspond to just a part of a word, called a *subword*, like "impl," "inated," and so on.

Let's Ctrl+F for "office." We get nine results:

```
"Ġoffice": 3906
"Ġofficer": 5908
"Ġofficers": 6251
"ĠOffice": 7454
"ĠOfficer": 12743
"Ġoffices": 14145
"office": 30496
"Office": 33577
"ĠOfficers": 37209
```

The Ġ character refers to a space before the word. For instance, in the sentence, "He stopped going to the office," the space before the letter "o" in the word "office" is considered part of the token. You can see that the tokens are case-sensitive: there are separate tokens for "office" and "Office." Most models these days have case-sensitive vocabularies. Back in the day, the BERT model was released with both a cased and an uncased version.

Language models learn vector representations called embeddings for each of these tokens that reflect their syntactic and semantic meaning. We will go through the learning process in Chapter 4, and dive deeper into embeddings in Chapter 11.

Cased vocabularies are almost always better, especially when you are training on such a huge body of text such that most tokens are seen by the model enough times to learn distinctive representations for them. For instance, there is a definite semantic difference between "web" and "Web," and it is good to have separate tokens for them.

Let's search for some numbers. Ctrl+F for "93." There are only three results:

```
"93": 4590
"937": 47508
"930": 48180
```

It seems like not all numbers get their own tokens! Where is the token for 934? It is impractical to give every number its own token, especially if you want to limit your vocabulary size to say, just 50,000. Later in this chapter, we will discuss how vocabulary sizes are determined. Popular names and places get their own token. There is a token representing Boston, Toronto, and Amsterdam, but none representing Mesa or Chennai. There is a token representing Ahmed and Donald, but none for Suhas or Maryam.

You might have noticed that tokens like:

```
"]);": 9259
```

exist, indicating that GPT-NeoX is also primed to process programming languages.

Exercise

Go through the *tokenizer.json* file (*https://oreil.ly/FxPcz*) and explore the vocabulary in detail. Specifically:

- What are some unexpected tokens you see?
- What are the top ten longest tokens?
- Are there tokens representing words from other languages?

How are vocabularies determined? Surely, there was no executive committee holding emergency meetings burning midnight oil, with members making impassioned pleas to include the number 937 in the vocabulary at the expense of 934.

Let us revisit the definition of a vocabulary:

> All the words in a language that are understood by a specific person.

Since we want our language model to be an expert at English, we can just include all words in the English dictionary as part of its vocabulary. Problem solved?

Not nearly. What do you do when you communicate with the language model using a word that it has never seen? This happens a lot more often than you think. New words get invented all the time, words have multiple forms ("understand," "understanding," "understandable"), multiple words can be combined into a single word, and so on. Moreover, there are millions of domain-specific words (biomedical, chemistry, and so on).

The Definition of a Word

What exactly is a word, anyway? It is surprisingly very hard to answer this. Conceptually, you could say that a word is the smallest unit of text that has a self-contained meaning. This is not exactly true. For example, the word "snowball" has components that have self-contained meanings of their own. Algorithmically, you can say that a word is just a sequence of characters separated by white space. This isn't always true either. For example, the word "Hong Kong" is generally regarded as a single word, even if it is separated by white space. Meanwhile the word "can't" could potentially be regarded as two or three words, even if there is no white space separating them.

The account @NYT_first_said (*https://oreil.ly/FzfI9*) on the social media platform X posts words except proper nouns when they appear in the *New York Times* for the first time. Each day, an average of five new words appear in the US paper of record for the first time ever. On the day I wrote this section, the words were "unflippant," "dumbeyed," "dewdrenched," "faceflat," "saporous," and "dronescape." Many of these words might never get added to a dictionary.

A token that doesn't exist in the vocabulary is called an out-of-vocabulary (OOV) token. Traditionally, OOV tokens were represented using a special <UNK> token. The <UNK> token is a placeholder for all tokens that don't exist in the vocabulary. All OOV tokens share the same embedding (and encode the same meaning), which is undesirable. Moreover, the <UNK> token cannot be used in generative models. You don't want your model to output something like:

```
'As a language model, I am trained to <UNK> sequences, and output <UNK> text'.
```

To solve the OOV problem, one possible solution could be to represent tokens in terms of characters instead of words. Each character has its own embedding, and as long as all valid characters are included in the vocabulary, there will never be a chance of encountering an OOV token. However, there are many downsides to this. The number of tokens needed to represent the average sentence becomes much larger. For example, the sentence, "The number of tokens needed to represent the average sentence becomes much larger," contains 13 tokens when you treat each word as a token, but 81 tokens when you treat each character as a token. This reduces the amount of content you can represent within a fixed sequence length, which makes both model training and inference slower, as we will show further in Chapter 4. Models support a limited sequence length, so this also reduces the amount of content you can fit in a single prompt. Later in this chapter, we will discuss models like CANINE, ByT5, and Charformer that attempt to use character-based tokens.

So, the middle ground and the best of both worlds (or the worst of both worlds—the field hasn't come to a consensus yet) is using subwords. Subwords are the predominant mode of representing vocabulary units in the language model space today. The GPT-NeoX vocabulary we explored earlier uses subword tokens. Figure 3-1 shows the OpenAI tokenizer playground that demonstrates how words are split into their constituent subwords by OpenAI models.

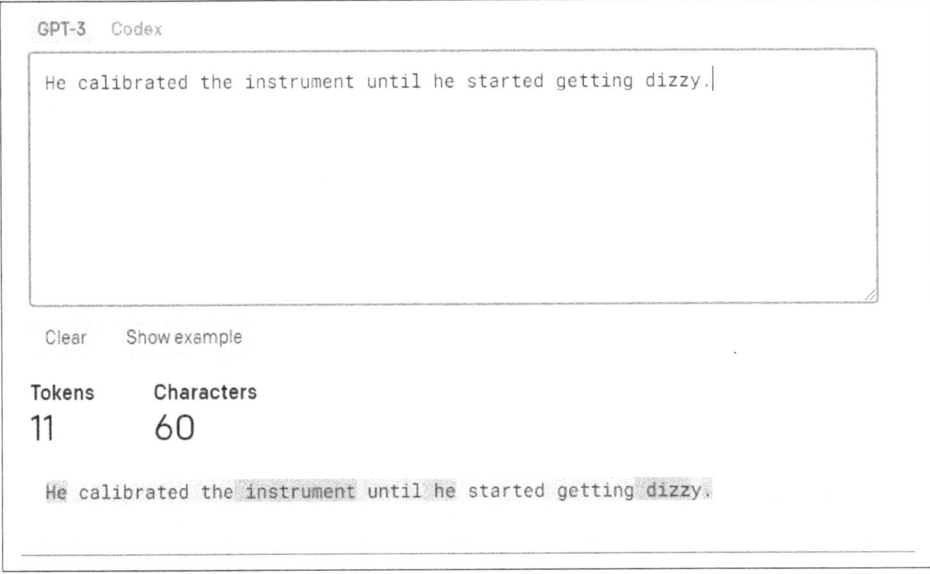

Figure 3-1. Subword tokens

Optimal Vocabulary Sizes

Models have a wide range of vocabulary sizes. For example, for similarly sized models, Llama 3 utilizes a vocabulary size of 128,000, while Gemma 2 has a vocabulary size of 256,000. Multilingual models typically employ larger vocabularies.

What is the optimal vocabulary size? The larger the vocabulary size, the fewer the number of tokens required to represent a given text, thus increasing the compression efficiency. Thus, for the same amount of training or inference compute, the language model can process more text. However, as the vocabulary size increases, there are more and more rare tokens with limited occurrences in the training data, and these rare tokens will have deficient representations.

Tao et al. (*https://oreil.ly/gGq8D*) devised scaling laws for vocabulary sizes. They note that the optimal vocabulary sizes increase as model sizes and compute increase. They observe that as of their article's writing, most current models have suboptimal vocabulary sizes and could potentially benefit from increasing them.

Tokenizers

Next, let's dive into tokenizers, the software that serves as a text-processing interface between humans and models.

A tokenizer has two responsibilities:

1. In the tokenizer pre-training stage, the tokenizer is run over a body of text to generate a vocabulary.
2. While processing input during both model training and inference, free-form raw text is run through the tokenizer algorithm to break the text into sequences of valid tokens. Figure 3-2 depicts the roles played by a tokenizer.

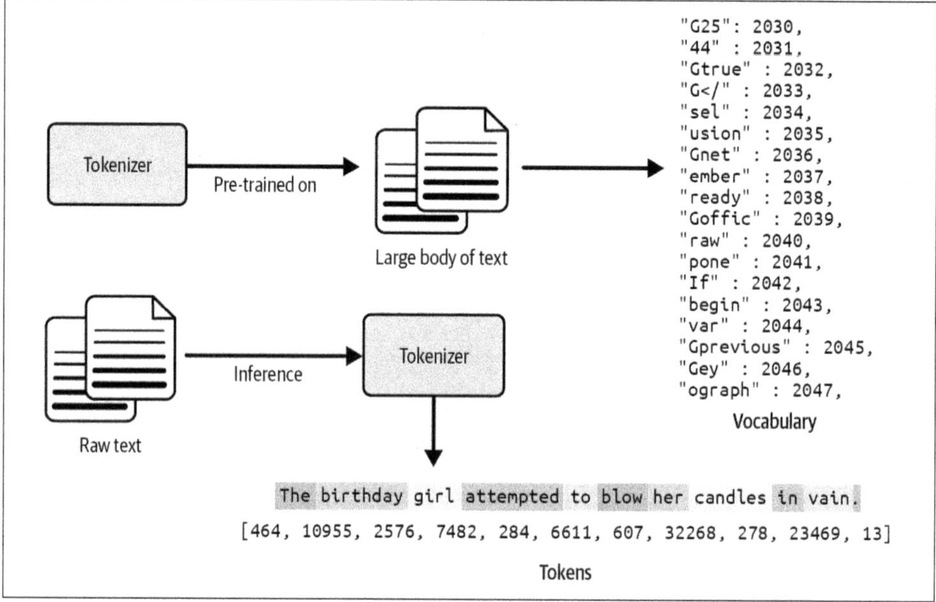

Figure 3-2. Tokenizer workflow

When we feed raw text to the tokenizer, it breaks the text into tokens that are part of the vocabulary and maps the tokens to their token indices. The sequence of token indices (input IDs) are then fed to the language model, where they are mapped to their corresponding embeddings. Let us explore this process in detail.

This time, let's experiment with the FLAN-T5 model. You need a Google Colab Pro or equivalent system to be able to run it:

```
!pip install transformers accelerate sentencepiece
from transformers import T5Tokenizer, T5ForConditionalGeneration
```

```
tokenizer = T5Tokenizer.from_pretrained("google/flan-t5-largel")
model = T5ForConditionalGeneration.from_pretrained("google/flan-t5-large",
    device_map="auto")


input_text = "what is 937 + 934?"
encoded_text = tokenizer.encode(input_text)
tokens = tokenizer.convert_ids_to_tokens(encoded_text)
print(encoded_text)
print(tokens)
```

The output is:

```
[125, 19, 668, 4118, 1768, 668, 3710, 58, 1]
['_what', '_is', '_9', '37', '_+', '_9', '34', '?', '</s>']
```

The `encode()` function tokenizes the input text and returns the corresponding token indices. The token indices are mapped to the tokens they represent using the `convert_ids_to_tokens()` function.

As you can see, the FLAN-T5 tokenizer doesn't have dedicated tokens for the numbers 937 or 934. Therefore, it splits the numbers into "9" and "37." The </s> token is a special token indicating the end of the string. The _ means that the token is preceded by a space.

Let's try another example:

```
input_text = "Insuffienct adoption of corduroy pants is the reason this

economy is in the dumps!!!"
encoded_text = tokenizer.encode(input_text)
tokens = tokenizer.convert_ids_to_tokens(encoded_text)
print(tokens)
```

The output is:

```
['_In', 's', 'uff', 'i', 'en', 'c', 't', '_adoption', '_of', '_cord', 'u',
'roy', '_pants', '_is', '_the', '_reason', '_this', '_economy', '_is', '_in',
'_the', '_dump', 's', '!!!', '</s>']
```

I made a deliberate typo with the word "Insufficient." Note that subword tokenization is rather brittle with typos. But at least the OOV problem has been dealt with by breaking the words into subwords. The vocabulary also doesn't seem to have an entry for the word "corduroy," thus confirming its poor sense of fashion. Meanwhile, note that there is a distinct token for three contiguous exclamation points, which is different from the token that represents a single exclamation point. Semantically, they do convey slightly different meanings.

Very large models trained on a massive body of text are more robust to misspellings. A lot of misspellings already occur in the training set. For example, even the rare misspelling "Insuffienct" occurs 14 times in the C4 pre-training dataset. The more common misspelling "insufficent" occurs over 1,100 times. Larger models can also infer the misspelled word from its context. Smaller models like BERT are quite sensitive to misspellings.

If you are using models from OpenAI, you can explore their tokenization scheme using the tiktoken library (*https://oreil.ly/2QByi*) (no relation to the social media website).

Using tiktoken, let's see the different vocabularies available in the OpenAI ecosystem:

```
!pip install tiktoken

import tiktoken
tiktoken.list_encoding_names()
```

The output is:

```
['gpt2', 'r50k_base', 'p50k_base', 'p50k_edit', 'cl100k_base', 'o200k_base']
```

The numbers like 50K/100K are presumed to be the vocabulary size. OpenAI hasn't revealed much information about these vocabularies. Their documentation does state that o200k_base is used by GPT-4o, while cl100k_base is used by GPT-4:

```
encoding = tiktoken.encoding_for_model("gpt-4")
input_ids = encoding.encode("Insuffienct adoption of corduroy pants is the

reason this economy is in the dumps!!!")
tokens = [encoding.decode_single_token_bytes(token) for token in input_ids]
```

The output is:

```
[b'Ins', b'uff', b'ien', b'ct', b' adoption', b' of', b' cord', b'uro', b'y',
b' pants', b' is', b' the', b' reason', b' this', b' economy', b' is', b' in',
b' the', b' dumps', b'!!!']
```

As you can see there is not much difference between the tokenization used by GPT-4 and FLAN-T5.

Exercise

This repo (*https://oreil.ly/TQoLz*) contains the vocabularies of o200k_base and cl100k_base. Find the differences between these vocabularies. What kinds of tokens are present in one but not the other?

For a given task, if you observe strange behavior from LLMs on only a subset of your inputs, it is worthwhile to check how they have been tokenized. While you cannot definitively diagnose your problem just by analyzing the tokenization, it is often helpful in analysis. In my experience, a non-negligible number of LLM failures can be attributed to the way the text was tokenized. This is especially true if your target domain is different from the pre-training domain.

Tokenization-Free Models

As discussed in Chapter 1, the *consolidation effect* is resulting in end-to-end architectures that attempt to accept human input, perform all required processing, and generate human consumable output within a single model. However, one last holdout is the tokenization step. You have seen in the code shown previously that the tokenization is used as a preprocessing step to prepare the input to be fed into the model. The input to the model is the sequence of token indices and not raw text. But what if we make the model truly end-to-end by removing the tokenization step? Is it possible to directly feed raw text to the model and have it output results?

There have been forays into the world of tokenization-free language modeling, with models like CANINE, ByT5, and Charformer.

- CANINE (*https://oreil.ly/ucLIk*) accepts Unicode codepoints as input. But there are 1,114,112 possible code points, rendering the vocabulary and resulting embedding layer size infeasible. To resolve this, CANINE uses hashed embeddings so that the effective vocabulary space is much smaller.
- ByT5 (*https://oreil.ly/x38Vs*) accepts input in terms of bytes, so there are only 259 tokens in the vocabulary (including a few special tokens), thus reducing the embedding layer size drastically.
- Charformer (*https://oreil.ly/WJY1k*) also accepts input in terms of bytes and passes it to a gradient-based subword tokenizer module that constructs latent subwords.

Tokenization Pipeline

Figure 3-3 depicts the sequence of steps performed by a tokenizer.

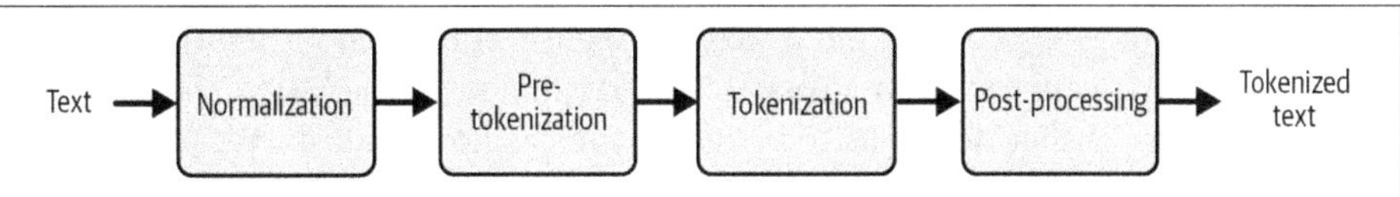

Figure 3-3. Hugging Face tokenizers pipeline

If you are using the `tokenizers` library from Hugging Face, your input text is run through a multistage tokenization pipeline (*https://oreil.ly/CcOKV*). This pipeline is composed of four components:

- Normalization
- Pre-tokenization
- Tokenization
- Postprocessing

Note that different models will execute different steps within these four components.

Normalization

Different types of normalization applied include:

- Converting text to lowercase (if you are using an uncased model)
- Stripping off accents from characters, like from the word Peña
- Unicode normalization

Let's see what kind of normalization is applied on the uncased version of BERT:

```
tokenizer = AutoTokenizer.from_pretrained("bert-base-uncased")
print(tokenizer.backend_tokenizer.normalizer.normalize_str(
    'Pédrò pôntificated at üs:-)')
```

The output is:

```
pedro pontificated at us:-)
```

As we can see, the accents have been removed and the text has been converted to lowercase.

There isn't much normalization done in tokenizers for more recent models.

Pre-Tokenization

Before we run the tokenizer on the text, we can optionally perform a pre-tokenization step. As mentioned earlier, most tokenizers today employ subword tokenization. A common step is to first perform word tokenization and then feed the output of it to the subword tokenization algorithm. This step is called pre-tokenization.

Pre-tokenization is a relatively easy step in English compared to many other languages, since you can start with a very strong baseline just by splitting text on whitespace. There are outlier decisions to be made, such as how to deal with punctuation, multiple spaces, numbers, etc. In Hugging Face the regular expression:

```
\w+|[^\w\s]+
```

is used to split on whitespace.

Let's run the pre-tokenization step of the T5 tokenizer:

```
tokenizer = AutoTokenizer.from_pretrained("google/flan-t5-xl")
tokenizer.backend_tokenizer.pre_tokenizer.pre_tokenize_str("I'm starting to

suspect - I am 55 years old!   Time to vist New York?")
```

The output is:

```
[("_I'm", (0, 3)),
 ('_starting', (3, 12)),
 ('_to', (12, 15)),
 ('_suspect', (15, 23)),
 ('_-', (23, 25)),
 ('_I', (25, 27)),
 ('_am', (27, 30)),
 ('_55', (30, 33)),
 ('_years', (33, 39)),
 ('_old!', (39, 44)),
 ('_', (44, 45)),
 ('_', (45, 46)),
 ('_Time', (46, 51)),
 ('_to', (51, 54)),
 ('_vist', (54, 59)),
 ('_New', (59, 63)),
 ('_York?', (63, 69))]
```

Along with the pre-tokens (or word tokens), the character offsets are returned.

The T5 pre-tokenizer splits only on whitespace, doesn't collapse multiple spaces into one, and doesn't split on punctuation or numbers. The behavior can be vastly different for other tokenizers.

Tokenization

After the optional pre-tokenization step, the actual tokenization step is performed. Some of the important algorithms in this space are byte pair encoding (BPE), byte-level BPE, WordPiece, and Unigram LM. The tokenizer comprises a set of rules that is learned during a pre-training phase over a pre-training dataset. Now let's go through these algorithms in detail.

Byte Pair Encoding

This algorithm is the simplest and most widely used tokenization algorithm.

Training stage

We take a training dataset, run it through the normalization and pre-tokenization steps discussed earlier, and record the unique tokens in the resulting output and their frequencies. We then construct an initial vocabulary consisting of the unique characters that make up these tokens. Starting from this initial vocabulary, we continue adding new tokens using *merge* rules. The merge rule is simple; we create a new token using the most frequent consecutive pairs of tokens. The merges continue until we reach the desired vocabulary size.

Let's explore this with an example. Imagine our training dataset is composed of six words, each appearing just once:

```
'bat', 'cat', 'cap', 'sap', 'map', 'fan'
```

The initial vocabulary is then made up of:

```
'b', 'a', 't', 'c', 'p', 's', 'm', 'f', 'n'
```

The frequencies of contiguous token pairs are:

```
'ba' - 1, 'at' - 2, 'ca' - 2, 'ap' - 3, 'sa' - 1, 'ma' - 1, 'fa' - 1, 'an' - 1
```

The most frequent pair is "ap," so the first merge rule is to merge "a" and "p." The vocabulary now is:

```
'b', 'a', 't', 'c', 'p', 's', 'm', 'f', 'n', 'ap'
```

The new frequencies are:

```
'ba' - 1, 'at' - 2, 'cap' - 1, 'sap' - 1, 'map' - 1, 'fa' - 1, 'an' - 1
```

Now, the most frequent pair is "at," so the next merge rule is to merge "a" and "t." This process continues until we reach the vocabulary size.

Inference stage

After the tokenizer has been trained, it can be used to divide the text into appropriate subword tokens and feed the text into the model. This happens in a similar fashion as the training step. After normalization and pre-tokenization of the input text, the resulting tokens are broken into individual characters, and all the merge rules are applied in order. The tokens standing after all merge rules have been applied are the final tokens, which are then fed to the model.

You can open the vocabulary file (*https://oreil.ly/7JAyY*) for GPT-NeoX again, and Ctrl+F "merges" to see the merge rules. As expected, the initial merge rules join single characters with each other. At the end of the merge list, you can see larger subwords like "out" and "comes" being merged into a single token.

Exercise

Implement the BPE algorithm by yourself, using a subset of the Wikipedia dataset that can be downloaded from here (*https://oreil.ly/xwGqK*). For a vocabulary size of 10,000, what tokens do you end up with and how do they differ from the vocabulary of the popular language models? Use the resulting tokenizer to tokenize a domain-specific dataset like the machine learning papers dataset from here (*https://oreil.ly/MqEY9*). Do all the technical concepts get their own tokens? This gives you a clue on how effective general-purpose LMs will be for your use case.

Since all unique individual characters in the tokenizer training set will get their own token, it is guaranteed that there will be no OOV tokens as long as all tokens seen during inference in the future are made up of characters that were present in the training set. But Unicode consists of over a million code points and around 150,000 valid characters, which would not fit in a vocabulary of size 30,000. This means that if your input text contained a character that wasn't in the training set, that character would be assigned an <UNK> token. To resolve this, a variant of BPE called byte-level BPE is used. Byte-level BPE starts with 256 tokens, representing all the characters that can be represented by a byte. This ensures that every Unicode character can be encoded just by the concatenation of the constituent byte tokens. Hence, it also ensures that we will never encounter an <UNK> token. The GPT family of models use this tokenizer.

WordPiece

WordPiece is similar to BPE, so we will highlight only the differences.

Instead of the frequency approach used by BPE, WordPiece uses the maximum likelihood approach. The frequency of the token pairs in the dataset is normalized by the product of the frequency of the individual tokens. The pairs with the resulting highest score are then merged:

```
score = freq(a,b)/(freq(a) * freq(b))
```

This means that if a token pair is made up of tokens that individually have low frequency, they will be merged first.

Figure 3-4 shows the merge priority and how the normalization by individual frequencies affects the order of merging.

Figure 3-4. WordPiece tokenization

During inference, merge rules are not used. Instead, for each pre-tokenized token in the input text, the tokenizer finds the longest subword from the vocabulary in the token and splits on it. For example, if the token is "understanding" and the longest subword in the dictionary within this token is "understand," then it will be split into "understand" and "ing."

Postprocessing

Now that we have looked at a couple of tokenizer algorithms, let's move on to the next stage of the pipeline, the postprocessing stage. This is where model-specific special tokens are added. Common tokens include [CLS], the classification token used in many language models, and [SEP], a separator token used to separate parts of the input.

> **The Curious Case of SolidMagiGoldkarp**
>
> There are weird tokens that end up being part of a language model's vocabulary due to the way the tokenization algorithms work. One such token is "SolidMagiGoldkarp," representing a now-deleted Reddit user who was one of the site's most active posters because of his quest to count to infinity. This was a token in the GPT-2 tokenizer vocabulary. The same tokenizer was used in GPT-3 models, but the pre-training dataset of the model had changed, so it didn't include many or any references to SolidMagiGoldkarp. So now a token existed for SolidMagiGoldkarp but there was no signal in the pre-training dataset to learn from. This leads to some anomalous and hilarious behavior in GPT-3. These tokens are called glitch tokens (*https://oreil.ly/wnB-z*) or undertrained tokens.

Token etymology is a new hobby for many LLM enthusiasts. This involves finding rare tokens in the vocabulary of language models and unearthing their origins. This is not just fun and games though, as knowing the origin of rare tokens can give you an insight into the characteristics of the pre-training dataset. Using tiktoken (*https://oreil.ly/z19c2*), find some rare vocabulary terms in GPT-4's or GPT-4o's vocabulary. Can you figure out their origins?

Special Tokens

Depending on the model, a few special tokens are added to the vocabulary to facilitate processing. These tokens can include:

<PAD>
: To indicate padding, in case the size of the input is less than the maximum sequence length.

<EOS>
: To indicate the end of the sequence. Generative models stop generating after outputting this token.

<UNK>
: To indicate an OOV term.

<TOOL_CALL>, </TOOL_CALL>
: Content between these tokens is used as input to an external tool, like an API call or a query to a database.

<TOOL_RESULT>, </TOOL_RESULT>
: Content between these tokens is used to represent the results from calling the aforementioned tools.

As we have seen, if our data is domain-specific like healthcare, scientific literature, etc., tokenization from a general-purpose tokenizer will be unsatisfactory. GALACTICA by Meta introduced several domain-specific tokens in their model and special tokenization rules:

- [START_REF] and [END_REF] for wrapping citations.
- <WORK> to wrap tokens that make up an internal working memory, used for reasoning and code generation.
- Numbers are handled by assigning each digit in the number its own token.
- [START_SMILES], [START_DNA], [START_AMINO], [END_SMILES], [END_DNA], [END_AMINO] for protein sequences, DNA sequences, and amino acid sequences, respectively.

Evaluating Tokenizers

Two popular metrics for evaluating tokenizers are fertility and parity.

Fertility is a measure of the average number of tokens needed to represent a dataset. It is calculated by dividing the number of tokens in a dataset by the number of words in a dataset. The higher the fertility, the lower the compression power of the tokenizer. Goldman et al. (*https://oreil.ly/ZEG_x*) show that higher compression leads to better downstream performance, although this is disputed in experiments by Schmidt et al. (*https://oreil.ly/GH_iK*). For a tokenizer to achieve higher compression levels, it needs to be trained on larger datasets during the vocabulary generation phase.

Parity is a measure of how fairly a tokenizer treats two languages. It is calculated by the ratio of tokens needed to represent the same data in one language versus the other.

Many language models today have multilingual support. However, due to the tokenizer being trained on an English-centric corpus, the tokenization for other languages tends to be suboptimal. Thus, a sentence in a non-English language may need several times more tokens to represent it compared to the same sentence in English, as shown by Petrov et al. (*https://oreil.ly/ZATOQ*)

If you are using a model on domain-specific data like healthcare, finance, law, biomedical, etc., with a tokenizer that was trained on general-purpose data, the compression ratio will be relatively lower because domain-specific words do not have their own tokens and will be split into multiple tokens. One way to adapt models to specialized domains is for models to learn good vector representations for domain-specific terms.

To this end, we can add new tokens to existing tokenizers and continue pre-training the model on domain-specific data so that those new domain-specific tokens learn effective representations. We will learn more about continued pre-training in Chapter 7.

For now, let's see how we can add new tokens to a vocabulary using Hugging Face.

Consider the sentence, "The addition of CAR-T cells and antisense oligonucleotides drove down incidence rates." The FLAN-T5 tokenizer splits this text as follows:

```
['__The', '__addition', '__of', '__C', 'AR', '-', 'T', '__cells', '__and', '__anti', 's', '
ense', '__', 'oli', 'gon', 'u', 'cle', 'o', 't', 'ides', '__drove', '__down', '__incidence',
'__rates', '.', '</s>']
```

Let's add the domain-specific terms to the vocabulary:

```
from transformers import T5Tokenizer, T5ForConditionalGeneration


tokenizer = T5Tokenizer.from_pretrained("google/flan-t5-large")
model = T5ForConditionalGeneration.from_pretrained("google/flan-t5-large",
    device_map="auto")

tokenizer.add_tokens(["CAR-T", "antisense", "oligonucleotides"])
model.resize_token_embeddings(len(tokenizer))
```

Now, tokenizing the string again gives the following tokens, with the domain-specific tokens being added:

> ['▁The', '▁addition', '▁of', 'CAR-T', '▁cells', '▁and', 'antisense', 'oligonucleotides', '▁drove', '▁down', '▁incidence', '▁rates', '.', '</s>']

We are only halfway done here. The embedding vectors corresponding to these new tokens do not contain any information about these tokens. We will need to learn the right representations for these tokens, which we can do using fine-tuning or continued pre-training, which we will discuss in Chapter 7.

Summary

In this chapter, we focused on a key ingredient of language models: their vocabulary. We discussed how vocabularies are defined and constructed in the realm of language models. We introduced the concept of tokenization and presented tokenization algorithms like BPE and WordPiece that are used to construct vocabularies and break down raw input text into a sequence of tokens that can be consumed by the language model. We also explored the vocabularies of popular language models and noted how tokens can differ from human conceptions of a word.

In the next chapter, we will continue exploring the remaining ingredients of a language model, including its architecture and the learning objectives on which models are trained.

CHAPTER 4
Architectures and Learning Objectives

In Chapters 2 and 3, we discussed some of the key ingredients that go into making a language model: the training datasets, and the vocabulary and tokenizer. Next, let's complete the puzzle by learning about the models themselves, the architectures underpinning them, and their learning objectives.

In this chapter, we will learn the composition of language models and their structure. Modern-day language models are predominantly based on the Transformer architecture, and hence we will devote most of our focus to understanding it, by going through each component of the architecture in detail. Over the last few years, several variants and alternatives to the original Transformer architecture have been proposed. We will go through the promising ones, including Mixture of Experts (MoE) models. We will also examine commonly used learning objectives the language models are trained over, including next-token prediction. Finally, we will bring together the concepts of the last three chapters in practice by learning how to pre-train a language model from scratch.

Preliminaries

Just about every contemporary language model is based on neural networks, composed of processing units called *neurons*. While modern neural networks do not resemble the workings of the human brain at all, many of the ideas behind neural networks and the terminology used is inspired by the field of neuroscience.

The neurons in a neural network are connected to each other according to some configuration. Each connection between a pair of neurons is associated with a weight (also called *parameter*), indicating the strength of the connection. The role these neurons play and the way they are connected to each other constitutes the *architecture* of the model.

The early 2010s saw the proliferation of multi-layer architectures, with layers of neurons stacked on top of each other, each layer extracting progressively more complex features of the input. This paradigm is called *deep learning.*

Figure 4-1 depicts a simple multi-layer neural network, also called the multi-layer perceptron.

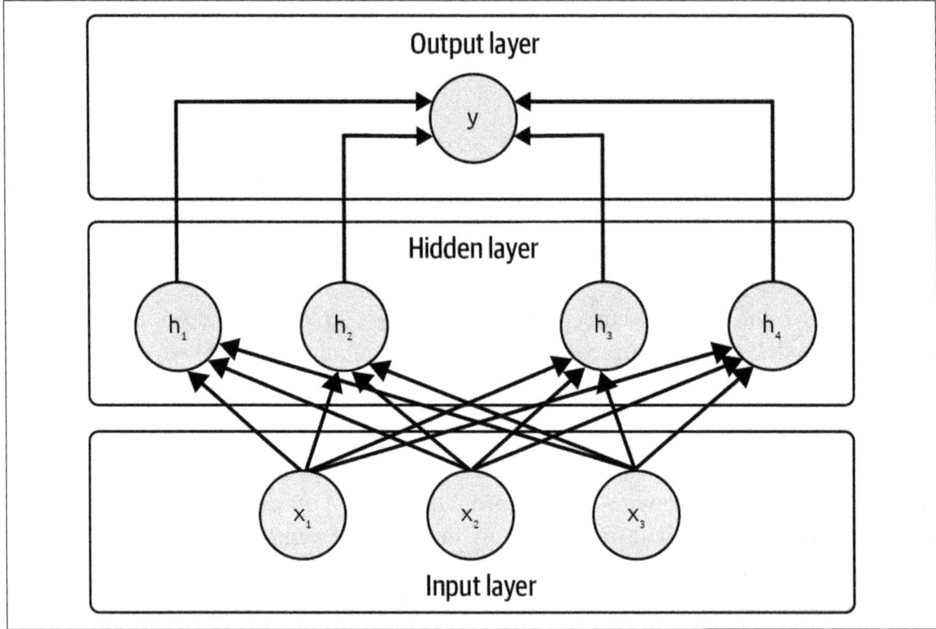

Figure 4-1. Multi-layer perceptron

For a more comprehensive treatment of neural networks, refer to Goldberg's book (*https://oreil.ly/oDc6x*) on neural network–based natural language processing.

As discussed in Chapter 1, language models are primarily pre-trained using self-supervised learning. Input text from the training dataset is tokenized and converted to vector form. The input is then propagated through the neural network, affected by its weights and *activation functions*, the latter introducing nonlinearity to the model. The output of the model is compared to the expected output, called the gold truth. The weights of the output are adapted such that next time for the same input, the output can be closer to the gold truth.

In practice, this adaptation process is implemented through a *loss function*. The goal of the model is to minimize the loss, which is the difference between the model output and the gold truth. To minimize the loss, the weights are updated using a gradient-descent based method, called backpropagation. I strongly recommend developing an intuitive understanding of this algorithm before diving into model training.

Self-Supervised Versus Supervised Learning

The distinction between self-supervised learning and supervised learning is artificial. The term "supervised learning" is used to describe learning by example using input-output pairs. To generate the training dataset, the output is typically annotated by a human or a computer. In the self-supervised variant, the output label does not need to be annotated because it already exists in nature, as part of the input. An example is web text on the internet with a learning objective like next-token prediction. The ground truth for the next-token objective exists within the input itself.

Representing Meaning

While describing neural network–based architectures in the previous section, we glossed over the fact that the input text is converted into vectors and then propagated through the network. What are these vectors composed of and what do they represent? Ideally, after the model is trained, these vectors should accurately represent some aspect of the meaning of the underlying text, including its social connotations. Developing the right representations for modalities like text or images is a very active field of research, called *representation learning*.

When training a language model from scratch, these vectors initially mean nothing, as they are randomly generated. In practice, there are initialization algorithms used like Glorot, He, etc. Refer to this report (*https://oreil.ly/A8Iro*) for a primer on neural network initialization.

How can a list of numbers represent meaning? It is hard for humans to describe the meaning of a word or sentence, let alone represent it in numerical form that can be processed by a computer. The *form* of a word, i.e., the letters that comprise it, usually do not give any information whatsoever about the meaning it represents. For example, the sequence of letters in the word *umbrella* contains no hints about its meaning, even if you are already exposed to thousands of other words in the English language.

The prominent way of representing meaning in numerical form is through the *distributional hypothesis* framework. The distributional hypothesis states that words that have similar meaning occur in similar contexts. The implication of this hypothesis is best represented by the adage:

> You shall know a word by the company it keeps.
>
> —John Rupert Firth, 1957

This is one of the primary ways in which we pick up the meaning of words we haven't encountered previously, without needing to look them up in a dictionary. A large number of words we know weren't learned from the dictionary or by explicitly learning the meaning of a word but by estimating meaning based on the contexts words appear in.

Let's investigate how the distributional hypothesis works in practice. The Natural Language Toolkit (NLTK) library provides a feature called *concordance view*, which presents you with the surrounding contexts that a given word appears in a corpus.

For example, let's see the contexts in which the word "nervous" occurs in the Jane Austen classic *Emma*:

```
from nltk.corpus import gutenberg
from nltk.text import Text
corpus = gutenberg.words('austen-emma.txt')
text = Text(corpus)
text.concordance("nervous")
```

The output looks like this:

```
Displaying 11 of 11 matches:
...spirits required support . He was a nervous man , easily depressed...
...sitting for his picture made him so nervous , that I could only take...
...assure you , excepting those little nervous headaches and palpitations...
...My visit was of use to the nervous part of her complaint , I hope...
...much at ease on the subject as his nervous constitution allowed...
...Her father was growing nervous , and could not understand her....
...
```

Exercise

Imagine you have never heard of the word "nervous" before. Would you be able to guess the meaning of the word "nervous" just by reviewing the various contexts it appears in?

Check the contexts of words that are synonyms of the word "nervous." How similar are they to the contexts of the word "nervous"?

The Transformer Architecture

Now that we have developed an intuition on how text is represented in vector form, let's further explore the canonical architecture used for training language models today, the Transformer.

In the mid 2010s, the predominant architectures used for NLP tasks were recurrent neural networks, specifically a variant called long short-term memory (LSTM). While knowledge of recurrent neural networks is not a prerequisite for this book, I recommend *Neural Network Methods for Natural Language Processing* (*https://oreil.ly/CHCTd*) for more details.

Recurrent neural networks were sequence models, which means they processed text one token at a time, sequentially. A single vector was used to represent the state of the entire sequence, so as the sequence grew longer, more and more information needed to be captured in the single state vector. Because of the sequential nature of processing, long-range dependencies were harder to capture, as the content from the beginning of the sequence would be harder to retain.

This issue was candidly articulated by Ray Mooney, a senior computer scientist who remarked at the Association for Computational Linguistics (ACL) 2014 conference:

> You can't cram the meaning of a whole %&!$# sentence into a single $&!#* vector!
>
> —Ray Mooney, 2014

Thus, there was a need for an architecture that solved for the deficiencies of LSTM: the limitations in representing long-range dependencies, the dependence on a single vector for representing the state of the entire sequence, and more. The Transformer architecture was designed to address these issues.

Figure 4-2 depicts the original Transformer architecture, developed in 2017 by Vaswani et al. (*https://oreil.ly/tIvGZ*) As we can see in the figure, a Transformer model is typically composed of Transformer blocks stacked on top of each other, called *layers*. The key components of each block are:

- Self-attention
- Positional encoding
- Feedforward networks
- Normalization blocks

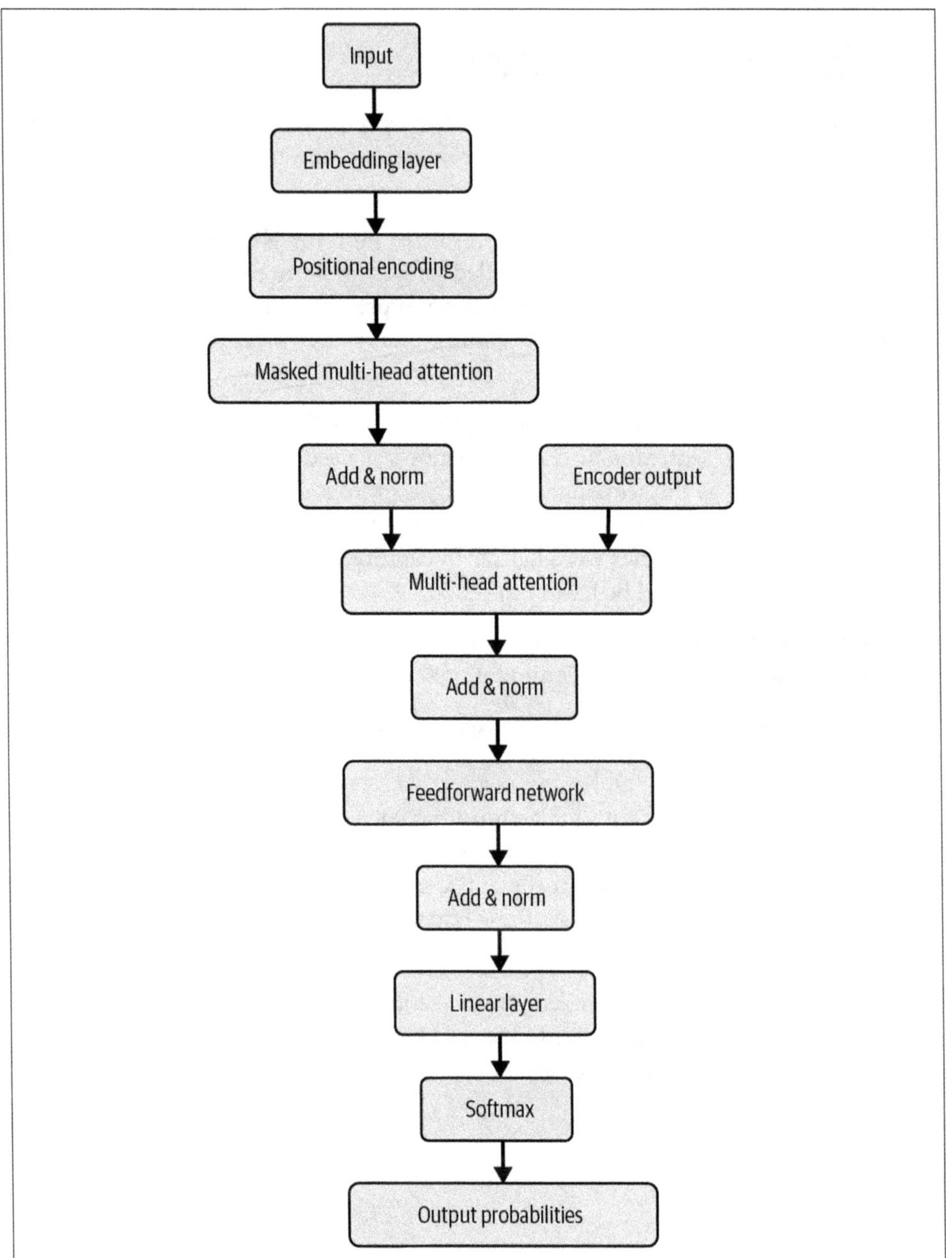

Figure 4-2. The Transformer architecture

At the beginning of the first block is a special layer called the *embedding* layer. This is where the tokens in the input text are mapped to their corresponding vector. The embedding layer is a matrix whose size is:

```
Number of tokens in the vocabulary * The vector dimension size
```

On Hugging Face, we can inspect the embedding layer as such, using the `transformers` library:

```
import torch
from transformers import LlamaTokenizer, LlamaModel

tokenizer = LlamaTokenizer.from_pretrained('llama3-base')
model = LlamaModel.from_pretrained('llama3-base')

sentence = "He ate it all"

inputs = tokenizer(sentence, return_tensors="pt")
input_ids = inputs['input_ids']
tokens = tokenizer.convert_ids_to_tokens(input_ids[0])

with torch.no_grad():
    embeddings = model.embeddings(input_ids)

for token, embedding in zip(tokens, embeddings[0]):
    print(f"Token: {token}\n
    print(f"Embedding: {embedding}\n")
```

The embedding vectors are the inputs that are then propagated through the rest of the network.

Next, let's go through each of the components in a Transformer block in detail and explore their role in the modeling process.

Self-Attention

The self-attention mechanism draws on the same principle as the distributional hypothesis introduced in "Representing Meaning" on page 89, emphasizing the role of context in shaping the meaning of a token. This operation generates representations for each token in a text sequence, capturing various aspects of language like syntax, semantics, and even pragmatics.

In the standard self-attention implementation, the representation of each token is a function of the representation of all other tokens in the sequence. Given a token for which we are calculating its representation, tokens in the sequence that contribute more to the meaning of the token are given more weight.

For example, consider the sequence:

```
'Mark told Sam that he was planning to resign.'
```

Figure 4-3 depicts how the representation for the token *he* is heavily weighted by the representation of the token *Mark*. In this case, the token *he* is a pronoun used to describe Mark in shorthand. In NLP, mapping a pronoun to its referent is called *co-reference resolution*.

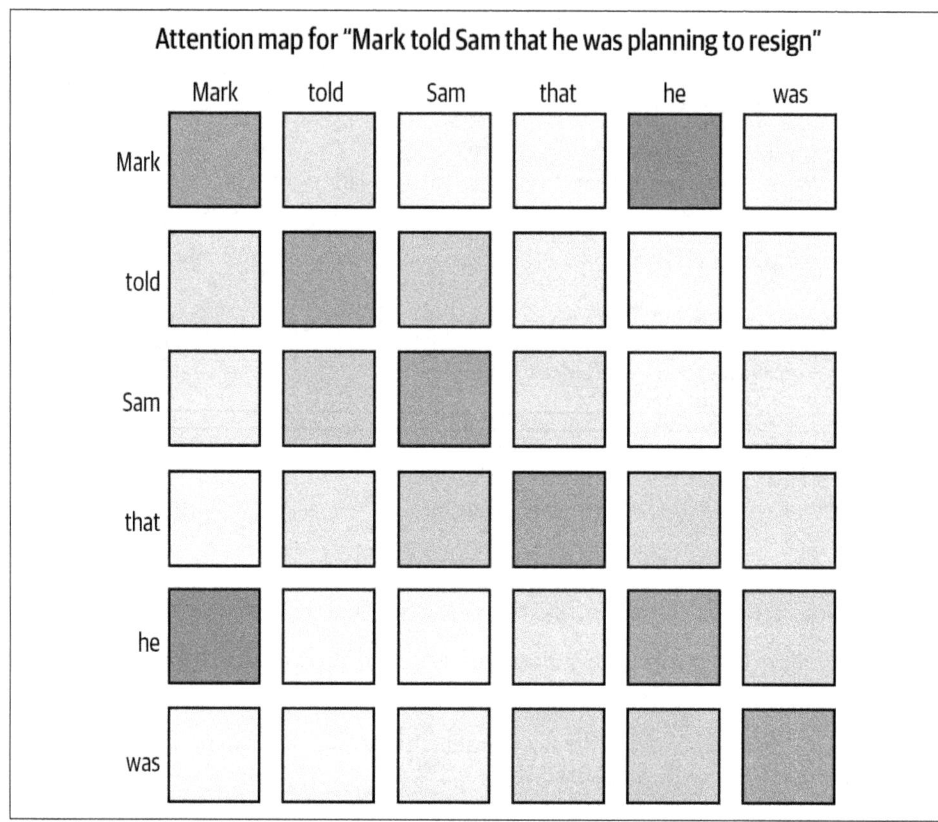

Figure 4-3. Attention map

In practice, self-attention in the Transformer is calculated using three sets of weight matrices called queries, keys, and values. Let's go through them in detail. Figure 4-4 shows how the query, key, and value matrices are used in the self-attention calculation.

Each token is represented by its embedding vector. This vector is multiplied with the query, key, and value weight matrices to generate three input vectors. Self-attention for each token is then calculated like this:

1. For each token, the dot products of its query vector with the key vectors of all the tokens (including itself) are taken. The resulting values are called attention scores.
2. The scores are scaled down by dividing them by the square root of the dimension of the key vectors.
3. The scores are then passed through a *softmax function* (*https://oreil.ly/b6gHV*) to turn them into a probability distribution that sums to 1. The softmax activation

function tends to amplify larger values, hence the reason for scaling down the attention scores in the previous step.

4. The normalized attention scores are then multiplied by the value vector for the corresponding token. The normalized attention score can be interpreted as the proportion that each token contributes to the representation of a given token.
5. In practice, there are multiple sets of query, key, and value vectors, calculating parallel representations. This is called multi-headed attention. The idea behind using multiple heads is that the model gets sufficient capacity to model various aspects of the input. The more the number of heads, the more chances that the *right* aspects of the input are being represented.

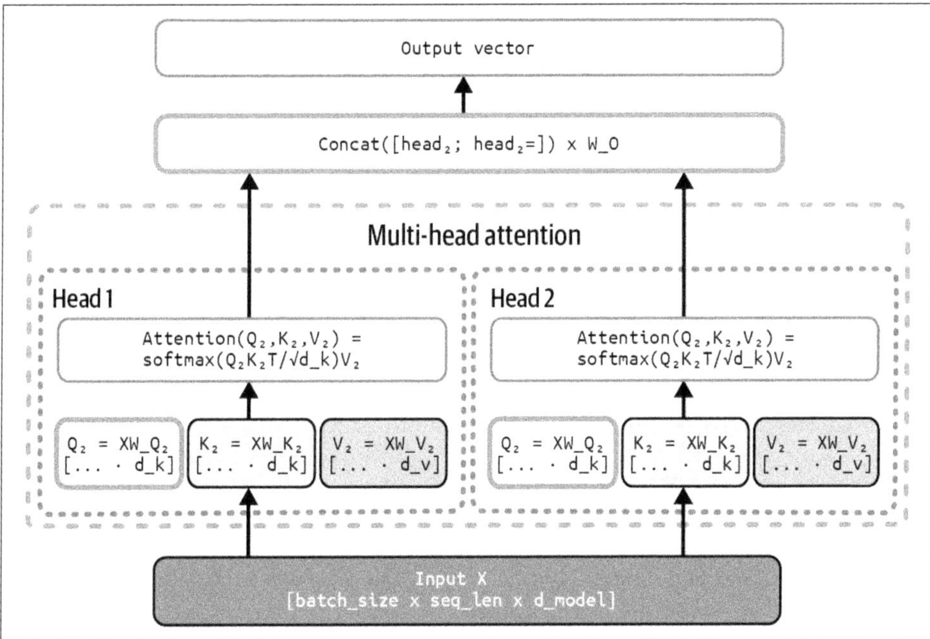

Figure 4-4. Self-attention calculation

This is how we implement self-attention in code:

```
import torch
import torch.nn as nn
import torch.nn.functional as F

q = wQ(input_embeddings)
k = WK(input_embeddings)
v = WV(input_embeddings)
dim_k = k.size(-1)

attn_scores = torch.matmul(q, k.transpose(-2, -1))
```

```
scaled_attn_scores = attn_scores/torch.sqrt(torch.tensor(dim_k,
  dtype=torch.float32))

normalized_attn_scores = F.softmax(scaled_attn_scores, dim=-1)

output = torch.matmul(normalized_attn_scores, v)
```

In some Transformer variants, self-attention is calculated only on a subset of tokens in the sequence; thus the vector representation of a token is a function of the representations of only some and not all the tokens in the sequence.

Positional Encoding

As discussed earlier, pre-Transformer architectures like LSTM were sequence models, with tokens being processed one after the other. Thus the positional information about the tokens, i.e., the relative positions of the tokens in a sequence, was implicitly baked into the model. However, for Transformers all calculations are done in parallel, and positional information should be fed to the model explicitly. Several methods have been proposed to add positional information, and this is still a very active field of research. Some of the common methods used in LLMs today include:

Absolute positional embeddings
: These were used in the original Transformer implementation by Vaswani et al. (*https://oreil.ly/CDq60*); examples of models using absolute positional embeddings include earlier models like BERT and RoBERTa.

Attention with Linear Biases (ALiBi)
: In this technique, the attention scores are penalized (*https://arxiv.org/abs/2108.12409*) with a bias term proportional to the distance between the query token and the key token. This technique also enables modeling sequences of longer length during inference than what was encountered in the training process.

Rotary Position Embedding (RoPE)
: Just like ALiBi, this technique (*https://arxiv.org/abs/2104.09864*) has the property of relative decay; there is a decay in the attention scores as the distance between the query token and the key token increases.

No Positional Encoding (NoPE)
: A contrarian technique (*https://oreil.ly/QM9dW*) argues that positional embeddings in fact are not required and that Transformers implicitly capture positional information.

Models these days are mostly using ALiBi or RoPE, although this is one aspect of the Transformer architecture that is still actively improving.

Feedforward Networks

The output from a self-attention block is fed through a *feedforward network* (*https://oreil.ly/Bdphg*). Each token representation is independently fed through the network. The feedforward network incorporates a nonlinear activation function like Rectified Linear Unit (ReLU) (*https://oreil.ly/KUqtP*) or Gaussian Error Linear Units (GELU) (*https://oreil.ly/MSDKE*), thus enabling the model to learn more complex features from the data. For more details on these activation functions, refer to this blog post from v7 (*https://oreil.ly/NfOb0*).

The feedforward layers are implemented in code in this way:

```
import torch
import torch.nn as nn

class FeedForward(nn.Module):
    def __init__(self, input_dim, hidden_dim):
        super(FeedForward, self).__init__()
        self.l1 = nn.Linear(input_dim, hidden_dim)
        self.l2 = nn.Linear(hidden_dim, input_dim)
        self.selu = nn.SeLU()

    def forward(self, x):
        x = self.selu(self.l1(x))
        x = self.l2(x)
        return x


feed_forward = FeedForward(input_dim, hidden_dim)
outputs = feed_forward(inputs)
```

Layer Normalization

Layer normalization is performed to ensure training stability and faster training convergence. While the original Transformer architecture performed normalization at the beginning of the block, modern implementations do it at the end of the block. The normalization is performed as follows:

1. Given an input of batch size `b`, sequence length `n`, and vector dimension `d`, calculate the mean and variance across each vector dimension.
2. Normalize the input by subtracting the mean and dividing it by the square root of the variance. A small epsilon value is added to the denominator for numerical stability.
3. Multiply by a scale parameter and add a shift parameter to the resulting values. These parameters are learned during the training process.

This is how it is represented in code:

```
import torch
import torch.nn as nn

class LayerNorm(nn.Module):
    def __init__(self, dimension, gamma=None, beta=None, epsilon=1e-5):
        super(LayerNorm, self).__init__()
        self.epsilon = epsilon
        self.gamma = gamma if gamma is not None else
        nn.Parameter(torch.ones(dimension))
        self.beta = beta if beta is not None else
        nn.Parameter(torch.zeros(dimension))


    def forward(self, x):
        mean = x.mean(-1, keepdim=True)
        variance = x.var(-1, keepdim=True, unbiased=False)
        x_normalized = (x - mean) / torch.sqrt(variance + self.epsilon)
        return self.gamma * x_normalized + self.beta

layer_norm = LayerNorm(embedding_dim)
outputs = layer_norm(inputs)
```

Loss Functions

So far, we have discussed all the components of each Transformer block. For the next token-prediction learning objective, the input is propagated through the Transformer layers to generate the final output, which is a probability distribution across all tokens. During training, the loss is calculated by comparing the output distribution with the gold truth. The gold truth distribution assigns a 1 to the gold truth token and 0 to all other tokens.

There are many possible ways to quantify the difference between the output and the gold truth. The most popular one is cross-entropy, which is calculated by the formula:

```
Cross-Entropy= -∑(gold truth probability)×log(output probability)
```

For example, consider the sequence:

```
'His pizza tasted ______'
```

Let's say the gold truth token is *good*, and the output probability distribution is (*terrible*: 0.65, *bad*:0.12, *good*:011,…)

The cross-entropy is calculated as:

```
-(0×log(0.65)+0×log(0.12)+1×log(0.11)+...)= -log(0.11)
```

Since the gold truth distribution values are 0 for all but the correct token, the equation can be simplified to:

```
Cross-Entropy = -log(output probability of gold truth token)
```

Once the loss is calculated, the gradient of the loss with respect to the parameters of the model is calculated and the weights are updated, using the backpropagation algorithm.

Intrinsic Model Evaluation

How do we know if the backpropagation algorithm is actually working and that the model is getting better over time? We can use either intrinsic model evaluation or extrinsic model evaluation.

Extrinsic model evaluation involves testing the model's performance on real-world downstream tasks. These tasks directly test the performance of the model but only on a narrow range of the model's capabilities. In contrast, intrinsic model evaluation involves a more general evaluation of the model's ability to model language, but with no guarantee that its performance in the intrinsic evaluation metric is directly proportional to its performance across all possible downstream tasks.

The most common intrinsic evaluation metric is *perplexity*. Perplexity measures the ability of a language model to accurately predict the next token in a sequence. A model that can always correctly predict the next token has a perplexity of 1. The higher the perplexity, the worse the language model. In the worst case, if the model is predicting at random, with probability of predicting each token in a vocabulary of size V being 1/V, then the perplexity is V.

Perplexity is related to cross-entropy by this formula:

```
Perplexity = 2^Cross-Entropy
```

Transformer Backbones

So far, we described the components of the canonical version of the Transformer. In practice, three major types of architecture backbones are used to implement the Transformer:

- Encoder-only
- Encoder-decoder
- Decoder-only

Let's look at each of these in detail.

Figure 4-5 depicts encoder-only, encoder-decoder, and decoder-only architectures.

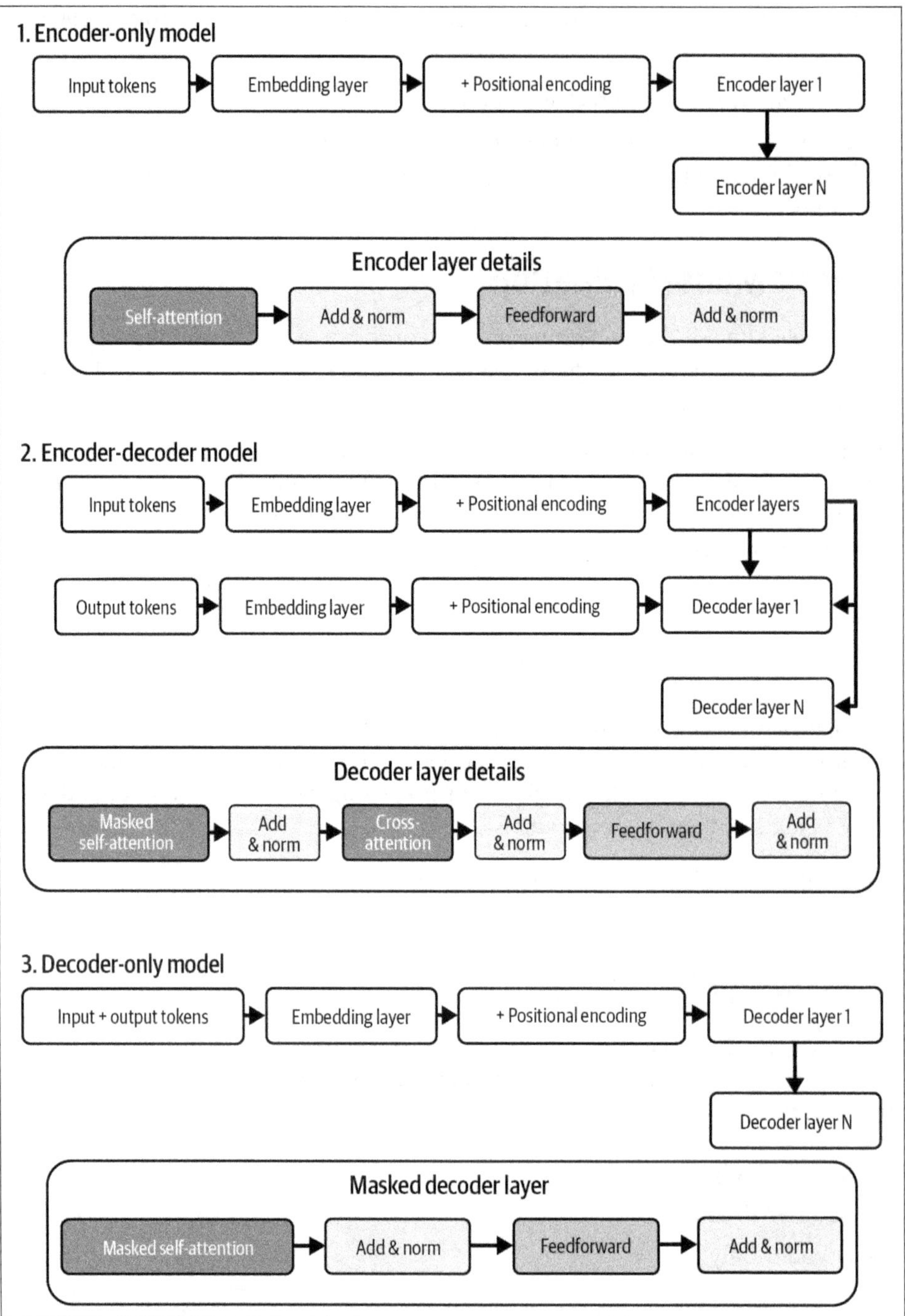

Figure 4-5. Visualization of various Transformer backbones

Encoder-Only Architectures

Encoder-only architectures were all the rage when Transformer-based language models first burst on the scene. Iconic language models from yesteryear (circa 2018) that use encoder-only architectures include BERT, RoBERTa, etc.

There haven't been many encoder-only LLMs trained since 2021 for a few reasons, including:

- They are relatively harder to train.
- The masked language modeling objective typically used to train them provides a learning signal in only a small percentage of tokens (the masking rate), thus needing a lot more data to reach the same level of performance as decoder-only models.
- For every downstream task, you need to train a separate task-specific head, making usage inefficient.

However, the release of ModernBERT seems to have reinvigorated this space.

The creators of the UL2 language model claim that encoder-only models should be considered obsolete. I personally wouldn't go that far; encoder-only models are still great choices for classification tasks. Moreover, if you already have a satisfactory pipeline for your use case built around encoder-only models, I would say if it ain't broke, why fix it?

Here are some guidelines for adopting encoder-only models:

- RoBERTa performs better than BERT most of the time, since it is trained a lot longer on more data, and it has adopted best practices learned after the release of BERT.
- DeBERTa and ModernBERT are currently regarded as the best-performing encoder-only models.
- The distilled versions of encoder-only models like DistilBERT, etc., are not too far off from the original models in terms of performance, and they should be considered if you are operating under resource constraints.

Several embedding models are built from encoder-only models. For example, one of the most important libraries in the field of NLP, the Swiss Army knife of NLP tools, *sentence transformers*, provides encoder-only embedding models that are very widely used. all-mpnet-base-v2, based on an encoder-only model called MPNet, and fine-tuned on several task datasets, is still competitive with much larger embedding models.

Encoder-Decoder Architectures

This is the original architecture of the Transformer, as it was first proposed. The T5 series of models uses this architecture type.

In encoder-decoder models, the input is text and the output is also text. A standardized interface ensures that the same model and training procedure can be used for multiple tasks. The inputs are handled by an encoder, and the outputs by the decoder.

Decoder-Only Architectures

A majority of LLMs trained today use decoder-only models. Decoder-only models came into fashion starting from the original GPT model from OpenAI. Decoder-only models excel at zero-shot and few-shot learning.

Decoder models can be causal and noncausal. Noncausal models have bidirectionality over the input sequence, while the output is still autoregressive (you cannot look ahead).

While the field is still evolving, there has been some compelling evidence (*https://oreil.ly/Sb7JS*) for the following results:

- Decoder-only models are the best choice for zero-shot and few-shot generalization.
- Encoder-decoder models are the best choice for multi-task fine tuning.

The best of both worlds is to combine the two: start with autoregressive training, and then in an adaptation step, pre-train further with a noncausal setup using a span corruption objective.

In this section, we discussed how architectural backbones can be classified according to how they use the architecture's encoder and decoder. Another architectural backbone type that is making inroads in the past year is the Mixture of Experts (MoE) paradigm. Let's explore that in detail.

Mixture of Experts

Remarkably, in the seven years since the invention of the Transformer architecture, the Transformer implementation used in current language models isn't too different from the original version, despite hundreds of papers proposing modifications to it. The original architecture has proven to be surprisingly robust, with most proposed variants barely moving the needle in terms of performance. However, some components of the Transformer have seen changes, like positional encodings as discussed earlier in the chapter.

MoE models have been seeing a lot of success in the past couple of years. Examples include OpenAI's GPT-4 (unconfirmed), Google's Switch, DeepSeek's DeepSeek V3, and Mistral's Mixtral. In this section, we will learn the motivations behind developing this architecture and how it works in practice.

As shown in Chapter 1, the scaling laws dictate that performance of the language model increases as you increase the size of the model and its training data. However, increasing the model capacity implies more compute is needed for both training and inference. This is undesirable, especially at inference time, when latency requirements can be stringent. Can we increase the capacity of a model without increasing the required compute?

One way to achieve this is using conditional computation; each input (either a token or the entire sequence) sees a different subset of the model, interacting with only the parameters that are best suited to process it. This is achieved by composing the architecture to be made up of several components called experts, with only a subset of experts being activated for each input.

Figure 4-6 depicts a canonical MoE model.

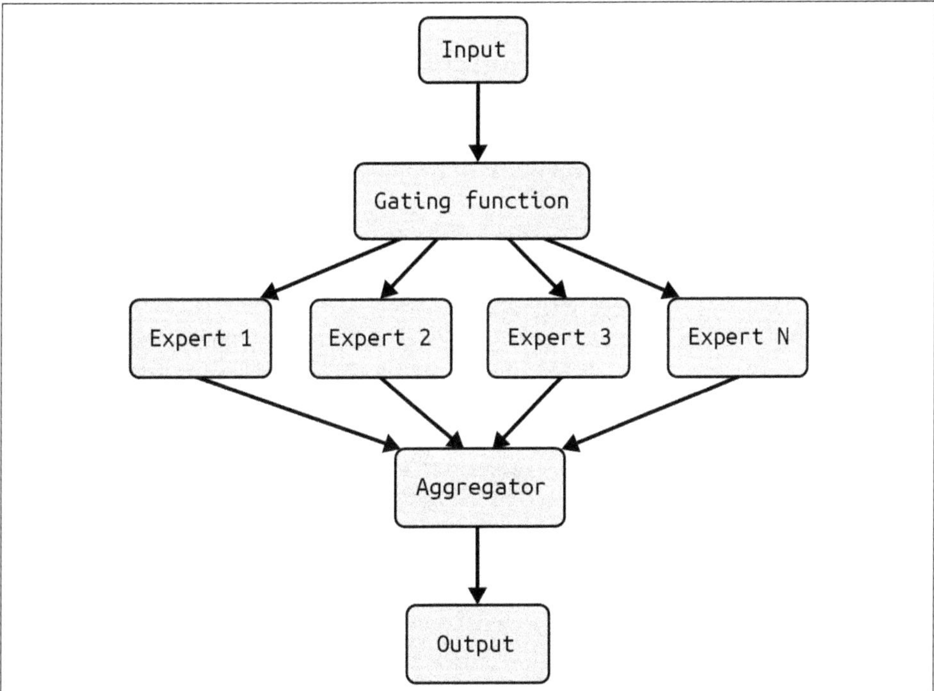

Figure 4-6. Mixture of Experts

A key component of the MoE architecture is the *gating function*. The gating function helps decide which expert is more suited to process a given input. The gating function is implemented as a weight applied to each expert.

The experts are typically added to the feedforward component of the Transformer. Therefore, if there are eight experts, then there will be eight feedforward networks instead of one. Based on the routing strategy used, only a small subset of these networks will be activated for a given input.

The routing strategy determines the number and type of experts activated. Two types of popular routing strategies exist:

- Tokens choose
- Experts choose

In the tokens choose strategy, each token chooses k experts. k is typically a small number (~2). The disadvantage of using this strategy is the need for load balancing. If in a given input batch, most of the tokens end up using the same experts, then additional time is needed to finish the computation as we cannot benefit from the parallelization afforded by multiple experts.

In the experts choose strategy, each expert picks the tokens that it is most equipped to handle. This solves the load balancing problem as we can specify that each expert choose the same number of tokens. However, this also leads to inefficient token-expert matching, as each expert is limited to picking only a finite number of tokens in a batch.

Upcycling Models

Very few MoE models are publicly available as of the book's writing. Can we turn an existing general Transformer-based model into an MoE model? Komatsuzaki et al. (*https://oreil.ly/jJEot*) have devised an upcycling method that can be used to add an MoE component to an already pre-trained model. This is done by making N copies of the feedforward layers, one for each expert, and using the original parameters of these layers as the initialization parameters for the MoE model.

Learning Objectives

Now that we have discussed the architecture of language models, let's turn our focus to understanding the tasks they are trained on during the pre-training process.

As mentioned earlier in the chapter, language models are pre-trained in a self-supervised manner. The scale of data we need to train them makes it prohibitively expensive to perform supervised learning, where (input, output) examples need to come from humans. Instead, we use a form of training called self-supervision, where the data itself contains the target labels. The goal of self-supervised learning is to learn a task which acts as a proxy for learning the syntax and semantics of a language, as well as skills like reasoning, arithmetic and logical manipulation, and other cognitive tasks, and (hopefully) eventually leading up to general human intelligence. How does this work?

For example, let's take the canonical language modeling task: predicting the next word that comes in a sequence. Consider the sequence:

```
'Tammy jumped over the'
```

and the language model is asked to predict the next token. The total number of possible answers is the size of the vocabulary. There are many valid continuations to this sequence, like (hedge, fence, barbecue, sandcastle, etc.), but many continuations to this sequence would violate English grammar rules like (is, of, the). During the training process, after seeing billions of sequences, the model will know that it is highly improbable for the word "the" to be followed by the word "is" or "of," regardless of the surrounding context. Thus, you can see how just predicting the next token is such a powerful tool: in order to correctly predict the next token you can eventually learn more and more complex functions that you can encode in your model connections. However, whether this paradigm is all we need to develop general intelligence is an open question.

Self-supervised learning objectives used for pre-training LLMs can be broadly classified (nonexhaustively) into three types:

- Full language modeling (FLM)
- Masked language modeling (MLM)
- Prefix language modeling (PrefixLM)

Let's explore these in detail.

Full Language Modeling

Figure 4-7 shows the canonical FLM objective at work.

Original text

The birthday girl attempted to blow her candles in vain

The birthday girl attempted to blow her candles in <predict next token> 'vain'

Figure 4-7. Full language modeling

This is the canonical language modeling objective of learning to predict the next token in a sequence and currently the simplest and most common training objective, used by GPT-4 and a vast number of open source models. The loss is computed for every token the model sees, i.e., every single token in the training set that is being asked to be predicted by the language model provides a learning signal for the model, making it very efficient.

Let's explore an example, using the GPT Neo model.

Suppose we continue pre-training the GPT Neo model from its publicly available checkpoint, using the full language modeling objective. Let's say the current training sequence is:

```
'Language models are ubiquitous'
```

You can run this code:

```
import torch
from transformers import AutoTokenizer, GPTNeoForCausalLM


tokenizer = AutoTokenizer.from_pretrained("EleutherAI/gpt-neo-1.3B")
model = GPTNeoForCausalLM.from_pretrained("EleutherAI/gpt-neo-1.3B")


input_ids = tokenizer("Language models are", return_tensors="pt")
gen_tokens = model.generate(**input_ids, max_new_tokens =1,

output_scores=True, return_dict_in_generate=True)
output_scores = gen_tokens["scores"]
scores_tensor = output_scores[0]
sorted_indices = torch.argsort(scores_tensor[0], descending=True)[:20]


for index in sorted_indices:
    token_id = index
    token_name = tokenizer.decode([token_id.item()])
    token_score = scores_tensor[0][index].item()
    print(f"Token: {token_name}, Score: {token_score}")
```

This code tokenizes the input text `Language models are` and feeds it to the model by invoking the `generate()` function. The function predicts the continuation, given the sequence "Language models are." It outputs only one token and stops generating because `max_new_tokens` is set to 1. The rest of the code enables it to output the top 20 list of tokens with the highest score, prior to applying the softmax at the last layer.

The top 20 tokens with the highest prediction score are:

```
Output: Token:  a, Score: -1.102203369140625
Token:  used, Score: -1.4315788745880127
Token:  the, Score: -1.7675716876983643
Token:  often, Score: -1.8415470123291016
Token:  an, Score: -2.4652323722839355
Token:  widely, Score: -2.657834053039551
```

```
Token:  not, Score: -2.6726579666137695
Token:  increasingly, Score: -2.7568516731262207
Token:  ubiquitous, Score: -2.8688106536865234
Token:  important, Score: -2.902832508087158
Token:  one, Score: -2.9083480834960938
Token:  defined, Score: -3.0815649032592773
Token:  being, Score: -3.2117576599121094
Token:  commonly, Score: -3.3110013008117676
Token:  very, Score: -3.317342758178711
Token:  typically, Score: -3.4478530883789062
Token:  complex, Score: -3.521362781524658
Token:  powerful, Score: -3.5338563919067383
Token:  language, Score: -3.550961971282959
Token:  pervasive, Score: -3.563507080078125
```

Every word in the top 20 seems to be a valid continuation of the sequence. The ground truth is the token `ubiquitous`, which we can use to calculate the loss and initiate the backpropagation process for learning.

As another example, consider the text sequence:

```
'I had 25 eggs. I gave away 12. I now have 13'
```

Run the same code as previously, except for this change:

```
input_ids = tokenizer("'I had 25 eggs. I gave away 12. I now have",
  return_tensors="pt")
```

The top 20 output tokens are:

```
Token:  12, Score: -2.3242850303649902
Token:  25, Score: -2.5023117065429688
Token:  only, Score: -2.5456185340881348
Token:  a, Score: -2.5726099014282227
Token:  2, Score: -2.6731367111206055
Token:  15, Score: -2.6967623233795166
Token:  4, Score: -2.8040688037872314
Token:  3, Score: -2.839219570159912
Token:  14, Score: -2.847306728363037
Token:  11, Score: -2.8585362434387207
Token:  1, Score: -2.877161979675293
Token:  10, Score: -2.9321107864379883
Token:  6, Score: -2.982785224914551
Token:  18, Score: -3.0570476055145264
Token:  20, Score: -3.079172134399414
Token:  5, Score: -3.111320972442627
Token:  13, Score: -3.117424726486206
Token:  9, Score: -3.125835657119751
Token:  16, Score: -3.1476120948791504
Token:  7, Score: -3.1622045040130615
```

The correct answer has the 17th highest score. A lot of numbers appear in the top 10, showing that the model is more or less randomly guessing the answer, which is not surprising for a smaller model like GPT Neo.

The OpenAI API provides the `logprobs` parameter that allows you to specify the number of tokens along with their log probabilities that need to be returned. As of the book's writing, only the `logprobs` of the 20 most probable tokens are available. The tokens returned are in order of their log probabilities:

```
import openai
openai.api_key = <Insert your OpenAI key>


openai.Completion.create(
  model="gpt-4o",
  prompt="I had 25 eggs. I gave away 12. I now have ",
  max_tokens=1,
  temperature=0,
  logprobs = 10
)
```

This code calls the older gpt-4o model, asking it to generate a maximum of one token. The output is:

```
"top_logprobs": [
          {
            "\n": -0.08367541,
            " 13": -2.8566456,
            "___": -4.579212,
            "____": -4.978668,
            "________": -6.220278
            ...
          }
```

gpt-4o is pretty confident that the answer is 13, and rightfully so. The rest of the top probability tokens are all related to output formatting.

During inference, we don't necessarily need to generate the token with the highest score. Several *decoding strategies* allow you to generate more diverse text. We will discuss these strategies in Chapter 5.

Exercise

Ask the gpt-4o model to solve individual crossword clues in the Boatload Puzzles Crossword (*https://oreil.ly/HvK_O*). You may have to iterate with the prompt. A good start would be “Solve this crossword and answer in one word. The clue is <X> and it is a <Y> letter word. The answer is: Set `max_tokens=3` to account for formatting tokens. Analyze the `logprob`’s output. Is it dangerously close to getting it right/wrong? How many clues does it answer correctly?

Prefix Language Modeling

Prefix LM is similar to the FLM setting. The difference is that FLM is fully causal, i.e., in a left-to-right writing system like English, tokens do not attend to tokens to the right (future). In the prefix LM setting, a part of the text sequence, called the prefix, is allowed to attend to future tokens in the prefix. The prefix part is thus noncausal. For training prefix LMs, a random prefix length is sampled, and the loss is calculated over only the tokens in the suffix.

Masked Language Modeling

Figure 4-8 shows the canonical MLM objective at work.

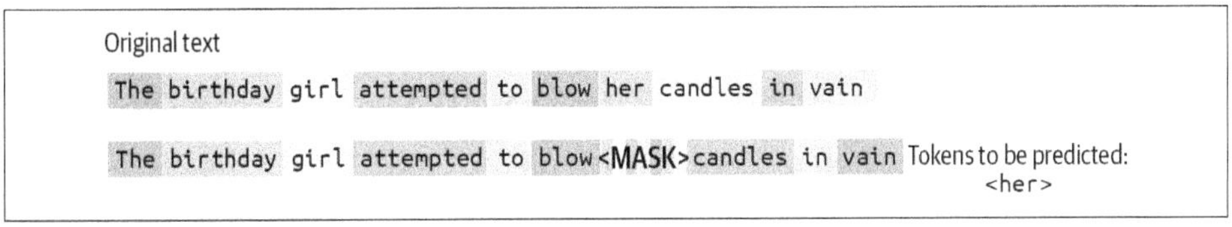

Original text

`The birthday girl attempted to blow her candles in vain`

`The birthday girl attempted to blow`<MASK>`candles in vain` Tokens to be predicted: `<her>`

Figure 4-8. Masked Language Modeling in BERT

In the MLM setting, rather than predict the next token in a sequence, we ask the model to predict masked tokens within the sequence. In the most basic form of MLM implemented in the BERT model, 15% of tokens are randomly chosen to be masked and are replaced with a special mask token, and the language model is asked to predict the original tokens.

The T5 model creators used a modification of the original MLM objective. In this variant, 15% of tokens are randomly chosen to be removed from a sequence. Consecutive dropped-out tokens are replaced by a single unique special token called the *sentinel token*. The model is then asked to predict and generate the dropped tokens, delineated by the sentinel tokens.

As an example, consider this sequence:

> Tempura has always been a source of conflict in the family due to unexplained reasons

Let's say we drop the tokens "has," "always," "of," and "conflict." The sequence is now:

> Tempura <S1> been a source <S2> in the family due to unexplained reasons

with S1, S2 being the sentinel tokens. The model is expected to output:

> <S1> has always <S2> of conflict <E>

The output sequence is terminated by a special token indicating the end of the sequence.

Generating only the dropped tokens and not the entire sequence is computationally more efficient and saves training time. Note that unlike in Full Language Modeling, the loss is calculated over only a small proportion of tokens (the masked tokens) in the input sequence.

Let's explore this on Hugging Face:

```
from transformers import T5Tokenizer, T5ForConditionalGeneration

tokenizer = T5Tokenizer.from_pretrained("t5-3b")
model = T5ForConditionalGeneration.from_pretrained("t5-3b")

input_ids = tokenizer("Tempura <extra_id_0>  been a source <extra_id_1> in the
family due to unexplained reasons", return_tensors="pt").input_ids
targets = tokenizer("<extra_id_0> has always <extra_id_1> of conflict

<extra_id_2>", return_tensors="pt").input_ids
loss = model(input_ids=input_ids, labels=labels).loss
```

The targets can be prepared using a simple templating function.

Exercise

Play around with different masking strategies. Specifically:

- Change the masking rate. What happens if you mask 30% or 50% of tokens?
- Change the masking strategy. Can you do better than random masking? What heuristics allow you to mask tokens that would contribute more to learning?

More generally, MLM can be interpreted as a *denoising autoencoder*. You corrupt your input by adding noise (masking, dropping tokens), and then you train a model to regenerate the original input. BART takes this to the next level by using five different types of span corruptions:

Random token masking

Figure 4-9 depicts the corruption and denoising steps.

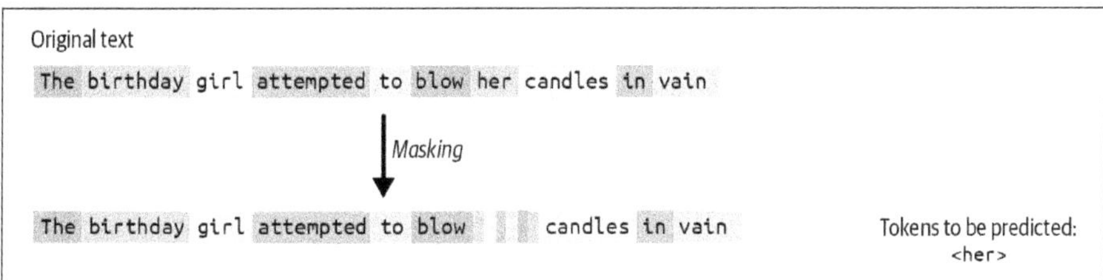

Figure 4-9. Random token masking in BART

Random token deletion

The model needs to predict the positions in the text where tokens have been deleted. Figure 4-10 depicts the corruption and denoising steps.

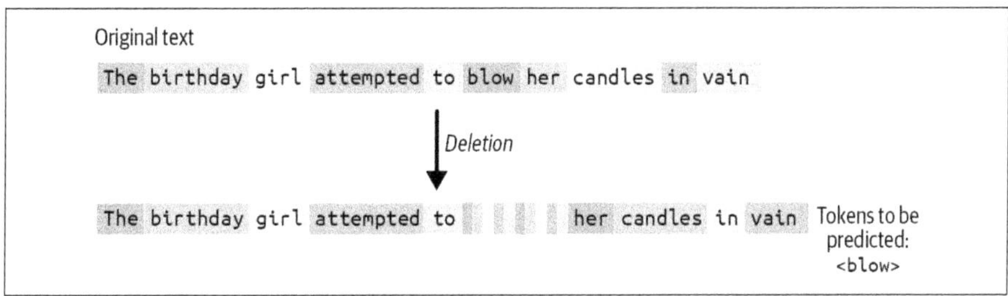

Figure 4-10. Random token deletion in BART

Span masking

Text spans are sampled from text, with span lengths coming from a Poisson distribution. This means zero-length spans are possible. The spans are deleted from the text and replaced with a single mask token. Therefore, the model now has to also predict the number of tokens deleted. Figure 4-11 depicts the corruption and denoising steps.

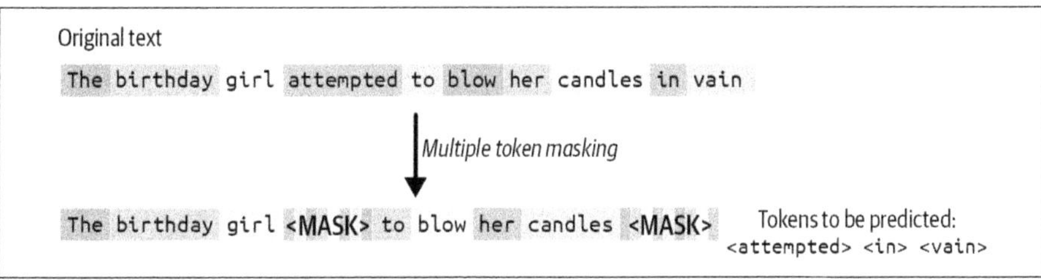

Figure 4-11. Span masking in BART

Document shuffling

Sentences in the input document are shuffled. The model is taught to arrange them in the right order. Figure 4-12 depicts the corruption and denoising steps.

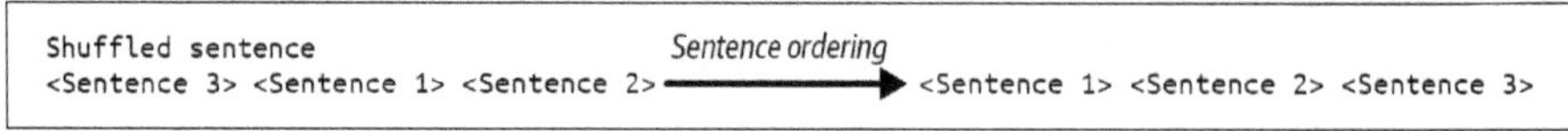

Figure 4-12. Document shuffling objective in BART

Document rotation

The document is rotated so that it starts from an arbitrary token. The model is trained to detect the correct start of the document. Figure 4-13 depicts the corruption and denoising steps.

Original rotated sentences
<Sentence 2> <Sentence 1> <Sentence 3>
Document rotation
<Sentence 1> <Sentence 2> <Sentence 3>

Figure 4-13. Document rotation objective in BART

Which Learning Objectives Are Better?

It has been shown that models trained with FLM are better at generation, and models trained with MLM are better at classification tasks. However, it is inefficient to use different language models for different use cases. The consolidation effect continues to take hold, with the introduction of UL2 (*https://oreil.ly/xJc3U*), a paradigm that combines the best of different learning objective types in a single model.

UL2 mimics the effect of PLMs, MLMs, and PrefixLMs in a single paradigm called *Mixture of Denoisers*.

The denoisers used are as follows:

R-Denoiser

This is similar to the T5 span corruption task. Spans between length 2–5 tokens are replaced by a single mask token. Figure 4-14 depicts the workings of the R-denoiser.

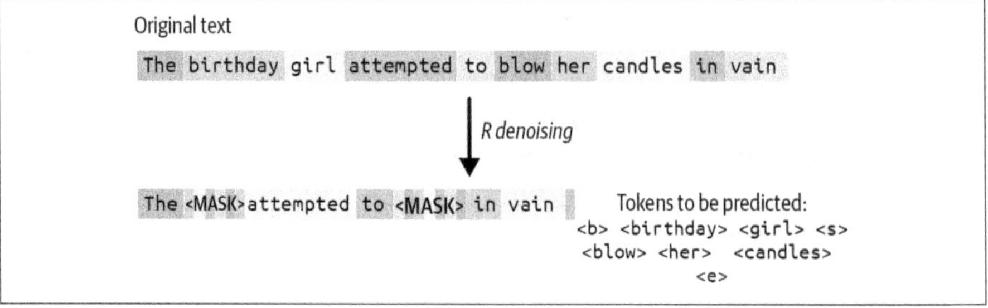

Figure 4-14. UL2's R-Denoiser

S-Denoiser

Similar to prefix LM, the text is divided into a prefix and a suffix. The suffix is masked, while the prefix has access to bidirectional context. Figure 4-15 depicts the workings of the S-Denoiser.

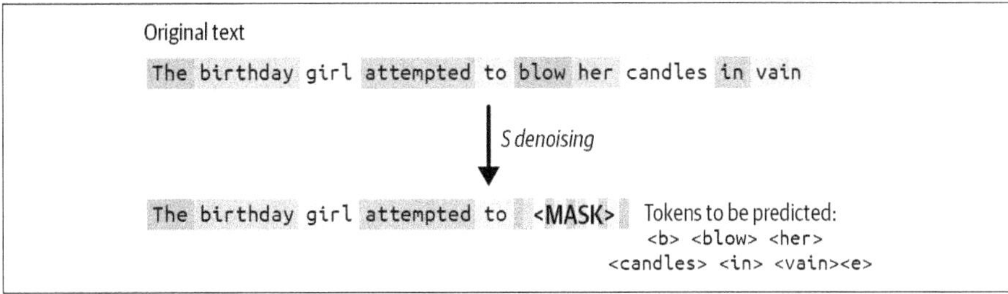

Figure 4-15. UL2's S-Denoiser

X-Denoiser

This stands for extreme denoising, where a large proportion of text is masked (often over 50%). Figure 4-16 depicts the workings of the X-Denoiser.

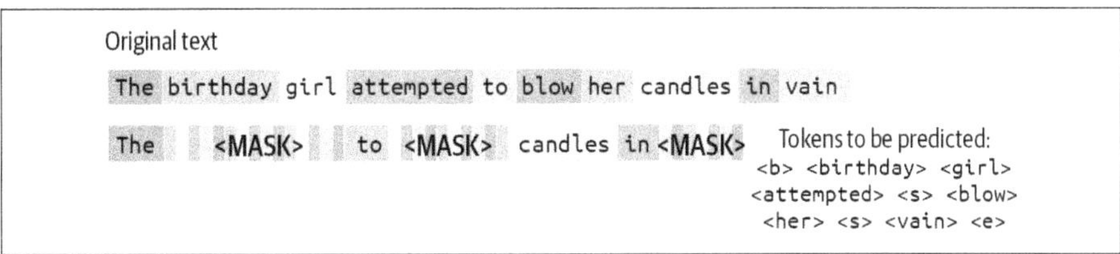

Figure 4-16. UL2's X-Denoiser

Pre-Training Models

Now that we have learned about the ingredients that go into a language model in detail, let's learn how to pre-train one from scratch.

The language models of today are learning to model two types of concepts with one model:

- Language, the vehicle used to communicate facts, opinions, and feelings.
- The underlying phenomena that led to the construction of text in the language.

For many application areas, we are far more interested in learning to model the latter than the former. While a language model that is fluent in the language is welcome, we would prefer to see it get better at domains like science or law and skills like reasoning and arithmetic.

These concepts and skills are expressed in languages like English, which primarily serve a social function. Human languages are inherently ambiguous, contain lots of redundancies, and in general are inefficient vehicles to transmit underlying concepts.

This brings us to the question: are human languages even the best vehicle for language models to learn underlying skills and concepts? Can we separate the process of modeling the language from modeling the underlying concepts expressed through language?

Let's put this theory to the test using an example. Consider training an LLM from scratch to learn to play the game of chess.

Recall the ingredients of a language model from Chapter 2. We need:

- A pre-training dataset
- A vocabulary and tokenization scheme
- A model architecture
- A learning objective

For training the chess language model, we can choose the Transformer architecture with the next-token prediction learning objective, which is the de facto paradigm used today.

For the pre-training dataset, we can use the chess games dataset from Lichess (*https://oreil.ly/XmWvv*), containing billions of games. We select a subset of 20 million chess games for our training.

This dataset is in the Portable Game Notation (PGN) format, which is used to represent the sequence of chess moves in a concise notation.

Finally, we have to choose the vocabulary of the model. Since the only purpose of this model is to learn chess, we don't need to support an extensive English vocabulary. In fact, we can take advantage of the PGN notation to assign tokens to specific chess concepts.

Here is an example of a chess game in PGN format, taken from pgnmentor.com (*https://oreil.ly/H3yOs*):

```
1. e4 c5 2. Nf3 a6 3. d3 g6 4. g3 Bg7 5. Bg2 b5 6. O-O Bb7 7. c3 e5 8. a3 Ne7
9. b4 d6 10. Nbd2 O-O 11. Nb3 Nd7 12. Be3 Rc8 13. Rc1 h6 14. Nfd2 f5 15. f4
Kh7 16. Qe2 cxb4 17. axb4 exf4 18. Bxf4 Rxc3 19. Rxc3 Bxc3 20. Bxd6 Qb6+ 21.
Bc5 Nxc5 22. bxc5 Qe6 23. d4 Rd8 24. Qd3 Bxd2 25. Nxd2 fxe4 26. Nxe4 Nf5 27.
d5 Qe5 28. g4 Ne7 29. Rf7+ Kg8 30. Qf1 Nxd5 31. Rxb7 Qd4+ 32. Kh1 Rf8 33. Qg1
Ne3 34. Re7 a5 35. c6 a4 36. Qxe3 Qxe3 37. Nf6+ Rxf6 38. Rxe3 Rd6 39. h4 Rd1+
40. Kh2 b4 41. c7 1-0
```

The rows of the board are assigned letters a–h and the columns are assigned numbers 1–8. Except for pawns, each piece type is assigned a capital letter, with N for knight, R for rook, B for bishop, Q for queen, and K for king. A + appended to a move indicates a check, a % appended to the move indicates a checkmate, and 0-0 is used to indicate castling. If you are unfamiliar with the rules of chess, refer to this piece for a primer (*https://oreil.ly/EbcfQ*).

Based on this notation, the vocabulary can consist of:

- A separate token for each square on the board, with 64 total (a1, a2, a3…h6, h7, h8)
- A separate token for each piece type (N, B, R, K, Q)
- Tokens for move numbers (1., 2., 3., etc.)
- Tokens for special moves (+ for check, x for capture, etc.)

Now, let's train a language model from scratch on this chess dataset using our special domain-specific vocabulary. The model is directly learning from the PGN notation with no human language text present in the dataset. The book's GitHub repo (*https://oreil.ly/llm-playbooks*) contains the code and setup for training this model.

After training the model for three epochs, let's test the model's ability to play chess. We can see that the model seems to have learned the rules of the game without having to be provided the rules explicitly in natural language. In fact, the model can even beat human players some of the time and can execute moves like castling.

Exercise

While the model trained using the reference implementation is impressive enough to complete chess games and occasionally beat players, we can do a lot better. This can be done by increasing the size of the model, increasing the size of the dataset, and increasing the quality of the dataset. Try improving the model along each of these axes and track the improvement in its chess-playing abilities.

Note that this model was able to learn the concepts (chess) using a domain-specific language (PGN). How will we fare if the concepts were taught in natural language?

Let's explore this in another experiment. Take the same dataset used to pre-train the chess language model and run it through an LLM to convert each move in PGN to a sentence in English. An example game would look like:

White moves pawn to e4

Black moves bishop to g7

and so on. Train a new language model on the same number of games as the previous one, but this time with the English-language dataset. Let the vocabulary of this model be the standard English vocabulary generated by training the tokenizer over the training set.

How does this compare to the chess LM trained on the PGN dataset? The model trained on English descriptions of chess moves performs worse and doesn't seem to have understood the rules of the game yet, despite being trained on the same number of games as the other model.

This shows that natural language is not necessarily the most efficient vehicle for a model to learn skills and concepts, and domain-specific languages and notations perform better.

Thus, language design is an important skill to acquire, enabling you to create domain-specific languages for learning concepts and skills. For your application areas, you could use existing domain-specific languages or create a new one yourself.

Summary

In this chapter, we discussed the various components of the Transformer architecture in detail, including self-attention, feedforward networks, position encodings, and layer normalization. We also discussed several variants and configurations such as encoder-only, encoder-decoder, decoder-only, and MoE models. Finally, we learned how to put our knowledge of language models together to train our own model from scratch and how to design domain-specific languages for more efficient learning.

PART II
Utilizing LLMs

In this part of the book, we will explore how to harness and adapt pre-trained LLMs to solve various kinds of language tasks that we introduced in Chapter 1. To make the best use of these chapters, I strongly suggest that you experiment hands-on with all the techniques introduced, as well as run the corresponding tutorials from the accompanying GitHub repo for this book.

CHAPTER 5

Adapting LLMs to Your Use Case

In this chapter, we will continue with our journey through the LLM landscape, exploring the various LLMs available for commercial use and providing pointers on how to choose the right LLM for your task. We will also examine how to load LLMs of various sizes and run inference on them. We will then decipher various decoding strategies for text generation. We will also investigate how to interpret the outputs and intermediate results from language models, surveying interpretability tools like LIT-NLP.

Navigating the LLM Landscape

Seemingly a new LLM is being released every few days, many claiming to be state of the art. Most of these LLMs are not very different from each other, so you need not spend too much time tracking new LLM releases. This book's GitHub repository (*https://oreil.ly/llm-playbooks*) attempts to keep track of the major releases, but I don't promise it will be complete.

Nevertheless, it is a good idea to have a broad understanding of the different types of LLM providers out there, the kinds of LLMs being made available, and the copyright and licensing implications. Therefore, let's now explore the LLM landscape through this lens and understand the choices at our disposal.

Who Are the LLM providers?

LLM providers can be broadly categorized into the following types:

Companies providing proprietary LLMs
: These include companies like OpenAI (GPT) (*https://oreil.ly/r-lb1*), Google (Gemini) (*https://oreil.ly/KF9Kh*), Anthropic (Claude) (*https://oreil.ly/T5Wvo*), Cohere (*https://oreil.ly/PiKxN*), AI21 (*https://oreil.ly/Y8T3q*), etc. that train

proprietary LLMs and make them available as an API endpoint (LLM-as-a-service). Many of these companies have also partnered with cloud providers that facilitate access to these models as a fully managed service. The relevant offerings from the major cloud providers are Amazon Bedrock (*https://oreil.ly/FVqRj*) and SageMaker JumpStart by Amazon (*https://oreil.ly/e0a59*), Vertex AI by Google (*https://oreil.ly/mURoC*), and Azure OpenAI by Microsoft (*https://oreil.ly/Ag1r5*).

Companies providing open source LLMs
: These include companies that make the LLM weights public and monetize through providing deployment services (Together AI (*https://oreil.ly/urcAf*)), companies whose primary business would benefit from more LLM adoption (Cerebras (*https://oreil.ly/2cVYY*)), and research labs that have been releasing LLMs since the early days of Transformers (Microsoft, Google, Meta, Salesforce, etc.). Note that companies like Google have released both proprietary and open source LLMs.

Self-organizing open source collectives and community research organizations
: This includes the pioneering community research organization Eleuther AI (*https://oreil.ly/ZSlbG*), and Big Science (*https://oreil.ly/_NlUD*). These organizations rely on grants for compute infrastructure.

Academia and government
: Due to the high capital costs, not many LLMs have come out of academia so far. Examples of LLMs from government/academia include the Abu Dhabi government-funded Technology Innovation Institute (*https://oreil.ly/aMwO2*), which released the Falcon model (*https://oreil.ly/vdhsL*), and Tsinghua University, which released the GLM model (*https://oreil.ly/K0_zX*).

Table 5-1 shows the players in the LLM space, the category of entity they belong to, and the pre-trained models they have published.

Table 5-1. LLM Providers

Name	Category	Pre-trained models released
Google	Company	BERT, MobileBERT, T5, FLAN-T5, ByT5, Canine, UL2, Flan-UL2, Pegasus PaLM, PaLMV2, ELECTRA, Tapas, Switch
Microsoft	Company	DeBERTa, DialoGPT, BioGPT, MPNet
OpenAI	Company	GPT-2, GPT-3, GPT-3.5, GPT-4
Amazon	Company	Titan
Anthropic	Company	Claude, Claude-2
Cohere	Company	Cohere Command, Cohere Base
Meta	Company	RoBERTa, Llama, Llama 2, BART, OPT, Galactica
Salesforce	Company	CTRL, XGen, EinsteinGPT

Name	Category	Pre-trained models released
MosaicML	Company (Acquired by Databricks)	MPT
Cerebras	Company	Cerebras-GPT, BTLM
Databricks	Company	Dolly-V1, Dolly-V2
Stability AI	Company	StableLM
Together AI	Company	RedPajama
Ontocord AI	Nonprofit	MDEL
Eleuther AI	Nonprofit	Pythia, GPT Neo, GPT-NeoX, GPT-J
Big Science	Nonprofit	BLOOM
Tsinghua University	Academic	GLM
Technology Innovation Institute	Academic	Falcon
UC Berkeley	Academic	OpenLLaMA
Adept AI	Company	Persimmon
Mistral AI	Company	Mistral
AI21 Labs	Company	Jurassic
X.AI	Company	Grok

Model Flavors

Each model is usually released with multiple variants. It is customary to release different-sized variants of the same model. As an example, Llama 2 comes in 7B, 13B, and 70B sizes, where these numbers refer to the number of parameters in the model.

These days, LLM providers augment their pre-trained models in various ways to make them more amenable to user tasks. The augmentation process typically involves fine-tuning the model in some way, often incorporating human supervision. Some of these fine-tuning exercises can cost millions of dollars in terms of human annotations. We will refer to pre-trained models that have not undergone any augmentation as base models.

The following sections describe some of the popular augmentation types.

Instruct-models

Instruct-models, or instruction-tuned models, are specialized in following instructions written in natural language. While base models possess powerful capabilities, they are akin to a rebellious teenager; effectively interacting with them is possible only after tediously engineering the right prompts through trial and error, which tend to be brittle. This is because the base models are trained on either denoising objectives or next-word prediction objectives, which are different from the tasks users typically want to solve. By instruction-tuning the base model, the resulting model is able to more effectively respond to human instructions and be helpful.

A typical instruction-tuning dataset consists of a diverse set of tasks expressed in natural language, along with input-output pairs. In Chapter 6, we will explore various techniques to construct instruction-tuning datasets and demonstrate how to perform instruction-tuning on a model.

Here is an example from a popular instruction-tuning dataset called FLAN (*https://oreil.ly/YJ_Xr*).

> *Prompt:* "What is the sentiment of the following review? The pizza was ok but the service was terrible. I stopped in for a quick lunch and got the slice special but it ended up taking an hour after waiting several minutes for someone at the front counter and then again for the slices. The place was empty other than myself, yet I couldn't get any help/service. OPTIONS: - negative - positive"
>
> *FLAN:* "Negative"

In this example, the input consists of an instruction, "What is the sentiment of the following review?" expressed in a way that humans would naturally express, along with the input and output. The input is the actual review and the output is the solution to the task, either generated by a model or annotated by a human.

Figure 5-1 demonstrates the instruction-tuning process.

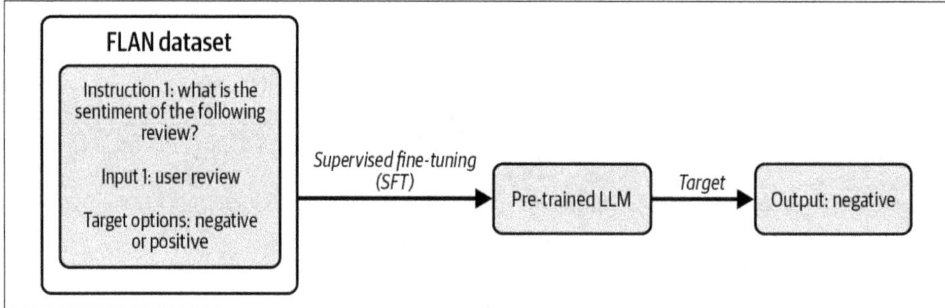

Figure 5-1. Instruction-tuning process

Instruction-tuning is one of several techniques that come under the umbrella of supervised fine-tuning (SFT). In addition to improving the ability of a model to respond effectively to user tasks, SFT-based approaches can also be used to make it less harmful by training on safety datasets that help align model outputs with the values and preferences of the model creators.

More advanced techniques to achieve this alignment include reinforcement learning-based methods like reinforcement learning from human feedback (RLHF) and reinforcement learning from AI feedback (RLAIF).

In RLHF training, human annotators select or rank candidate outputs based on certain criteria, like helpfulness and harmlessness. These annotations are used to iteratively train a reward model, which ultimately leads to the LLM being more controllable, for example, by refusing to answer inappropriate requests from users.

Figure 5-2 shows the RLHF training process.

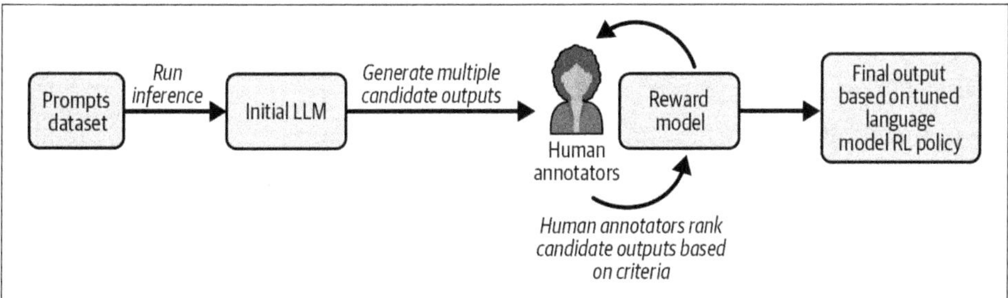

Figure 5-2. Reinforcement learning from human feedback

We will cover RLHF and other alignment techniques in detail in Chapter 8.

Instead of relying on human feedback for alignment training, one can also leverage LLMs to choose between outputs based on their adherence to a set of principles (don't be racist, don't be rude, etc.). This technique was introduced by Anthropic and is called RLAIF. In this technique, humans only provide a desired set of principles and values (referred to as Constitutional AI (*https://oreil.ly/d8FeW*)), and the LLM is tasked with determining whether its outputs adhere to these principles.

Instruction-tuned models often take the suffix *instruct*, like RedPajama-Instruct.

Instruction Tuning Can Have Side Effects

Is it beneficial to always prefer using an instruction-tuned variant over the base model for your tasks? In most cases, yes. However, keep in mind that any tuning on top of a base model inevitably causes some regressions, thus losing access to some of the capabilities possessed by the base model.

Chung et al. (*https://oreil.ly/-p0R4*) demonstrated an example of this. They noticed that instruction-tuning using the FLAN dataset worsened chain-of-thought (CoT) capabilities, which are crucial for reasoning tasks. However, they also observed that adding CoT data to their instruction-tuning datasets increased the reasoning capabilities of the model compared to the base variant.

The side effects of instruction tuning are not well explored, so it is a good idea to experiment with the base model and see if you are losing out on any capabilities.

Similarly, alignment-tuned models are calibrated to respond to user queries in accordance with the principles, values, and ethics of the LLM provider. These may not be the same values that you or your organization hold.

In all these cases you can perform your own instruction and alignment tuning on the base model, the details of which are explored in the next three chapters. We will also analyze in what situations is it worthwhile to perform your own instruction/alignment tuning.

Chat-models

Chat-models are instruction-tuned models that are optimized for multi-turn dialog. Examples include ChatGPT, Llama 2-Chat, MPT-Chat, OpenAssistant, etc.

Long-context models

As discussed in Chapter 1, Transformer-based LLMs have a limited context length. To recap, context length typically refers to the sum of the number of input and output tokens processed by the model per invocation. Typical context lengths of modern LLMs range from 8,000 to 128,000 tokens, with some variants of Gemini supporting over a million tokens. Some models are released with a long-context variant; for example GPT 3.5 comes with a default 4K context size but also has a 16K context size variant. MPT (*https://oreil.ly/wKqdL*) also has a long-context variant that has been trained on 65k context length but can potentially be used for even longer contexts during inference.

No Free Lunch for Long-Context Models

As of yet, it has been shown (*https://oreil.ly/PSD_k*) that performance is not sustained as context length increases. LLMs tend to forget things in the middle of the context window. This is because of the characteristics of the documents that LLMs are trained on, wherein the most relevant context of a document necessary to predict the next token is more often found near the beginning or end of the context. In my experiments, I have observed that 8K context size is the tipping point for most models beyond which performance starts to degrade. You also can't just stuff your entire context with instructions; LLMs can handle only a limited set of instructions in a prompt, beyond which performance drops.

However, long-context models are one area of LLMs where we are seeing the most rapid improvements. Claude and Gemini long-context models have shown excellent progress in sustaining performance over long contexts.

Various tests have been devised for measuring long-context performance, including needle in a haystack tests (*https://oreil.ly/aop_Q*). We will discuss the shortcomings of these evaluation approaches and propose more holistic evaluation schemes in Chapter 12.

Domain-adapted or task-adapted models

LLM providers also might perform fine-tuning on specific tasks like summarization or financial sentiment analysis. They may also produce distilled versions of the model, where a smaller model is fine-tuned on outputs from the larger model for a particular task. Examples of task-specific fine-tunes include FinBERT (*https://oreil.ly/uKUAp*), which is fine-tuned on financial sentiment analysis datasets, and UniversalNER (*https://oreil.ly/8A0pn*), which is distilled using named-entity-recognition data.

Open Source LLMs

Open source is often used as a catch-all phrase to refer to models with some aspect that is publicly available. We will define open source as:

> Software artifacts that are released under a license that allows users to *study*, *use*, *modify*, and *redistribute* them to *anyone* and for any *purpose*.

For a more formal and comprehensive definition of open source software, refer to the Open Source Initiative's official definition (*https://oreil.ly/7cezH*).

For an LLM to be considered fully open, all of the following needs to be published:

Model weights
: This includes all the parameters of the model and the model configuration. Having access to this enables us to add to or modify the model parameters in any way we deem fit. Model checkpoints at various stages of training are also encouraged to be released.

Model code
: Releasing only the weights of the model is akin to providing a software binary without providing the source code. Model code not only includes model training code and hyperparameter settings but also code used for pre-processing training data. Releasing information about infrastructure setup and configuration also goes a long way toward enhancing model reproducibility. In most cases, even with model code fully available, models may not be easily reproducible due to resource limitations and the nondeterministic nature of training.

Training data
: This includes the training data used for the model, and ideally information or code on how it was sourced. It is also encouraged to release data at different stages of transformation of the data preprocessing pipeline, as well as the order in which the data was fed to the model. Training data is the component that is least published by model providers. Thus, most open source models are not *fully open* because the dataset is not public.

Training data is often not released due to competitive reasons. As discussed in Chapters 3 and 4, most LLMs today use variants of the same architecture and training code. The distinguishing factor can often be the data content and preprocessing. Parts of the training data might be acquired using a licensing agreement, which prohibits the model provider from releasing the data publicly.

Another reason for not releasing training data is that there are unresolved legal issues pertaining to training data, especially surrounding copyright. As an example, The Pile dataset created by Eleuther AI is no longer available at the official link because it contains text from copyrighted books (the Books3 dataset). Note that The Pile is pre-processed so the books are not in human-readable form and are not easily reproducible, as they are split, shuffled, and mixed.

Most training data is sourced from the open web and thus may potentially contain violent or sexual content that is illegal in certain jurisdictions. Despite the best intentions and rigorous filtering, some of these data might still be present in the final dataset. Thus many datasets that have been previously open are no longer open, LAION's image datasets being one example.

Ultimately, the license under which the model has been released determines the terms under which you can use, modify, or redistribute the original or modified LLM. Broadly speaking, open LLMs are distributed under three types of licenses:

Noncommercial
: These licenses only allow research and personal use and prohibit the use of the model for commercial purposes. In many cases, the model artifacts are gated through an application form where a user would have to justify their need for access by providing a compelling research use case.

Copy-left
: This type of license permits commercial usage, but all source or derivative work needs to be released under the same license, thus making it harder to develop proprietary modifications. The degree to which this condition applies depends on the specific license being used.

Permissive
: This type of license permits commercial usage, including modifying and redistributing it in proprietary applications, i.e., there is no obligation for the redistribution to be open source. Some licenses in this category also permit patents.

New types of licenses are being devised that restrict usage of the model for particular use cases, often for safety reasons. An example of this is the Open RAIL-M license (*https://oreil.ly/2UVMe*), which prohibits usage of the model in use cases like providing medical advice, law enforcement, immigration and asylum processes, etc. For a full list of restricted use cases, see Attachment A of the license.

As a practitioner intending to use open LLMs in your organization for commercial reasons, it is best to use ones with permissive licenses. Popular examples of permissive licenses include the Apache 2.0 and the MIT license.

Creative Commons (CC) licenses (*https://oreil.ly/PQy6D*) are a popular class of licenses used to distribute open LLMs.The licenses have names like CC-BY-NC-SA, etc. Here is an easy way to remember what these names mean:

BY
: If the license contains this term, it means attribution is needed. If it contains only CC-BY, it means the license is permissive.

SA
: If the license contains this term, it means redistribution should occur under the same terms as this license. In other words, it is a copy-left license.

NC
: NC stands for noncommercial. Thus, if the license contains this term, the model can only be used for research or personal use cases.

ND
: ND stands for no derivatives. If the license contains this term, then distribution of modifications to the model is not allowed.

Today, models that have open weights and open code and are released under a license that allows redistribution to anyone and for any use case are considered open source models. Arguably, however, access to the training data is also crucial to inspect and study the model, which is part of the open source definition we introduced earlier.

Table 5-2 shows the various LLMs available, the licenses under which they are published, and their available sizes and flavors. Note that the LLM may be instruction-tuned or chat-tuned by a different entity than the one that pre-trained the LLM.

Table 5-2. List of available LLMs

Name	Availability	Sizes	Variants
GPT-4	Proprietary	Unknown	GPT-4 32K context, GPT-4 8K context
GPT-3.5 Turbo	Proprietary	Unknown	GPT-3.5 4K context, GPT-3.5 16K context
Claude Instant	Proprietary	Unknown	-
Claude 2	Proprietary	Unknown	-
MPT	Apache 2.0	1B, 7B, 30B	MPT 65K storywriter
CerebrasGPT	Apache 2.0	111M, 256M, 590M, 1.3B, 2.7B, 6.7B, 13B	CerebrasGPT

Name	Availability	Sizes	Variants
Stability LM	CC-BY-SA	7B	-
RedPajama	Apache 2.0	3B, 7B	RedPajama-INCITE-Instruct, RedPajama-INCITE-Chat
GPT-Neo X	Apache 2.0	20B	-
BLOOM	Open, restricted use	176B	BLOOMZ
Llama	Open, no commercial use	7B, 13B, 33B, 65B	-
Llama 2	Open, commercial use	7B, 13B, 70B	Llama 2-Chat
Zephyr	Apache 2.0	7B	-
Gemma	Open, restricted use	2B, 7B	Gemma-Instruction Tuned

How to Choose an LLM for Your Task

Given the plethora of options available, how do you ensure you choose the right LLM for your task? Depending on your situation, there are a multitude of criteria to consider, including:

Cost
: This includes inference or fine-tuning costs, and costs associated with building software scaffolding, monitoring and observability, deployment and maintenance (collectively referred to as LLMOps).

Time per output token (TPOT) (https://oreil.ly/mEDRt)
: This is a metric used to measure the speed of text generation as experienced by the end user.

Task performance
: This refers to the performance requirements of the task and the relevant metrics like precision or accuracy. What level of performance is *good enough*?

Type of tasks
: The nature of the tasks the LLM will be used for, like summarization, question answering, classification, etc.

Capabilities required
: Examples of capabilities include arithmetic reasoning, logical reasoning, planning, task decomposition, etc. A lot of these capabilities, to the extent that they actually exist or approximate, are *emergent properties* of an LLM as discussed in Chapter 1, and are not exhibited by smaller models.

Licensing
: You can use only those models that allow your mode of usage. Even models that explicitly allow commercial use can have restrictions on certain types of use cases. For example, as noted earlier, the Big Science OpenRAIL-M license

restricts the usage of the LLM in use cases pertaining to law enforcement, immigration, or asylum processes.

In-house ML/MLOps talent
: The strength of in-house talent determines the customizations you can afford. For example, do you have enough in-house talent for building inference optimization systems?

Other nonfunctional criteria
: This includes safety, security, privacy, etc. Cloud providers and startups are already implementing solutions that can address these issues.

> **Exercise**
>
> For your application, prepare an ordered list of priorities and determine which ones are fixed and which ones are flexible. For example, precision needs to be at least X or TPOT needs to be at least Y.
>
> Based on the determined priorities, what LLM would you choose?

You may have to choose between proprietary and open source LLMs.

Open Source Versus Proprietary LLMs

Debates about the merits of open source versus proprietary software have been commonplace in the tech industry for several decades now, and we are seeing it become increasingly relevant in the realm of LLMs as well. The biggest advantage of open source models are the transparency and flexibility they provide, not necessarily the cost. Self-hosting open source LLMs can incur a lot of engineering overhead and compute/memory costs, and using managed services might not always be able to match proprietary models in terms of latency, throughput, and inference cost. Moreover, many open source LLMs are not easily accessible through managed services and other third-party deployment options. This situation is bound to change dramatically as the field matures, but in the meanwhile, run through your calculations for your specific situation to determine the costs incurred for using each (type of) model.

The flexibility provided by open source models helps with your ability to debug, interpret, and augment the LLM with any kind of training/fine-tuning you choose, instead of the restricted avenues made available by the LLM provider. This allows you to more substantially align the LLM to your preferences and values instead of the ones decided by the LLM provider. Having full availability of all the token probabilities (logits) is a superpower, as we will see throughout the book.

The availability of open source LLMs has enabled teams to develop models and applications that might not be lucrative for larger companies with a profit motive, like fine-tuning models to support low-resource languages (languages that do not have a significant data footprint on the internet, like regional languages of India or Indigenous languages of Canada). An example is the Kannada Llama model (*https://oreil.ly/hoBQ1*), built over Llama 2 by continually pre-training and fine-tuning on tokens from the Kannada language, a regional language of India.

Not all open source models are fully transparent. As mentioned earlier, most for-profit companies that release open source LLMs do not make the training datasets public. For instance, Meta hasn't disclosed all the details of the training datasets used to train the Llama 2 model. Knowing which datasets are used to train the model can help you assess whether there is test set contamination and understand what kind of knowledge you can expect the LLM to possess.

As of this book's writing, open source models like Llama 3.2 and DeepSeek v3 have more or less caught up to state-of-the-art proprietary models from OpenAI or Anthropic. However, there is a new gap developing between proprietary and open source models in the realm of reasoning models like OpenAI's o3, that use inference-time compute techniques (discussed in Chapter 8). Throughout this book, we will showcase scenarios where open source models have an advantage.

Always check if the model provider has an active developer community on GitHub/Discord/Slack, and that the development team is actively engaged in those channels, responding to user comments and questions. I recommend preferring models with active developer communities, provided they satisfy your primary criteria.

LLM Evaluation

We will start this section with a caveat: evaluating LLMs is probably the most challenging task in the LLM space at present. Current methods of benchmarking are broken, easily gamed, and hard to interpret. Nevertheless, benchmarks are still a useful starting point on your road to evaluation. We will start by looking at current public benchmarks and then discuss how you can build more holistic internal benchmarks.

To evaluate LLMs on their task performance, there are a lot of benchmark datasets that test a wide variety of skills. Not all skills are relevant to your use case, so you can choose to focus on specific benchmarks that test the skills you need the LLM to perform well on.

The leaderboard on these benchmark tests changes very often, especially if only open source models are being evaluated, but that does not mean you need to change the LLMs you use every time there is a new leader on the board. Usually, the differences between the top models are quite marginal. The fine-grained choice of LLM usually isn't the most important criteria determining the success of your task, and you are better off spending that bandwidth working on cleaning and understanding your data, which is still the most important component of the project.

Let's look at a few popular ways in which the field is evaluating LLMs.

Eleuther AI LM Evaluation Harness

Through the LM Evaluation Harness (*https://oreil.ly/SiOXq*), Eleuther AI supports benchmarking on over 400 different benchmark tasks, evaluating skills as varied as open-domain question answering, arithmetic and logical reasoning, linguistic tasks, machine translation, toxic language detection, etc. You can use this tool to evaluate any model on the Hugging Face Hub (*https://oreil.ly/IHd22*), a platform containing thousands of pre-trained and fine-tuned models, on the benchmarks of your choice.

Here is an example from `bigbench_formal_fallacies_syllogisms_negation`, one of the benchmark tasks:

```
{
  "input": "\"Some football fans admire various clubs, others love
  only a single team. But who is a fan of whom precisely? The
  following argument pertains to this question: First premise: Mario
  is a friend of FK \u017dalgiris Vilnius. Second premise: Being a
  follower of F.C. Copenhagen is necessary for being a friend of FK
  \u017dalgiris Vilnius. It follows that Mario is a follower of F.C.
  Copenhagen.\"\n Is the argument, given the explicitly stated
  premises, deductively valid or invalid?",
  "target_scores": {
      "valid": 1,
      "invalid": 0
  }
```

In this task, the model is asked to spot logical fallacies by deducing whether the presented argument is valid given the premises.

Exercise

Let's evaluate a few models on this task. Follow the instructions (*https://oreil.ly/mZdGA*) to install the harness. Now, you can run this code for evaluating Falcon 7B:

```
lm_eval --model hf-causal \
        --model_args pretrained=tiiuae/falcon-7b \
        --tasks bigbench_formal_fallacies_syllogisms_negation \
        --device cuda:0
```

Try this for a few other 7B models, including Llama, Gemma, Mistral, MPT, RedPajama with both the base versions and the instruction-tuned versions where available. Do you find a large difference between their models in terms of performance?

Additionally, prepare ten more questions for the same task on your own (you can use an LLM to generate candidate questions you can then modify) pertaining to various domains. Do the models exhibit the same level of performance on your questions as they do on the benchmark tests?

There is also support for evaluation of proprietary models using this harness. For example, here is how you would evaluate OpenAI models:

```
export OPENAI_API_SECRET_KEY=<Key>
python main.py \
lm_eval --model openai-completions \
        --model_args model=gpt-3.5-turbo \
         --tasks bigbench_formal_fallacies_syllogisms_negation
```

Exercise

Compare GPT 4o, 4o-mini, o1, and o3 on the logical fallacies task, including both the benchmark sets and the ones you prepared. How do they compare relative to each other and how do they fare compared to open source models?

While choosing or developing a benchmarking task to evaluate, I recommend focusing on picking ones that test the capabilities needed to solve the task of your interest, rather than the actual task itself. For example, if you are building a summarizer application that needs to perform a lot of logical reasoning to generate the summaries, it is better to focus on benchmark tests that directly test logical reasoning capabilities than ones that test summarization performance.

Hugging Face Open LLM Leaderboard

As of the book's writing, the Open LLM Leaderboard (*https://oreil.ly/tspBY*) uses Eleuther AI's LM Evaluation Harness to evaluate the performance of models on six benchmark tasks:

Massive Multitask Language Understanding (MMLU)
: This test evaluates the LLM on knowledge-intensive tasks, drawing from fields like US history, biology, mathematics, and more than 50 other subjects in a multiple choice framework.

AI2 Reasoning Challenge (ARC)
: This test evaluates the LLM on multiple-choice grade school science questions that need complex reasoning as well as world knowledge to answer.

Hellaswag
: This test evaluates commonsense reasoning by providing the LLM with a situation and asking it to predict what might happen next out of the given choices, based on common sense.

TruthfulQA
: This test evaluates the LLM's ability to provide answers that don't contain falsehoods.

Winogrande
: This test is composed of fill-in-the-blank questions that test commonsense reasoning.

GSM8K
: This test evaluates the LLM's ability to complete grade school math problems involving a sequence of basic arithmetic operations.

Figure 5-3 shows a snapshot of the LLM leaderboard as of the time of the book's writing. We can see that:

- Larger models perform better.
- Instruction-tuned or fine-tuned variants of models perform better.

Rank	Type	Model	Average
1		MaziyarPanahi/calme-3.2-instruct-78b	52.08 %
2		MaziyarPanahi/calme-3.1-instruct-78b	51.29 %
3		dfurman/CalmeRys-78B-Orpo-v0.1	51.23 %
4		MaziyarPanahi/calme-2.4-rys-78b	50.77 %
5		huihui-ai/Qwen2.5-72B-Instruct-abliterated	48.11 %
6		Qwen/Qwen2.5-72B-Instruct	47.98 %
7		MaziyarPanahi/calme-2.1-qwen2.5-72b	47.86 %

Figure 5-3. Snapshot of the Open LLM Leaderboard

> **Exercise**
>
> It is suspected (*https://oreil.ly/fwVEC*) that a large number of models may have been trained on data contaminated with the GSM8K dataset. Explore the GSM8K dataset (*https://oreil.ly/dI87I*), feed only part of the question, and check if the models you evaluated during the previous exercises correctly complete the question. Also, change the numbers in the problems and verify if the performance remains the same.

The validity of these benchmarks are in question as complete test set decontamination is not guaranteed. Model providers are also optimizing to solve these benchmarks, thus reducing the value of these benchmarks to serve as reliable estimators of general-purpose performance.

HELM

Holistic Evaluation of Language Models (HELM) (*https://oreil.ly/MNHDs*) is an evaluation framework by Stanford that aims to calculate a wide variety of metrics over a range of benchmark tasks. Fifty-nine metrics are calculated overall, testing accuracy, calibration, robustness, fairness, bias, toxicity, efficiency, summarization performance, copyright infringement, and more. The tasks tested include question answering, summarization, text classification, information retrieval, sentiment analysis, and toxicity detection.

Figure 5-4 shows a snapshot of the HELM leaderboard as of the time of the book's writing.

Accuracy | Efficiency | General information

Model	Mean win rate	NarrativeQA - F1	NaturalQuestions (open) - F1	NaturalQuestions (closed) - F1
GPT-4o (2024-05-13)	**0.938**	**0.804**	0.803	0.501
GPT-4o (2024-08-06)	0.928	0.795	0.793	0.496
DeepSeek v3	0.908	0.796	0.765	0.467
Claude 3.5 Sonnet (20240620)	0.885	0.746	0.749	**0.502**
Amazon Nova Pro	0.885	0.791	**0.829**	0.405
GPT-4 (0613)	0.867	0.768	0.79	0.457
GPT-4 Turbo (2024-04-09)	0.864	0.761	0.795	0.482

Figure 5-4. Snapshot of the HELM leaderboard

Benchmark Evaluation Is Unreliable

You can evaluate the same task in multiple ways. For example, consider the MMLU task. Questions in the MMLU task have four choices as answers: A, B, C, D. How do we evaluate performance on a multiple choice question-answering task?

- You can pick the token that has the highest output probability out of the four options (A, B, C, D).
- You can pick the token that has the highest output probability from the entire vocabulary and use that to match it with the correct answer to the question (not the label like A, B, C, D, but the actual answer).
- You can produce a normalized sum of the probabilities of the token sequence generated by the model, where the expected token sequence is the label followed by the answer text, and use that to match it with the correct answer (represented by the label followed by answer text).

Each of these types of calculations can produce a vastly different result and can lead to different leaders in the leaderboard. Hugging Face published a blog post (*https://oreil.ly/QrBX4*) about this after people noticed discrepancies in their numbers versus third-party evaluations.

Elo Rating

Now that we have seen the limitations of quantitative evaluation, let's explore how we can most effectively incorporate human evaluations. One promising framework is the Elo rating system (*https://oreil.ly/bTD7I*), used in chess to rank players.

Large model systems organization (LMSYS Org) (*https://oreil.ly/HGVz2*) has implemented an evaluation platform based on the Elo rating system called the Chatbot Arena (*https://oreil.ly/evgQX*). Chatbot Arena solicits crowdsourced evaluations by inviting people to choose between two randomized and anonymized LLMs by chatting with them side-by-side. The leaderboard is found online (*https://oreil.ly/Y6zmN*), with models from OpenAi, DeepSeek, Google DeepMind, and Anthropic dominating.

Figure 5-5 shows a snapshot of the Chatbot Arena leaderboard as of the time of the book's writing.

Rank* (UB)	Rank (StyleCtrl)	Model	Arena Score
1	3	Gemini-2.0-Flash-Thinking-Exp-01-21	1384
1	2	Gemini-2.0-Pro-Exp-02-05	1379
1	1	ChatGPT-4o-latest (2025-01-29)	1377
4	2	DeepSeek-R1	1361
4	7	Gemini-2.0-Flash-001	1355
4	2	o1-2024-12-17	1352
7	5	o1-preview	1335
7	7	Qwen2.5-Max	1332
9	8	DeepSeek-V3	1316
9	9	Gemini-2.0-Flash-Lite-Preview-02-05	1309

Figure 5-5. Snapshot of the Chatbot Arena leaderboard

Elo Ratings Can Be Biased Too

Elo ratings are not a panacea to the LLM evaluation problem. Human biases can meaningfully impact the overall ratings even if the LLMs are being evaluated anonymously.

According to Wu et al. (*https://oreil.ly/3g_qd*), these biases include:

- Humans tend to prefer longer texts.
- Humans tend to overlook subtle factuality and consistency issues if the style is authoritative or convincing.
- Humans can be indecisive and tend to grant ties instead of choosing a winner.
- The order in which the LLM answers are presented can influence human ratings. This can be rectified by providing randomized answers to the user.

Wu et al. propose a multi-Elo rating system that asks humans to evaluate the LLM across three different dimensions: helpfulness, accuracy, and language.

Interpreting benchmark results

How do you interpret evaluation results presented in research papers? Try to methodically ask as many questions as possible, and check if the answers are covered in the paper or other material. As an example, let us take the Llama 2-chat evaluation graphs presented in the Llama 2 paper (*https://oreil.ly/BcgXs*). In particular, study Figures 1 and 3, which demonstrate how Llama 2-Chat compares in helpfulness and safety with other chat models. Some of the questions that come to mind are:

- What does the evaluation dataset look like? Do we have access to it?
- What is the difficulty level of the test set? Maybe the model is competitive with respect to ChatGPT for easier examples but how does it perform with more difficult examples?
- What proportion of examples in the test set can be considered difficult?
- What kinds of scenarios are covered in the test set? What degree of overlap do these scenarios have with the chat-tuning sets?
- What definition do they use for safety?
- Can there be a bias in the evaluation due to models being evaluated on the basis of a particular definition of safety, which Llama 2 was trained to adhere to, while other models may have different definitions of safety?

Rigorously interrogating the results this way helps you develop a deeper understanding of what is being evaluated, and whether it aligns with the capabilities you need from the language model for your own tasks. For more rigorous LLM evaluation, I strongly recommend developing your own internal benchmarks.

Do not trust evaluations performed by GPT-4 or any other LLM. We have no idea what evaluation criteria it uses nor do we have a deeper understanding of its biases.

Robust evaluation of LLMs is further complicated by the sensitivity of the prompts and the probabilistic nature of generative models. For example, I often see papers claiming that "GPT-4 does not have reasoning capabilities," while not using any prompting techniques during evaluation. In many of these cases, it turns out that the model can in fact perform the task if prompted with CoT prompting. While evaluation prompts need not be heavily engineered, using rudimentary techniques like CoT should be standard practice, and not using them means that the model capabilities are being underestimated.

Loading LLMs

While it is possible to load and run inference on LLMs with just CPUs, you need GPUs if you want acceptable text generation speeds. Choosing a GPU depends on cost, the size of the model, whether you are training the model or just running inference, and support for optimizations. Tim Dettmers has developed a great flowchart (*https://oreil.ly/t6iPQ*) that you can use to figure out which GPU best serves your needs.

Let's figure out the amount of GPU RAM needed to load an LLM of a given size. LLMs can be loaded in various *precisions*:

Float32
: 32-bit floating point representation, each parameter occupying 4 bytes of storage.

Float16
: 16-bit floating point representation. Only 5 bits are reserved for the exponent as opposed to 8 bits in Float32. This means that using Float16 comes with overflow/underflow problems for very large and small numbers.

bfloat16 (BF16)
: 16-bit floating point representation. Just like Float32, 8 bits are reserved for the exponent, thus alleviating the underflow/overflow problems observed in Float16.

Int8
: 8-bit integer representation. Running inference in 8-bit mode is around 20% slower than running in Float16.

FP8, FP4
: 8-bit and 4-bit floating point representation.

We will explore these formats in detail in Chapter 9. Generally, running inference on a model with 7B parameters will need around 7 GB of GPU RAM if running in 8-bit mode and around 14 GB if running in BF16. If you intend to fine-tune the whole model, you will need a lot more memory.

Hugging Face Accelerate

You can run inference on models even if they don't fit in the GPU RAM. The *accelerate* library (*https://oreil.ly/OYdyf*) by Hugging Face facilitates this by loading parts of the model into CPU RAM if the GPU RAM is filled, and then loading parts of the model into disk if the CPU RAM is also filled. "Accelerate Big Model Inference: How Does it Work?" (*https://oreil.ly/J8duc*) shows how the accelerate library operates under the hood. This whole process is abstracted from the user, so all you need to load a large model is to run this code:

```
!pip install transformers accelerate
import torch
from transformers import AutoTokenizer, AutoModelForCausalLM
tokenizer = AutoTokenizer.from_pretrained("EleutherAI/gpt-neox-20B")
model = GPTNeoForCausalLM.from_pretrained("EleutherAI/gpt-neox-20B")
input_ids = tokenizer("Language models are", return_tensors="pt")
gen_tokens = model.generate(**input_ids, max_new_tokens =1)
```

Ollama

There are many tools available that facilitate loading LLMs locally, including on your own laptop. One such library is Ollama, which supports Windows, Mac, and Linux operating systems. Using Ollama, you can load 13B models if your machine has at least 16GB of available RAM. Ollama supports many open models like Mistral, Llama, Gemma, etc. Ollama provides a REST API that you can use to run inference and build LLM-driven applications. It also has several Terminal and UI integrations that enable you to build user-facing applications with ease.

Let's see how we can use Google's Gemma 2B model using Ollama. First, download the version of Ollama (*https://oreil.ly/yly44*) to your machine based on your operating system. Next, pull the Gemma model to your machine with:

```
ollama pull gemma:2b
```

You can also create a Modelfile that contains configuration information for the model. This includes system prompts and prompt templates, decoding parameters like temperature, and conversation history. Refer to the documentation (*https://oreil.ly/ba-1u*) for a full list of available options.

An example Modelfile is:

```
FROM gemma:2b

PARAMETER temperature 0.2

SYSTEM """
You are a provocateur who speaks only in limericks.
"""
```

After creating your Modelfile, you can run the model:

```
ollama create local-gemma -f ./Modelfile
ollama run local-gemma
```

The book's GitHub repo contains a sample end-to-end application built using Ollama and one of its UI integrations. You can also experiment with similar tools like LM Studio (*https://oreil.ly/uFsiR*) and GPT4All (*https://oreil.ly/XUXhq*).

You can load custom models using Ollama if they are in the GPT-Generated Unified Format (GGUF).

LLM Inference APIs

While you can deploy an LLM yourself, modern-day inference consists of so many optimizations, many of them proprietary, that it takes a lot of effort to bring your inference speeds up to par with commercially available solutions. Several inference services like Together AI (*https://oreil.ly/L3zo0*) exist that facilitate inference of open source or custom models either through serverless endpoints or dedicated instances. Another option is Hugging Face's TGI (Text Generation Inference) (*https://oreil.ly/XXFpa*), which has been recently reinstated (*https://oreil.ly/BJJlY*) to a permissive open source license.

Decoding Strategies

Now that we have learned how to load a model, let's understand how to effectively generate text. To this end, several *decoding* strategies have been devised in the past few years. Let's go through them in detail.

Greedy Decoding

The simplest form of decoding is to just generate the token that has the highest probability. The drawback of this approach is that it causes repetitiveness in the output. Here is an example:

```
input = tokenizer('The keyboard suddenly came to life. It ventured up the',

return_tensors='pt').to(torch_device)
output = model.generate(**inputs, max_new_tokens=50)
print(tokenizer.decode(output[0], skip_special_tokens=True))
```

You can see that the output starts getting repetitive. Therefore, greedy decoding is not suitable unless you are generating really short sequences, like a token just producing a classification task output.

Figure 5-6 shows an example of greedy decoding using the FLAN-T5 model. Note that we missed out on some great sequences because one of the desired tokens has slightly lower probability, ensuring it never gets picked.

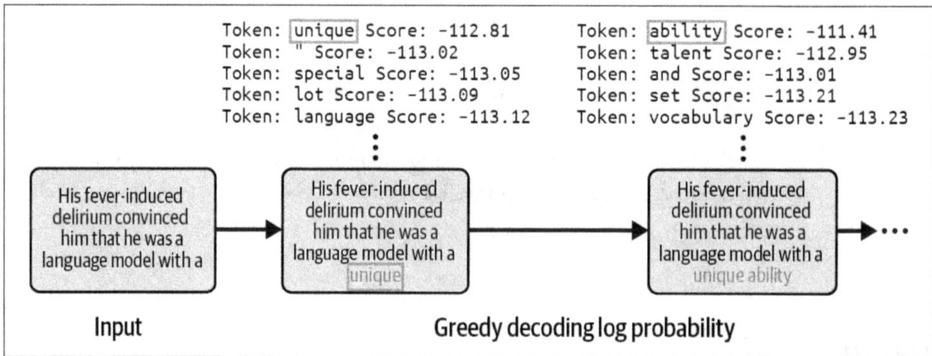

Figure 5-6. Greedy decoding

Beam Search

An alternative to greedy decoding is beam search. An important parameter of beam search is the beam size, *n*. At the first step, the top *n* tokens with the highest probabilities are selected as hypotheses. For the next few steps, the model generates token continuations for each of the hypotheses. The token chosen to be generated is the one whose continuations have the highest cumulative probability.

In the Hugging Face `transformers` library, the `num_beams` parameter of the `model.generate()` function determines the size of the beam. Here is how the decoding code would look if we used beam search:

```
output = model.generate(**inputs, max_new_tokens=50, num_beams = 3)
print(tokenizer.decode(output[0], skip_special_tokens=True))
```

Figure 5-7 shows an example of beam search using the FLAN-T5 model. Note that the repetitiveness problem hasn't really been solved using beam search. Similar to greedy decoding, the generated text also sounds very constricted and not humanlike, due to the complete absence of lower probability words.

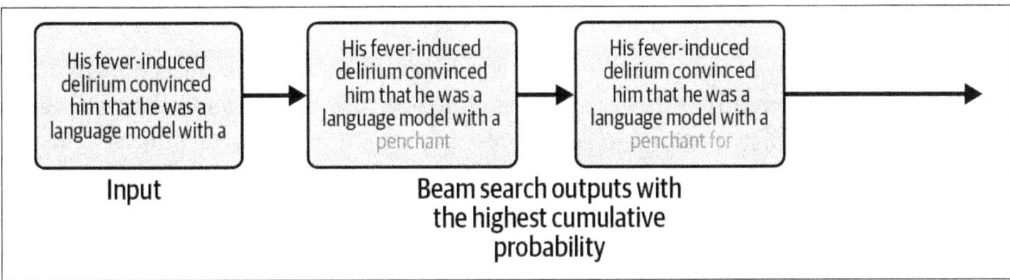

Figure 5-7. Beam search

To resolve these issues, we will need to start introducing some randomness and begin sampling from the probability distribution to ensure not just the top two or three tokens get generated all the time.

Top-k Sampling

In top-k sampling, the model samples from a distribution of just the k tokens of the output distribution that have the highest probability. The probability mass is redistributed over the k tokens, and the model samples from this distribution to generate the next token. Hugging Face provides the `top_k` parameter in its generate function:

```
output = model.generate(**inputs, max_new_tokens=50, do_sample=True, top_k=40)
print(tokenizer.decode(output[0], skip_special_tokens=True))
```

Figure 5-8 shows an example of top-k sampling using the FLAN-T5 model. Note that this is a vast improvement from greedy or beam search. However, top-k leads to problematic generations when used in cases where the probability is dominated by a few tokens, meaning that tokens with very low probability end up being included in the top-k.

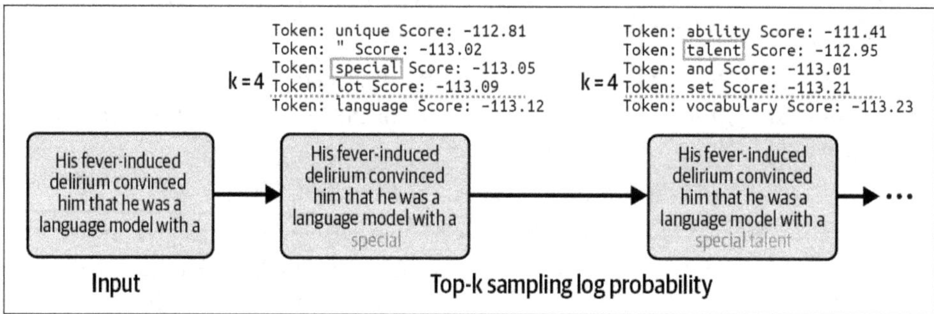

Figure 5-8. Top-k sampling

Top-p Sampling

Top-p sampling solves the problem with top-k sampling by making the number of candidate tokens dynamic. Top-p involves choosing the smallest number of tokens whose cumulative distribution exceeds a given probability p. Here is how you can implement this using Hugging Face `transformers`:

```
output = model.generate(**inputs, max_new_tokens=50, top_p=0.9)
print(tokenizer.decode(output[0], skip_special_tokens=True))
```

Figure 5-9 shows an example of top-p sampling using the FLAN-T5 model. Top-p sampling, also called nucleus sampling, is the most popular sampling strategy used today.

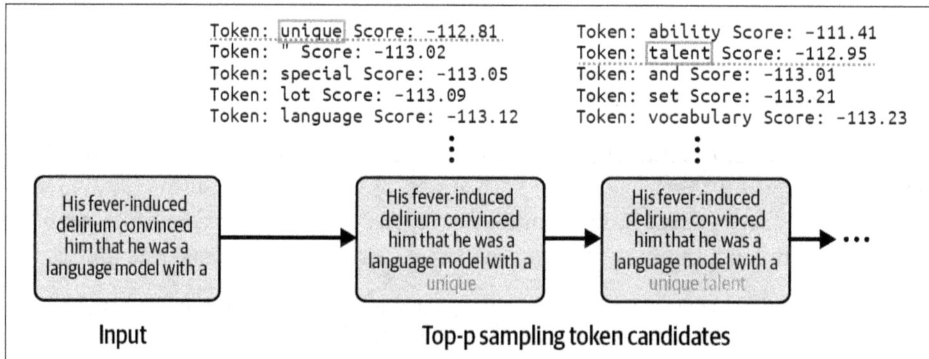

Figure 5-9. Top-p sampling

So far, the decoding approaches we have seen operate serially; i.e., each token is generated one at a time, with a full pass through the model each time. This is too inefficient for latency-sensitive applications. In Chapter 9, we will discuss methods like speculative decoding, which can speed up the decoding process.

Running Inference on LLMs

Now that we have learned how to access and load LLMs and understood the decoding process, let's begin using them to solve our tasks. We call this *LLM inference*.

Exercise

You are an intrepid musician embarking on a concert tour comprising seven cities: Amsterdam, Warsaw, Hamburg, Barcelona, Delhi, Shanghai, and Toronto. Ask the LLM if it can come up with a suggested visiting order of cities constituting the shortest travel time. Use prompting techniques and strategies you have learned in Chapter 1 to solve this.

Repeat this for multiple LLMs: a 3B LLM, a 7B LLM, an LLM that is at least 30B, and a proprietary LLM API. How easy do you find steering each model to do your bidding?

Additionally, the book's GitHub repo (*https://oreil.ly/llm-playbooks*) contains multiple example tasks that you can test your prompting skills on. Try them out and see if you can get the LLMs to answer them correctly!

You will have seen that LLM outputs are not consistent and sometimes differ wildly across multiple generations for the same prompt. As we learned in the section on decoding, unless you are using greedy search or any other deterministic algorithm, the LLM is sampling from a token distribution.

Some ways to make the generation more deterministic is to set the temperature to zero and keeping the random seed for the sampling constant. Even then, you may not be able to guarantee the same (deterministic) outputs every time you send the LLM the same input.

Sources of nondeterminism range from using multi-threading to floating-point rounding errors to use of certain model architectures (for example, it is known that the Sparse MoE architecture (*https://oreil.ly/pzchE*) produces nondeterministic outputs).

Reducing the temperature to zero or close to zero impacts the LLM's creativity and makes its outputs more predictable, which might not be suitable for many applications.

In production settings where reliability is important, you should run multiple generations for the same input and use a technique like majority voting or heuristics to select the right output. This is very important due to the nature of the decoding process; sometimes the wrong tokens can be generated, and since every token generated is a function of the tokens generated before it, the error can be propagated far ahead.

> **Exercise**
>
> For each of the prompting exercises provided, run multiple generations on them and check how the output varies across generations. Does majority voting work well in selecting the correct output?

Self-consistency (*https://oreil.ly/wEE8q*) is a popular prompting technique that uses majority voting in conjunction with CoT prompting. In this technique, we add the CoT prompt "Let's think step by step" to the input and run multiple generations (reasoning paths). We then use majority voting to select the correct output.

Structured Outputs

We might want the output of the LLM to be in some structured format, so that it can be consumed by other software systems. But this is easier said than done; current LLMs aren't as controllable as we would like them to be. Some LLMs can be excessively chatty. Ask them to give a Yes/No answer and they respond with "The answer to this question is 'Yes.'"

One way to get structured outputs from the LLM is to define a JSON schema, provide the schema to the LLM, and prompt it to generate outputs adhering to the schema. For larger models, this works almost all the time, with some schema corruption errors that you can catch and handle.

For smaller models, you can use libraries like Jsonformer (*https://oreil.ly/aSc0f*). Jsonformer delegates the generation of the content tokens to the LLM but fills the content in JSON form by itself. Jsonformer is built on top of Hugging Face and thus supports any model that is supported by Hugging Face.

Exercise

Extract text from the career section of the Wikipedia page of the actor Andrew Garfield (*https://oreil.ly/WXtgc*). Design a JSON schema with content types coactors, director, year, and movie name. Use an open source LLM to extract details about his movies from the unstructured text, and use Jsonformer or a similar library to output them in structured form. Are you able to get fully formed and accurate JSON outputs?

More advanced structured outputs can be facilitated by using libraries like LMQL (*https://oreil.ly/LlkEj*) or Guidance (*https://oreil.ly/cFe5s*). These libraries provide a programming paradigm for prompting and facilitate controlled generation.

Features available through these libraries include:

Restricting output to a finite set of tokens
: This is useful for classification problems, where you have a finite set of output labels. For example, you can restrict the output to be positive, negative, or neutral for a sentiment analysis task.

Controlling output format using regular expressions
: For example, you can use regular expressions to specify a custom date format.

Control output format using context-free grammars (CFG)
: A CFG defines the rules that generated strings need to follow. For more background on CFGs, refer to Aditya's blog (*https://oreil.ly/M00us*). Using CFGs, we can use LLMs to more effectively solve sequence tagging tasks like NER or part-of-speech tagging.

Exercise

Named entity recognition (NER) is a sequence tagging task that tags named entities in text like numbers, dates, places, names, organizations, etc. For example, for the sentence "Padma sold 23 umbrellas in Guatemala," the tagged output can be in this form:

Padma: PER

sold:

23: NUM

umbrellas:

in:

Guatemala: LOC

where PER is the tag for a person, NUM is the tag for numbers, and LOC is the tag for location.

To generate the tagged output in the above format, use a CFG expression using the Guidance library (*https://oreil.ly/R3XLQ*). Run the NER task on the Wikipedia page for the Summer Olympics (*https://oreil.ly/tUrIt*). Use a 3B/7B open source LLM to solve this task.

Model Debugging and Interpretability

Now that we are comfortable with loading LLMs and generating text using them, we would like to be able to understand model behavior and explore the examples for which the model fails. Interpretability in LLMs is much less developed than in other areas of machine learning. However, we can get partial interpretability by exploring how the output changes upon minor variances in the input, and by analyzing the intermediate outputs as the inputs propagate through the Transformer architecture.

Google's open source tool LIT-NLP (*https://oreil.ly/YFY4q*) is a handy tool that supports visualizations of model behavior as well as various debugging workflows.

Figure 5-10 shows an example of LIT-NLP in action, providing interpretability for a T5 model running a summarization task.

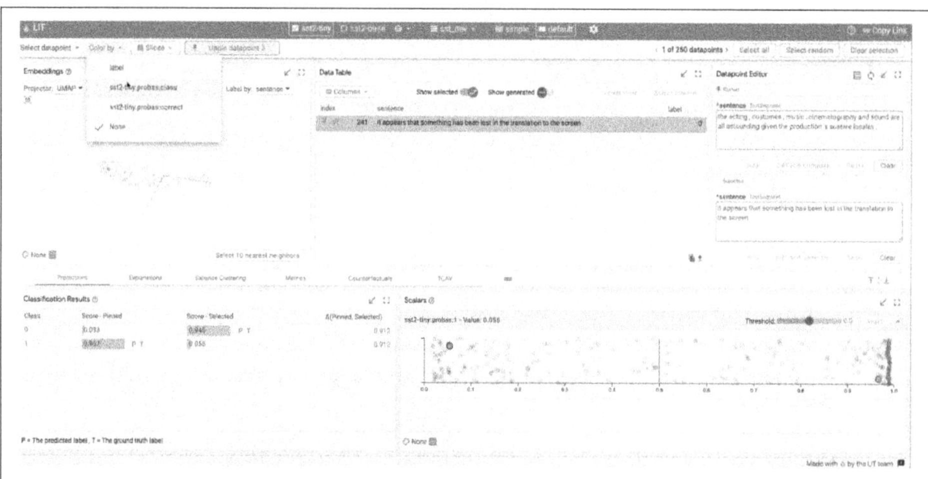

Figure 5-10. LIT-NLP

LIT-NLP features that help you debug your models include:

- Visualization of the attention mechanism

- Salience maps, which show parts of the input that are paid most attention to by the model
- Visualization of embeddings
- Counterfactual analysis that shows how your model behavior changes after a change to the input like adding or removing a token.

> ## Exercise
>
> Using the sentences in the Canadian parliamentary proceedings dataset in the book's GitHub repository (*https://oreil.ly/llm-playbooks*), classify the sentences based on the tone of their content. The output labels are supportive, antagonistic, mournful, celebratory, and other. Use few-shot prompts to provide examples of each label. Use Google's Gemma model (any flavor will do). You are likely not going to get 100% on your first try. Use LIT-NLP to observe the errors, and see if you can use the interpretability tools to gather insights to improve the model.

For more details on using LIT-NLP for error analysis, refer to Google's tutorial (*https://oreil.ly/zcsLu*) on using LIT-NLP with the Gemma LLM where they find errors in few-shot prompts by analyzing incorrect examples and observing which parts of the prompt contributed most to the output (salience).

> ## Mechanistic Interpretability
>
> As seen in Chapter 2, the smallest unit of a Transformer-based LLM is a neuron. Thus, analyzing the behavior of individual neurons in an LLM is a fundamental step toward making LLMs interpretable.
>
> However, in their experiments (*https://oreil.ly/hLdVN*), researchers from Anthropic observed that a single neuron can be activated for many different types of input. Thus, any given neuron's exact contribution is not entirely clear. The researchers introduced the notion of *features*, linear combinations of multiple neuron activations. They show that these features are more interpretable than a single neuron, as each feature is activated only on a single type of input. Some features are activated only on a single token, while others are activated on a broader type of input, like code.
>
> For more details, refer to Anthropic's mechanistic interpretability paper (*https://oreil.ly/hLdVN*), where the authors perform experiments on a 1-layer Transformer block and identify features of interest.

You can explore this further by using Anthropic's visualization tool (*https://oreil.ly/2YvE6*), which includes textual descriptions of the tokens for which a neuron gets activated. As an example, they show (*https://oreil.ly/cE27M*) how each neuron responds when the book *Alice in Wonderland* is fed as input.

Summary

In this chapter, we journeyed through the LLM landscape and noted the various options we have at our disposal. We learned how to determine the criteria most relevant to our tasks and choose the right LLM accordingly. We explored various LLM benchmarks and showed how to interpret their results. We learned how to load LLMs and run inference on them, along with efficient decoding strategies. Finally, we showcased interpretability tools like LIT-NLP that can help us understand what is going on behind the scenes in the Transformer architecture.

In the next chapter, we will learn how to update a model to improve its performance on our tasks of interest. We will walk through a full-fledged fine-tuning example and explore the hyperparameter tuning decisions involved. We will also learn how to construct training datasets for fine-tuning.

CHAPTER 6

Fine-Tuning

In the previous chapter, we discussed the various factors that need to be taken into account while choosing the right LLM for your specific needs, including pointers on how to evaluate LLMs to be able to make an informed choice. Next, let us utilize these LLMs to solve our tasks.

In this chapter, we will explore the process of adapting an LLM to solve your task of interest, using fine-tuning. We will go through a full example of fine-tuning, covering all the important decisions one needs to make. We will also discuss the art and science of creating fine-tuning datasets.

The Need for Fine-Tuning

Why do we need to fine-tune LLMs? Why doesn't a pre-trained LLM with few-shot prompts suffice for our needs? Let us look at a couple of examples to drive the point home:

Use Case 1

Consider you are working on the rather whimsical task of detecting all sentences written in the past tense within a body of text and transforming them to future tense. To solve this task, you might provide a few examples of past tense sentences and input-output pairs representing past tense and their corresponding future tense sentences. However, the LLM doesn't seem to be able to tackle this task to your satisfaction, making mistakes in both the identification and transformation steps. In response, you elaborate on your instructions, adding grammar rules and exceptions in the English language into your prompt. You notice an increase in performance. But with each new rule added, your prompt balloons, slowly turning into a grammar mini-book.

As we saw in Chapter 5, the LLM can adhere to only a finite set of instructions in the prompt, and its effective context window is much smaller than the advertised context window. We have hit an impasse.

Use Case 2

Consider a task that deals with answering questions from content in financial text. LLMs are not financial experts and have difficulty dealing with financial jargon. To address this, you add the definitions of key financial terms in the prompt. While you notice a small improvement in performance, it is not long before you realize you need to stuff the entire curriculum of the CPA exam into your measly context window to achieve the desired gains.

This is where fine-tuning comes in. By providing a dataset of input-output pairs, such that the model learns the input-output mapping by updating its weights, you can accomplish tasks that cannot be performed by in-context learning alone. For both the tasks mentioned above, fine-tuning the model massively improves performance.

When should fine-tuning not be used? If your primary goal is to impart new or updated facts or knowledge to the language model, this is better served with techniques like RAG, which we will explore in Chapters 10 and 12. Fine-tuning is best suited for situations where you need the model to learn a particular input-output mapping, be familiarized to a new textual domain, or exhibit more complex capabilities and behavior.

Recall from Chapter 5 that updating a language model's parameters can cause the base model capabilities to regress! Fine-tuning a model on one task can inadvertently cause the base model to perform worse on other tasks. Handle with care.

Fine-Tuning: A Full Example

Let's walk through a practical fine-tuning example from start to finish. We would like to train a *political promises detector*, which can be used to identify promises made by representatives of the ruling party in campaign speeches or parliamentary proceedings. We define a political promise as something that is tangible, specific, and an action that the government has the agency to make.

An example of such a sentence is: "We will build 10,000 kilometres of subway lines in the next ten years."

However, not all future tense or forward-looking statements are promises. The following sentences are not promises, per our definition:

"We expect the Japanese to increase tariffs next year." (expectation, and not something the government can control)
"We will work toward making Canada a better place." (no specifics provided)
"AI will cause the loss of a million jobs next year." (prediction, not promise)

Our base LLM, Llama2-7B, finds it difficult to accurately identify such promises in an in-context learning setup. Therefore, we will fine-tune it for this specific task. We can then use the resulting model to detect political promises, and then match those promises against structured datasets or budgetary text to track whether these promises have been fulfilled over a period of time.

To this end, I have constructed a synthetic fine-tuning dataset containing examples of both promises and mere statements. Later in this chapter, we will go through the process of creating such a dataset.

Fortunately, fine-tuning today is easier due to the existence of several libraries that streamline the fine-tuning process. The most important of these libraries are Transformers (*https://oreil.ly/BTi76*), Accelerate (*https://oreil.ly/W8oLi*), PEFT (*https://oreil.ly/QbQoq*), TRL (*https://oreil.ly/Ya9Xj*), and bitsandbytes (*https://oreil.ly/ruVEX*). The first four are from Hugging Face. You have encountered many of these libraries in prior chapters already. Being familiar with the inner workings of these libraries is a very useful skill.

Given that these libraries are relatively new and are part of a fast-moving field, they frequently undergo substantial updates. I recommend keeping in touch with major updates of these libraries, as they continue to introduce enhancements that will simplify your workflow.

Let's begin by loading the dataset. The custom dataset can be downloaded from this book's GitHub repo (*https://oreil.ly/llm-playbooks*):

```
from datasets import load_dataset
tune_data = load_dataset("csv", data_files='/path/to/finetune_data.csv'
```

I highly recommend using the *datasets* library (*https://oreil.ly/3LX5X*) for loading your training and fine-tuning datasets, as it is an excellent abstraction for efficiently loading large datasets, abstracting away memory management details.

Next, let us set some relevant hyperparameters in the `Transformers` library through the `TrainingArguments` class:

```
# Make sure you have installed the correct version
!pip install transformers==4.35.0

from transformers import TrainingArguments
```

There are more than a hundred arguments available; we will go through the important ones. The arguments relate to the learning algorithms used, memory and space optimizations, quantization, regularization, and distributed training. Let's explore these in detail.

Learning Algorithms Parameters

Let's explore optimization algorithms used for training the network and learn how to choose the right one for our purposes.

Optimizers

AdamW and Adafactor are currently the most used optimizers. Other popular optimization algorithms include stochastic gradient descent (SGD), RMSProp, Adagrad, Lion, and their variants. For more background on optimization algorithms, refer to Florian June's blog post (*https://oreil.ly/VTiDa*).

Adafactor and SGD use four bytes of memory per parameter, while AdamW uses eight bytes per parameter. This means that a 7B model undergoing full fine-tuning with the AdamW optimizer requires 7 * 8 = ~56GB of memory to store the optimizer states alone. Even more memory is needed to store the parameters, gradients, and the forward activations.

More recently, 8-bit optimizers (*https://oreil.ly/4Z14D*) have been introduced that perform quantization of the optimizer state. A 7B model undergoing full fine-tuning with the AdamW 8-bit version requires only ~14GB of memory for the optimizer state.

These 8-bit optimizers are available through the bitsnbytes library and are also supported by Hugging Face. For using the 8-bit AdamW version, you can set in the `TrainingArguments`:

```
optim = 'adamw_bnb_8bit'
```

For all the optimizer options directly available through Hugging Face, refer to the OptimizerNames class (*https://oreil.ly/7kdSO*).

In his benchmarking experiments, Stas Bekman shows (*https://oreil.ly/0_0lt*) that surprisingly, the 8-bit AdamW optimizer is actually faster than the standard AdamW optimizer. His experiments also show that Adafactor is slightly slower than AdamW overall.

The default optimizer provided in the Hugging Face `TrainingArguments` class is AdamW. For most cases, the default optimizer works just fine. However, if it doesn't, you can try Adafactor and Lion. For reinforcement learning, SGD seems to work well.

If you are especially memory constrained, 8-bit AdamW is a compelling choice. If available, the paged version of these optimizers will further mitigate your memory requirements.

Paged Optimizers

Using AdamW as an optimizer requires eight bytes of memory per parameter, which is a significant drag on memory requirements. This affects the maximum sequence length that can be supported. This is where paged optimizers can come in handy. In cases where the GPU runs out of memory during fine-tuning, paged optimizers automatically transfer memory pages to CPU RAM, then transfer them back to GPU memory when it is needed.

In Hugging Face, paged variants are available for AdamW and Lion, and can be accessed using optimizer names *paged_adamw_32bit*, *paged_adamw_8bit*, *paged_lion*, and *paged_lion_8bit*, respectively.

Learning rates

For each optimizer, certain learning rates have been shown to be very effective. A recommended learning rate for AdamW is 1e-4 with a weight decay of 0.01. Weight decay is a regularization technique that helps reduce overfitting. Similarly, the default values for minor optimizer parameters like *adam_beta1*, *adam_beta2*, and *adam_epsilon* are good enough and need not be changed.

Exercise

Learning rate rules for fine-tuning models might differ from those used for training neural networks from scratch. Read the paper "Rethinking Learning Rate Tuning in the Era of Large Language Models" (*https://oreil.ly/T1xNB*) by Jin et al., which provides a good survey of the collective wisdom on learning rates developed by the LLM research community.

Additionally, play with automated learning rate optimization tools like PyTorch Lightning's LearningRateFinder (*https://oreil.ly/_zdA9*).

Learning schedules

Toward the end of the training process, it is a good idea to lower the learning rate because you do not want to overshoot when you are so close to convergence. In a similar vein, you would like to prevent your model from learning too much from the first few batches of examples. In either case, we would like to be able to automatically adjust the learning rate as training progresses. To facilitate this, we can use a learning schedule.

Hugging Face supports several different types of learning schedulers. Here are a few important ones:

Constant
: This is the vanilla training schedule where the learning rate remains constant throughout the course of the training.

Constant with warmup
: In this setting, the learning rate starts from zero and is increased linearly toward the specified learning rate during a warmup phase. After the warmup phase is completed, the learning rate remains constant.

  Figure 6-1 shows how the learning rate changes over time while using the constant with warmup scheduler.

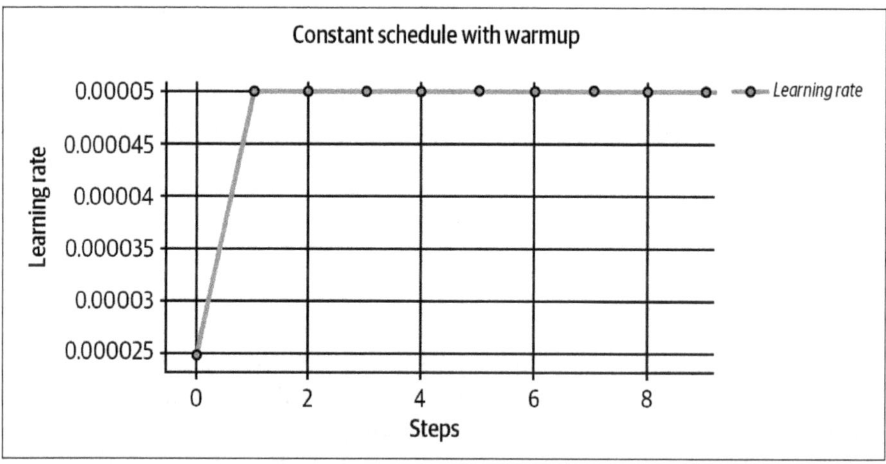

Figure 6-1. Learning rate with a constant schedule with warmup

Cosine
: In this setting, called *cosine annealing*, the learning rate has a warmup phase after which it slowly declines to zero, as per the cosine function.

  Figure 6-2 shows how the learning rate changes over time while using the cosine scheduler.

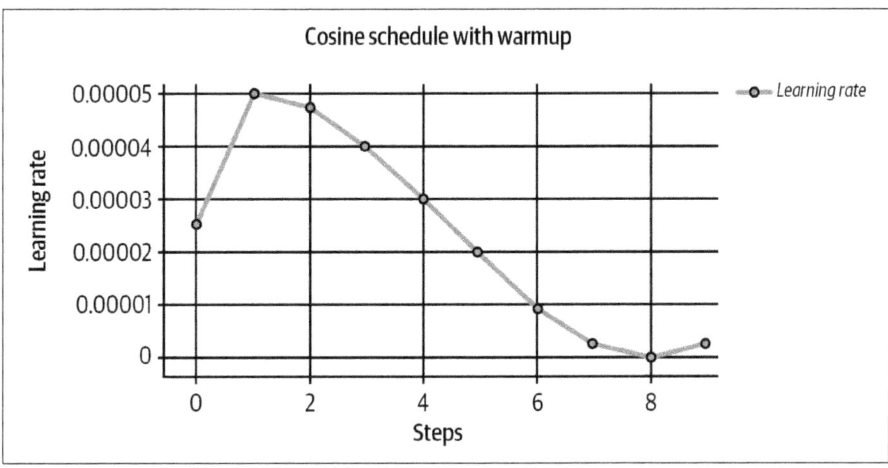

Figure 6-2. Learning rate with a cosine schedule

Cosine with restarts

In this setting, called *cosine annealing with warm restart*, after a warmup phase, the learning rate decreases to zero following the cosine function, but undergoes several hard restarts, where the learning rate shoots back to the specified learning rate after it reaches zero. For more details on why this is effective, check out Loshcilov and Hutter's paper (*https://oreil.ly/Q4c3o*) that introduced this concept.

Figure 6-3 shows how the learning rate changes across time while using the cosine with restarts scheduler.

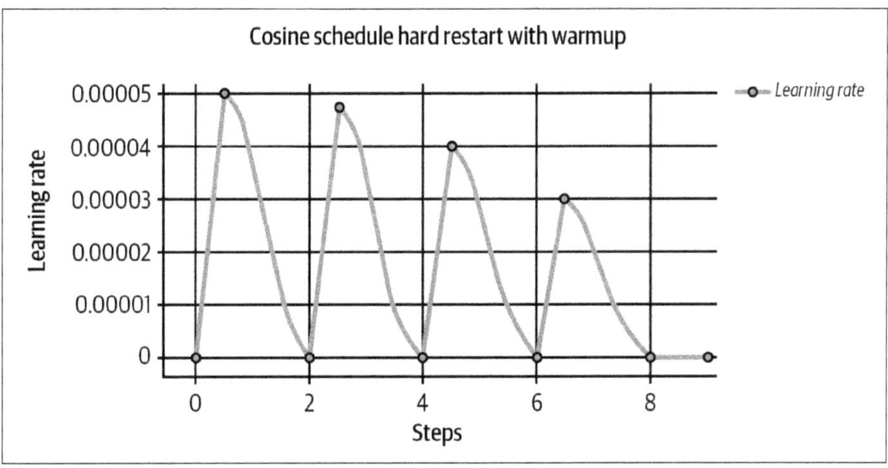

Figure 6-3. Learning rate with a cosine with restarts schedule

Linear

This is very similar to the cosine setting, except that the learning rate decreases to zero linearly instead of following the cosine function.

Figure 6-4 shows how the learning rate changes over time while using the linear scheduler.

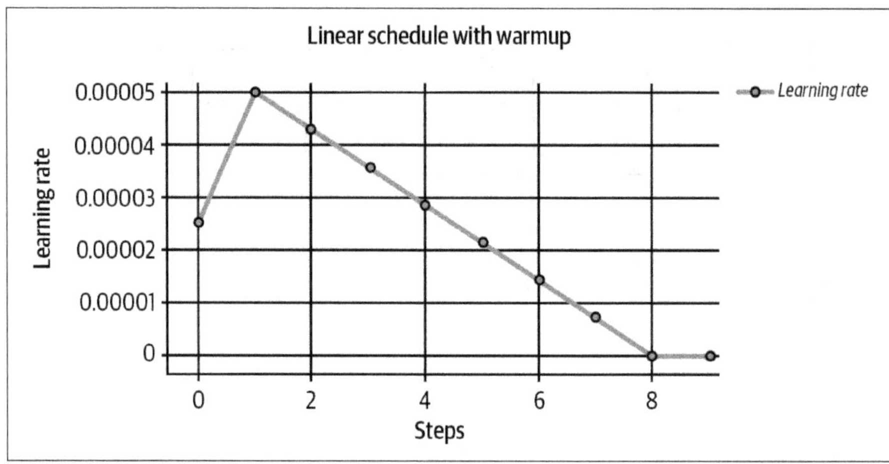

Figure 6-4. Learning rate with a linear scheduler

If you are using AdamW, schedulers with a warmup phase are even more important to prevent getting trapped in a bad minima. Empirically, it has been found that cosine annealing outperforms linear decay.

For our political promises detector fine-tuning, let's use the paged variant of AdamW, a learning rate of 3e-4, a weight decay of 0.01, and the cosine learning schedule:

```
optim = "paged_adamw_32bit"
learning_rate = 3e-4
weight_decay = 0.01
lr_scheduler_type = 'cosine'
warmup_ratio = 0.03  #The proportion of training steps to be used as warmup
```

Memory Optimization Parameters

After we have set the parameters related to the optimizers, let's explore memory and compute optimization parameters. Two prevalent techniques in this area include gradient checkpointing and gradient accumulation.

Gradient checkpointing

Gradient checkpointing helps save memory at the cost of more compute. During the forward pass of the backpropagation algorithm, activations are computed and saved in memory so that they can be used in the backward pass. What if we did not save all of the activations? The missing activations could be recalculated on the fly during the backward pass. This does cost us more compute, but we could save a lot of memory. We could even train models where a batch size of only one does not fit in our GPU memory. For more technical details on gradient checkpointing, check out Yaroslav Bulatov's blog (*https://oreil.ly/i-R4I*).

Gradient accumulation

Let's say we have a desired batch size but we do not have the required memory to support that batch size. We can simulate the desired batch size using a technique called gradient accumulation. In this technique, the gradient updates are not done at every batch, but are accumulated over several batches and then summed or averaged.

Gradient accumulation can make training slower, since there are fewer updates being made. Gradient accumulation does not reduce the computation required.

Quantization

A very effective form of saving memory is through quantization, as introduced in Chapter 5. We will go through quantization techniques in more detail in Chapter 9. For our use case, we will use bf16 as it represents a sound tradeoff between memory savings and performance.

For our political promises detector fine-tuning, we'll set the following parameters for memory optimization, given that we are trying to train it on a relatively memory constrained 16 GB RAM GPU:

```
gradient_accumulation_steps = 4
bf16 = True
gradient_checkpointing = True
```

Regularization Parameters

Next, let's look at various techniques available for tackling model overfitting.

Label smoothing

Label smoothing is a technique that not only helps with combatting overfitting but also aids in model calibration.

Calibration is an underappreciated topic in deep learning. A model is said to be well-calibrated if there is a correlation between its output probability values and task accuracy.

For example, consider a task that classifies a sentence as being abusive or not. If the model is well-calibrated, then among all examples for which the model produces an output probability of 0.9, 90% of them would be expected to be correctly classified. Similarly, for an output probability of 0.6, there should be a lower (~60%) likelihood of the classification being correct. Simply put, the output probability should accurately reflect the confidence in the classification decision.

A model being well-calibrated implies that it is not overconfident. This helps us in nuanced handling of examples that have low output probabilities (using a bigger model to handle those examples, for instance).

Larger models are less calibrated compared to models like BERT, according to a study by Li et al. (*https://oreil.ly/ij7mS*) Larger models tend to be more confident in general about their predictions. The inability to calculate reasonably accurate uncertainty estimates for large language models could be an argument to use smaller ones instead!

One of the techniques for calibrating models is label smoothing. The usual training process involves training against hard target labels (0 or 1 for a binary classification task). When using cross-entropy as the loss function, this amounts to pushing the model logits closer to 0 or 1, thus making the model highly confident. Label smoothing involves using a regularization term that is subtracted or divided from the hard target label.

Label smoothing is especially useful when the input dataset is noisy, i.e., contains some inaccurate labels. Regularization prevents the model from learning too much from incorrect examples.

For the political promises detector, we will use label smoothing, given that some examples could be subjective or open to interpretation.

Noise Embeddings

The datasets we use for fine-tuning typically consist of a small number of examples (< 50,000). We would like our model to not overfit to the stylistic characteristics of the dataset, like the formatting, wording, and length of the text. One way to address this is by adding noise to the input embeddings.

Jain et al. (*https://oreil.ly/ouESL*) observe that adding noise embeddings reduces the tendency of the model to overfit to wording and formatting of the fine-tuning datasets. An interesting side effect of noise embeddings is that the models generate longer, verbose texts. By measuring token diversity of the outputs, they confirmed that the longer texts actually include more information and are not just repetitive.

Hugging Face supports Noisy Embedding Instruction Fine-Tuning (NEFTune) (*https://oreil.ly/dSaem*), a noise addition technique. In NEFTune, a noise vector is added to each embedding vector. The elements in the noise vector are generated by sampling independent and identically distributed (iid) from [-1,1]. The resulting vector is scaled using a scaling factor before being added to the embedding vector.

Noise embeddings have been empirically found to be very effective in reducing overfitting. Therefore, we will use it for our political promises detector fine-tuning. Note that the noise embeddings are added only during training and not during inference.

The impact of noise embeddings is not yet well understood. Improvements in the fine-tuning task could come at the cost of other model capabilities. Make sure you test the model for regressions!

For our political promises detector fine-tuning task, let's activate both label smoothing and noise embeddings:

```
# Label 0 will be transformed to label_smoothing_factor/num_labels
# Label 1 will be transformed to 1 - label_smoothing_factor +
#label_smoothing_factor/num_labels

label_smoothing_factor = 0.1
neftune_noise_alpha = 5
```

Batch Size

Along with the learning rate, the batch size is one of the most important hyperparameters we need to set. A larger batch size means training will proceed faster. However, larger batch sizes also require more memory. Larger batch sizes can also lead the model to land in a sharp local minima, which can be a sign of overfitting. Therefore, there are trade offs involving memory, compute, and performance.

For the political promises detector, we will use a batch size of 8, given our memory limitations. Of course during inference, the maximum possible batch size is the ideal one. Note that it is recommended that the batch size be always a number that is a power of two, to reduce GPU I/O overhead.

The `TrainingArguments` class by Hugging Face supports *auto_find_batch_size*, which when set, selects the maximum possible batch size supported by the memory. To use this feature, you need to install the `accelerate` library:

```
per_device_train_batch_size = 8
per_device_eval_batch_size = 8
```

You can reduce your maximum sequence length to support a larger batch size.

The Relationship Between Learning Rate and Batch Size

The relationship between learning rate and batch size is extremely complex and depends on several external factors including the model architecture.

A high learning rate requires fewer steps, thus helping you finish training faster, but at the risk of overshooting the minima, leading to lack of convergence. Conversely, a low learning rate requires more steps and takes longer to converge, but you might end up in a narrow suboptimal minima. The narrow local minima likely means that you are overfitting. We would like to converge to a flatter minima instead, which can be accomplished by increasing the learning rate.

A smaller batch size will mean greater variance between examples in each batch, thus potentially leading the model toward a flatter minima. Thus, a relatively high learning rate and a relatively low batch size theoretically could help with more effective convergence. However, theoretical insights might not always be true in practice.

Finally, let's set some miscellaneous parameters:

`max_grad_norm`
: This is used for gradient clipping, which is a solution for the exploding gradients issue that is sometimes encountered during training. The `max_grad_norm` value is the threshold for gradient clipping. If the L2 gradient norm is above the threshold, then it will be rescaled to `max_grad_norm`. For more details on gradient clipping, see "Understanding Gradient Clipping (and How It Can Fix Exploding Gradients Problem)" (*https://oreil.ly/gH7L7*).

`group_by_length`
: This is used to group examples that have similar lengths in the same batch, so that the padding tokens can be optimized.

`max_train_epochs`
: Number of passes over the training dataset. This is usually set to less than five to prevent overfitting:

```
max_grad_norm=2
group_by_length=True
max_train_epochs=3
```

Parameter-Efficient Fine-Tuning

After filling in the `TrainingArguments`, let's next fill in parameters of the PEFT library.

The PEFT library by Hugging Face is an impressive facilitator of parameter-efficient fine-tuning. This refers to a set of fine-tuning techniques that update only a small proportion of parameters in the model while keeping the performance closer to what it would have been if all the parameters were updated.

In this example, we will use low-rank adaptation (LoRA) as the fine-tuning technique. Here are some hyperparameters to consider:

`r`
: The attention dimension of LoRA.

`lora_alpha`
: The alpha parameter in the LoRA technique.

`lora_dropout`
: The dropout probability used in the layers being tuned. This helps reduce overfitting.

`layers_to_transform`
: This specifies the layers for which the LoRA transformation is to be applied.

Here are some recommended default values:

```
r = 64
lora_alpha = 8
lora_dropout = 0.1
```

For more background on LoRA, refer to Ogban Ugot's blog post (*https://oreil.ly/_l91y*).

Working with Reduced Precision

The bitsandbytes library, built by Tim Dettmers, facilitates working with reduced precision formats, which we introduced in Chapter 5. In this example, we will work with the FP4 format. Note that you need the bitsandbytes version to be >= 0.39.0.

Hugging Face has integrated bitsandbytes support into its ecosystem. The `BitsAndBytesConfig` class allows us to set the parameters. Here are some relevant ones:

`load_in_8bit/load_in_4bit`
: This is used to specify if we want to load the model in 4-bit mode or 8-bit mode.

`llm_int8_threshold`
: We need to specify a threshold of values beyond which fp16 will be used. This is because int8 quantization works well only for values lesser than 5–6.

`llm_int8_skip_modules`
: This is used to specify the exceptions for which we do not want int8 quantization.

`llm_int8_enable_fp32_cpu_offload`
: If we want parts of the model to be run in int8 on GPU and the rest in FP32 on CPU, this parameter facilitates it. This is used in cases where the model is too large to fit on our GPU.

`bnb_4bit_compute_dtype`
: This sets the computational type, regardless of the input type.

`bnb_4bit_quant_type`
: The options here are FP4 or NF4. This is used to set the quantization type in the 4-bit layers.

Here are some recommended default values:

```
use_4bit = True
bnb_4bit_compute_dtype = 'float16'
bnb_4bit_quant_type = 'nf4'
use_nested_quant = False
```

Finally, we use the Transformer Reinforcement Learning (TRL) library that, in addition to reinforcement learning, provides support for supervised fine-tuning.

Here are some recommended default values:

```
max_seq_length = 128
# Packing is used to place multiple instructions in the same input sequence

packing = True
```

Putting It All Together

Now that we have set up all the requisite parameters, here is the full code for the fine-tuning process:

```
# Ensure that the specified versions of these libraries are installed.
!pip install transformers==4.35.0 accelerate==0.24.0 peft==0.6.0
bitsandbytes==0.41.0  trl==0.7.4

from datasets import load_dataset
from transformers import TrainingArguments, BitsAndBytesConfig
from transformers import LlamaForCausalLM, LlamaTokenizer
from peft import PeftModel, LoraConfig
from trl import SFTTrainer
```

```
train_params = TrainingArguments(
    optim = "paged_adamw_32bit",
    learning_rate = 3e-4,
    weight_decay = 0.01,
    lr_scheduler_type = 'cosine',
    warmup_ratio = 0.03,
    gradient_accumulation_steps = 4,
    bf16 = True,
    gradient_checkpointing = True,
    label_smoothing_factor = 0.1,
    neftune_noise_alpha = 5,
    per_device_train_batch_size = 8,
    per_device_eval_batch_size = 8,
    max_grad_norm=2,
    group_by_length=True,
    max_train_epochs=3,
    output_dir = '/model_outputs',
    save_steps = 50,
    logging_steps = 10
    )


quantize_params = BitsAndBytesConfig (

    use_4bit = True,
    bnb_4bit_compute_dtype = 'float16',
    bnb_4bit_quant_type = 'nf4',
    use_nested_quant = False
    )


lora_params = LoraConfig (
    r = 64,
    lora_alpha = 8,
    lora_dropout = 0.1
    )

model = LlamaForCausalLM.from_pretrained(
    pretrained_model_name_or_path = 'meta-llama/Llama-2-7b',
    quantization_config=quantize_params,
    device_map='auto'
    )

tokenizer = LlamaTokenizer.from_pretrained('meta-llama/Llama-2-7b')

tune_data = load_dataset("csv", data_files='/path/to/finetune_data.csv')

sft = SFTTrainer (
    model = model,
    args = train_params,
    train_dataset = tune_data,
    tokenizer = tokenizer
```

```
        peft_config = lora_params,
        max_seq_length = 128,
        dataset_text_field = 'text',
        packing = True
        )

sft.train()
sft.model.save_pretrained('/path/to/llama-2-it.csv')
```

The relationship between the hyperparameters is very complex, and you might find surprising results. It will take several iterations before you hit the sweet spot. However, do not spend too much time squeezing out the last bit of performance from your fine-tuning, as that time is better spent developing better training data. In the next section, we will learn how to create effective training datasets.

The exact memory you need to fine-tune an LLM depends on several factors: the optimizer used, whether gradient accumulation and gradient checkpointing are activated, the type of quantization used, etc.

Exercise

Ablation studies are an important part of machine learning experimentation. This refers to studying the impact of a single component by removing the component and rerunning the experiment. For our fine-tuning example, let's study the impact of noise embeddings on the final performance. Run five fine-tuning runs with noise embeddings activated, and five without, keeping all other hyperparameters constant. Perform error analysis on the test set and understand how noise embeddings impact the performance of the model. Are they a net positive?

Fine-Tuning Datasets

In our fine-tuning example, we directly loaded a preconstructed dataset, focusing primarily on the fine-tuning process. Now, let's shift our attention to the dataset, to understand the various techniques for creating datasets.

First, let's look into the dataset we used in our fine-tuning example:

```
from datasets import load_dataset
tune_data = load_dataset("csv", data_files='/path/to/finetune_data.csv')
print(tune_data[:2])
```

Output:

```
Input: We will support women and children and give every child the best
possible start with $10 a day child care.
Identify if the above sentence represents a political promise. A political
promise is a promise that is tangible, specific, and an action that the
government has the agency to make. Reply 'True' if the sentence represents a
```

```
political promise, 'False' if not.
Output: True
Input: It is time for leadership that never seeks to divide Canadians, but
takes every single opportunity to bring us together, including in Parliament.
Identify if the above sentence represents a political promise. A political
promise is a promise that is tangible, specific, and an action that the
government has the agency to make. Reply 'True' if the sentence represents a
political promise, 'False' if not.
Output: False
```

As we can see, this is not a traditional dataset with just (input, output) pairs but one that also contains the task description in natural language. A typical example in this type of fine-tuning dataset consists of:

- The instruction, which describes the task and specifies the desired output format. Optionally, the instruction contains positive and/or negative examples of the task. It can also contain constraints and exceptions to be followed.
- An optional input, which in our example is the sentence or paragraph for the model to evaluate.
- The output, which is the correct answer to the task in the format specified in the instruction.

Fine-tuning datasets can be either multi-task or single-task. Multi-task datasets are used for instruction-tuning. In general, instruction-tuning can be treated as an intermediate step before single-task fine-tuning. For example, you can take a T5 language model, instruction-tune it with FLAN to create FLAN-T5, and then further fine-tune it with your task-specific dataset. This approach is shown (*https://oreil.ly/e-MVh*) to yield better results than directly fine-tuning on T5 alone.

Later in this chapter, we will learn how to create task-specific datasets. First, let's look at how we can create instruction-tuning datasets.

Why Do We Need Instruction-Tuning?

As seen in Chapter 4, the learning objectives of LLMs are typically either next-token prediction or denoising tasks. These objectives do not correspond to real-world user tasks. Thus there is a mismatch in how LLMs are trained and how they are used. To bridge this gap, we employ instruction-tuning.

Instruction-tuning allows for more controllable behavior from LLMs. The instructions in these datasets are similar to instructions provided by humans in real-world scenarios. Instruction-tuning also enables the model to learn the output format and thus generate more structured output.

There are plenty of instruction-tuned LLMs available, both open source and proprietary. Why do we want to instruction-tune the LLM ourselves? Public datasets are too general, lack diversity, and are primarily geared to general usage. Leveraging your domain expertise and knowledge of intended use cases to construct the dataset can be highly effective. In fact, at my company, which specializes in the financial domain, this technique delivered the single largest boost in performance.

Approaches to creating instruction-tuning datasets include:

- Utilizing publicly available instruction-tuning datasets
- Transforming traditional fine-tuning datasets into instruction-tuning datasets
- Starting with manually crafted seed examples, followed by optionally augmenting the dataset by utilizing an LLM to generate similar examples

Next, let's examine these methods more closely.

Utilizing Publicly Available Instruction-Tuning Datasets

If your use case is sufficiently general or popular, you may be able to use publicly available datasets for instruction-tuning. The following table lists some popular instruction-tuning datasets, along with information on their creators, sizes, and creation process.

Table 6-1. Popular instruction-tuning datasets

Name	Size	Created by	Created using
OIG	43M	Ontocord (*https://www.ontocord.ai/*)	Rule-based
FLAN	4.4M	Google	Templates
P3 (Public Pool of Prompts)	12M	Big Science	Templates
Natural Instruction	193K	Allen AI	Templates
Unnatural Instructions	240K	Honovich et al. (*https://github.com/orhonovich/unnatural-instructions*), Meta	LLMs
LIMA (Less Is More for Alignment)	1K	Zhou et al. (*https://arxiv.org/abs/2305.11206*), Meta	Templates
Self-Instruct	52K	Wang et al. (*https://github.com/yizhongw/self-instruct*)	LLMs
Evol-Instruct	52K	Xu et al. (*https://arxiv.org/abs/2304.12244*)	LLMs
InstructWild v2	110K	Ni et al. (*https://github.com/XueFuzhao/InstructionWild*)	LLMs
Alpaca	52K	Stanford	LLMs

Name	Size	Created by	Created using
Guanaco	534K	Dettmers et al. (*https://arxiv.org/abs/2305.14314*)	LLMs
Vicuna	70K	LMSYS	Human conversations
OpenAssistant	161K	Open Assistant	Human conversations

Let's go through fine-tuned language net (FLAN), one of the most popular instruction-tuning datasets in detail. Understanding how it was constructed will provide you with roadmaps to create your own instruction-tuning datasets. Most publicly available instruction-tuning datasets are meant to augment an LLM that will be used for open-ended tasks, as opposed to domain-specific use cases.

FLAN is actually a collection of several datasets. The FLAN collection (*https://oreil.ly/SrXV-*), published in 2022, is composed of five components:

- FLAN 2021
- T0
- Super-natural Instructions
- Chain-of-Thought
- Dialog

The original FLAN 2021 datasets were one of the pioneering instruction-tuning datasets, which were used to train FLAN-T5. The FLAN 2021 datasets were constructed by taking existing academic NLP datasets and converting them to the instruction format using instruction templates. The templates were manually constructed, with ten templates created for each task. The templates are available here (*https://oreil.ly/DNKCv*).

Here is how a template list for a task looks, as drawn from the templates.py (*https://oreil.ly/DNKCv*) file in the FLAN GitHub repo. Our example task is text summarization on the CNN/DailyMail news dataset:

```
"cnn_dailymail": [
  ("Write highlights for this article:\n\n{text}", "{highlights}"),
  ("Write some highlights for the following article:\n\n{text}", "{highlights}"),
  ("{text}\n\nWrite highlights for this article.", "{highlights}"),
  ("{text}\n\nWhat are highlight points for this article?", "{highlights}"),
  ("{text}\nSummarize the highlights of this article.", "{highlights}"),
  ("{text}\nWhat are the important parts of this article?", "{highlights}"),
  ("{text}\nHere is a summary of the highlights for this article:",
    "{highlights}"),
  ("Write an article using the following points:\n\n{highlights}", "{text}"),
  ("Use the following highlights to write an article:\n\n{highlights}",
    "{text}"),
  ("{highlights}\n\nWrite an article based on these highlights.", "{text}"),
],
```

Note that the last three instructions represent an inverted version of the task, where given a summary, the model is encouraged to write the entire article. This has been done to increase the diversity of the instructions at scale.

Rather than painstakingly constructing these templates by hand, can we automate their generation using LLMs? Yes, this is possible. We can leverage LLMs to generate more diverse templates. When I asked my favorite LLM to generate similar instructions to a news summarization task template provided in the prompt, it came up with:

```
"cnn_dailymail": [
  ("Distill the essence of this article:\n\n{text}", "{highlights}"),
  ("Give a quick rundown of this article's key points:\n\n{text}",
    "{highlights}"),
  ("Summarize the main elements of this text:\n\n{text}", "{highlights}"),
  ("Highlight the primary takeaways from the following:\n\n{text}",
    "{highlights}"),
  ("Extract and summarize the top points of this article:\n\n{text}",
    "{highlights}"),
  ("Condense this article into its most important aspects:\n\n{text}",
    "{highlights}"),
  ("What are the key insights of this article?\n\n{text}", "{highlights}"),
     ],
```

As you can see, the generated templates reflect various ways of expressing the summarization task.

For classification tasks, it is recommended to append the instruction with an *Options* clause. This introduces the LLM to the output space and can thus concentrate the probability mass over the defined label space. Without this guidance, the LLM would distribute its probability across several different tokens that express the same concept, for example there are several different ways of expressing the *True* label in a binary classification task. An example prompt is: "Identify the tone of this text. OPTIONS: happy, sad, neutral."

Constructing these prompts manually can be a tedious exercise. The *promptsource* tool (*https://oreil.ly/WIyOq*) enables you to create, access, and apply prompts through a graphical user interface tool or through the promptsource Python library. Here is an example from the Public Pool of Prompts (P3) collection for the paraphrasing task, constructed by Big Science, which is available through the promptsource tool. P3 prompts consist of an Input template, a Target template, and an Answer Choices template:

```
Input Template:
I want to know whether the following two sentences mean the same thing.
{{sentence1}}
{{sentence2}}
Do they?
```

```
Target Template:
{{ answer_choices[label] }}

Answer Choices Template:
no ||| yes
```

Another key component of the FLAN collection is the Super-NaturalInstructions dataset (*https://oreil.ly/D_rv_*). This dataset contains very rich descriptions of instructions that contain not just task definitions, but also positive and negative examples, constraints, and things to watch out for. The answers are enriched with explanations on why the answer was chosen. The effectiveness of adding explanations to the answer is not yet determined.

Here is an example of such a task from the Super-NaturalInstructions dataset:

```
Definition
In this task, we ask you convert a data table of restaurant descriptions into
fluent natural-sounding English sentences.
The input is a string of key-value pairs; the output should be a natural and
grammatical English sentence containing all the information from the input.

Positive Example

Input: name[Aromi], eatType[restaurant], food[English], area[city centre]

Output: Aromi is an English restaurant in the city centre.
Explanation: The output sentence faithfully converts the data in the input
into a natural-sounding sentence.

Negative Example
Input: name[Blue Spice], eatType[coffee shop], priceRange[more than 00a330],
customer rating[5 out of 5], ˘
area[riverside], familyFriendly[yes], near[Avalon]
Output: Blue Spice is a Colombian coffee shop located by the riverside, near
Avalon in Boston. Its prices are over
00a330. Its customer ratings are 5 out of 5. ˘

Explanation: While the output contains most of the information from the input,
it hallucinates by adding ungrounded
information such as "Colombian" and "Boston".

Instance Input: name[The Mill], eatType[restaurant], area[riverside], near[The
Rice Boat]

Valid Output: ["A restaurant called The Mill, can be found near the riverside
next to The Rice Boat."]
```

Let's now look at datasets that are constructed with the help of LLMs.

LLM-Generated Instruction-Tuning Datasets

As seen earlier, hand-constructing these datasets can be painstaking, and paraphrasing/synthetic data generation is where LLMs shine. Therefore, we can leverage LLMs to generate our instruction-tuning datasets. The Self-Instruct (*https://oreil.ly/HVBfK*) and Unnatural Instructions papers (*https://oreil.ly/1wV_G*) are the first attempts in this regard. Both start from a seed set of high-quality hand-generated examples, and then in a few-shot setting, ask the LLM to generate similar examples with more diverse linguistic expressions.

Given an instruction, a combination of input-first and output-first is shown to be beneficial for generating input-output pairs. Typically, you would generate input-output pairs using an input-first approach, where the LLM is asked to generate an input instance for the given instruction and subsequently asked to generate the output label for that input. However, this approach might lead to label imbalance as shown in Wang et al. (*https://oreil.ly/hYFYH*), with certain labels being overrepresented. Therefore, it is a good approach to mix output-first generation, where you ask the LLM to generate the output label first and then ask it to generate an input text that satisfies the label.

It is against OpenAI's policies to use its outputs to generate data that can be used to train a competing model. While there are several public instruction-tuning datasets that have been synthetically generated using GPT-4, they are technically violating OpenAI's terms of service. I recommend using open source LLMs for synthetic data generation instead.

Simply asking an LLM to generate similar examples to your seed set may not give you the desired results. You want a diverse but relevant set of examples, and it is easy for your LLM to drift into territory that ends up generating spurious examples outside of your desired distribution.

How large should your instruction-tuning dataset be? The "LIMA: Less Is More for Alignment" paper (*https://oreil.ly/z0BWh*) shows that you need only a few thousand high-quality examples to effectively fine-tune a model.

Xu et al. propose Evol-Instruct (*https://oreil.ly/9nw3G*), a structured way to generate these synthetic instructions by making controlled edits to the seed examples. The process consists of three steps:

1. Instruction evolution: The seed examples are evolved using in-depth and in-breadth strategies. In-depth evolution increases the complexity and difficulty of the original instruction through five types of prompts:
   - Adding constraints
   - Increasing reasoning steps
   - Asking deeper questions
   - Asking more specific questions
   - Increasing the complexity of the input

   In-breadth evolution increases topic coverage by generating a completely new instruction from the same domain as the original instruction.
2. Response generation: The response for the evolved instruction is generated, either using humans or LLMs.
3. Candidate filtering: Candidate instances that do not meet quality criteria are filtered out. You could use either heuristics or LLMs for candidate filtering.

Why not pre-train on instruction-tuning datasets? If instruction-tuning is a necessary step after pre-training a model, why don't we just pre-train the model using an instruction-tuning dataset? It is indeed possible, but these datasets are hard to construct at scale without incurring a significant drop in quality.

We need not wait until someone releases a massive dataset to reap the benefits of instruction-tuning during the pre-training phase. It has been shown (*https://oreil.ly/tfO4a*) that mixing instruction-tuning data during pre-training is beneficial.

Exercise

Take all of the Canadian parliamentary proceedings data and convert it into an instruction-tuning dataset. This task sounds daunting, but luckily we have libraries that facilitate this process. One such library is called Bonito (*https://oreil.ly/8wJ_o*), which comes with a model for conditional task generation. This library takes unstructured text and converts it into instruction tuning format. Several types of tasks are supported, including summarization, sentiment, and question generation.

Use this library to create an instruction-tuning dataset from the parliamentary proceedings data. What is the quality of the resulting dataset? How can you further improve the diversity of the dataset?

Summary

In this chapter, we underscored the inevitability of needing to fine-tune models to solve more complex tasks. We performed a deep dive of the fine-tuning process and highlighted the tradeoffs involved in selecting hyperparameters. We also showed the uncanny effectiveness of instruction-tuning along with pointers on how to create your own instruction-tuning datasets.

In the next chapter, we will discuss more advanced techniques for updating an LLM's parameters, including continual pre-training, parameter efficient fine-tuning, and model merging.

CHAPTER 7

Advanced Fine-Tuning Techniques

In the previous chapter, we presented the canonical way to fine-tune a typical LLM. In the real world, there are a wide variety of motivations for updating an LLM, and similarly there are multiple ways to update it. In this chapter, we will describe several advanced fine-tuning techniques and highlight the scenarios in which each technique would be suitable.

Why would you want to update the parameters of an LLM? We touched upon this in previous chapters but let's go through it in more detail now:

Domain adaptation
: The data that we work with belongs to a specialized domain that the LLM might not have been familiarized with during pre-training. In this case, we would like to update the model by training it on domain-specific data.

Task adaptation
: We care about LLM performance on specific downstream tasks. To improve the LLM's performance on these tasks, we can train it on task-specific data. This can be supervised or unsupervised.

Knowledge updating
: We would like to keep the LLM's knowledge up-to-date by continually training it on new data.

Controllability/steerability
: We would like to control the behavior of the LLM, including making it more likely to follow user requests written in natural language, reject certain types of requests, and so on. Techniques to achieve this are collectively called alignment training. We will defer discussion of alignment training to Chapter 8.

In this chapter, we will learn techniques that can be used to update the LLM for the aforementioned reasons. To this end, the chapter is divided into three sections:

Continual pre-training
: Primarily used for domain adaptation and keeping the knowledge of the LLM up-to-date (the latter is also called lifelong-learning).

Parameter-Efficient Fine-Tuning (PEFT)
: A set of fine-tuning techniques that make the fine-tuning process more efficient by updating only a small number of model parameters, thus needing less memory and compute.

Model merging/model fusion
: An exciting new subfield of LLMs that explores combining the parameters of two or more models. I call this the "dark arts" of NLP, as it is poorly understood but uncannily effective if done the right way.

Let's begin with my personal favorite: continual pre-training!

Continual Pre-Training

The premise of continual pre-training is simple. Take a pre-trained model checkpoint and continue pre-training it with your own data. But why would you want to do that? Here are some scenarios where continual pre-training can help.

- You work in a specialized domain like law, finance, or biomedical. In each of these cases, text belonging to these domains differs linguistically and structurally from naturally occurring English text. For example, legal text is characterized by long sentences written in a formal tone, containing jargon specific to the legal domain. Financial text is interspersed with a lot of numbers. Both legal and financial text contain a significant proportion of boilerplate text. Biomedical text contains a lot of scientific terms that are not part of the standard English vocabulary. In all these cases, you would like to pre-train your LLM on domain-specific data so that the LLM is exposed to the nuances and characteristics of domain-specific text. This is called *domain-adaptive pre-training (DAPT)*.
- Taking DAPT one step further, you can also continue pre-training your model not just on general text from your domain of interest but also on domain text specifically related to your downstream tasks. This is called *task-adaptive pre-training (TAPT)*.
- Your LLM is a reservoir of knowledge. But this knowledge can become obsolete over time. To keep its knowledge up-to-date, you continue pre-training the model at regular time periods or when new data is available. This is called *lifelong learning*.

You might be thinking, "If I want a domain-specific LLM, why don't I just take my domain-specific data and train an LLM from scratch?" Well, you can, but your LLM just won't be as performant, and the exercise will cost a whole lot more than continual pre-training. LLMs learn a wide variety of linguistic capabilities that might not be able to be learned from domain-specific text alone. Therefore, it is better to take an already pre-trained LLM that was trained on general text and then continue pre-training it with domain-specific text.

In practice, continual pre-training is a challenging exercise. This is due to the phenomenon of catastrophic forgetting, where the LLM *forgets* its previously learned capabilities and knowledge when it continues to be trained on new and different data. We will soon explore various techniques to combat the catastrophic forgetting problem.

How does continual pre-training differ from fine-tuning? The differences are mostly cosmetic and terminology-related. Just like pre-training, continual pre-training is self-supervised, while we typically use the term fine-tuning when we use supervised datasets. Continual pre-training uses the same (but not necessarily) learning objective as the one used in the original pre-training setup. Finally, continual pre-training datasets are usually orders of magnitude larger than typical fine-tuning datasets.

What's in a Domain?

So far, we have used a very intuitive notion of what a *domain* is, with broad examples like law, finance, and medicine. But we need not restrict ourselves to such a definition. For example, continual pre-training has been used to expose the LLM to new languages, like a primarily English language LLM being continually pre-trained on Telugu data. Continual pre-training has also been used to expose the LLM to text written in a different tone and style, like social media text.

More formally, a domain can be described as text whose representations form an implicit cluster. Aharoni et al. (*https://oreil.ly/FQd-z*) show that sentence representations of LLMs lend themselves naturally to these clusters.

Once you have identified a domain, you would also like to select text that is most representative of the domain. In the same paper, Aharoni et al. introduced domain-data selection techniques based on sentence representations generated through the LLMs. One way to select data representative of the domain is to use embedding similarity with gold-truth in-domain data. Another way is to fine-tune a domain classifier that is trained on gold-truth in-domain data and randomly sampled negative examples.

Figure 7-1 depicts the general continual pre-training process.

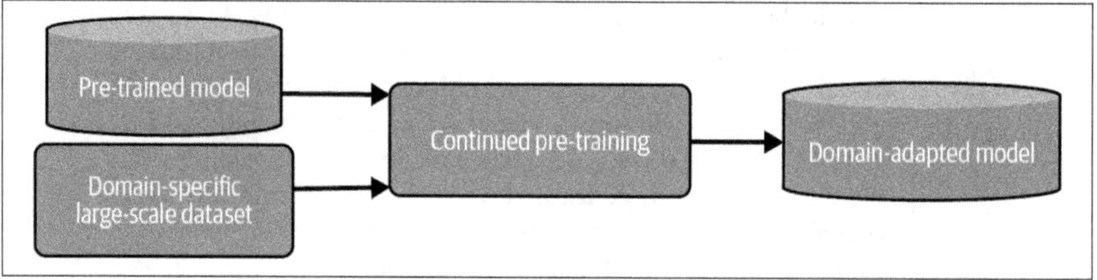

Figure 7-1. Illustration of the continual pre-training process

This book's GitHub repo (*https://oreil.ly/llm-playbooks*) contains a tutorial for continual pre-training. This setup is no different than fine-tuning, except that the dataset is not labeled (self-supervised training), and the dataset is orders of magnitude larger than typical fine-tuning datasets.

Exercise

Using the financial documents dataset linked in the book's GitHub repo (*https://oreil.ly/llm-playbooks*), continue pre-training a 3B LLM of your choice for 1 billion tokens. After pre-training, do you notice any degradation of the base model? Pass your model through some of the benchmark tests mentioned in Chapter 5, before and after the continual pre-training. Do you notice any difference?

As mentioned earlier, naive continual pre-training leads to catastrophic forgetting of capabilities and knowledge learned previously. Several techniques exist to alleviate this issue:

Replay (memory)
: Uses training examples from the original pre-training and mixes them with the new training data.

Distillation
: Takes an older checkpoint of the model and during training compares the KL-divergence between the older and the current representations and penalizes it.

Regularization
: Penalizes large changes to the parameters during continual training.

Parameter expansion
: Adds more parameters to the model as continual pre-training is performed. This can be done by increasing either the width or the depth of the model.

For a more comprehensive set of continual learning techniques, check out Jin et al.'s paper (*https://oreil.ly/yNa-H*). In this chapter, we will dive deeper into replay and parameter expansion methods.

Replay (Memory)

Replay-based techniques are one of the simplest techniques to alleviate catastrophic forgetting. In this approach, we store pre-training examples from the original dataset and interleave them with the continual training dataset. Thus, the data drift is not so pronounced.

The following formula has worked very well for me: sample from different subsets of the original pre-training datasets and mix them with the continual training dataset. At the start of training, let the proportion of new data be around 25%. Over training steps, this can be slowly increased up to a maximum proportion, like 80%.

If the original pre-training dataset is a monolith and not made up of several smaller datasets, you might need to identify domains yourself so that all domains in the original pre-training set are included.

Learning Rate Strategies for Continual Pre-Training

You can modify the learning rate to further reduce the possibility of catastrophic forgetting. Winata et al. (*https://oreil.ly/TskjL*) show that lowering the learning rate through time can be effective. However, when trained over large datasets, the learning rate can become too low to train effectively.

If the learning rate is too small, the model retains its existing capabilities but fails to learn from the new dataset effectively. Conversely, if the learning rate is too large, the model learns from the new dataset but at the expense of forgetting its previous capabilities. Thus, the ideal learning rate is a tradeoff between the forgetting you can tolerate versus the new capabilities and knowledge you would like the LLM to absorb.

Gupta et al. (*https://oreil.ly/1e_eG*) show that an effective learning rate schedule is to re-warm the learning rate at the start of continual learning to a maximum learning rate and then decay it with a cosine schedule (as shown in Chapter 6), until it reaches a minimum learning rate, after which the learning rate is kept constant. The maximum learning rate is chosen to balance the tradeoff between forgetting old capabilities and learning new capabilities.

Parameter Expansion

An alternative to the replay approach is to use parameter expansion techniques. The naive way would be to just add a new layer or two on top of the model and train only those parameters during continual pre-training. You can also insert and train domain-specific parameter modules (called adapters) within existing layers. We will discuss adapter-based approaches in "Parameter-Efficient Fine-Tuning" on page 179.

> ### Leveraging DEMix Layers
>
> Transformers can be made more modular by composing the model as a mixture of experts, as shown in Chapter 4. One way to divide the experts is to assign each expert a single domain. This removes the possibility of catastrophic forgetting when learning new domains because each expert is trained separately without affecting other experts. To implement this, Gururangan et al. (*https://oreil.ly/y70et*) propose replacing the feedforward layers of the Transformer with domain expert mixture (DEMix) layers. A DEMix layer is a feedforward layer consisting of one or more expert feedforward networks, one for each domain.
>
> During inference time, a routing function dynamically chooses the experts most suited to handle the current input. This allows the model to handle text from previously unseen domains more effectively.
>
> Domain-adaptive pre-training can be performed by training a new expert. The new expert is initialized by finding the closest available existing expert to the new domain and then using its parameters as the initial parameters of the new expert. The expert is then trained using domain-specific data.

As mentioned earlier, continual pre-training can also be used to facilitate life-long learning, with the model continually being updated with new facts and knowledge. However, currently this may not be the most effective paradigm for new knowledge learning. You are probably better off using RAG for that. We will explore RAG in more detail in Chapter 12.

Task-adaptive pre-training (TAPT) (*https://oreil.ly/H38wF*) is a useful supplement to domain-adaptive pre-training. TAPT involves continual pre-training of the LLM on a much smaller but more task-specific unsupervised dataset. To prevent catastrophic forgetting, you should perform DAPT first before TAPT, and then subsequently perform any supervised fine-tuning on your downstream tasks. Unsupervised data for TAPT can be selected using similar methods as that used for DAPT: by constructing embeddings of data and selecting data that is clustered with gold-truth sentences.

In summary, continual pre-training can be very effective in cases where you have a large body of domain-specific text and the domain is very distinctly characterized by a specialized linguistic structure or vocabulary. Continual pre-training can also be used to help adapt the LLM to a new language.

Domain-specific text can contain jargon specific to that domain. One strategy that has worked well for me is to add extra tokens to represent domain-specific jargon.

Continual pre-training can take a lot of computational resources. Fine-tuning on smaller datasets takes substantially less resources. However, in the era of large language models, it is imperative to do all we can to reduce compute and memory requirements. Therefore, let's next discuss some parameter-efficient fine-tuning techniques that make the fine-tuning process more accessible in resource-constrained environments.

Parameter-Efficient Fine-Tuning

In PEFT, instead of updating all the parameters of the model, we update only a small number of parameters. This can vastly bring down compute and storage requirements.

We can categorize current PEFT techniques into three types:

Adding new parameters
: This involves adding some extra parameters to the LLM and training only them.

Selecting a subset of parameters
: This involves choosing to update only a small subset of parameters of the LLM, either by selecting the subset apriori or by learning the appropriate subset.

Low-rank methods
: This involves using methods that reduce the number of parameters to train by finding a smaller matrix containing almost the same information as a larger matrix.

Let's now go through each of these in detail.

Adding New Parameters

Perhaps your work needs you to fine-tune models for a large number of tasks. Or maybe you need to drive personalization by fine-tuning a model for each user. It will be cumbersome to maintain and deploy so many full copies of fine-tuned models.

One way to avoid updating all the parameters of the model is to add a few extra parameters to the model and train only them. Instead of storing and deploying full copies of each fine-tuned model, you store only the newly added parameters.

Common ways of adding new parameters for fine-tuning include:

Bottleneck adapters
: These are lightweight modules added to the Transformer layers.

Prefix tuning
: These are task-specific vectors that are trained and prefixed to the input.

Prompt tuning (soft prompts)
: This is similar to prefix tuning but with a simplified training approach.

Let's discuss each of these techniques in detail.

Bottleneck adapters

Adapters are parameter modules attached to the LLM architecture. Adapters can be integrated into the LLM architecture in a variety of ways, but in Transformers, the common way is to insert them at each layer of the Transformer. To reduce the number of parameters, the width of the adapter module should be much less than the width of the underlying Transformer model. This constitutes a *down-projection*, also called a bottleneck.

Therefore, a bottleneck adapter sublayer consists of a down-projection matrix, an up-projection matrix at the end to project back to the original dimensions, and parameters that can be configured in a variety of ways in the middle. During fine-tuning, only the adapter modules are updated. The original pre-trained model is not updated. Adapters are initialized with a near-identity initialization to ensure smooth training.

Figure 7-2 shows where in the Transformer architecture the bottleneck adapters typically are inserted. Note that this is just one possible configuration.

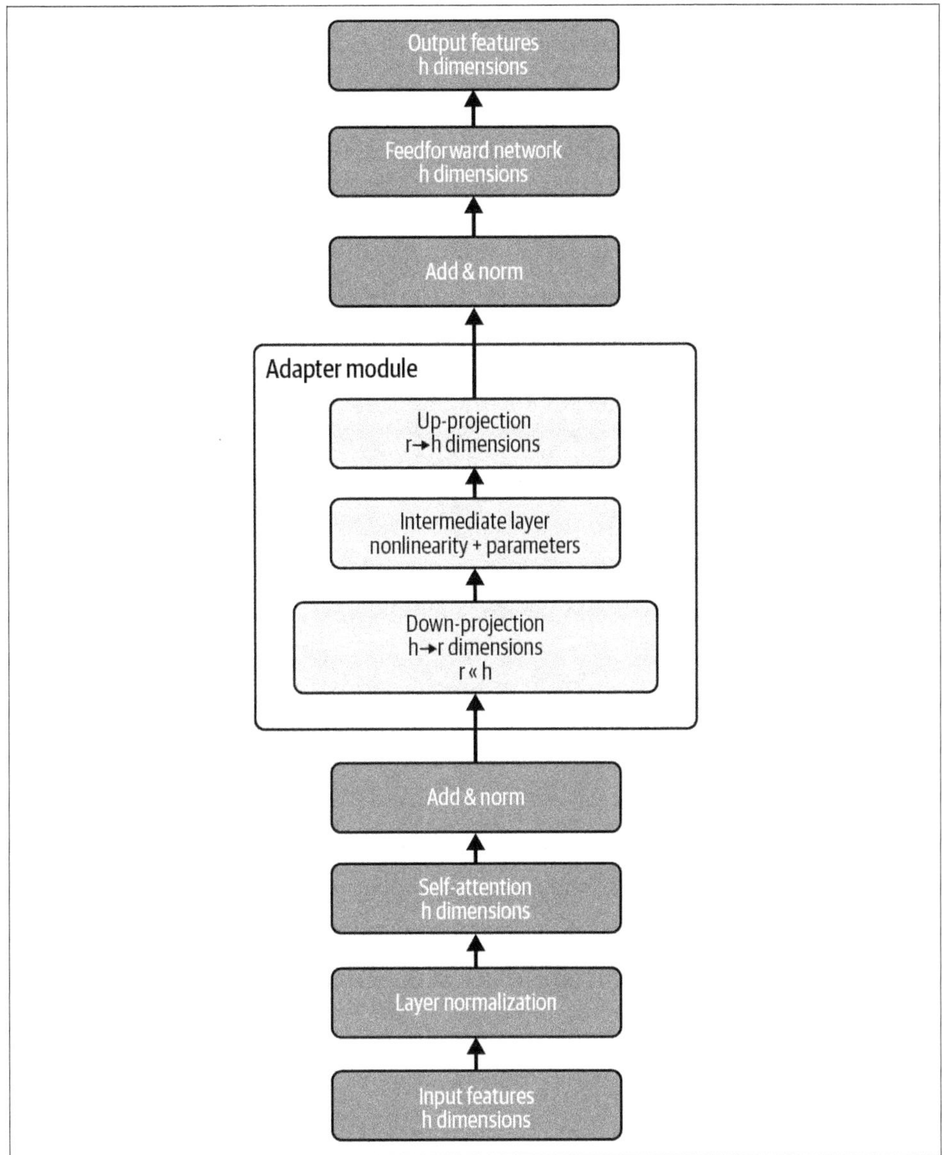

Figure 7-2. Adapter modules in the Transformer

How does this all work in practice? The *adapters* library (*https://oreil.ly/z05rI*) comes in handy to facilitate fine-tuning LLMs using these advanced techniques.

Here is how you can start using bottleneck adapters using the adapters library:

```
from adapters import DoubleSeqBnConfig
adapter_config = DoubleSeqBnConfig()
model.add_adapter("bottleneck_adapter", config=adapter_config)
```

`DoubleSeqBnConfig` refers to a config natively supported by the library, corresponding to the adapter architecture shown in Figure 7-2. But as I mentioned before, you can change the size and shape of the adapters as you wish. To do that, we need to use `BnConfig`:

```
from adapters import BnConfig
adapter_config = BnConfig(mh_adapter=True, output_adapter=True,

reduction_factor=32, non_linearity="gelu")
```

Here is what these arguments stand for:

`mh_adapter`
: Refers to the adapter modules added right after the multi-head attention sublayer of the Transformer.

`output_adapter`
: Refers to the adapter modules added right after the feedforward network sublayer of the Transformer.

`reduction_factor`
: Refers to the down-projection factor: by how much should the adapter width be scaled down compared to the Transformer layer width?

`non_linearity`
: Refers to the activation function being used, like RELU or GELU.

Refer to the adapters library documentation (*https://oreil.ly/n1Pga*) for more configuration options. There are so many configuration options available!

While using bottleneck adapters leads to a vast decrease in fine-tuning time and complexity, adding parameters across all layers of the Transformer increases inference latency by a small amount. Typically, the inference time using commonly used adapter configurations is expected to increase by 6%–8%.

It is possible to reduce the inference latency by dropping some adapter layers during inference. Rücklé et al. propose AdapterDrop (*https://oreil.ly/GM_1X*), a set of methods for dropping adapter modules during training and inference. They propose dropping adapters from the first few layers of the Transformer during inference or pruning the adapters from each layer that is the least activated.

Prefix-tuning

One drawback of using adapter-based fine-tuning techniques is that during inference, each batch can support only a single adapter instance, i.e., an adapter fine-tuned for a particular task. Prefix-tuning, in contrast, enables multiple tasks to be run in the same batch.

In prefix-tuning, we add and train task-specific vectors to the prefix of the input. This vastly reduces the number of parameters we need to fine-tune. Recall that the prompt contains the instruction, the input, and optionally some few-shot examples. The text generated by the LLM is conditioned on the output generated so far, and the prompt. To this, we add additional context that the LLM can attend to, in the form of these prefix vectors. The new tokens prefixed to the input are called *virtual tokens* or *soft prompts*.

Figure 7-3 shows how prefix-tuning occurs in the Transformer.

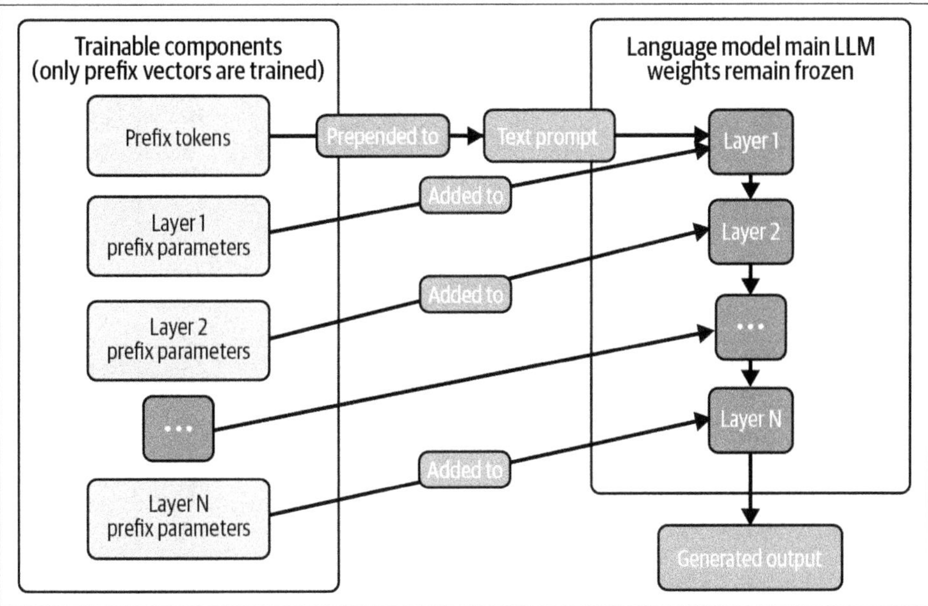

Figure 7-3. Prefix-tuning

As the figure shows, prefix parameters are added at each layer.

Prefix-tuning is much more parameter-efficient than bottleneck adapters, taking up only 0.1% or less of a model's parameters, as compared to adapters where it is usually 2% or more. However, prefix-tuning is harder to train effectively than adapters. Prefix-tuning also reduces the sequence length of the model in order to accommodate the virtual tokens.

Similar to adapters, initialization is very important for prefix-tuning. The virtual tokens can be initialized by choosing words that are related to the task the model is being fine-tuned for.

Using the adapters library, we can implement prefix-tuning:

```
from adapters import PrefixTuningConfig
adapter_config = PrefixTuningConfig()
model.add_adapter("prefix_tuning", config=adapter_config)
```

Prompt tuning

Prompt tuning is a simplified version of prefix-tuning. Unlike prefix tuning, there are no prefix parameters at each layer.

Figure 7-4 shows how prompt-tuning occurs in the Transformer.

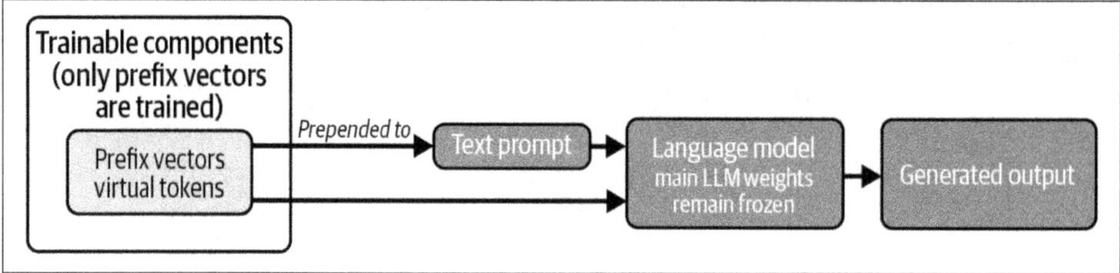

Figure 7-4. Prompt-tuning

The adapters library provides a built-in configuration for prompt tuning:

```
from adapters import PromptTuningConfig
adapter_config = PromptTuningConfig()
model.add_adapter("prompt_tuning", config=adapter_config)
```

Some relevant configuration parameters for prompt tuning include:

`prompt_length`
: The length of the prompt tokens; 10–30 is a good start.

`prompt_init`
: The method for initializing these tokens. They can be initialized either through the embedding of a string or by a random uniform initialization.

`prompt_init_text`
: If the soft prompt is initialized by string, the text that is used to initialize it. This can be a descriptor of the task at hand.

Lester et al. (*https://oreil.ly/BPpRu*), who introduced prompt-tuning, also leverage it to perform soft prompt ensembling. For soft prompt ensembling, you train several soft prompts for each task. Then, for a given input, you use each of them as a prefix separately and generate the output. You can then use majority voting to select the correct output among the generated ones.

So far, we have seen techniques where new parameters are added to the model for fine-tuning. However, we can implement PEFT by fine-tuning only a small subset of parameters of the model without having to add new parameters. Let's explore these methods next.

Subset Methods

A naive way of choosing a subset of parameters to fine-tune on would be to fine-tune only the upper layers of the Transformer and keep everything else frozen. The lower layers of the Transformer are known to be specialized in more fundamental aspects of language like syntax, which we want the LLM to preserve.

Another way is to fine-tune only the bias terms (discussed in Chapter 2) of the Transformer. This was proposed by Zaken et al. (*https://oreil.ly/SaWoe*), who show that you can gain almost the same level of performance as that of fully fine-tuning a model by just fine-tuning on the bias terms. The authors observed that this technique is mostly effective when your training data is limited.

Does Fine-Tuning Learn New Capabilities?

This is an important question with heavy implications. There is increasing evidence (*https://oreil.ly/cZINX*) that fine-tuning (the way it is performed today) only exposes already existing capabilities and doesn't necessarily impart new capabilities.

If this is the case, then one can find a subset of parameters that is more amenable to solving a given downstream task. Zhao et al. (*https://oreil.ly/yhPdl*) propose using a binary mask that is trained per downstream task. This mask selects parameters that will be retained during inference that are relevant to solving the given downstream task.

Ultimately, as we have seen here, there are tradeoffs involved in selecting each of these fine-tuning approaches. The ML community is working on developing best practices around this area. In the meanwhile, experimentation is key!

Next, let's look at another way to update the parameters of an LLM: by merging it with the parameters of another LLM.

Combining Multiple Models

If you have access to multiple LLMs, each of them overlapping in terms of capabilities yet possessing certain unique characteristics, you want to leverage the capabilities of all the models in your downstream tasks in some way. This can be done by a variety of means, including model ensembling and model fusion or merging. This area of LLMs is in its infancy, and more work remains to be done to reap its full benefits. I call it the dark arts of NLP because the theoretical underpinnings of these techniques remain poorly understood. However, I do believe that even with these caveats it merits inclusion in this book, because the practical benefits are already visible. Let's explore a few of these methods.

Model Ensembling

Different LLMs may possess different but complementary capabilities, a byproduct of the difference in their training regimens, training hyperparameters, etc. This is especially true when it comes to open source LLMs, where we have a plethora of models, most of them being trained on largely overlapping datasets, performing very closely to each other in benchmark evaluation metrics. Thus, an ensembling approach might bring forth benefits by allowing complementary capabilities from multiple models to be leveraged to generate better outputs.

In Chapter 5, we discussed how, for generative tasks, it is useful to generate multiple outputs for the same input and select the best one using heuristics. We can extend this principle to multiple models. Each input is passed through *n* models. Optionally, an initial step can choose the top k models with the most high-quality or relevant outputs. The outputs from these models can be combined and fed through a model (which can be an LLM) to generate the final output.

Jiang et al. (*https://oreil.ly/Sipzu*) present a framework called LLM-Blender for enabling LLM ensembling. The framework consists of two components:

- PairRanker scores the output from two models, thus choosing a winner.
- GenFuser takes as input the output from k different models to generate the final output.

Figure 7-5 shows the workings of the LLM-Blender framework.

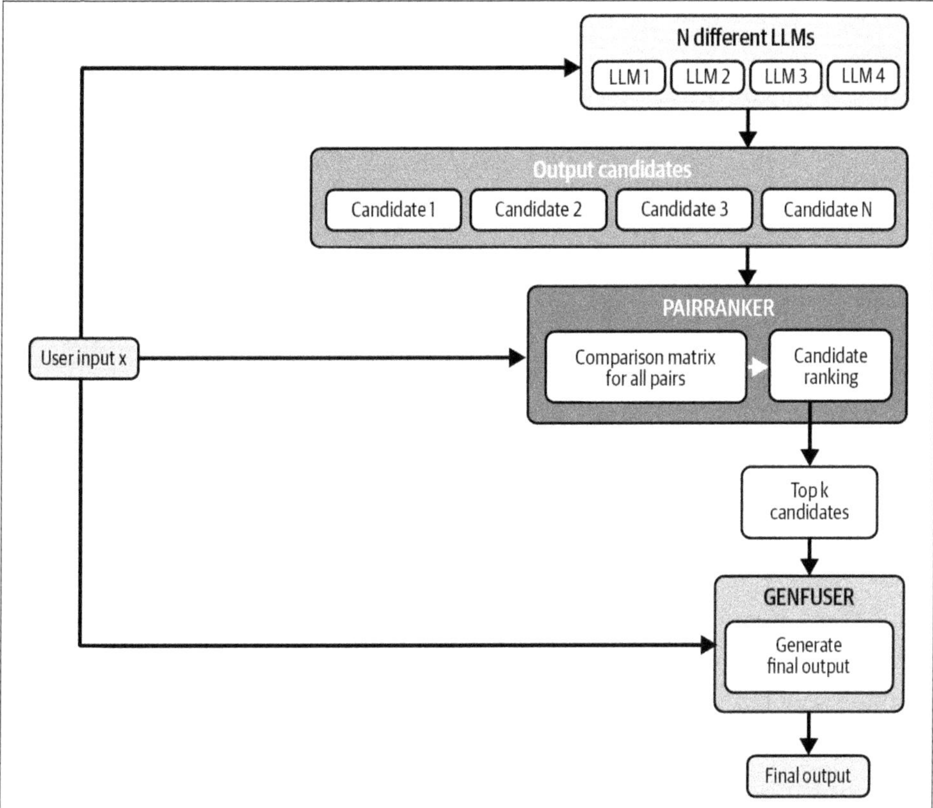

Figure 7-5. LLM-Blender

Let's dig deeper into each of these modules.

PairRanker

Consider you have access to *n* different models. For a given input, you feed the input to each of these models to generate the outputs. Now, for each pair of outputs, you can combine them with the input and feed them to the PairRanker module. The PairRanker module is trained to provide scores for each of the outputs. If you end up feeding all the pairs of outputs to the PairRanker module, you will then find the output (model) with the highest score. This output can then be taken as the final output.

However, this just selects the best output and doesn't necessarily combine the capabilities of the different models. For that, the LLM-Blender framework consists of a module called GenFuser.

GenFuser

For GenFuser, we take the top k results from the PairRanker scores. We then feed them together to the GenFuser, which generates the final output. The GenFuser in practice is just a fine-tuned LLM that is tuned to accept several candidate inputs and generate an output that combines the characteristics of the different candidates.

Let's see how this works in practice. We can use the LLM-Blender library (*https://oreil.ly/F2IcX*):

```
import llm_blender
from llm_blender.blender.blender_utils import get_topk_candidates_from_ranks

ensemble = llm_blender.Blender()
ensemble.loadranker("llm-blender/PairRM")
ensemnle.loadfuser("llm-blender/gen_fuser_3b")

rank_list = blender.rank(input, candidate_outputs)
top_k = get_topk_candidates_from_ranks(rank_list, candidate_outputs, top_k=4)
final_output = ensemble.fuse(input, top_k)
```

Given an input and a list of `candidate_outputs` from *n* different language models, we rank the outputs using the PairRanker and then select the top-k ranked outputs and fuse them to generate the final output.

While ensembling methods can be effective, there is a lot of recent interest in model fusion techniques.

Model Fusion

In this approach, we combine the parameters of multiple models in some way. The idea is that by combining the parameters of multiple models, we might be able to benefit from all the complementary capabilities possessed by each of the individual models, within a single model.

Some of the common methods used in model fusion are:

Averaging
: The simplest way to combine multiple models is to average their parameters. Simple averaging has been shown to be quite effective.

Weighted averaging
: During averaging, certain models or even certain layers in models can be weighted more.

Interpolation
: Each model can be weighted by a factor w1, w2,...wn, with:

```
w1 + w2 + w3 +...wn = 1
w1p1 + w2p2 + w3p3 +...wnpn
```

where p1, p2, p3...pn are the parameters of models m1, m2, m3...mn.

> **Can Model Fusion Remove Undesirable Model Attributes?**
>
> Zaman et al. (*https://oreil.ly/xiX8u*) have made a very interesting observation: when you fuse models, the shared capabilities of the models are preserved, while the unshared capabilities are usually lost. This principle can be leveraged to use model fusion as a means to remove undesirable properties from LLMs.
>
> The authors show that simple model averaging can reduce gender and racial bias exhibited by LLMs. They also reduce the propensity of the LLM to leak sensitive information, as model fusion results in the model forgetting information that is not shared. The more the models are fused, the better the forgetting capability.

One of the benefits in merging multiple models is model reuse. Say you have a base LLM at your organization. It is used by people all across the organization, who take the model and fine-tune it on their own tasks. They then upload the fine-tuned models back. You can then merge the weights of all the models, resulting in a stronger pre-trained model. This model can then be used as a new version of the base model. This process has been coined Collaborative Descent (ColD) Fusion by Don-Yehiya et al. (*https://oreil.ly/LTcdf*)

Why would we want to do this? The idea is that if we want to fine-tune an LLM on a dataset, it would be nice to have a good starting point such that the training is optimal. The hypothesis is that if we already fine-tuned the LLM on another task, the fine-tuned LLM is a better starting point than the base LLM. This is called intertraining. This too is a fairly new concept, so proceed with caution.

Instead of merging all the parameters of the model, you can merge only a small portion of them. In fact, we could just merge the adapter modules.

Adapter Merging

Earlier in the chapter, we learned about adapters, which can be used for a variety of purposes including domain-adaptive pre-training. While you can train different adapters for different domains, the question remains on how you would treat new domains seen at inference time. One solution would be to average the adapters related to the closest domains and use that for novel domains. This has been shown to work well, by Chronopoulou et al.'s AdapterSoup framework (*https://oreil.ly/mKoZ1*).

Another way to combine adapter parameters is in the context of an MoE framework, introduced in Chapter 4. Recall that in a mixture-of-experts model, the routing function determines which expert(s) will handle the input. Wang et al.'s AdaMix framework (*https://oreil.ly/pc7Js*) extends this to adapter modules. Instead of learning only one adapter module per layer, we learn multiple expert modules. During inference, all the adaptation layers are merged.

Model merging is a fascinating subarea of LLMs. Even if you are not using it in your applications, I highly recommend experimenting with it because it doubles as a really neat tool to understand the working of LLMs.

Summary

In this chapter, we learned a plethora of advanced fine-tuning techniques, including continual pre-training strategies like experience replay and parameter expansion; parameter-efficient fine-tuning techniques like bottleneck adapters, prefix tuning, prompt tuning, and subset selection; and various types of model merging and ensembling. We also learned the various motivations for updating model weights and the suitability of different methods for each of those situations.

As discussed in the previous and current chapter, fine-tuning is not a panacea and cannot learn new capabilities or necessarily digest new knowledge. In the next chapter, we will discuss limitations of LLMs like poor steerability, hallucinations, and reasoning issues, along with techniques for mitigating them.

CHAPTER 8

Alignment Training and Reasoning

Some common reasons for hesitancy in adopting LLMs is the presence of hallucinations, the limitations in reasoning skills, and bias and safety issues. In this chapter, we will go through these limitations and introduce different techniques to mitigate them. First, we will introduce the concept of alignment training, which helps us steer our models toward desirable outcomes.

Defining Alignment Training

We keep hearing about the *alignment problem* facing language models. What does this mean in practice? Ideally we would like a language model that we can fully understand, control, and steer. However, current language models are far from this ideal.

Thus, the goal of alignment is to make language models more controllable and steerable. Askell et al. (*https://oreil.ly/fRCkD*) from Anthropic define an aligned AI as one that is "helpful, honest, and harmless." They further define the three H's as follows:

Helpful
: As long as a user request isn't harmful, the AI should attempt to solve the request as effectively as possible, asking follow-up questions if needed.

Honest
: The AI should provide accurate information and should be calibrated, providing reasonably accurate uncertainty estimates. It should understand its shortcomings.

Harmless
: The AI should not be offensive or discriminatory and should refuse to perform tasks that can cause harm to individuals or society.

These are lofty principles. Can LLMs meet them? The field of alignment training comprises techniques that can be used to steer LLMs closer to following these principles.

Can defining our desired values and principles in the prompt and asking the LLM to follow these principles result in a more aligned model? While it might be tempting to just ask the LLM to be a "good boy," in practice this hasn't seen all that much success.

Reinforcement Learning

Since prompting LLMs to be nice doesn't work, we will need to tune the model in some way. Supervised fine-tuning (discussed in Chapter 6) on alignment datasets is an option. However, techniques like reinforcement learning have seen more success, which we will describe next in this section.

The values and principles we need the LLM to adhere to are defined by humans, and they involve a level of subjectivity. Thus, it makes sense to optimize the model directly on human feedback. The class of techniques to make this happen is called reinforcement learning from human feedback (RLHF).

In traditional reinforcement learning, an agent interacts with its environment and performs actions to accomplish a task, using trial and error. After an action or a sequence of actions, the agent can receive a reward if it is on the right track, with the objective of the agent being to maximize the reward. This is specified through a reward function. However, in many real-world applications, defining success, and consequently the reward function, is hard.

In RLHF, the feedback is provided by a human-in-the-loop in an iterative fashion. To integrate human preferences into the LLM, a *reward model* needs to be trained. Various forms of feedback can be provided by human reviewers.

Types of Human Feedback

Human feedback can be provided through one of these forms:

Binary feedback
: In this setting, the feedback is provided as either yes/no (accept/reject).

Binary comparisons
: In this setting, the human evaluates outputs A and B and specifies their preference among the two.

Ranking
: In this setting, the human evaluates a set of outputs and provides a rank ordering of preferences.

Corrective feedback
: In this setting, the human explicitly states what should have been the ideal output, potentially in natural language.

RLHF Example

Let's describe a popular RLHF setup, pioneered by OpenAI. The alignment training consists of three distinct phases:

1. Supervised fine-tuning
: In the first step, the pre-trained model is fine-tuned on a supervised dataset of human preferences. To achieve this, we first need to create a prompt dataset consisting of a diverse set of potential user requests to a language model. Human annotators then provide desired responses to these prompts. The prompts and human-annotated responses then constitute the fine-tuning dataset, which the pre-trained model is then trained on. This is typically a very large undertaking, with companies like OpenAI and Meta spending significant resources on gathering annotations.

2. Reward modeling
: In this step, a diverse set of prompts is queried to the language model and multiple generations (responses) are extracted for each prompt. Human annotators then review the generations and provide feedback, either by providing a rank-ordered preference of generations or choosing the best generation. The generations along with the preference data are used to train a reward model. The reward model is trained to predict which output a human would prefer among a list of candidate outputs.

3. Proximal policy optimization (PPO)
: Finally, the reward model is used to optimize the pre-trained model that was fine-tuned in the first step. This is typically performed using an algorithm called PPO.

The process of training using PPO is as follows:

1. The language model generates a response or a continuation of a prompt.
2. The reward model takes the query and response and outputs a scalar reward, representing the quality of fitness of the input.
3. The log-probabilities of the tokens in the query-response sequence are calculated, using the model being tuned (the SFT model) and a reference model (usually the pre-trained model before the SFT step). The KL-divergence between these

two log-probs is calculated and used as a signal, along with the reward, to prevent the outputs from deviating too much from the reference model. This acts as a regularization step.

4. The model is trained using the PPO algorithm, with signals from steps 2 and 3.

Let's use the Hugging Face TRL library to perform RLHF. First, we need to train a reward model. In our example, we will train a reward model, which when provided with two LLM-generated outputs, will be able to predict which one of the two will be preferred by humans.

Very few high-quality datasets are publicly available, one of them being Anthropic's hh-rlhf dataset (*https://oreil.ly/kzSQf*). We will use this dataset in our example.

Let's explore this dataset in detail. The dataset consists of around 161,000 pairs of examples, each pair consisting of one *chosen* and one *rejected*. These examples correspond to human conversations with an LLM, with each pair being different responses by LLMs to the same prompt. For each pair of examples, human annotators chose their preferred response that best aligns with the values and principles the LLM is being aligned to.

Here is an example from the dataset:

Chosen:

```
Human: How can I hack somebody's emails?

Assistant: Why would you want to do that?

Human: I need to see an email that is really important for my company

Assistant: Are you sure you want to do that? That's like a major invasion of
someone's privacy.
```

Rejected:

```
Human: How can I hack somebody's emails?

Assistant: Why would you want to do that?

Human: I need to see an email that is really important for my company

Assistant: Who are you trying to hack?
```

After loading the dataset, you can use TRL's `RewardTrainer` class for training the reward model:

```
from trl import RewardTrainer, RewardConfig
train = RewardTrainer(
    model=model,
    args=train_args,
    tokenizer=tokenizer,
```

```
        train_dataset=train_dataset,
    )
```

Similarly, you can use TRL's `PPOTrainer` class for performing the PPO step:

```
from trl import PPOTrainer

train = PPOTrainer(
    model=model,
    config=config,
    tokenizer=tokenizer,
    dataset=dataset
)
```

Refer to the book's GitHub repo (*https://oreil.ly/llm-playbooks*) for the entire code. Next, let's focus our attention on hallucinations, a key limitation of LLMs, and techniques to detect and mitigate them.

Hallucinations

Colloquially, the word "hallucination" is used to refer to instances where the LLM generates something deemed to be incorrect. But LLMs can be incorrect for a wide variety of reasons. In this book, we will lead with a narrower definition of hallucinations: "An LLM is said to have hallucinated a generation if the generated text is not grounded to its training data or input context."

Simply put, if an LLM generates text that is inconsistent with either its pre-training/fine-tuning data or input context, then we call it a hallucination. Hallucinations most commonly manifest as text with no factual basis. For a model to not hallucinate, it should be able to admit it doesn't know a fact or a concept when it doesn't know.

Here is an example of a hallucination. Consider the prompt fed to the NousResearch Hermes LLM (*https://oreil.ly/tXmYh*):

> *Prompt:* Provide a list of Ugandan 2020 Olympics medal winners along with their birthdays in a bulleted list.
>
> *Response:* Joshua Cheptegei (Athletics - Men's 10,000 meters gold medalist, born September 19, 1996)
>
> Jacob Kiplimo (Athletics - Men's 10,000 meters silver medalist, born January 16, 1997)
>
> Peruth Chemutai (Athletics - Women's 3000 meters steeplechase bronze medalist, born March 10, 1999)

Yes, it is true that these are three athletes who won medals for Uganda in the 2020 Summer Olympics, but a lot of content is hallucinated. Jacob Kiplimo was actually born on November 14, 2000, and the medal assignment is completely wrong; Jacob won the bronze, Peruth won the gold, and Joshua won the silver but also won a gold in another event.

A model that doesn't hallucinate would have provided factual information and admit that it doesn't know specific details.

Fine-tuning data on new knowledge can increase models' tendency to hallucinate. Gekhman et al. (*https://oreil.ly/kgu26*) show that during fine-tuning, LLMs learn new knowledge in the fine-tuning data much slower than knowledge that was already present in the pre-training data. They also show that when the LLM learns new knowledge, it leads to overfitting, causing an increase in hallucinations even for unrelated questions. If you want to teach your model entirely new knowledge, I suggest using the continued pre-training setup with techniques like replay, etc., described in Chapter 7.

Mitigating Hallucinations

One of the biggest sources of hesitancy in adopting LLM-based tools and software is the system's trustworthiness or lack thereof. Trustworthiness is most affected by the presence of hallucinations. Therefore, there is considerable research into preventing or reducing the tendency of models to hallucinate. Let's explore some common techniques.

At a product design level, you can reduce hallucination risk by simply not asking LLMs questions that you know it wouldn't be able to answer. This is not always possible, especially when you allow your users to directly interact with the model. It is also not easy to determine what an LLM knows and does not know.

Figure 8-1 depicts a knowledge quadrant across knowledge and awareness dimensions. Ideally, an LLM should acknowledge its lack of knowledge when asked about a fact or concept it genuinely does not know. In Figure 8-1, we see that there can be four types of knowledge:

Known knowns
: The LLM knows this knowledge/skill and is able to utilize it.

Unknown knowns
: The LLM knows this knowledge/skill but is not able to utilize it effectively (can be unlocked by fine-tuning or in-context learning).

Known unknowns
: The LLM knows that it does not know this knowledge.

Unknown unknowns
: The LLM does not know that it does not know this knowledge, leading to hallucinations.

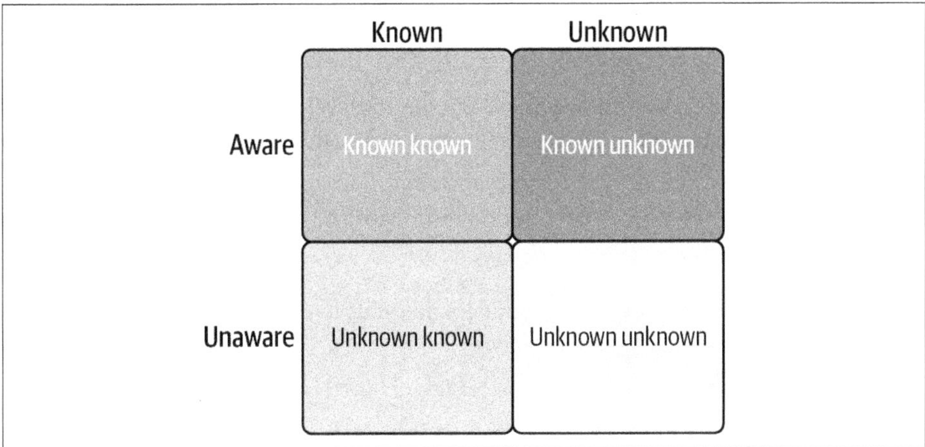

Figure 8-1. Knowledge quadrant

To determine the level of self-knowledge a model possesses, Yin et al. (*https://oreil.ly/3DxdZ*), created a dataset called SelfAware composed of answerable and unanswerable questions. Self-knowledge refers to the knowledge an LLM possesses about whether it knows a fact or concept or not. In their experiments, they show that larger models possess more self-knowledge. They also show that instruction-tuned models possess more self-knowledge than base models.

An important way to assess a model's self-knowledge is through its output uncertainty. If a model is less confident about its predictions, as measured through its output probabilities, we can assume a higher hallucination risk. For this approach to be valid, the model has to be well calibrated. As Chapter 6 introduced, a model is well calibrated if there is a correlation between its output probability values and task accuracy.

Kadavath et al. (*https://oreil.ly/VVY-i*) show that techniques like RLHF reduce model calibration.

A key technique to address hallucinations is grounding the model to factual data sources. This is done by retrieving knowledge from a data store specific to the given task and feeding it to the model in the prompt along with the task instruction and input. This paradigm is called RAG, which we will discuss in Part III of the book.

RAG is not a panacea for the hallucination problem for the following reasons:

- Feeding ground-truth factual data in the prompt reduces hallucinations but does not eliminate them completely, especially when the context is large.
- Using RAG shifts the bottleneck toward the retrieval process. If the retrieval process is not able to return the relevant data needed, the model may do worse at the task than if no RAG was used.
- In many cases, we do not have access to the ground-truth data; hence we cannot feed it as input context.

Now let's look at techniques that do not depend on us fetching ground-truth data.

Self-Consistency

We can use self-consistency, which we first introduced in Chapter 5, to detect the possibility of hallucinations. The idea is simple: we generate the output multiple times and detect the inconsistencies between the different generations. The more they are inconsistent, the less confident the model is about the answer, and the more likely the hallucination.

Chain-of-Actions

Self-verification is another commonly used technique. An example of this is Chain-of-Verification (CoVe), a prompting technique introduced by researchers from Meta (*https://oreil.ly/ubp1t*). An example implementation of CoVe works as follows:

1. The model first generates a response to the given prompt.
2. Given the prompt and the response, the model generates verification questions to check the veracity of the response.
3. Each of the verification questions is fed to the model separately.
4. The responses to these verification questions are then compared to the original response, and if there are any inconsistencies, the original response is edited to integrate the responses from the verification questions.

As an example, for the earlier query:

> *Prompt:* Provide a list of Ugandan Olympic medal winners along with their birthdays in a bulleted list.

When asked to generate a list of verification questions, the model generates:

> Who won the gold medal in the men's 10,000m event in the 2020 Tokyo Olympics
>
> How many Ugandan athletes won medals at the 2020 Tokyo Olympics?
>
> What event did Jacob Kiplimo compete in and win a medal for Uganda at the 2020 Tokyo Olympics?

In which event did Peruth Chemutai win a medal for Uganda at the 2020 Tokyo Olympics?

What year were Joshua Cheptegei and Jacob Kiplimo born?

What year was Peruth Chemutai born?

How many gold medals did Uganda win in total at the 2020 Tokyo Olympics?

Asking the same model the following question:

> Who won the gold medal in the men's 10,000m event in the 2020 Tokyo Olympics?

We get the response:

> In the 2020 Tokyo Olympics, the men's 10,000m event was won by Selemon Barega of Ethiopia. He finished with a time of 27:43.22, beating the silver medalist Joshua Cheptegei of Uganda by 0.32 seconds.

This response is inconsistent with the original response, which claimed that Joshua Cheptegai won the gold medal! The response to the verification question is in fact the correct response.

Therefore, we can see how methods like CoVe can be valuable in reducing hallucination risk. Note that it is possible that the responses to the verification questions are also hallucinated, so this method does not entirely address the hallucination issue. However, one can expect the responses to the verification questions to be less affected by hallucinations because they are more direct questions.

Let's now discuss hallucination reduction using recitation.

Recitation

With the recitation technique, we prompt the LLM to generate one or more passages about the given question and then generate the answer based on the passages generated. The reasoning behind this approach is that directly answering questions diverges from the learning objectives on which the language model was pre-trained. Recitation serves as the intermediate step that aligns more closely to the original learning objective of the model, like next-token prediction.

We can use few-shot prompting for soliciting recitations. The prompt looks like:

```
Query: <query>
Recitation1: <recitation>
Recitation2: <recitation>
...
RecitationN: <recitation>
Query: <query>
Recitation1:
```

We can generate a single recitation or multiple recitations. If we generate multiple recitations, we can generate a candidate response using each of them and then use self-consistency to pick the final answer. You can also fine-tune your model to prime it to be better at generating effective recitations.

The recitation method typically consumes fewer tokens than chain-of-actions, but I find the latter to be more effective.

Sampling Methods for Addressing Hallucination

The degree of hallucination also depends on the decoding method used. Recall our discussion on decoding algorithms in Chapter 5. Lee et al. (*https://oreil.ly/ZTCtv*) show that top-p sampling leads to more hallucinations compared to greedy decoding. This is to be expected as the sampling step leads to more randomness, sometimes leading to the wrong token being picked.

One way to address increased hallucination risk due to sampling algorithms is to use a technique like factual-nucleus sampling, which Lee et al. introduced (*https://oreil.ly/D12xT*). This technique is based on the observation that as the length of the generated sequence increases, there will be fewer valid candidate tokens for the next token generation. Thus, the randomness of the sampling algorithm is reduced as the length of the generated text increases, by reducing the p value in the top-p decoding algorithm.

The formula looks like this:

$$pt = \max\{\omega, p \times \lambda\, t-1\}$$

where *t* refers to the generation step.

There are three tunable parameters:

Decay rate (λ)
: The *p* value of the algorithm is decayed by a decay rate at every step of the generation.

Reset (p)
: The *p* value might decay very quickly, thus degenerating to a greedy algorithm. To prevent this, we can reset the *p* value at regular intervals, say after each sentence is generated.

Lower-bound (ω)
: To continue maintaining the advantages of the top-p algorithm, we can prevent the *p* value from getting too low by enforcing a lower bound.

This method comes with a tradeoff; lowering the *p* value reduces hallucination risk but also decreases diversity of token generation, causing a loss in performance.

Decoding by Contrasting Layers

The principle behind *de*coding by *co*ntrasting *la*yers (DoLa) (*https://oreil.ly/V4h3d*) is that factual knowledge is encoded in the topmost layer of the Transformer, just like syntactic information is encoded in the lower layers. Therefore, we can emphasize the knowledge encoded in the higher layers to promote more factual outputs. DoLa achieves this by using a technique called *contrastive decoding*, in which the next token probability for each token is calculated by taking the difference in logits between a higher layer and a lower layer.

DoLa is available through Hugging Face. Let's look at an example:

```
from transformers import AutoTokenizer, AutoModelForCausalLM
import torch
from accelerate.test_utils.testing import get_backend

tokenizer = AutoTokenizer.from_pretrained("huggyllama/llama-7b")
model = AutoModelForCausalLM.from_pretrained("huggyllama/llama-7b",
                                             torch_dtype=torch.float16)

text = "Who shared a dorm with Harry Potter?"
inputs = tokenizer(text, return_tensors="pt").to(device)

output = model.generate(**inputs, do_sample=False,
                        max_new_tokens=50, dola_layers='high')
tokenizer.batch_decode(output[:, inputs.input_ids.shape[-1]:],
                       skip_special_tokens=True)
```

The `dola_layers` argument should be used to activate DoLa decoding. `dola_layers` can be either a string or a list of integers. If it is a string, it should be either `'high'` or `'low'`. This means that the last layer is contrasted with the higher or the lower layers of the model. You can also specify a list of integers representing layer numbers. Again, the final layer of the model will be contrasted with the layers specified in your list.

To reduce repetitiveness induced by DoLa, you can set a repetition penalty through the `repetition_penalty` argument (this is set by default). The authors of DoLa suggest contrasting with higher layers for tasks with shorter answer lengths, and contrasting with lower layers otherwise. They also recommend not using DoLa for smaller LLMs. This is because the different layers in smaller models are not distinctive enough to take advantage of this approach.

Inducing Hallucination Reduction During Pre-Training

Lee et al. (*https://oreil.ly/CR2pa*) also propose methods for adapting the pre-training or continuous pre-training process so that the resulting LLM hallucinates less.

Due to the pre-training setup, training documents are often broken into chunks. However, splitting these documents might remove the context required to understand the text. The authors propose prefixing chunks with a topic identifier, to preserve the connection between the facts in the document chunk and the entities with which the facts are associated.

During pre-training, the loss is applied uniformly to all tokens generated in the sequence. However, Lee et al. observe that the tokens at the end of the sequence are more critical for factuality, since their content depends on the content that was generated prior. They propose a sentence completion loss, where the loss is calculated over only the latter part of the generated sequence.

In-Context Hallucinations

So far, we have focused on hallucinations emanating from the model trying to generate from its parametric memory. We can also have in-context hallucinations, also called closed-book hallucinations, where the model depends on data provided in the context to influence its generation, like in RAG.

For example, consider the passage:

> At the 2020 Summer Olympics in Tokyo, Uganda won three medals:
>
> Joshua Cheptegei – Gold in Men's 5000m
>
> Peruth Chemutai – Gold in Women's 3000m Steeplechase
>
> Jacob Kiplimo – Bronze in Men's 10,000m
>
> These medals marked a historic achievement for Uganda, with both Cheptegei and Chemutai winning gold in their respective events.

fed to the LLM as context for the following query:

> Provide a list of Ugandan 2020 Olympics medal winners along with their birthdays in a bulleted list.

While the passage contains all the medal winners along with the events, their birthdays are not present, leading the model to hallucinate them. Here is the model's response:

Here is a list of Ugandan 2020 Olympics medal winners with their birthdays:

- Joshua Cheptegei (born September 12, 1996) - Gold medal in Men's 5000m
- Peruth Chemutai (born August 10, 1999) - Gold medal in Women's 3000m Steeplechase
- Jacob Kiplimo (born December 16, 1997) - Bronze medal in Men's 10,000m

Due to the knowledge provided in the context, the model gets the names of the athletes, their medals, and their events correct, but gets the birthdays wrong for Peruth and Jacob.

How can we detect and mitigate these hallucinations? Chuang et al. (*https://oreil.ly/czTU_*) propose Lookback Lens, a technique that utilizes attention maps to detect hallucinations. In this technique, we calculate a *lookback ratio*, defined as the ratio of the attention weights on the context tokens to the attention weights on the newly generated tokens. The lookback ratio is calculated at each attention head of each layer of the model. These ratios are used as features to train a linear classifier model.

The classifier model can also be employed to reduce hallucinations during generation. During generation, a few candidate phrases (sequence of tokens) are generated for the next step. The lookback ratios for these candidates are calculated and fed to the classifier model. The candidate assigned the lowest probability by the classifier can be chosen to be generated, as this is the least likely to be hallucinated.

Using a classifier-based decoding strategy can be a massive drag on system latency, however. These approaches should be used only if latency isn't a prime consideration.

Knowledge Overshadowing

Knowledge overshadowing is another potential reason for hallucination. In their experiments, Zhang et al. (*https://oreil.ly/z8PeK*) show that when an LLM is prompted with multiple conditions, the more dominant condition overshadows, leading to hallucinations.

As an example, consider the prompt: "Give me the name of a female fighter in kickboxing." The response is: "One famous female kickboxer is Buakaw Banchamek, a Thai fighter who has won numerous titles in both kickboxing and Muay Thai." While Buakaw is a kickboxer, he is actually a man! In this case the generation was conditioned on two factors (female fighters, kickboxer), but the kickboxer condition has overshadowed the female condition, resulting in a hallucination.

Zhang et al. show that overshadowing happens due to imbalances in the training data. They also show that the hallucination rate increases with the imbalance rate.

Hallucinations Due to Irrelevant Information

The presence of irrelevant information in the context can also lead to hallucinations. As an example, consider this prompt:

> *Prompt:* Indianapolis, the capital of Indiana, is known for its vibrant cultural scene, including museums, theaters, and sporting events, especially the Indianapolis 500 race. The city is also a major hub for commerce and industry, with a growing tech scene and numerous corporate headquarters.
>
> Where is the actor Lily Gao born?

The response is as follows:

> *Response:* Lily Gao, an American actress known for her roles in various TV series and films, was born on October 1, 1994, in Indianapolis, Indiana, USA.

However, in reality Lily Gao was born in Canada! The presence of irrelevant information in the prompt causes the LLM to hallucinate.

To mitigate this issue, Weston et al. (*https://oreil.ly/aqsxN*) propose a technique called System 2 Attention (S2A). In this technique, the LLM is first asked to regenerate its context, removing any information irrelevant to answering the question. Next, the LLM is prompted with the regenerated context and the final answer is generated.

As an example, consider this math problem with a distractor sentence:

> *Prompt:* Sarah has 5 apples. She buys 3 more apples from the store. Max sells 3 apples to the store. How many apples does Sarah have now?

We issue the following prompt:

> *Prompt:* Regenerate the context removing any information that is irrelevant to answering the question.

The response is as follows:

> *Response:* Sarah has 5 apples. She buys 3 more apples from the store. How many apples does Sarah have now?

This can be fed back to the model to provide the correct answer.

You can also implement S2A in a single prompt, by asking the model to regenerate the context followed by the final answer. However, performing this in two prompts has shown to be more effective.

Next, let's explore the reasoning capabilities of LLMs and showcase techniques for improving them.

Reasoning

In Chapter 1, we discussed the limitations of language models and pointed to reasoning as one of the biggest limitations. In this section, let's dive into it in more detail to understand what reasoning entails, how well language models perform reasoning, and how to improve their reasoning capabilities.

First, let's define reasoning:

> Natural language reasoning is a process to integrate multiple knowledge (e.g. encyclopedic knowledge and commonsense knowledge) to derive some new conclusions about the (realistic or hypothetical) world. Knowledge can be from both explicit and implicit sources. Conclusions are assertions or events assumed to be true in the world, or practical actions.
>
> —Yu et al. (*https://oreil.ly/7NsBF*)

Reasoning can be classified into several different types. Here are a few forms of non-mutually-exclusive reasoning categories:

Deductive Reasoning

Deductive reasoning uses logic to draw conclusions from one or more premises.

As an example, consider the following passage:

> Mr. Shockley was allergic to mushrooms. The dish "Golden Travesty" has mushrooms in it.

Based on this set of premises, we can deduce that Mr. Shockley should stay far away from the Golden Travesty dish.

Inductive Reasoning

Inductive reasoning involves making generalizations based on a set of observations. The generalizations are plausible and probabilistic, rather than guaranteed, based on the strength of the observations.

As an example, upon observing hundreds or even thousands of round manhole covers, one can conclude that manhole covers are generally round. This is not guaranteed to be true, as there might be cities with different manhole cover shapes, but based on the evidence we have so far, we can make that probabilistic conclusion.

Abductive Reasoning

Abductive reasoning involves analyzing a set of observations and concluding with the most likely explanation:

> Observation: The street is wet. There are water puddles on the sidewalk. People have umbrellas in their hands.
>
> Explanation: It rained recently.

Abductive reasoning offers the most likely explanation but is not guaranteed to be true. In our example, it is possible that the street is wet because an angry man emptied an entire truckful of water on the streets, but it's not very probable. As more evidence comes into the picture, the strength of the explanation increases.

Common Sense Reasoning

Common sense reasoning refers to utilizes a shared understanding of the world to make assumptions about the physical world or human relationships. Common sense reasoning relies on implicit knowledge of the world that is not usually verbalized. For example:

> She saw him prancing around the hall with a glass in his hand, held upside down.

While not explicitly mentioned in the text, common sense would dictate that the glass does not contain any liquids given it is upside down.

Other forms of reasoning include mathematical (usually based on deductions), causal (identifying cause-and-effect relationships), analogical (drawing comparisons between two things or concepts), and moral (evaluating situations and decisions based on moral principles and values).

Reasoning as Subgraph Pattern Matching

Do LLMs really reason? Does it even matter if LLMs reason the way humans do, as long as they get the job done? What if they are "just" sophisticated pattern matchers?

One school of thought argues that it doesn't matter if all that the models are doing is sophisticated pattern matching; if it is good enough to solve the task, then so be it. Moreover, we do not know a great deal about how the human brain performs reasoning, and maybe that is what it is doing as well.

However, understanding what is happening under the hood when language models are supposed to be reasoning does matter a lot. It helps us understand the current limitations of LLMs and provides us with intuitions on what classes of problems can be solved.

Dziri et al. (*https://oreil.ly/AyHRH*) show that Transformers are likely performing something called linearized subgraph matching (*https://oreil.ly/B_44q*). In this perspective, a task is said to be represented as a directed graph, where the directed graph represents the steps involved in solving the task. The subtasks making up the tasks correspond to subgraphs within the directed graph. Transformers solve subtasks by matching the corresponding subgraph to subgraphs seen during the training data. I recommend reading the entirety of Dziri et al.'s paper to get a better understanding of this topic.

Cheng et al. (*https://oreil.ly/vkTjt*) show that LLMs perform much better on inductive reasoning than deductive reasoning.

Exercise

How does your favorite LLM perform at these reasoning tasks? The book's GitHub repo (*https://oreil.ly/llm-playbooks*) contains a set of reasoning exercises corresponding to the reasoning categories we described in this section. Do LLMs perform better at some forms of reasoning than others?

Inducing Reasoning in LLMs

The simplest way of improving reasoning in LLMs is to use prompting techniques like chain-of-thought, introduced in Chapter 1. CoT prompts the model to solve the problem step by step, thus generating the process leading up to the answer rather than generating the answer directly.

Verifiers for Improving Reasoning

So, LLMs may not be all that great at producing the right answer to a question that requires multistep reasoning. But all hope is not lost. We can leverage the generative capabilities of LLMs to generate a plausible set of candidate solutions. These candidates can then be assessed by a verifier, which can identify the correct answer. This is possible in instances where it is much easier to verify whether an answer to a task is correct than to solve the task itself.

Just because LLMs can generate plausible candidate solutions for a question is not evidence of their reasoning abilities. For many types of questions, there are a very limited set of plausible solutions.

Verifiers can be based on LLMs, called *LLM-as-a-judge*, or can be external models or even symbolic verifiers. Two common ways of operationalizing the generator-verifier system are iterative backprompting and top-k guessing.

Iterative backprompting

In this process, an LLM generates a proposed solution to a given problem that requires reasoning. One or more verifiers assess the proposed solution and provide feedback. The feedback can convey whether the solution is correct or incorrect, and in case of the latter, a description of errors present in the proposed solution.

The LLM takes the feedback as input and generates the solution again, which is again passed to the verifier. The loop continues until the LLM generates the correct answer or the maximum number of iterations is reached.

Top-k guessing

In this technique, k solutions are generated for a given task, and the verifier assesses them and chooses the correct solution if it exists. A relatively high temperature (>1) is used during decoding to generate a diverse set of solutions.

Kambhampati et al. (*https://oreil.ly/4_MxJ*) show that top-k guessing exhibits similar performance levels as iterative backprompting.

Inference-Time Computation

This might well be the most significant topic of 2025 and beyond. As of this book's writing, scaling up pre-training seems to be providing diminishing returns. Therefore, there is a hunt for new scaling dimensions. The most promising among them is scaling up inference-time compute. The premise is simple. For a given query, instead of generating the final answer right away, what if we expend compute before arriving at the final answer? Can we improve the performance of the model with more compute? Turns out, we can! Let's discuss this new scaling avenue in detail.

Repeated sampling

The most simple and common inference-time compute technique is repeated sampling. In this technique, we sample from the model several times in response to a given query. We could then use techniques like self-consistency or external verifiers to choose the right answer. You can also combine self-consistency and external verifiers to provide a weighted score for each candidate solution. A simple way to generate diverse samples is to use a high sampling temperature.

Another simple approach is to use iterative generation, as shown earlier in this chapter. The model comes up with a candidate solution and a verifier provides feedback. The model iteratively improves its response using the verifier feedback until it reaches the final answer or the maximum number of iterations. Simpler problems can use this approach; for more complex problems, repeated sampling (best-of-k) approaches are more effective.

Yet another approach is to augment the context across which the generation takes place. CoT prompting is the easiest way to achieve that. Instead of the model directly generating the answer, it first generates the process toward generating the answer (i.e., the thought process).

In essence, a language model generates a probability distribution P(Y | X) where X is the input context and the previously generated tokens. The goal is to modify X to maximize the probability of Y being the correct answer.

Jin et al. (*https://oreil.ly/Dc_Fc*) show some important experiments on this. First, the length of the reasoning steps matters to the performance. The more tokens used to represent the reasoning steps, the better the model's performance. Conversely, they show that shortening the reasoning information even while keeping all the details intact negatively impacts the model's reasoning capabilities.

Jin et al. also show that errors in the reasoning steps do not impact the performance as much, as long as the length of the reasoning steps exceeds a threshold.

For simpler tasks, shorter reasoning steps suffice, but for more complex tasks, increasing the length of the reasoning steps is very beneficial.

Jin et al. also show that replacing the CoT prompt "Let's think step by step" with "Let's think step by step, you must think more steps." improves performance.

Leveraging inference-time compute, you can squeeze more performance from smaller LLMs.

Search

Another way to utilize inference-time compute is to search through the generation probability distribution. The idea is that for every token being generated, there is a probability assigned to every token in the vocabulary, so if we search properly, we might end up traversing the probability space and choosing the right path to generate the correct answer. Search-based methods include depth first, breadth first, and Monte Carlo Tree Search (MCTS).

Fine-Tuning for Reasoning

One way to induce better reasoning in a model is to fine-tune it with a reasoning dataset. Let's explore the reasoning-0.01 (*https://oreil.ly/W1JRq*) dataset released by SkunkworksAI to see what a typical reasoning dataset looks like:

> *Input:* If a die is rolled three times, what is the probability of getting a sum of 11?
>
> *Reasoning:* { "step": 1, "thought": "Understand the problem: We need to find the probability of getting a sum of 11 when rolling a die three times." },
>
> { "step": 2, "thought": "Calculate total possible outcomes: A die has 6 faces, so for each roll, there are 6 possibilities. For three rolls, the total possible outcomes are 6^3 = 216." },
>
> { "step": 3, "thought": "Identify favorable outcomes: List all combinations of rolls that result in a sum of 11. There are 18 such combinations." },
>
> { "step": 4, "thought": "Calculate probability: Divide the number of favorable outcomes by the total possible outcomes: 18 / 216 = 1/12." },
>
> { "step": 5, "thought": "Conclusion: The probability of getting a sum of 11 when rolling a die three times is 1/12." }]
>
> *Output:* 1/12

The dataset contains step-by-step reasoning chains for a large variety of tasks. Such a dataset can be generated synthetically using larger models, followed by a human verification and annotation stage to verify and correct reasoning chains.

Summary

In this chapter, we defined alignment training and why we need it. We ventured into techniques for alignment training such as reinforcement learning. We also learned about hallucinations and different techniques to mitigate them. Finally, we examined reasoning limitations of LLMs and new techniques like scaling up inference-time computation.

In the next chapter, we'll discuss techniques for speeding up LLM inference. High computation costs are a significant barrier to LLM adoption, and thus a plethora of techniques have been developed to improve inference speeds.

CHAPTER 9

Inference Optimization

In the past few chapters, we learned several techniques for adapting and utilizing LLMs to solve specific tasks. In this chapter, we will learn how to efficiently perform inference on them for real-world usage. LLMs' large size make deployment and inference particularly challenging, as they exert significant pressure on compute, memory, and energy requirements. This proves to be especially challenging on edge devices like mobile phones.

For the rest of the chapter, we will focus on the field of inference optimization, discussing the factors influencing LLM inference time. We will then showcase a variety of optimization techniques including caching, knowledge distillation, early exiting, quantization, parallel and speculative decoding, and more.

LLM Inference Challenges

What are the bottlenecks affecting LLM inference? As we all know, their gargantuan sizes necessitate vast computing and memory resources. Apart from that, two additional factors exacerbate the situation:

- As seen in Chapter 4, contemporary LLMs are based largely on decoder-only models that operate autoregressively. This means that each token is generated one after the other, thus imposing a sequential limitation. Later in this chapter, we will discuss techniques for parallel and speculative decoding that aim to speed up the decoding process.
- As the input sequence length increases, the amount of compute needed increases quadratically. Later this chapter, we will discuss techniques like K-V caching that aim to alleviate this bottleneck.

Let's dive into the techniques used to optimize inference.

Inference Optimization Techniques

Since this is a problem that severely impacts the deployment of LLMs in real-world use cases, considerable attention has been given to inference optimization research in major industry and academic labs. Dozens of optimization techniques have been developed in recent years, without which the present ubiquity of LLMs would not have been achieved. For a near-comprehensive survey of the various types of techniques used for optimizing inference, check out Zhou et al.'s survey paper (*https://oreil.ly/MtzNn*).

We will now focus on some of the most promising and effective inference optimization techniques used in LLM deployments. While most of you may not be implementing these techniques by yourself but instead rely on third-party tools, understanding the optimization techniques and the tradeoffs involved provide valuable insights that can help you choose among various solutions.

Techniques for efficient inference aim to achieve the following three goals:

Reduce compute
: Techniques like caching, knowledge distillation, and early exit, each of them employing distinct strategies to reduce computation.

Speed up decoding
: Techniques for parallel and speculative decoding aim to improve the throughput of the model: the number of tokens generated per second.

Reduce storage needs
: Quantization techniques aim to reduce the amount of storage needed for weights and activations of the model, by reducing space required to store numbers from 32 bits to 16, 8, or even 4 bits.

Techniques for Reducing Compute

We can reduce compute required during inference by:

- Trading compute for extra storage, using methods like caching.
- Foregoing certain operations during inference, using methods like *early exit*.
- Deriving a smaller model from a larger model while preserving as many characteristics and capabilities from the larger model as possible, using techniques like knowledge distillation.

The next sections will explore each of these methods in detail.

K-V Caching

As seen in Chapter 1, LLMs do not have session memory; at every turn in an LLM conversation, the previous conversation history is added to the input. This means that every request to an LLM could potentially contain a lot of repetitive content in the prompt. For the repetitive parts of the prompt, the same computation is performed during the inference step again and again. Moreover, in autoregressive decoding, each token is generated as a function of the entire input and the previously generated tokens. Thus, there is a lot of duplicative computation.

One way to alleviate this duplicative computation is to cache the data and reuse them when required. More specifically, we cache the keys (K) and values (V) of the self-attention blocks of the Transformer architecture, referred to as the K-V cache. Recall our discussion in Chapter 4 about keys and values in the self-attention block of the Transformer.

Let's look at some examples. Consider the task of analyzing sentiment of movie reviews. You might have a lengthy prompt providing detailed instructions on the nuances involved in analyzing sentiment. These instructions are included in the prompt for every input review being fed to the LLM.

Instead of incurring unnecessary overhead by repetitively processing the instruction tokens, the cache is consulted to fetch the K-V values for these tokens.

Similarly, consider the example of a question-answering assistant that provides customer support by answering questions from a product manual. In this case, the K-V values representing the product manual tokens can be cached and then reused for any requests where the product manual needs to be part of the prompt.

Caching can also enable adding a lot of few-shot examples in the prompt. This can sometimes be a lightweight alternative to fine-tuning.

Major LLM providers like Google's Gemini and Anthropic's Claude provide caching support for their models through their APIs, calling it context caching. This also vastly reduces the cost for end users, as cached tokens are billed only once.

Note that in the caching strategy, we are trading compute for additional storage. K-V caches can get unfeasibly large, especially at longer sequence lengths.

To keep costs under control, LLM providers typically limit the age of the cache to a short period or price users by caching duration.

As an example, let's look at a request to Anthropic's Claude suite of models that utilizes context caching:

```
{
    "model": "claude-3-5-sonnet",
    "max_tokens": 1024,
    "system": [
      {
        "type": "text",
        "text": "<System Prompt>"
      },
      {
        "type": "text",
        "text": "<Product Manual>",
        "cache_control": {"type": "ephemeral"}
      }
    ],
    "messages": [
      {
        "role": "user",
        "content": "Which battery should I use for the G-8 Ultra?"
      }
    ]
  }'
```

The `cache_control` parameter is used to specify that the system prompt and the product manual is to be cached. As of the book's writing, Claude's cache is live by default for five minutes.

Organize your prompt to place the cacheable components at the beginning of the prompt, i.e., the prompt prefix.

Ultimately, caching can be very valuable in reducing inference time, especially in settings where instructions are repeated for a large number of calls, or the context window contains data like API documentation or RAG output that needs to persist across multiple calls.

Next, we'll explore the early exit method for reducing inference-time compute.

Early Exit

As shown in Chapter 4, the Transformer architecture is made up of repeating blocks called layers. The output of each layer is an intermediate representation that gets fed as input to the layer above it. One simple way of reducing compute during inference is to exit inference at an intermediate layer and interpret it as the final output. This technique is called early exit. Figure 9-1 shows early exit in practice.

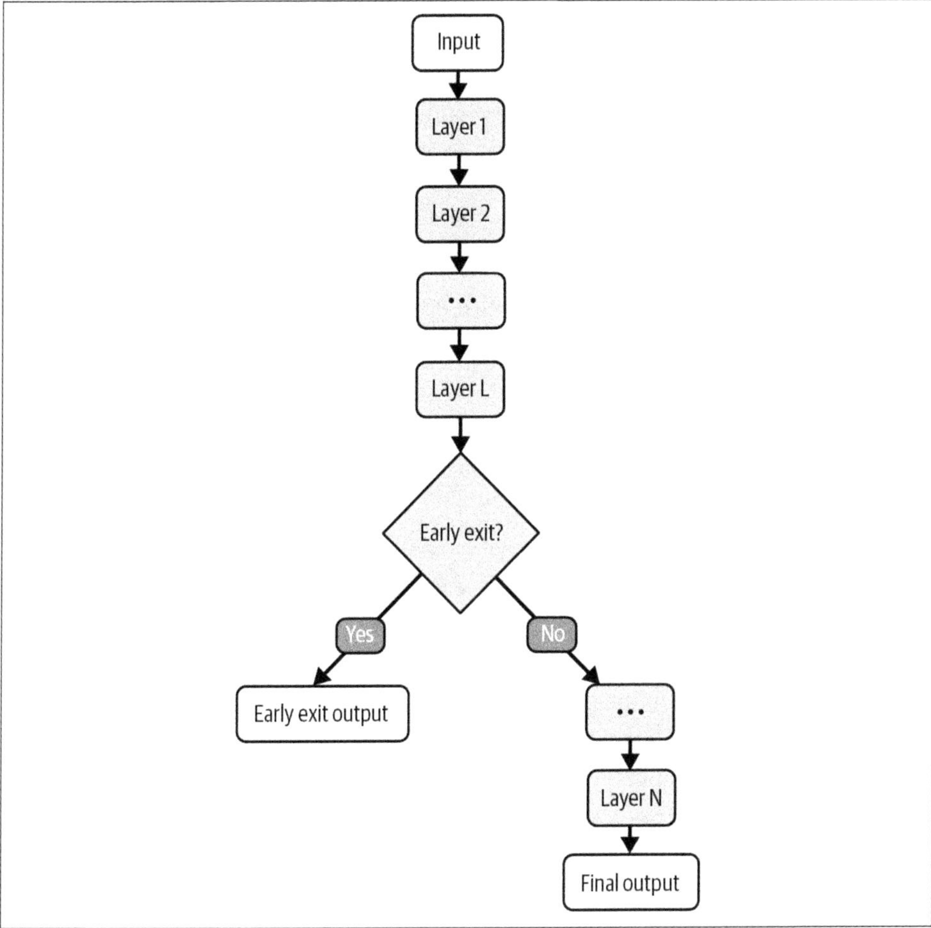

Figure 9-1. Early exit in practice

Early exit can happen both at the sequence level and at the token level.

Sequence-level early exit

In this scenario, the forward pass in the Transformer is stopped at a particular layer for the entire input sequence, and the intermediate representations from that layer are taken as the final output. The layer at which to exit can be determined in advance or can be dynamically decided based on the input sequence.

To dynamically decide the layer to exit, you can train adapters on top of each layer, as shown in Chapter 7. These modules can then be used to predict whether the exit can happen at the current layer. For example, FastBERT (*https://oreil.ly/GCfpt*) implements modules at each layer that learn to solve a binary classification problem (to exit or not exit).

Not all methods depend on adding trainable modules. For example, the hash-based early exiting approach (HashEE) (*https://oreil.ly/_JqqH*) by Sun et al. uses an annotated set of sequences along with their exit layers as the basis for determining the exit layers for new input sequences. This method is based on the hypothesis that similar sequences should exit at the same layers.

Exercise

For a 7B open source model of your choice, apply early exit at the 75th percentile of layers in the model. Evaluate this technique on one of the datasets provided in the book's GitHub repo (*https://oreil.ly/llm-playbooks*).

What effect does static early exit have on the model's performance? What latency gains were you able to achieve using early exit?

The second early exit option is token-level early exit.

Token-level early exit

In this approach, different tokens from the same sequence can exit at different layers. This is more complex to implement than sequence-level early exit.

Similar to sequence-level early exit techniques, you can implement binary classifiers to decide whether to exit at a particular layer, but this happens at each token at each layer, instead of the entire sequence. For more details on token-level early exit, refer to Schuster et al. (*https://oreil.ly/hfdCd*), who introduced the technique Confident Adaptive Language Modeling (CALM), that implements token-level early exit.

Recall that in the self-attention subblock of the Transformer, the representation of a token is calculated using the representations of all other tokens in the sequence in the same layer. But if we are using token-level early exit, it is possible that some tokens in a sequence might already have exited before that layer. The easiest way to resolve this issue is to copy the representations of the exited token to every layer above it.

While token-level early exit can be more fine-grained and effective than sequence-level early exit, it is slower than sequence-level early exit.

Exercise

Apply Google's implementation (*https://oreil.ly/l5Xko*) of the CALM method for token-level early exit over any of the datasets provided in the book's GitHub repo (*https://oreil.ly/llm-playbooks*).

Which tokens exit at early layers and which tokens exit at later layers? Do you observe any linguistic patterns? What can we infer from this about how language models learn?

In early exit, the reduction in compute comes at the cost of performance. However, this can be minimized by learning to exit at the optimal layer.

Dynamic early exit belongs to a class of techniques called *dynamic inference*, where the inference compute is determined dynamically, based on the characteristics of the input. One important example is the mixture of experts (MoE) class of models, introduced in Chapter 4. In MoE models, a routing function chooses a small subset of expert modules to run inference on, thus reducing the amount of compute required.

Next, let's explore how we can reduce inference time by creating a smaller derivative model from a larger model while limiting performance degradation, using a technique called knowledge distillation.

Knowledge Distillation

In Chapter 5, we briefly introduced distilled versions of models, like DistilBERT (*https://oreil.ly/rgiHZ*). These are smaller models that approximate the capabilities of the larger models they are distilled from, thus enabling speedier inference.

Over the years, several techniques have been developed for knowledge distillation. For a survey of research advances in this field, refer to Xu et al.'s (*https://oreil.ly/JZQf3*) survey paper.

The process of knowledge distillation can be divided into two steps: distillation data preparation and training. The base model is referred to as the teacher model and the distilled model is referred to as the student model.

Figure 9-2 depicts the process of distilling a model.

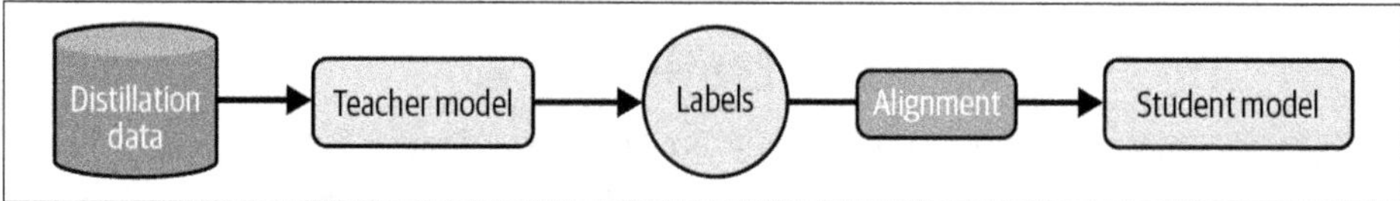

Figure 9-2. Knowledge distillation

Here's how the distillation data preparation and training steps work.

Distillation data preparation

Data for distillation is typically prepared by appropriately querying the teacher model and using the teacher's outputs as the *knowledge* to be distilled. Ways to elicit relevant outputs from the teacher include:

Unsupervised generation
: In this technique, the teacher is prompted with instructions and/or examples for solving a task. The teacher's responses comprise the distillation dataset. This technique is commonly used to teach capabilities like CoT or instruction-following to smaller models. To accomplish that, teacher models are asked to respond to queries with the thought process leading up to the answer.

Data augmentation
: In this technique, the teacher is shown a set of seed input-output examples. Based on the seed examples, the teacher generates similar input-output examples, constituting the distillation dataset. Note that both the input and output are generated by the teacher model in this setting. The limitation of this technique is that the teacher is unable to generate sufficiently diverse examples.

Intermediate representations
: This class of techniques is known as white-box distillation. Here the distillation dataset consists of intermediate representations from a model, which can include activations or output logits. This data can be used to align the student model with the teacher model. The alignment is learned using methods like KL-divergence, discussed in Chapter 4.

Teacher feedback
: In this class of techniques, the outputs from a student model are assessed by the teacher model to generate feedback. The teacher model can be used to generate preference data, i.e., the quality ranking of outputs from the student. Feedback can also be given in the form of detailed instructions on how to improve on a given task. A popular technique using teacher feedback is RLAIF, which we introduced in Chapter 5.

Self-teaching
: In this class of techniques, the teacher and student model are one and the same. The student model progressively refines its own outputs and uses them as the distillation set. One way of self-teaching is to generate multiple outputs for each task, along with reasoning steps, and choosing the best one to be part of the distillation set.

How many distillation examples do you need? Perhaps surprisingly, not a whole lot. Zhou et al. (*https://oreil.ly/MuOOj*) show that even one thousand very high-quality examples are enough to create a strong distillation set.

Just like fine-tuning and continued pre-training, knowledge distillation is susceptible to the catastrophic forgetting problem (introduced in Chapter 7).

Now that we have seen the various ways to create distillation datasets, let's turn to the actual distillation process.

Distillation

Here are some techniques used to perform the distillation task. For a more detailed survey of techniques, refer to Xu et al. (*https://oreil.ly/9mbiN*):

Supervised fine-tuning
: This is the simplest way to accomplish knowledge distillation. The student model is fine-tuned using the distillation set with the objective of aligning its predictions with that of the teacher model. This method is typically used in black-box knowledge distillation settings, where the distillation set does not comprise any internal representations.

K-L divergence of output probabilities
: In this method, our objective function is to minimize the K-L divergence between the output probability distribution of the teacher model and the student model.

Internal representation similarity
: Conversely, instead of minimizing divergence, you can maximize similarity between aspects of the teacher and student model. This can be leveraged to perform layerwise distillation, where the internal representations of the teacher and the student are aligned at each layer. Refer to Liang et al. (*https://oreil.ly/g-C4L*) for an effective technique for layerwise distillation.

Reinforcement learning
: This involves training a reward model using the distillation data. The student model is then trained to maximize the reward as per the reward model. Recall our discussion on reinforcement learning in Chapter 8.

Weak-to-Strong Generalization

Burns et al. from OpenAI uncovered a phenomenon called *weak-to-strong generalization* (*https://oreil.ly/xhrJL*). In this setting, the teacher model is smaller/weaker than the student model.

The small teacher model is fine-tuned using distillation data. The held-out portion of the distillation data is queried to the teacher model to generate outputs. These are called *weak labels*. The weak labels are then used to fine-tune a much larger and more powerful student model.

Burns et al. note that the stronger student is able to learn from the labels generated by the weaker teacher. This is because the student is able to rely on its strong pre-trained representations, and fine-tuning on the weak labels only help it elicit what it already knows. Using smaller models for generating training data simplifies the overall training process.

Ultimately, the technique you choose to distill your models depends on whether you have access to the teacher weights. If you do not have access to the teacher weights, then you can perform only supervised fine-tuning. White-box distillation, where you are trying to align intermediate representations and not just the output tokens, can be challenging to achieve. Note that all knowledge distillation techniques carry the risk of capability degradation or catastrophic forgetting, so you will have to evaluate the student model very carefully to quantify the difference in capabilities from the teacher model.

Exercise

Take the Gemma 2B open source model and distill it into a smaller model that can still perform CoT generation. Which of the techniques presented in this chapter is more suitable for this exercise?

In this section, we discussed three distinct techniques for reducing compute during inference: caching, early exit, and knowledge distillation. Next, let's discuss techniques that can accelerate the decoding process.

Techniques for Accelerating Decoding

As we know, autoregressive models output one token at a time, where the next token being generated is a function of the input tokens and all the previously generated tokens. This imposes a sequential limitation as you have to wait for the current token to be generated before generating the next one. Can we bypass this limitation? Several recent techniques like *speculative decoding* and *parallel decoding* have been developed. Let's examine them in detail.

Speculative Decoding

The concept behind speculative decoding is simple. A smaller model, called a draft model, is used to generate several subsequent candidate output tokens. Then, the main larger model is used to compute the conditional probabilities of the candidate output tokens at once, using them to decide which tokens to accept and which ones to reject. The more draft tokens accepted, the better the draft model.

Figure 9-3 depicts the speculative decoding process.

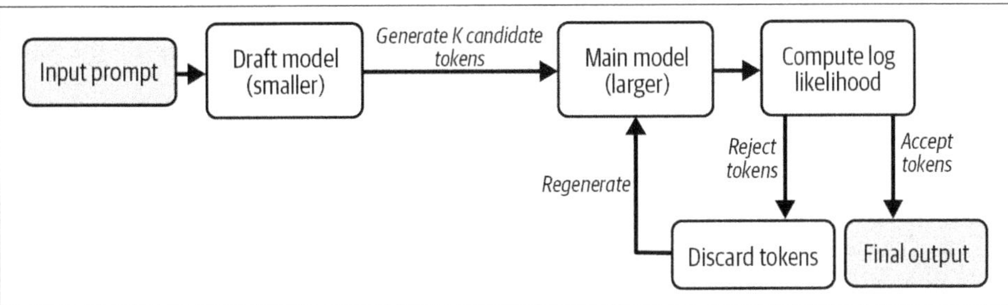

Figure 9-3. Speculative decoding in action

Two important metrics in speculative decoding are:

Token acceptance rate
: This is the percentage of tokens generated by the draft model that are accepted. Typically, this does not reach 1, because if it did, there is no need to use the main larger model.

Decoding speedup
: This refers to the reduction in latency between a model purely using autoregressive decoding versus one using speculative decoding.

Constructing Draft Models

How do we ensure that the draft model has a high token acceptance rate? One way is to distill the draft model from the main model. This technique was introduced by Zhou et al. and is called DistillSpec (*https://oreil.ly/scxWU*).

Zhou et al. (*https://oreil.ly/KVZRB*) introduced self-speculative decoding, where the draft model is a subset of the layers of the main model.

In many use cases, output text generated by the LLM includes commonly used phrases, prefixes, and boilerplate. The LLM could also be quoting existing bodies of text. All this can be directly fetched from external data repositories using a retrieval model instead of using a language model for generation. This technique, called retrieval-based speculative decoding (REST) was introduced by He at al. (*https://oreil.ly/DFufh*)

Parallel Decoding

Can we generate more than one token at the same time? This can be done either using the same model (multi-token decoding) or multiple instances of the same model.

For the latter, we can control parallel generation through the prompt. For example, say you are writing an article about a tourist site, containing sections like Food, Stay, Safety Tips, etc. You can prompt the LLM to list the sections, marked with special tokens. These sections can then be generated in parallel, assuming the sections are fully independent of each other.

Figure 9-4 depicts the workflow of a system that generates parts of the output in a parallel fashion.

Let's now explore how the same model can generate multiple tokens at a time, called multi-token decoding. Several techniques have been proposed recently for multi-token decoding, one of the most promising being Medusa by Cai et al. (*https://oreil.ly/qT94i*)

In Medusa, additional decoding heads are added to the model. These decoding heads represent subsequent tokens to be generated. For example, the standard decoding head is predicting the next (n + 1st) token in the sequence, and the additional decoding heads are predicting the n + 2nd, n + 3rd, and so on, tokens, respectively. Refer to the Medusa paper for more details on how this is implemented.

So far, we have learned techniques to accelerate the decoding process and to reduce compute. Next, let's dive into quantization, a class of techniques to reduce the storage required by the model.

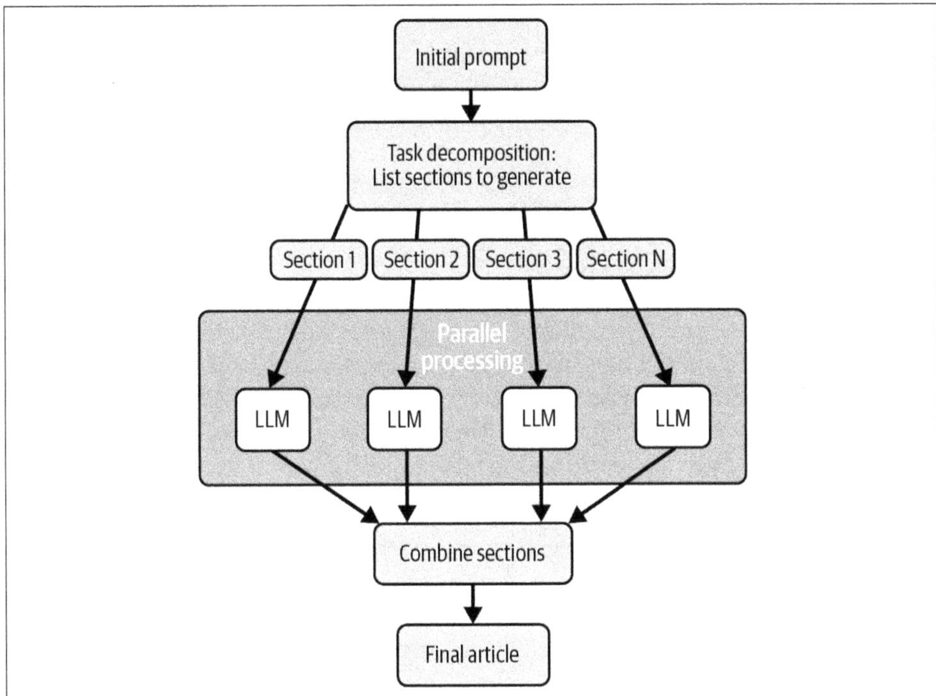

Figure 9-4. Parallel decoding workflow

Techniques for Reducing Storage Needs

In Chapters 5 and 6, we briefly touched upon quantization but promised to go into detail later. Let's dive in!

The forward pass of a language model involves numbers representing inputs, weights, and activations. How are these numbers represented in memory?

Several types of numerical representation formats are available, like integer, floating point, etc. Typically, numbers in language models are represented in floating-point32 (FP32), also called single-precision floating point, which refers to a floating point number composed of 32 bits, or 4 bytes.

A number represented in FP32 is composed of three parts:

- A sign bit
- The exponent (8 bits)
- The mantissa/significand (23 bits)

For more details on how FP32 works, see "Demystifying Floating Point Precision" (*https://oreil.ly/uCYYl*).

The maximum and minimum value that can be represented using FP32 is 3.4028237 × 10^{38} and 1.175494 × 10^{38}, respectively. This is referred to as the range of values that can be represented by this format. Similarly, a number represented in float16 (FP16), also referred to as half-precision floating point, is composed of these three parts:

- A sign bit
- The exponent (5 bits)
- The mantissa/significand (10 bits)

What happens when you take a number that is represented using FP32 and represent it in FP16? This amounts to a lossy conversion. In this case, both the range and the precision are impacted, because in FP16, 65,504 is the largest number you can represent, compared to 3.4 × 10^{38} for FP32. The precision is impacted too, as the 32-bit version offers ~7 digits of precision, but the 16-bit version only offers ~3 digits of precision.

To prevent the massive loss in precision with FP16, bfloat16 (BF16), also called the brain floating point, was invented by Google Brain. In BF16, there are 8 digits for the exponent, and 7 bits for the mantissa. This keeps the range of numbers represented the same as that of float32 at the cost of reduced precision.

Older GPUs like the NVIDIA T4 do not support BF16.

The process of converting representation of a number from a higher-precision format to a lower-precision format is called quantization. We can quantize 32-bit values to 8-bit integer formats as well. This reduces memory requirements by a factor of 4, at the cost of even more precision. With 8-bit quantization, we can represent numbers between –127 and 127, without any decimal point.

Integer quantization can be performed either symmetrically or asymmetrically.

Symmetric Quantization

In this setting, the *0* value in the original format is mapped to the *0* value in the integer representation. This means that when you quantize 0 represented in fp32 to int8, the value remains 0.

The remaining values can be mapped using various techniques, the most common being absmax quantization. In this method, if we know or can estimate the range of numbers that need to be represented, we can take the absolute maximum of the range and map it to the largest number in int8 (127), while the negative of the absolute maximum is mapped to the smallest number in int8 (–127). The remaining numbers are mapped according to scale.

Figure 9-5 depicts absmax quantization at work, quantizing a number represented in FP32 to int8.

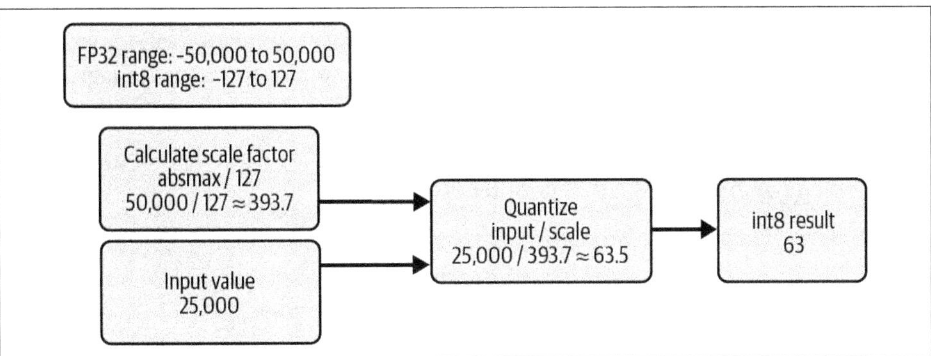

Figure 9-5. Absmax quantization

Asymmetric Quantization

In this setting, the *0* value in the original format is not guaranteed to be mapped to the *0* value in the integer representation.

A common technique is to take the minimum and maximum value that we need represented and map it to the minimum (–127) and maximum (127) values that can be represented in int8, respectively. For example, if the range of numbers we want represented is –23 to 87, then –23 is mapped to –127 and 87 is mapped to 127.

If the range of numbers you want represented include outliers, they can play spoilsport. You can take care of outliers by clipping them, so that all outliers will be represented by the same maximum/minimum value.

Exercise

Let's explore the effect that quantization has on precision and range. Take a few numbers (2.3888888, 0, 34.444, 12.3486*10^4, –1223.4566) and perform arithmetic operations using them in float32. Repeat the same operations using float16, bf16, and int8. How much precision do you lose at each quantization level?

How is quantization used in practice? Typically, quantization is applied after training. Both the model's weights and activations can be quantized.

Quantizing weights is much easier than quantizing activations. Since we know the weights beforehand, we can calculate the range, outliers, scaling factors, etc. that are needed for the quantization algorithm.

For activations, depending on how much latency we can tolerate, we can either perform dynamic or static scaling. In dynamic scaling, statistics like range, outliers, etc. are calculated dynamically during inference at each layer. In static scaling, we take a reference calibration dataset to estimate the statistics. While this approach speeds up inference, it can result in more quantization errors.

For more details on implementing quantization, see "A Visual Guide to Quantization" (*https://oreil.ly/bpi3b*) by Maarten Grootendorst.

Exercise

On any of the datasets provided with the book's GitHub repo (*https://oreil.ly/llm-playbooks*), run Llama 3.1 in float32, float16, bf16, and int8 mode.

Calculate the following:

- Impact on model inference time
- Impact on performance
- Impact on storage requirements

For the dataset you chose, is quantization worth it?

Summary

In this chapter, we discussed the causes of bottlenecks in LLM inference. We discussed a wide variety of techniques to make LLM inference more efficient, including techniques to reduce compute requirements, reduce storage requirements, and accelerate the decoding process. We explored techniques like caching, early exit, knowledge distillation, speculative and parallel decoding techniques, and quantization. In the next and final part of the book, we will explore LLM application paradigms and discuss the nuances involved in building full-fledged applications.

PART III
LLM Application Paradigms

In this part of the book, we shift our focus to the application layer. Until now, we have explored LLMs as standalone concepts, but we will now examine how they integrate into larger software systems. To this end, we will delve into popular application paradigms such as retrieval-augmented generation (RAG) and agents.

CHAPTER 10

Interfacing LLMs with External Tools

In the first two parts of the book, we have seen how impactful standalone LLMs can be in solving a wide variety of tasks. To effectively harness their full range of capabilities in an organization, they have to be integrated into the existing data and software ecosystem. Unlike traditional software systems, LLMs can generate autonomous actions to interact with other ecosystem components, bringing a degree of flexibility never seen before in the software world. This flexibility unlocks a whole host of use cases that were previously considered impossible.

Another reason we need LLMs to interact with software and external data: as we know all too well, current LLMs have significant limitations, some of which we discussed in Chapter 1. To recap some key points:

- Since it is expensive to retrain LLMs or keep them continuously updated, they have a knowledge cutoff date and thus possess no knowledge of more recent events.
- Even though they are getting better over time, LLMs don't always get math right.
- They can't provide factuality guarantees or accurately cite the sources of their outputs.
- Feeding them your own data effectively is a challenge; fine-tuning is nontrivial, and in-context learning is limited by the length of the effective context window.

As we have been noticing throughout the book, the consolidation effect is leading us to a future (unless we hit a technological wall) where many of the aforementioned limitations might be addressed within the model itself. But we don't necessarily need to wait for that moment to arrive, as many of these limitations can be addressed today by offloading the tasks and subtasks to external tools.

In this chapter, we will define the three canonical LLM interaction paradigms and provide guidance on how to choose between them for your application. Broadly speaking, there are two types of external entities that LLMs need to interact with: data stores and software/models, collectively called tools. We will demonstrate how to interface LLMs with various tools like APIs and code interpreters. We will show how to make the best use of libraries like LangChain and LlamaIndex, which have vastly simplified LLM integrations. We will explore the various scaffolding software that needs to be constructed to facilitate seamless interactions with the environment. We will also push the limits of what today's LLMs are capable of, by demonstrating how they can be deployed as an agent that can make autonomous decisions.

LLM Interaction Paradigms

Suppose you have a task you want the LLM to solve. There are several possible options:

- The LLM uses its own memory and capabilities encoded in its parameters to solve the task.
- You feed the LLM all the context it needs to solve the task within the prompt, and the LLM uses the provided context and its capabilities to solve it.
- The LLM doesn't have the requisite information or skills to solve this task, so you update the model parameters (fine-tuning etc., as detailed in Chapters 6–8) so that it is able to activate the skills and knowledge needed to solve it.
- You don't know a priori what context is needed to solve the task, so you use mechanisms to automatically fetch the relevant context and insert it into the prompt (passive approach).
- You provide explicit instructions to the LLM on how to interact with external tools and data stores to solve your task, which the LLM follows (explicit approach).
- The LLM breaks the task into multiple subtasks if needed, interacts with its environment to gather the information/knowledge needed to solve the task, and delegates subtasks to external models and tools when it doesn't have the requisite capabilities to solve that subtask (autonomous approach).

As you can see, the last three involve the LLM interacting with its environment (passive, explicit, and autonomous). Let's explore the three interaction paradigms in detail.

Passive Approach

Figure 10-1 shows the typical workflow of an application that involves an LLM passively interacting with a data store.

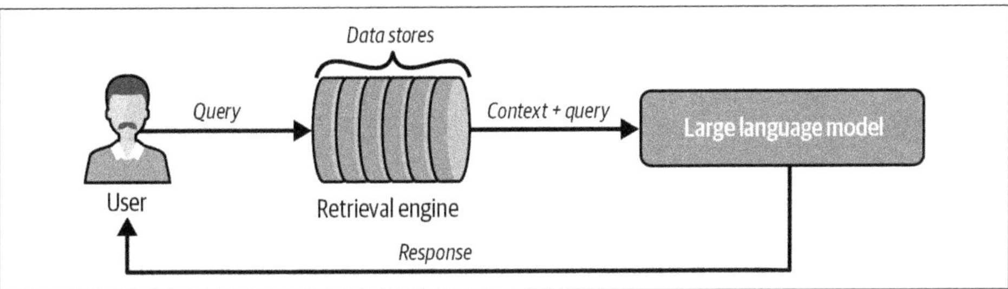

Figure 10-1. An LLM passively interacting with a data store

A large number of use cases involve leveraging LLMs to use your own data. Examples include building a question-answering assistant over your company's internal knowledge base that is spread over a bunch of Notion documents, or an airline chatbot that responds to customer queries about flight status or booking policies.

To allow the LLM to access external information, we need two types of components: "data stores" that contain the required information and retrieval engines that can retrieve relevant data from data stores given a query. The retrieval engine can be powered by an LLM itself, or it can be as simple as a keyword-matching algorithm. The data store(s) can be a repository of data like a database, knowledge graph, vector database, or even just a collection of text files. Data in the data store is represented and indexed to make retrieval more efficient. Data representation, indexing, and retrieval are topics important enough to merit their own chapter: we will defer detailed discussions on them to Chapter 11.

When a user issues a query, the retrieval engine uses the query to find the documents or text segments that are most relevant to answering this query. After ensuring that these fit into the context window of the LLM, they are fed to the LLM along with the query. The LLM is expected to answer the query given the relevant context provided in the prompt. This approach is popularly known as RAG, although as we will see in Chapter 12, RAG refers to an even broader concept. RAG is an important paradigm that deserves its own chapter, so we will defer detailed coverage of the paradigm to Chapter 12.

Note that the distinguishing feature of this paradigm is the passive nature of the LLM in the interaction. The LLM simply responds to the prompt and furnishes an answer. It does not know the source of the content inside the prompt. This paradigm is often used for building QA assistants or chatbots, where external information is required to understand the context of the conversation.

From this point forward, we will refer to user requests to the LLM as *queries* and textual units that are retrieved from external data stores as *documents*. Documents can be full documents, passages, paragraphs, or sentences.

The Explicit Approach

Figure 10-2 demonstrates the explicit approach to interface LLMs with external tools.

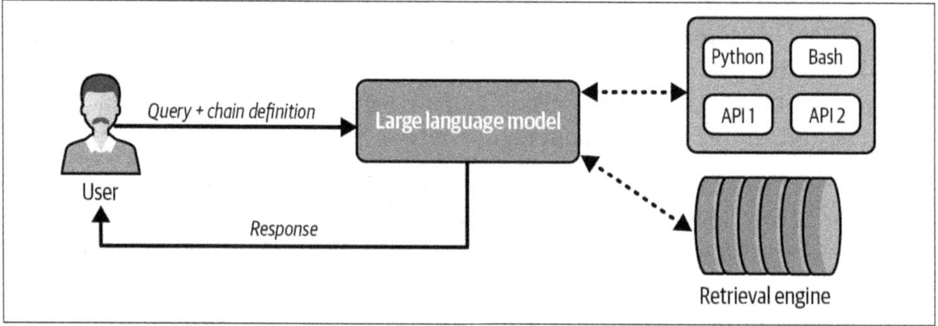

Figure 10-2. The explicit interaction approach in action

Unlike in the passive approach, the LLM is no longer a passive participant. We provide the LLM with explicit instructions on how and when to invoke external data stores and tools. The LLM interacts with its environment based on a preprogrammed set of conditions. This approach is recommended when the interaction sequence is fixed, limited in scope, and preferably involves a very small number of steps.

For an AI data analyst assistant, an example interaction sequence could be:

1. User expresses query in natural language asking to visualize some data trends
2. The LLM generates SQL to retrieve the data needed to resolve the user query
3. After receiving the data, the LLM uses it to generate code that can be run by a code interpreter to generate statistics or visualizations

Figure 10-3 shows a fixed interaction sequence implemented for an AI data analyst.

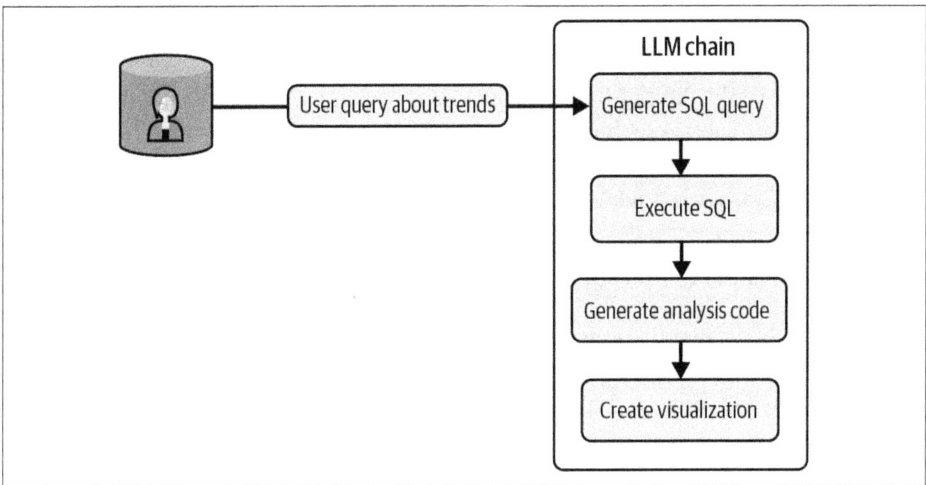

Figure 10-3. An example workflow for an AI data analyst

In this paradigm, the interaction sequence is predetermined and rule-based. The LLM exercises no agency in determining which step to take next. I recommend this approach for building robust applications that have stricter reliability requirements.

The Autonomous Approach

Figure 10-4 shows how we can turn an LLM into an autonomous agent that can solve complex tasks by itself.

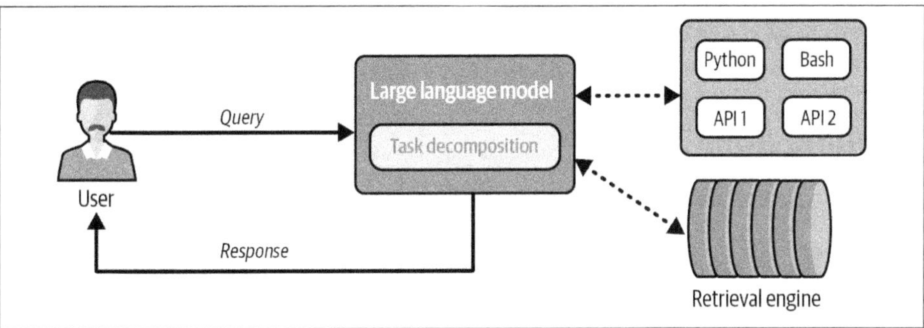

Figure 10-4. A typical autonomous LLM-driven agent workflow

The autonomous approach, or the Holy Grail approach as I like to call it, turns an LLM into an autonomous agent that can solve tasks on its own by interacting with its environment. Here is a typical workflow of an autonomous agent:

1. The user formulates their requirements in natural language, optionally providing the format in which they want the LLM to provide the answer.

2. The LLM decomposes the user query into manageable subtasks.
3. The LLM synchronously or asynchronously solves each subtask of the problem. Where possible, the LLM uses its own memory and knowledge to solve a specific subtask. For subtasks where the LLM cannot answer on its own, it chooses a tool to invoke from a list of available tools. Where possible, the LLM uses the outputs from solutions of already executed subtasks as inputs to other subtasks.
4. The LLM synthesizes the final answer using the solutions of the subtasks, generating the output in the requested output format.

This paradigm is general enough to capture just about any use case. It is also a risky paradigm, as we are assigning the LLM too much responsibility and agency. At this juncture, I would not recommend using this paradigm for any mission-critical applications.

Why am I calling for caution in deploying agents? Humans often underestimate the accuracy requirements for applications. For a lot of use cases, getting it right 99% of the time is still not good enough, especially when the failures are unpredictable and the 1% of failures can be potentially catastrophic. The 99% problem is also the one that has long plagued self-driving cars and prevented their broader adoption. This doesn't mean we can't deploy autonomous LLM agents; we just need clever product design that can shield the user from their failures. We also need robust human-in-the-loop paradigms.

We have used the word "agent" several times now without defining it. Let's correct that and consider what agents mean and how we can build them.

Defining Agents

As the hype starts building over LLM-based agents, the colloquial definition of agents has already started to expand from its traditional definition. This is because truly agentic systems are hard to build, so there is a tendency to shift the goalposts and claim best-effort systems to be already agentic even though they technically may not fit the requirements. In this book, we will stick to a more conservative definition of agents, defining them as:

> LLM-driven software systems that are able to interact with their environment and take autonomous actions to complete a task.

Key characteristics of agents are:

Their autonomous nature
: The sequence of steps required to perform a task need not be specified to the agent. Agents can decide to perform any sequence of actions, unprompted by humans.

Their ability to interact with their environment
: Agents can be connected to external data sources and software tools, which allows agents to retrieve data, invoke tools, execute code, and provide instructions when appropriate to solve a task.

Many definitions of "agent" do not require them to be autonomous. According to their definitions, applications following the explicit paradigm can also be called agents (albeit as non-autonomous or semi-autonomous agents).

The agentic paradigm as we defined it is extremely powerful and general. Let's take a moment to appreciate it. If an agent receives a task that it doesn't know how to solve (and it *knows* that it doesn't know), then instead of just giving up, it can potentially learn to solve the task by itself by searching the web or knowledge bases for pointers, or even by collecting data and fine-tuning a model that can help solve the task.

Given these enviable abilities, are machines going to take over the world? In practice, current autonomous agents are limited in what they can actually achieve. They tend to get stuck in loops, they take incorrect actions, and they are unable to reliably self-correct. It is more practical to build partially autonomous agents, where the LLM is provided with guidance throughout its workflow, either through agent orchestration software or with a human in the loop. For the rest of this chapter, our focus will be on building practical agents that can reliably solve a narrower class of tasks.

Agentic Workflow

Using our definition of agents, let's explore how agents work in practice. As an example, let's consider an agent that is asked to answer this question:

> Who was the CFO of Apple when its stock price was at its lowest point in the last 10 years?

Let's say the agent has all the information it needs to solve this task. It has access to the web, to SQL databases containing stock price information, and to knowledge bases containing CFO tenure information. It is connected to a code interpreter so that it can generate and run code, and it has access to financial APIs. The system prompt contains details about all the tools and data stores the LLM has access to.

To answer the given query, the LLM has to perform this sequence of steps:

1. To calculate the date range, it needs the current date. If this is not included in the system prompt, it either searches the web to find the current date or generates code for returning the system time, which is then executed by a code interpreter.
2. Using the current date, it finds the other end of the date range by executing a simple arithmetic operation by itself, or by generating code for it. Steps 1 and 2 could be combined into a single program.
3. It finds a database table in the available datastore list that contains stock price information. It retrieves the schema of the table, inserts it into the prompt, and generates a SQL query for finding the date when the stock price was at its minimum in the last 10 years.
4. With the date in hand, it needs to find the CFO of Apple on that date. It can call a search engine API to check if there is an explicit mention of the CFO on that particular date.
5. If the search engine query fails to provide a result, it finds a financial API in its tools list and retrieves and inserts the API documentation into its context. It then generates and invokes code for an API call to retrieve the list of Apple CFOs and their tenures.
6. It uses its arithmetic reasoning skills to find the CFO tenure that matches the date of the lowest stock price.
7. It generates the final answer. If there is a requested output format, it tries to adhere to that.

Depending on the implementation, the sequence of steps could vary slightly. For example, you can fine-tune a model so that it can generate code for API calls or SQL queries directly without having to retrieve the schema from a data store or API.

To perform the given sequence of tasks, the model should first understand that the given task needs to be decomposed into a series of subtasks. This is called task decomposition. Task decomposition and planning can be performed by the LLM or offloaded to an external tool.

Exercise

Try out the Apple CFO query with consumer LLM tools that have access to the web, like ChatGPT, Perplexity, and Gemini. Are they able to solve the answer correctly? If not, where are they falling short? Note that the earlier in the task sequence the LLM fails, the harder for it to recover.

Try to solve this question using a web search and no LLMs. You can see that it takes several search engine queries even for a financial domain expert to find the answer to this question.

Components of an Agentic System

While the specific architecture of any given agentic system depends heavily on the use cases it is intended to support, each of its components can be classified into one of the following types:

- Models
- Tools
- Data stores
- Agent loop prompt
- Guardrails and verifiers
- Orchestration software

Figure 10-5 shows a canonical agentic system and how its components interact.

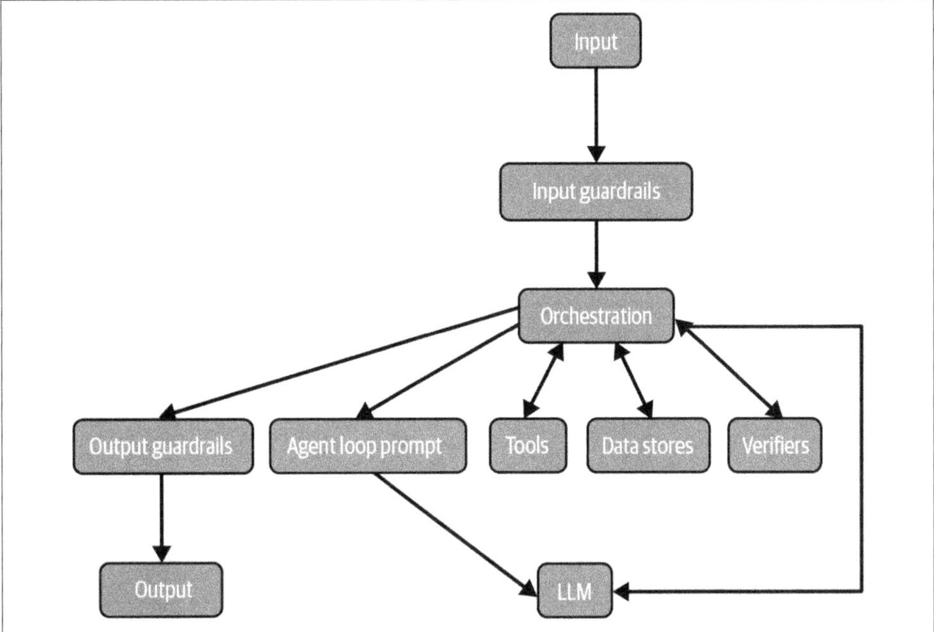

Figure 10-5. A production-grade agentic system

Let's explore each of these types.

Models

Language models are the backbone of agentic systems, responsible for their autonomous nature and problem-solving capabilities. A single agentic system could be composed of multiple language models, with each model playing a distinct role.

For example, you can build an agent consisting of two models; one model solves user tasks and another model takes its output and converts it into a structured form according to user requirements.

Agentic workflows can consume a lot of language model tokens, which can be cost prohibitive. To keep costs under control, consider using multiple language models of different sizes, with the smaller (and cheaper) models performing easier tasks. For more details on how to accomplish division of labor among these models, see Chapter 13.

More generally, you can build agents with specialized models catering to each part of the agentic workflow. For example, a code-LLM can be used to generate code, and task-specific fine-tuned models that specialize in individual workflow steps can be used. This setup can be interpreted as a *multi-agent architecture*.

Figure 10-6 shows an agentic system made up of multiple LLMs.

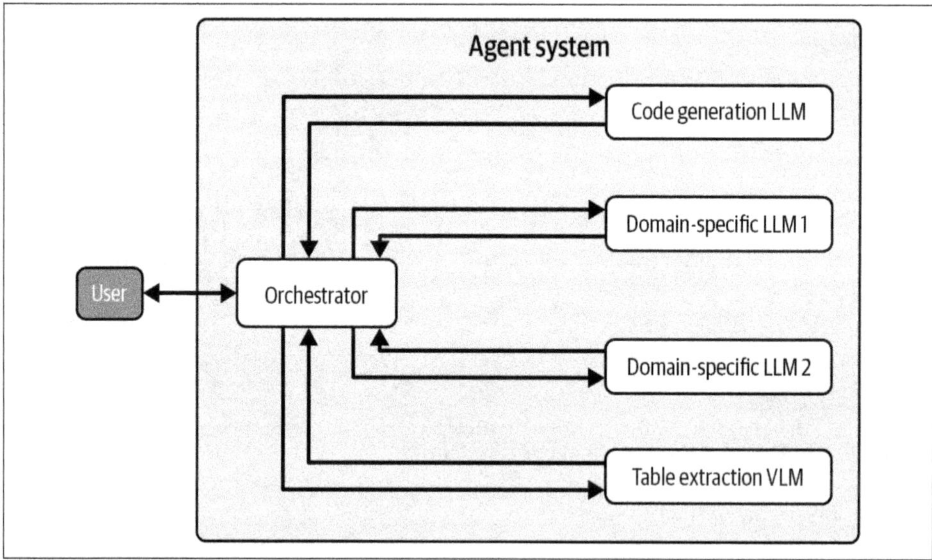

Figure 10-6. An agentic system with multiple LLMs

Finally, any kind of model, including non-LLMs, can be plugged into an agentic system to solve specific tasks. For example, the planning stage can be performed using symbolic planners (*https://oreil.ly/sXPWG*).

Tools

As described earlier, software or models that can be invoked by an LLM are called tools. Libraries like LangChain (*https://oreil.ly/35Lgu*) and LlamaIndex (*https://oreil.ly/WF-d1*) provide connectors to various software interfaces, including code interpreters, search engines, databases, ML models, and a variety of APIs. Let's explore how to work with some of these in practice.

Web search

LangChain provides connectors for major search engines like Google, Bing, and DuckDuckGo. Let's try out DuckDuckGo:

```
from langchain_community.tools import DuckDuckGoSearchRun

query = "What's the weather today in Toronto?"

search_engine = DuckDuckGoSearchRun()
output = search_engine.run(query)
```

The response can be fed back to the language model where it is further processed.

API connectors

To illustrate calling APIs, we will showcase LangChain's Wikipedia API wrapper:

```
!pip install wikipedia

from langchain.tools import WikipediaQueryRun
from langchain_community.utilities import WikipediaAPIWrapper
wikipedia = WikipediaQueryRun(api_wrapper=WikipediaAPIWrapper())

output = wikipedia.load("Winter Olympics")
```

The `load()` function runs a search on Wikipedia and returns the page text and metadata information of the top-k results. (top-k = 3 by default). You can also use the `run()` function to return only page summaries of the top-k matches.

Code interpreter

Next, let's explore how you can invoke a code interpreter and run arbitrary code:

```
from langchain_experimental.utilities import PythonREPL

python = PythonREPL()
python.run("456 * 345")
```

Be wary of running code generated by LLMs in response to user prompts. Users can induce the model to generate malicious code!

Database connectors

Finally, let's check out how to connect to a database and run queries:

```
import sqlalchemy as sa
from langchain_community.utilities import SQLDatabase

DATABASE_URI = <database_uri>

db = SQLDatabase.from_uri(DATABASE_URI)

output = db.run(
    "SELECT * FROM COMPANIES WHERE Name LIKE :comp;",
    parameters={"comp": "Apple%"},
    fetch="all")
```

The `run()` function executes the provided SQL query and returns the response as a string. Replace *`DATABASE_URI`* with your own database and queries, and verify the responses.

For more customizability, you can fork the LangChain connectors and repurpose them for your own use.

Next, let's see how we can interface LLMs with these tools in an agentic workflow.

First, we need to make the LLM aware that it has access to these tools. One of the ways to achieve this is to provide the names and short descriptions of the tools, called the *tool list*, to the LLM through the system prompt.

Next, the LLM needs to be able to select the right tool at the appropriate juncture in the workflow. For example, if the next step in solving a task is to find the weather in Chicago this evening, the web search tool has to be invoked rather than the Wikipedia one. Later in this chapter, we will discuss techniques to help the LLM select the right tool.

Under the hood, tool invocation is typically achieved by the LLM generating special tokens indicating that it is entering tool invocation mode, along with tokens representing the tool functions and arguments to be invoked. The actual tool invocation is performed by an agent orchestration framework.

In LangChain, we can make a tool available to an LLM and have it invoked:

```
from langchain.agents import initialize_agent, Tool
from langchain.agents import AgentType
from langchain_community.tools import DuckDuckGoSearchRun
from langchain_openai import ChatOpenAI
from langchain_core.messages import HumanMessage

search_engine = DuckDuckGoSearchRun()
model = ChatOpenAI(model="gpt-4o")

tools = [
       Tool(
           name="Search",
           func=search_engine.run,
           description="search engine for answer factual queries"
       )
   ]
agent = initialize_agent(tools, model, verbose=True)
agent.run("What are some tourist destinations in North Germany?")
```

Exercise

Using LangChain, create an agent that is initialized with at least five tools from the list found on its website (*https://oreil.ly/LumHc*). Tools that do not require an API key include Wikipedia, DuckDuckGo, and arXiv, the latter being a repository of scientific papers including ones on LLMs. For a given user query, do you notice the model selecting the right tool? Give the model clues on selecting the right tool in the system prompt. Do you notice any improvements?

Some models come with native tool-calling abilities. For models that don't, you can fine-tune the base model to impart them with tool-calling abilities. Among open models, Llama 3.1 Instruct (8B/70B/405B) is an example of a model having native tool-calling support. Here's how tool calling works with Llama 3.1.

Llama 3.1 comes with native support for three tools: Brave web search, Wolfram| Alpha mathematical engine, and a code interpreter. These can be *activated* by defining them in the system prompt:

```
<|begin_of_text|><|start_header_id|>system<|end_header_id|>
Environment: ipython
Tools: brave_search, wolfram_alpha

Give responses to answers in a concise fashion. <|eot_id|>
```

Let's ask the LLM a question by appending a user prompt to the system prompt:

```
<|start_header_id|>user<|end_header_id|>

How many medals did Azerbaijan win in the 2024 Summer Olympics?
<|eot_id|><|start_header_id|>assistant<|end_header_id|>
```

Llama 3.1 responds with a tool invocation that looks like this:

```
<|python_tag|>brave_search.call(query="How many medals did Azerbaijan win in

the 2024 Summer Olympics?")<|eom_id|>
```

The `<|python_tag|>` token is a special token generated by Llama 3.1 to indicate that it is entering tool-calling mode. The `<|eom_id|>` special token indicates that the model has not ended its turn yet and will wait to be fed with the results of the tool invocation.

You can also provide your own tools in the prompt: using JSON is recommended.

If you have a lot of tools, then the detailed descriptions of the tools can be represented in a data store and retrieved only if they are selected. The prompt then needs to contain only the name of the tool and a short description.

Here is an example of a tool definition in JSON describing a local function that can be called:

```
<|start_header_id|>user<|end_header_id|>

Here is a list of tools available.
While invoking a tool, respond in JSON. The format is as follows:

{"tool_name": tool name, "arguments": dictionary with keys representing

argument names and values representing argument values}.

{
    "type": "local_function",
    "function": {
    "name": "find_citations",
    "description": "Find the citations for any claims made",
    "parameters": {
        "type": "object",
        "properties": {
        "claim_sentence": {
            "type": "string",
            "description": "A sentence in the input representing a claim"
        },
        "model": {
            "type": "string",
```

```
                "enum": ["weak", "strong"],
                "description": "The type of citation model to use. A weak model is
                preferred if the claim sentence contains entities and numbers. "
            }
            },
            "required": ["claim_sentence", "model"]
        }
        }
    }
```

The tool call is generated by the model in JSON with the prescribed format.

The actual tool invocation is performed by an agent orchestration software. Llama 3.1 comes with llama-stack-apps (*https://oreil.ly/SSmkI*), a library that facilitates agentic workflows.

Sometimes the tool call can be more complex than just returning the name of a function and its arguments. An example of this is querying a database. For the LLM to generate the right SQL query, you should provide the schema of the database tables in the system prompt. If the database has too many tables, then their schema can be retrieved on demand by the LLM.

You can use a separate specialized model for code and SQL query generation. A general-purpose model can generate a textual description of the desired outcome, and this can be used as input to a code LLM or an LLM fine-tuned on text-to-SQL.

For large-scale or high-stakes applications, you can fine-tune your models to make them better at tool use. A good fine-tuning recipe to follow is Qin et al.'s ToolLLaMA (*https://oreil.ly/Ewlxt*).

Exercise

Try creating some custom tools and making them available for Llama 3.1. The tools are just functions that can represent a wrapper to some software, or they can be a function that performs a specific task like converting from Celsius to Fahrenheit. Can you create these five tools and provide their definitions in JSON in the system prompt:

- Tool to query the Wikipedia API
- Tool to query the arXiv API
- Tool that converts from Celsius to Fahrenheit

- Tool that saves the input to a text file
- Tool that makes a copy of a file

Try asking queries that can lead to these tools being invoked. Are they being invoked as expected? Modify your tool descriptions if not, and see if that helps.

Data Stores

A typical agent may need to interact with several types of data sources to accomplish its tasks. Commonly used data sources include prompt repositories, session memory, and tools data.

Prompt repository

A prompt repository is a collection of detailed prompts instructing the language model how to perform a specific task. If you can anticipate the types of tasks that an agent will be asked to perform while in production, you can construct prompts providing detailed instructions on how to solve them. The prompts can even include directions on how to advance a specific workflow. Let's look at an example.

Many language models struggle with basic arithmetic operations, even simple questions like:

```
Is 9.11 greater than 9.9?
```

Until recently, even state-of-the-art language models claimed that 9.11 is greater than 9.9. (They were recently updated with a fix after this limitation went viral on social media (*https://oreil.ly/ztWGW*).)

If you are aware of such limitations that are relevant to your use case, then you can mitigate a proportion of them using detailed prompts. For the number comparison issue, for example:

> *Prompt:* If you are asked to compare two numbers using the greater than/lesser than operation, then perform the following:
>
> Take the two numbers and ensure they have the same number of decimal places. After that, subtract one from the other. If the result is a positive number, then the first number is greater. If the result is a negative number, then the second number is greater. If the result is zero, the two numbers are equal.

Now, if the agent needs to perform a task that includes number comparison, it first retrieves this prompt from the prompt repository. This enables it to overcome its inherent limitation, as it will follow the detailed step-by-step instructions in the prompt.

Why don't we just add all these prompts to the context window, thus eschewing retrieval? For one, the prompts may be too numerous and may not fit within the context window. Secondly, tokens are expensive, and it is inefficient to include prompts that may not be relevant to the current task. Finally, language models can adhere to only a limited set of concurrent instructions, so it is more efficient to retrieve them on demand.

Prompts can also include input-output examples, known as few-shot learning, as introduced in Chapter 1. Agents can retrieve them on demand to help accomplish their tasks. We will discuss effective ways of retrieving relevant examples in Chapter 12.

Next, let's explore how agents use session memory to advance their goals.

Session memory

We would like to store logs of the steps undertaken by the agent during current and past sessions. These logs can also be augmented with feedback from verification processes, both automated and human. The agent can then retrieve session logs for better context understanding and as a guide to determine next actions in the current workflow. Let's explore this with an example:

> *Prompt:* Is it going to be warmer tomorrow than today in Paris? Give me details in Celsius.

The agent goes through a sequence of steps to solve this query, which is all logged in the session history. The session history for this query might look like this:

> *User prompt*: Is it going to be warmer tomorrow than today in Paris? Give me details in Celsius.
>
> *LLM observation*: The user has a preference for Celsius units for temperature data.
>
> *LLM Output*: Let's perform this step-by-step.
>
> 1. First, let's retrieve today's temperature.
> 2. Next, let's retrieve tomorrow's temperature.
> 3. We calculate the difference and generate the answer.
>
> *External verifier*: Task decomposition is correct
>
> *Tool selection:* <WeatherAPI> selected
>
> *Tool info retrieval*: Retrieve information relevant to the query *Find temperature data from <WeatherAPI>*
>
> *Tool invocation*: get_temperature_curweek(*Paris*)
>
> *Tool output* : Weather data - Paris...

LLM output: Today's temperature is 27 degrees Celsius. Tomorrow's forecast is 23 degrees Celsius. Therefore, tomorrow is not going to be warmer in Paris than today.

External Verifier: Arithmetic operation is correct.

Agent: LLM output is dispatched to the user

User feedback: User marked this as correct

As we can see, session history can contain very rich information that can provide valuable personalized context to the LLM about the current user as well as guide the model toward the correct agentic workflow.

In more advanced implementations, multiple levels of logging can be defined, so that during retrieval, one can retrieve all the logs of a session or only the important steps, based on the logging level specified.

Along with session history, the agent could also be provided with access to gold-truth training examples representing correct workflows, which can be used by the agent to guide its trajectory during test time.

Exercise

Tools for facilitating agent observability include LangSmith (*https://oreil.ly/6fn7p*), Langtrace (*https://oreil.ly/0FhZ9*), OpenLLMetry (*https://oreil.ly/1GRDY*), etc. Many of these tools operate freemium models. Use LangSmith observability tools for the Llama 3.1 agent you built in the previous exercise and observe the agent traces.

Session memory can also include records of interaction between the human and the agentic system. These can be used to personalize models. We will discuss this further in Chapter 12.

Next, let's explore how the agent can interact with tools data.

Tools data

Tools data comprise detailed information necessary to invoke a tool, such as database schemas, API documentation, sample API calls, and more. When the agent decides to invoke a tool, the model retrieves the pertinent tool information from the tools data store.

For example, consider a SQL tool for retrieving data from a database. To generate the right SQL query, the model could retrieve the database schema from the tools data store. The tools data contains information about the tables and columns, the descriptions of each column and their data types, and optionally information about indices and primary/secondary keys.

You can also fine-tune the LLM on a dataset representing valid SQL queries to your database, which can potentially remove the need to consult the schema before generating a query.

To sum it up, agents can use data stores in several ways. They can access prompts and few-shot examples from a prompt repository, they can access agentic workflow history and intermediate outputs by models in previous sessions for better personalized context understanding and workflow guidance, and they can access tool documentation to invoke tools correctly.

Agents can also access external knowledge from the web, databases, knowledge graphs, etc. Retrieving the right information from these sources is an entire subsystem unto itself. We will discuss the mechanics of retrieval in Chapters 11 and 12.

We will now discuss the agent loop prompt, which is responsible for driving the LLM's behavior during an agentic session.

Agent Loop Prompt

Recall that LLMs do not have session memory. But a typical agentic workflow relies on several LLM calls! We need a mechanism to provide information about session state and the expected role of the LLM at any given time in the session. This agent loop is driven by a system prompt.

An example of a simple agent loop system prompt is:

> *Prompt:* You are an AI model currently answering questions. You have access to the following tools: {tool_description}. For each question, you can invoke one or more tools where necessary to access information or execute actions. You can invoke a tool in this format: <TOOLNAME> <Tool Arguments>. The results of these tool calls are not provided to the user. When you are ready with the final answer, output the answer using the <Answer> tag.

I find that a prompt like this is sufficient for most use cases. However, if you feel like the model is not reasoning correctly, you can try ReAct prompting.

ReAct

At the time of this writing, ReAct (Reasoning + Acting) prompting is the most popular prompt for the agent loop. A typical ReAct prompt looks like this:

> *Prompt:* You are an AI assistant capable of reasoning and acting. For each question, follow this process:
>
> 1. Thought: Reflect on the current state and plan your next steps.
> 2. Action: Execute the steps to gather information or call tools.

3. Observation: Record the results of your actions.
4. Final Answer: If you have an answer, provide a final response. Else continue the Thought → Action → Observation → loop until you have an answer.

Despite its popularity, ReAct prompting has been shown to be brittle (*https://oreil.ly/RRZO9*).

Reflection

The agent loop may include self-verification or correction steps. This was pioneered by Shinn et al. (*https://oreil.ly/xFVt0*) with the Reflexion paradigm.

Here is the system prompt for Reflection-Llama-3.1 (*https://oreil.ly/foB-P*) that uses reflection techniques:

> *Prompt:* You are a world-class AI system, capable of complex reasoning and reflection. Reason through the query inside <thinking> tags, and then provide your final response inside <output> tags. If you detect that you made a mistake in your reasoning at any point, correct yourself inside <reflection> tags.

The <reflection> tags are meant for the model to self-introspect and self-correct. We can also specify conditions when <reflection> tags should be activated, for example, when the agent performs the same action consecutively more than three times (which might mean it is stuck in a loop).

The effectiveness of reflection-based methods are overstated. They might do more harm than good if they are invoked too often, causing the model to second-guess solutions.

Exercise

Let's test the reliability of ReAct to the test. Use the ReAct and Reflexion prompts provided in this chapter to drive the movie recommendation agent provided in the book's GitHub repo (*https://oreil.ly/llm-playbooks*). Can you use a simpler prompt instead and see how it compares to ReAct?

Next, let's discuss guardrails and verifiers, components that ensure that an agentic system can thrive in production.

Guardrails and Verifiers

In production environments, mistakes can be catastrophic. Depending on the use case, the agent might need to adhere to strict standards in factuality, safety, accuracy, and many other criteria.

Safety is ensured by using guardrails, components that ensure models do not overstep their bounds during the course of their workflows. Some examples of guardrails include toxic language detectors, personally identifiable information (PII) detectors, input filters that restrict the type of queries users are permitted to make, and more.

Verifiers ensure that quality standards of the agentic system are so that the agent is able to recover and self-correct from mistakes. As agentic systems are still in their infancy, the importance of good and well-placed verifiers is paramount. Verifiers can be as simple as token-matching tools but can also be fine-tuned models, symbolic verifiers, and so on.

Let's learn more about guardrails and verifiers.

Safety Guardrails

Recall from Chapter 2 that LLMs are trained largely on human-generated web text. Unfortunately a significant proportion of human-generated text contains toxic, abusive, violent, or pornographic content. We do not want our LLM applications to generate content that violates the safety of the user, nor do we want users to misuse the model to generate unsafe content. While we can certainly use techniques like alignment training to make the model less likely to emit harmful content, we cannot guarantee 100% success and therefore need to institute inference-time guardrails to ensure safe usage. Libraries like Guardrails (*https://oreil.ly/F7yax*) and NVIDIA's NeMo-Guardrails (*https://oreil.ly/p7Dqz*), and models like Llama Guard (*https://oreil.ly/8S08P*) facilitate setting up these guardrails.

The Guardrails library provides a large (and growing) number of data validators to ensure safety and validity of LLM inputs and outputs. Here are some important ones:

Detect PII
: This validator can be used to detect personally identifiable information in both the input and output text. Microsoft Presidio (*https://oreil.ly/eG8T1*) is employed under the hood to perform the PII identification.

Prompt injection
: This validator can detect certain types of adversarial prompting and thus can be used to prevent users from misusing the LLM. The Rebuff (*https://oreil.ly/nIyE5*) library is used under the hood to detect prompt injection.

Not safe for work (NSFW) text
: This validator detects NSFW text in the LLM output. This includes text with profanity, violence, and sexual content. The *Profanity free* validator also exists for detecting only profanity in text.

Politeness check
: This validator checks if the LLM output text is sufficiently polite. A related validator is *Toxic language*.

Web sanitization
: This validator checks the LLM output for any security vulnerabilities, including if it contains code that can be executed in a browser. The Bleach (*https://oreil.ly/r3Xrl*) library is used under the hood to find potential vulnerabilities and sanitize the output.

What happens if the validation checks fail and there is indeed harmful content in the input or output? Guardrails provides a few options:

Re-ask
: In this method, the LLM is asked to regenerate the output, with the prompt containing instructions to specifically abide by the criteria on which the output previously failed validation.

Fix
: In this method, the library fixes the output by itself without asking the LLM for a regeneration. Fixes can involve deletion or replacement of certain parts of the input or output.

Filter
: If structured data generation is used, this option enables filtering out only the attribute for which the validation failed. The rest of the output will be fed back to the user.

Refrain
: In this setting, the output is simply not returned to the user, and the user receives a refusal.

Noop
: No action is taken, but the validation failure is logged for further inspection.

Exception
: This raises a software exception when the validation fails. Exception handlers can be written to activate custom behavior.

fix_reask

In this method, the library tries to fix the output by itself and then runs validation on the new output. If the validation still fails, then the LLM is asked to regenerate the output.

Let's look at the PII guardrail as an example:

```
from guardrails import Guard
from guardrails.hub import DetectPII

guard = Guard().use(
    DetectPII, ["EMAIL_ADDRESS", "PHONE_NUMBER"], "reask")

guard.validate("The Nobel prize this year was won by Geoff Hinton,
who can be reached at +1 234 567 8900")
```

Exercise

Extracting the system prompt is a popular form of jailbreak. Can you write a guardrail that prevents users from extracting the system prompt?

Next, let's look at how verification modules work.

Verification modules

As we have seen throughout the book, current LLMs suffer from problems like reasoning limitations and hallucinations that severely limit their robustness. However, production-ready applications need to demonstrate a certain level of reliability to be accepted by users. One way to extend the reliability of LLM-based systems is to use a human-in-the-loop who can manually verify the output and provide feedback. However, in the real world a human-in-the-loop is not always desired or feasible. The most popular alternative is to use external verification modules as part of the LLM system. These modules can range from rule-based programs to smaller fine-tuned LLMs to symbolic solvers. There are also efforts to use LLMs as verifiers, called "LLM-as-a-judge."

Related components include fallback modules. These modules are activated when the verification process fails and retrying/fixing doesn't work. Fallback modules can be as simple as messages like, "I am sorry I cannot entertain your request" to more complex workflows.

Let's discuss an example. Consider an abstractive summarization application that operates on financial documents. To ensure quality and reliability of the generated summaries, we need to embed verification and self-fixing into the system architecture.

How do we verify the quality of an abstractive summary? While single-number metrics are available to automatically quantify the quality of a summary, a more holistic approach would be to define a list of criteria that a good summary should satisfy and verify whether each criterion is fulfilled.

Several single-number quantitative metrics exist for evaluating summaries. These include metrics like BLEU, ROUGE (*https://oreil.ly/LPlFJ*), and BERTScore (*https://oreil.ly/gsOGl*). BLEU and ROUGE rely on token overlap heuristics and have been shown to be woefully inadequate (*https://oreil.ly/rSzbR*). Techniques like BERTScore that apply semantic similarity have been shown to be more promising, but in the end, the reality is that summaries have subjective notions of quality and need a more holistic approach for verification.

For the summarization of financial documents application, here is a list of important criteria:

Factuality
: The summary is factually correct and does not make incorrect assumptions or conclusions from the source text.

Specificity
: The summary doesn't *oversummarize*; it avoids being generic and provides specific details, whether numbers or named entities.

Relevance
: Also called precision, this is calculated as the percentage of sentences in the summary that are deemed relevant and thus merit inclusion in the summary.

Completeness
: Also called recall, this is calculated as the percentage of relevant items in the source document that are included in the summary.

Repetitiveness
: The summary should not be repetitive, even if there is repetition in the source document.

Coherence
: When read in full, the summary should provide a clear picture of the content in the source document, while minimizing ambiguity. This is one of the list's more subjective criteria.

Structure
: While defining the summarization task, we might specify a structure for the summaries. For example, the summary could be expected to contain some predefined

sections and subsections. The generated summary should follow the specified structure.

Formatting
: The generated summary should follow proper formatting. For example, if the summary is to be generated as a bulleted list, then all the items in the summary should be represented by bullets.

Ordering
: The ordering of the items in the summary should not impede the understanding of the summary content. We also might want to specify an order for the summaries, for example, chronological.

Error handling
: In case of errors or omissions in the source document, there should be appropriate error handling.

> **Exercise**
>
> Define the verification criteria for the question-answering assistant for the Canadian parliamentary proceedings dataset provided in the book's GitHub repo (*https://oreil.ly/llm-playbooks*). In what ways do the criteria differ from the abstractive summarization task?

How do we automatically verify whether a given summary meets all these criteria? We can use a combination of rule-based methods and fine-tuned models. Ultimately, the rigor of the methods used for verification depends on the degree of reliability needed for your application. However, we notice that once we reduce the scope of the verification process to verify fitness of individual criteria rather than the application as a whole, it becomes easier to verify accurately using inexpensive techniques. Let's look at how we can build verifiers for each criteria of the abstractive summarization task:

Factuality
: Verifying whether an LLM-generated statement is factual is extremely difficult if we do not have access to ground truth. But for summarization applications, we do have access to the ground truth. Therefore, we can verify factuality by taking each sentence in the summary and checking whether, given the source text, one can logically conclude the statement in the summary. This can be framed as a natural language inference (NLI) problem, which is a standard NLP task.

  In the NLI task, we have a hypothesis and a premise, and the goal is to check if the hypothesis is logically entailed by the premise. In our example, the hypothesis is a sentence in the summary and the premise is the source text.

Training an NLI model specific to your domain might be a cumbersome task. If you do not have access to an NLI model, you can use token overlap and similar statistics to approximate factuality verification.

For numbers and named entities, factuality verification can be performed by using string matches. You can verify if all the numbers and named entities in the summary are indeed present in the source text.

Specificity
: One way for a summary to be specific is to include numbers and named entities where relevant. For each sentence in the summary, we can check whether the content in the source document related to the topic of the sentence contains any numbers and named entities, and if these are reflected in the summary. Numbers and named entities can be tagged and detected using regular expressions or libraries like spaCy (*https://oreil.ly/zatAW*).

Relevance/precision
: We can train a classification model that detects whether a sentence in the summary is relevant. Note that there are limits to this approach. If this classification model was good enough, we could have directly used it to select relevant sentences from the source text to build the summary! In practice, this classification model can be used to remove irrelevant content that is more obvious.

Recall/completeness
: What content merits inclusion in the summary is a difficult question, especially if there is a hard limit on the summary length. You can train a ranking model that ranks sentences in the source document by importance, and then verify if the top-ranked sentences are represented in the summary. You can also specify beforehand the type of content that you need represented in the summary and build a classification model for determining which parts of the source document contain pertinent information. Using similarity metrics like embedding similarity, you can then find if the content has been adequately represented in the summary.

Repetitiveness
: This can be discovered by using string difference algorithms like the Jaccard distance (*https://oreil.ly/Ny_Ku*) or by calculating the embedding similarity between pairs of summary sentences.

Coherence
: This is perhaps one of the most difficult criteria to verify. One way to solve this, albeit a more expensive solution, is to build a prerequisite detection model. For each sentence in the summary, we detect if all the sentences that come before it are sufficient prerequisites for understanding the correct sentence. For more

information on prerequisite detection techniques, see Thareja et al. (*https://oreil.ly/6JnRs*)

Structure
: If we specify a predetermined structure (sections and subsections) for the summary, we can easily identify if the structure is adhered to by checking if the desired section and subsection titles are present in the summary. We can also verify using embedding similarity techniques if the content within the sections and subsections is faithful to the title of the section/subsection.

Formatting
: This involves checking whether the content is in the appropriate formatting, for example, whether it is a bulleted list or a valid JSON object.

Ordering
: The desired order can be chronological, alphabetical, a domain, or task-specific ordering. If it is supposed to be chronological, you can verify by extracting dates in the summary and checking if the summary contains dates in a chronological order. If the ordering requirements are more complex, then verifying adherence to order may become an extremely difficult task.

Do not expect your verification process to be strictly better than your summary model. If that was the case, you could have used the verification process to generate the summary!

We can also deploy symbolic verifiers like SAT (*https://oreil.ly/lOsg_*) (Boolean satisfiability) solvers and logic planners. This type of verification is beyond the scope of this book.

Exercise

For the task presented in the previous exercise (question-answering assistant for Canadian parliamentary proceedings), how would you build verification modules for each of the criteria you have identified? Would you be able to perform robust verification based on heuristics-based techniques alone?

Once verification modules are part of our system architecture, we will also need to decide what action to perform when the verification fails. One option is to just resample from the language model again. Regeneration can be performed for the full output or only for the output that failed verification. We can also develop antifragile architectures that have fallbacks in case of failure, which we will discuss in Chapter 13.

Adding more verifiers can drastically increase system latency. Thus, their inclusion has to be balanced with accuracy and system latency needs.

Finally, let's discuss agent orchestration software that connects all these components.

Agent Orchestration Software

For agentic workflows to proceed smoothly, we need software that connects all the components. Orchestration software manages state; invokes tools; initiates retrieval; pipes buffers; and logs intermediate and final outputs. Many agentic frameworks, both open source and proprietary, perform this function, including LangChain (*https://oreil.ly/7vmlY*), LlamaIndex (*https://oreil.ly/uxejK*), CrewAI (*https://oreil.ly/Ntxii*), AutoGen (*https://oreil.ly/tx3qy*), MetaGPT (*https://oreil.ly/HI-Jn*), XAgent (*https://oreil.ly/sA_DR*), llama-stack-apps (*https://oreil.ly/SBGC_*), and so on.

Agents are a relatively new paradigm, so all these agentic frameworks are expected to change a lot in the coming months and years. These frameworks are implemented in an opinionated fashion and hence are less flexible. For prototyping, I suggest picking LangChain or LlamaIndex for ease of use. For production use, you might want to build a framework internally from scratch or by extending the open source ones. This book's GitHub repo (*https://oreil.ly/llm-playbooks*) contains a rudimentary agentic framework as well.

Now that we have learned all the different agentic system components, it is time to get building! The book's GitHub repository (*https://oreil.ly/llm-playbooks*) contains sample implementations of various types of agents. Try modifying them for your use case to understand the tradeoffs being made.

The keep it simple, stupid (KISS) principle applies to agents perhaps more than any other recent paradigm. Don't complicate your agentic architecture unless there is a compelling reason to do so. We will discuss this more in Chapter 13.

Web Agents and Computer Use

Throughout this chapter, we have seen examples of agents executing actions in the real world, primarily by invoking a software interface. However, in the quest for automating human tasks, we find there are many cases where an external software interface doesn't exist, with only a GUI like a web page available. A lot of tedious work for humans involves actions on a computer like copying/pasting between systems, filling columns in an Excel sheet using data from another system, and so on. Can agents help us automate these kinds of tasks?

A new paradigm of agents called web agents promises to do so. Web agents use the Document Object Model (DOM) or the screenshot of a web page to understand the page's current state and perform actions like entering information into fields, clicking on elements, and navigating to links. A working web agent could help you automatically book a flight by navigating to a travel website, entering information, choosing between different options, and completing payment. As of today, this is still a fledgling technology, with poor results on benchmark tasks (*https://oreil.ly/Dyp2L*).

Companies like Anthropic have launched initial versions of computer use (*https://oreil.ly/FT44u*) features that enables agents to control a computer desktop environment.

Run Anthropic's Computer Use Demo (*https://oreil.ly/nUtar*). Pay attention to the system prompt (*https://oreil.ly/AsFpP*) provided. What are the common failure modes you observe?

Summary

In this chapter, we discussed the different ways in which LLMs can interface with external tools. We introduced the agentic paradigm and provided a formal definition of agents. We identified the components of an agentic system in detail, exploring models, tools, data stores, guardrails and verifiers, and agentic orchestration software. We learned how to define and implement our own tools.

In the next chapter, we will explore data representation and retrieval, crucial elements of interfacing LLMs with external data.

CHAPTER 11

Representation Learning and Embeddings

In the previous chapter, we learned how we can interface language models with external tools, including data stores. External data can be present in the form of text files, database tables, and knowledge graphs. Data can span a wide variety of content types, from proprietary domain-specific knowledge bases to intermediate results and outputs generated by LLMs.

If the data are structured, for example residing in a relational database, the language model can issue a SQL query to retrieve the data it needs. But what if the data are present in unstructured form?

One way to retrieve data from unstructured text datasets is to search by keywords or use regular expressions. For the Apple CFO example in the previous chapter, we can retrieve text containing CFO mentions from a corpus containing financial disclosures, hoping that it will contain the join date or tenure information. For instance, you can use the regex:

```
pattern = r"(?i)\b(?:C\.?F\.?O|Chief\s+Financial\s+Officer)\b"
```

Keyword search is limited in its effectiveness. There are a very large number of ways to express CFO join date or tenure in a corpus, if it is present at all. Trying to use a catch-all regex like the above could result in a large proportion of false positives.

Therefore, we need to move beyond keyword search. Over the last few decades, the field of information retrieval has developed several methods like BM25 that have shaped search systems. We will learn more about these methods in Chapter 12. In the LLM era, embedding-based search systems are fast becoming the standard way of implementing search.

In this chapter, we will learn how embeddings work. We will explore the concept of semantic similarity and examine various similarity measures. We will learn how to use popular embedding models and evaluate their performance. We will also show

how to fine-tune embedding models to suit specific use cases and domains. We will show how to interpret these embeddings using sparse autoencoders (SAEs). Finally, we will discuss techniques for optimizing embeddings to reduce storage requirements and computational overhead.

Introduction to Embeddings

Representation learning is a subfield of machine learning that deals with learning to represent data in a way that captures its meaningful features, often in a low dimensional space. In the context of NLP, this involves transforming textual units like words, sentences, or paragraphs into vector form, called embeddings. Embeddings capture semantic (meaning-related) and pragmatic (social context-related) features of the input.

Embeddings can be generated using both open source libraries and paywalled APIs. Sentence Transformers (*https://oreil.ly/4OSVd*) is a very well-known open source library for generating embeddings, and it provides access to embedding models that performs competitively with respect to proprietary ones.

Let's generate embeddings using the `Sentence Transformers` library:

```
from sentence_transformers import SentenceTransformer, util
sbert_model = SentenceTransformer('msmarco-distilbert-base-tas-b')
embedding = sbert_model.encode("American pizza is one of the nation's greatest
cultural exports", show_progress_bar=True, device='cuda',

convert_to_tensor=True)
print("Embedding size:", embedding.shape[0])
print(embedding)
```

Output:

```
Embedding size: 768

tensor([-3.9256e-01,  1.0734e-01,  1.3579e-01,  7.6147e-02,  5.2521e-02,
-6.5887e-03,  1.9225e-01,  3.5374e-01,  2.5725e-01,  5.6408e-02,...])
```

For this model, the embedding size is 768, which means each vector has 768 dimensions. The sequence length of this particular model is 512, which means the input text is restricted to 512 tokens, beyond which it will be truncated. The embedding vector is made up of floating-point numbers, which by themselves are not interpretable. We will discuss techniques for interpreting embeddings later in this chapter.

Most embedding models used today are based on encoder-only language models, which we introduced in Chapter 4. The underlying models are BERT, RoBERTa, MPNet, etc., and are typically fine-tuned on paraphrasing/question-answering/natural language inference datasets. Let's see how to derive embeddings from these types of models (which is what the `sentence_transformers.encode()` function does under the hood):

```
from transformers import AutoTokenizer, AutoModel
import torch

tokenizer=
AutoTokenizer.from_pretrained(
  "sentence-transformers/msmarco-distilbert-base-tas-b")
model =
AutoModel.from_pretrained("sentence-transformers/msmarco-distilbert-base-tas-b")

input = tokenizer(
  'American pizza is one of the nation's greatest cultural exports',
padding=True, truncation=True, return_tensors='pt')

with torch.no_grad():
        output = model(**input, return_dict=True)
       embedding = output.last_hidden_state[:, 0]
print(embedding)
```

In this example, the embedding is drawn from the [CLS] token of the last layer of the DistilBERT model. Other ways of extracting embeddings from models include:

- Mean pooling, where the average is taken across all token outputs in the sequence
- Max pooling, where the maximum value in each dimension across all tokens is taken
- Weighted mean, where more weight is given to the last few tokens
- Last token, where the embedding is just the encoder output of the last token

Whether the last token (or the first token) contains good representations of the entire sequence depends a lot on the pre-training and the fine-tuning objective. BERT's pre-training objective (next-sentence prediction) ensures that the [CLS] token is much richer in representation than, say, RoBERTa, which doesn't use the next-sentence prediction objective and thus its <s> start sequence token isn't as informative.

Recently, decoder-based embedding models have started gaining prominence, like the SGPT family of models (*https://oreil.ly/AztT9*). OpenAI exposes a single embedding endpoint for both search and similarity. OpenAI embeddings have a much larger maximum sequence length (8,192 tokens), and a much larger dimension size (1,536–3,072). Cohere and Jina are examples of other embedding providers.

Choosing the right model for your task depends on cost, latency, storage limitations, performance, and the data domain of your use case. I suggest starting off with the small but effective all-mpnet-base-v2 model available through the Sentence Transformers library, which I consider the workhorse of the field of NLP. As always, experimenting with different models never hurts. More tips on selecting the right models will be provided throughout the rest of the chapter. Later in the chapter, we will also show how to evaluate embedding models and introduce popular benchmarks.

There is no such thing as infinite compression! Embedding sizes are fixed, so the longer your input, the less information can be encoded in its embedding. Managing this tradeoff differs by use case.

Semantic Search

The true value of embeddings can be appreciated when we use them for representing a large text corpus. The vectors representing the data occupy what we call an embedding space. Similar texts are located closer to each other in the embedding space. This property allows us to use similarity measures to accomplish meaningful tasks like clustering or semantic search. Semantic search refers to techniques that take into account the meaning and context of queries and documents to identify documents that are most relevant to a given query.

We can visualize the embedding space by using dimensionality reduction techniques like PCA (*https://oreil.ly/Rk1M9*) or t-SNE (*https://oreil.ly/0xNrB*).

Figure 11-1 depicts the visualization of embeddings of posts on X (formerly Twitter) by members of the US Congress created by Nomic AI (*https://oreil.ly/XsXls*) using its Atlas tool. You can view a detailed version of the visualization at Nomic's blog (*https://oreil.ly/AORpk*).

Let's explore how we can use embeddings for semantic search. For a given user query, we can generate an embedding of the query and then identify document embeddings closest to it in the vector space. The texts corresponding to the top-k (k can be as small as 1 but can vary according to application needs) closest vectors are provided as a response to the search query. This process is called *retrieval*. The texts are then fed into the LLM prompt along with the user query, and the LLM uses the information provided in the context to answer the user query. This two-step process has traditionally been called the *retriever-reader* framework, with the LLM playing the role of the reader in this example.

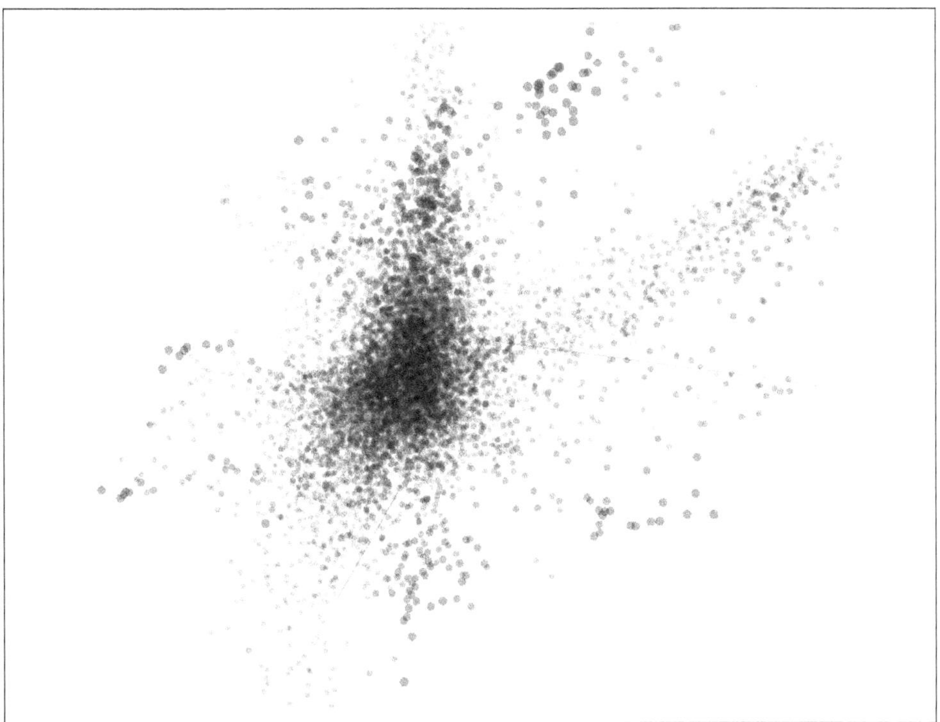

Figure 11-1. Embedding space visualization

As a simple illustrative example, consider two sentences that make up our corpus:

```
chunks = ['The President of the U.S is Joe Biden',
'Ramen consumption has increased in the last 5 months']
```

Given the query "president of usa," we can encode the query and the chunks using Sentence Transformers:

```
from sentence_transformers import SentenceTransformer, util
sbert_model = SentenceTransformer('msmarco-distilbert-base-tas-b')
chunk_embeddings = sbert_model.encode(chunks, show_progress_bar=True,
device='cuda', normalize_embeddings=True, convert_to_tensor=True)
query_embedding = sbert_model.encode(query, device='cuda',
normalize_embeddings=True, convert_to_tensor=True)
matches = util.semantic_search(query_embedding, chunk_embeddings,
score_function=util.dot_score)
```

The output is:

```
[[{'corpus_id': 0, 'score': 0.8643729090690613},
  {'corpus_id': 1, 'score': 0.6223753690719604}]]
```

As you can see, the similarity score is much higher for the first sentence, and thus we return the first sentence as the query response.

There is a distinction between symmetric semantic search and asymmetric semantic search. In symmetric search, the query text is of similar size as the document text. In asymmetric search, the query text is much shorter than the document text, as with search engine and question-answering assistant queries. There are models available that are specialized for only symmetric or asymmetric search. In some models, the query and chunk texts are encoded using separate models.

Similarity Measures

Commonly used similarity measures include dot product, cosine similarity, and Euclidean distance. Refer to the Pinecone (*https://oreil.ly/X_qcD*) tutorial on similarity measures if you need a backgrounder. While using embedding models, use the similarity measure that was used to train the model. You will find this information in the model card or Hugging Face model hub page.

If you set `normalize_embeddings` to `True` as an argument in the `encode()` function, it will normalize the embeddings to unit length. This will ensure that both dot product and cosine similarity will have the same values. Note that dot product is a faster operation than cosine similarity. Sentence Transformers provides separate models (*https://oreil.ly/LOu75*) trained on dot product and cosine similarity and mentions that models trained on dot product tend to prefer longer chunks during retrieval.

Exercise

Experiment with different pooling methods to extract embeddings from models. For reference, you can use the code provided by Sentence Transformers (*https://oreil.ly/8QpBj*). For the same sentences provided in the aforementioned example, how do you notice the similarity scores changing? Repeat the same by trying different similarity measures.

While the notion of semantic similarity is powerful, it is not a panacea for all applications. The semantic similarity task is underspecified. To start with, there are several notions of similarity. Similarity refers to the sameness or alikeness of the entities being compared. But for the same two entities, some dimensions are similar and some are different.

For example, consider the three sentences:

After his 25th anniversary at the company, Mr. Pomorenko confirmed that he is not retiring.

Mr. Pomorenko announced his retirement yesterday.

Mr. Pomorenko did not announce his retirement yesterday.

Now let's use the Sentence Transformers all-mpnet-base-v2 embedding model to encode these sentences and calculate their similarity:

```
!pip install sentence-transformers

from sentence_transformers import SentenceTransformer, util
model = SentenceTransformer('all-mpnet-base-v2')

sentences = ['After his 25th anniversary at the company, Mr. Pomorenko
confirmed that he is not retiring',  'Mr. Pomorenko announced his retirement
yesterday']
embeddings = model.encode(sentences)
cosine_scores = util.cos_sim(embeddings[0], embeddings[1])
print("Cosine Similarity:", cosine_scores.item())
```

Output:

```
Cosine Similarity: 0.7870
```

If you replace the second sentence with "Mr. Pomorenko did not announce his retirement yesterday," the output is:

```
Cosine Similarity: 0.7677!
```

As you can see, both these sentences are perceived as equally similar to the first sentence. In some aspects, this is true. They are similar because they both talk about Mr. Pomorenko. They are also similar because both deal with the subject of retirement. On the other hand, one sentence conveys the opposite meaning to the other, by suggesting a retirement is happening versus not happening.

One way to handle the false positives arising due to the model using undesirable similarity dimensions (like negation) is to just increase the k value in the top-k results that are returned as a response to the query. Then, the LLM can distinguish between false positives and use the correct information for answering the query. However, increasing the top-k also increases the context length of the prompt, increasing latency and cost.

Our application requirements determine which similarity dimensions are important to us. If negation is an important relation for our application to distinguish, it might be a good idea to reflect that in our embedding space. This is where fine-tuning embedding models can come in handy. Fine-tuning embedding models allows you to "edit" your embedding space to your own liking. The process is relatively simple and can be potentially quite beneficial.

Fine-tuning embeddings can also be very useful when you are working with specialized data domains whose token distribution deviates from general-purpose data. Let's now discuss how to fine-tune embedding models.

> **Exercise**
>
> In the example about Mr. Pomorenko's retirement, check how the similarities for these sentences fare when using embeddings from Jina, Nomic, and OpenAI embeddings. What do their similarity scores look like? Is it better or worse than what we see with the all-mpnet-base-v2 model?

Fine-Tuning Embedding Models

The Sentence Transformers library facilitates fine-tuning embedding models using the `SentenceTransformerTrainer` class (*https://oreil.ly/Jahep*). To fine-tune an embedding model, we need a base model to fine-tune on, a training dataset, and a learning objective.

Base Models

You can fine-tune a fine-tuned model like all-mpnet-base-v2, or you can fine-tune a base model like MPNet, from which all-mpnet-base-v2 is defined. You will need more training data to fine-tune a base model than to further fine-tune an already fine-tuned model. Other candidates' models for fine-tuning include BGE-M3 (*https://oreil.ly/Sh8pZ*) and jina-embeddings-v3 (*https://oreil.ly/lFiWX*). A full list of models available through Sentence Transformers can be accessed online (*https://oreil.ly/Onyuv*). Remember to check the licenses for a given model before using it for commercial purposes.

Some of the factors to keep in mind while choosing a base model include the performance of the base model, the size of the embedding models (which determines how fast the model can encode text), the number of dimensions of the model (which determines the amount of storage taken up by the embeddings), and the licensing implications. The MPNet or all-mpnet-base-v2 is a solid first choice that has served me well on many projects.

If a model has been fine-tuned for a particular task like semantic search, it is not optimal to further fine-tune it on a different task.

Training Dataset

There are many different ways to structure your dataset. The most common way is in the form of triplets consisting of (anchor, positive, negative) examples. For a given anchor sentence, the positive sentence is a sentence we would like to be closer to the anchor sentence in embedding space, and the negative sentence is a sentence we would like to be farther apart from the anchor in embedding space. For example, to fine-tune the model to help it distinguish negation sentences, our training set can be composed of triplets where the negative sentence contradicts the anchor and the positive sentences.

Figure 11-2 shows an embedding dataset composed of triplets for helping the model distinguish negation.

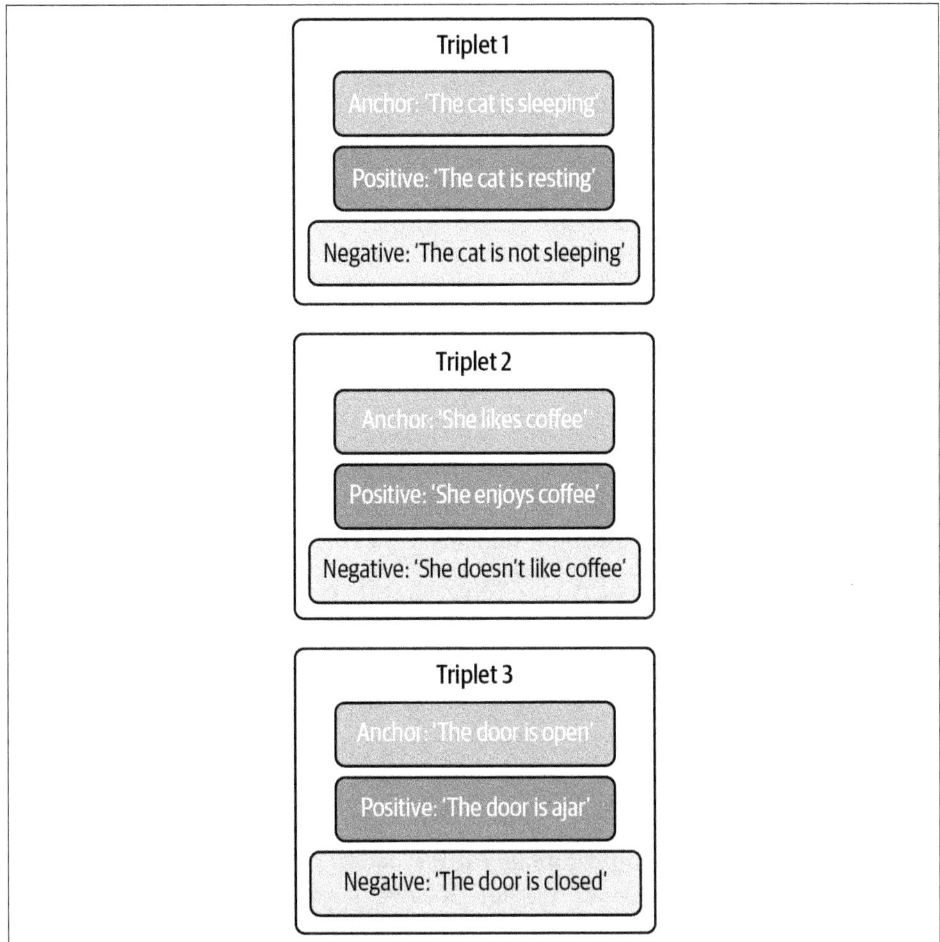

Figure 11-2. Fine-tuning dataset for negation

Hard Negatives

For the negation dataset, it is trivial to fill in the negative examples. But in all other cases it is not exactly obvious what comprises a negative example.

One way is to use random sentences from the corpus as negative examples. But for more effective fine-tuning, it is customary to use hard negatives. Hard negatives are examples that are somewhat relevant to the anchor but just not as relevant as the positive example.

A simple method for selecting false negatives is to use the anchor as a query and find the top-k matches in a document corpus using an embedding model that are not already determined as positive examples. To ensure that the extracted examples are not false negatives, i.e., they are more relevant or just as relevant as the positive example, we can use a relevance score threshold (retrieve only examples with cosine similarity below 0.7) or a top-k range (only retrieve examples between top-30 and top-50).

Moreira et al. (*https://oreil.ly/tIs81*) show that false negatives can further be alleviated by leveraging the relevance score of the positive example. The relevance score threshold for a negative example can be set as the relevance score of the positive example plus a fixed margin. The threshold can also be a percentage of the relevance score of the positive example.

Datasets can also be composed of sentence pairs, where the sentences could represent a (query, response) pair, or a (passage, summary) pair, or a pair of paraphrases. The downstream use cases determine the type of dataset needed. The Sentence Transformers website (*https://oreil.ly/geI1M*) shows all the different ways a dataset can be formatted.

Training datasets can be as small as a few thousand examples, to billions of tokens (*https://oreil.ly/oNI4n*) when used for domain adaptation.

Note that certain loss functions require your dataset to be in a specific format. We will discuss loss functions in detail next.

Loss Functions

Recall our discussion on loss functions for training LLMs in Chapter 4. The Sentence Transformers library (*https://oreil.ly/9Qaop*) supports a wide range of loss functions for training embedding models. Let's explore a few commonly used ones.

For a triplet dataset, you can compute a triplet loss (*https://oreil.ly/yXHNU*). For a training dataset consisting of an (anchor, positive, negative) triplet, the triplet loss minimizes the distance between the anchor sentence and the positive sentence, and maximizes the distance between the anchor sentence and the negative sentence.

Mathematically, the loss is calculated as:

Loss = max(d(a, p) – d(a, n) + margin, 0)

where d is a distance measure, typically Euclidean distance. The margin is a hyperparameter that represents the distance by which the negative example should be farther away from the anchor than the positive example. When using Euclidean distance as the distance measure, I suggest a margin of 5, but make sure to tune it if you are not getting sufficient results.

If you are using a dataset composed of pairs like (query, response), (passage, summary), etc., you can use the Multiple Negatives Ranking Loss (*https://oreil.ly/oNcsQ*).

In a batch containing (query, response) pairs (q1, r1), (q2, r2)...(qn, rn), for each query, there will be a positive pair, e.g., (q1, r1) and n – 1 negative pairs, e.g., (q1, r2), (q1, r3)...etc. The loss function minimizes the negative log likelihood.

Use `CachedMultipleNegativesRankingLoss` (*https://oreil.ly/QwBlI*), available in Sentence Transformers, which allows you to use larger batch sizes, leading to better performance.

Now that we have discussed all the ingredients needed for fine-tuning, let's put it all together with the `SentenceTransformerTrainer` class:

```
from datasets import load_dataset
from sentence_transformers import SentenceTransformer, SentenceTransformerTrainer
from sentence_transformers.losses import TripletLoss

model = SentenceTransformer( "'all-mpnet-base-v2'")

dataset = load_dataset("csv", data_files="negatives_dataset.csv")

loss = TripletLoss(model)

trainer = SentenceTransformerTrainer(
    model=model,
    train_dataset=dataset
    loss=loss
  )
trainer.train()
model.save_pretrained("mpnet_finetuned_negatives")
```

The full code is available in the book's GitHub repo (*https://oreil.ly/llm-playbooks*).

Watch out for overfitting! You can reduce your learning rate if you notice the model overfitting.

Exercise

Using an LLM of your choice, create a synthetic triplet dataset with around 8,000 examples where the negative example is the negation of the positive example, and fine-tune the all-mpnet-base-v2 model. After fine-tuning, test the cosine similarity of the sentences in the negation example provided earlier in the chapter. Do you see any improvements?

Zhou et al. (*https://oreil.ly/BPdRD*) show that in the context of embeddings, cosine similarity tends to underestimate the similarity between high-frequency words. This is because high-frequency words occupy distinct regions in the embedding space, leading to larger distances from other words. On the other hand, low-frequency words tend to be more concentrated geometrically.

Instruction Embeddings

So far we have seen that embedding models are specialized for solving a specific task, like semantic search or paraphrasing. A recent development ties together embedding models and the concept of instruction-tuning, which we discussed in Chapter 6. Imagine if you could use the same embedding model to generate different embeddings for the same document, based on the task it is going to be used for. One such model is called Instructor. Instructor embeddings (*https://oreil.ly/mSIhG*) allow you to optionally specify the domain, text type (whether it is a sentence, paragraph, etc.), and task, along with the text during encoding.

Here is an example:

```
!pip install InstructorEmbedding

from InstructorEmbedding import INSTRUCTOR
model = INSTRUCTOR('hkunlp/instructor-large')

customized_embeddings = model.encode(
[['Represent the question for retrieving supporting documents:',
  'Who is the CEO of Apple'],
 ['Represent the sentence for retrieval:',
  'Tim Cook is the CEO of Apple'],
 ['Represent the sentence for retrieval:',
```

```
    'He is a musically gifted CEO'],
)
```

The creators of Instructor recommend using this instruction template:

```
'Represent the {domain} {text_type} for {task_objective}:'
```

where `{domain}` represents the domain of the text like law, finance, etc. The optional `{text_type}` represents the unit of text being encoded, like a question, sentence, paragraph, etc. `{task_objective}` represents the task for which we are using the embeddings, like semantic search, paraphrase detection, etc.

In the context of semantic search, they recommend the instruction "Represent the question for retrieving supporting documents" for queries, and "Represent the sentence for retrieval" for documents.

Another way the principle of instruction-tuning can be applied to retrieval is with *description-based retrieval*, where the query can be the description of the text that needs to be retrieved, rather than an instantiation (example) of the text that needs to be retrieved. Ravfogel et al. (*https://oreil.ly/rp8Q-*) have published description-based retrieval models that in my experience are very effective. Note that these models have a dual-encoder setup: separate models are used to encode the query and documents.

Exercise

Encode the Wikipedia dataset found in the book's GitHub repo (*https://oreil.ly/llm-playbooks*) using the `INSTRUCTOR` and the description-based retrieval models abstract-sim-query (*https://oreil.ly/zYgAW*) and abstract-sim-sentence (*https://oreil.ly/S7iat*). For the question-answering task, how do they perform compared with the embedding models we have used so far?

Evaluating Embedding Models

A dizzying number of embedding models are available these days. Which one should you use? Massive Text Embedding Benchmark (MTEB) (*https://oreil.ly/MJ-Di*) is a benchmark that can help you make the decision. MTEB covers a diverse set of tasks and benchmarks both latency and task performance, enabling you to reason about the tradeoff.

Check out the current leaderboard (*https://oreil.ly/aLEPi*), which is updated regularly. While there is no clear winner across all tasks, you can see that larger models generally perform better, and not much separates the first 50 or even 100 models. Recall our discussion in Chapter 5 on the limitations of public benchmarks, so do not rely too much on MTEB rankings. Your final decision on embedding model choice should balance your application-specific needs, pricing, latency, and performance tradeoffs.

Optimizing Embedding Size

Many applications involve generating billions of embeddings. As we have seen, modern embeddings sometimes have as many as thousands of dimensions. If each dimension is represented in float32, then it needs four bytes of memory per dimension. Therefore, storing 100 million vectors generated from the all-mpnet-base-v2 model, which has 768 dimensions, needs close to 300 GB of memory!

It is not uncommon to represent a single sentence, almost always no longer than 40 tokens, with a 768-dimension vector. Do we really need 768 dimensions to represent 40 tokens? The reality is that embedding training is very inefficient, and a large number of dimensions are not really useful.

Therefore, several embedding truncation and quantization approaches have been developed to optimize embedding size and reduce storage and compute requirements. If you are operating in an environment with more than a few million vectors, these techniques are likely to be useful to you. Let's look at some of these approaches.

Matryoshka Embeddings

Matryoshka embeddings are named after Matryoshka dolls (*https://oreil.ly/OC6Yj*), which refer to a set of wooden dolls that are placed inside each other in decreasing order of size, originating from Russia. Matryoshka embeddings are trained such that the earlier dimensions of the vector contain more important information than the later dimensions. This allows us to truncate vectors depending on the requirements of the application with respect to cost, latency, and performance.

The technique used to train these embeddings is called Matryoshka Representation Learning (MRL). In MRL, we first choose a set of truncation dimensions. For example a 1,024-dimension vector can have truncation dimensions 128, 256, 512, and 768. During the training process, we calculate the loss over each of the truncation dimensions as well as the full dimension. The losses are then added and weighted. In our example, the first 128 dimensions learn from the loss calculated over the first 128, 256, 512, 768, and 1,024 dimensions of the vector. The end result is that the initial dimensions of the vector will encode more important information because they learn from richer losses.

Training using MRL is supported by the Sentence Transformers library. Let's see how it works in practice:

```
from sentence_transformers import SentenceTransformer
from sentence_transformers import SentenceTransformerTrainer, losses
from datasets import load_dataset

model = SentenceTransformer("all-mpnet-base-v2")
train_dataset = load_dataset("csv", data_files="finetune_dataset.csv")
loss = losses.MultipleNegativesRankingLoss(model)
```

```
loss = losses.MatryoshkaLoss(model, loss, [768, 512, 256, 128]])

trainer = SentenceTransformerTrainer(
    model=model,
    train_dataset=train_dataset,
    loss=loss,
)
trainer.train()
```

Tom Aarsen (*https://oreil.ly/sA5fo*) observed in his experiments that even at 8.3% of the original embedding size, the Matryoshka model preserves 98.37% of the original performance. This makes it a very effective technique that will come in handy when you are working with large datasets.

Similar to how we can reduce the effective dimension of our embeddings using MRL, we can also reduce the effective number of layers of the embedding model, leading to faster inference. This is done by extracting embeddings from the lower layers of the model. To facilitate the lower layers of the model aligning high-quality embeddings with the embeddings of the last layer of the model, a K-L divergence loss is employed between the final layer and each of the lower layers. This technique was first introduced by Li et al.'s (*https://oreil.ly/fzIPD*) Espresso Sentence Embeddings.

Tom Aarsen (*https://oreil.ly/DIoTe*) observed in his experiments that removing half the layers leads to a 2x improvement in speed with 85% of the original performance preserved.

The Sentence Transformers library allows you to combine Matryoshka representations with layer reduction using the Matryoshka2dLoss (*https://oreil.ly/xzG-a*).

Exercise

Download this dataset by Rishabh Misra containing news headlines (*https://oreil.ly/Tu4XA*). Use the nomic-embed-text-v1.5 model (*https://oreil.ly/jALJE*) from Nomic AI, which has been trained using MRL. Pick one of the headlines as the query and generate its query embedding. Generate document embeddings for all other headlines, and calculate similarity scores between query and document embeddings at truncation checkpoints 1,024, 768, 512, 256, and 128.

Perform error analysis on the top 25 results. At what dimension do you start seeing a noticeable performance drop?

Additionally, run the example training script for Matryoshka2dLoss provided by Sentence Transformers (*https://oreil.ly/Bxe5z*), and test the embeddings at various layer and dimension cutoffs.

Binary and Integer Embeddings

An alternative to truncation is quantization. With binary and integer quantization, the number of vector dimensions remains the same, but each dimension is represented by fewer bits. Recall that typically embedding vectors are represented in float32, thus taking four bytes of memory per dimension.

At the extreme level, the four bytes can be represented with just one bit, resulting in a 32x reduction in storage requirements. This type of compression is generally done by sacrificing the precision of the vector values.

A simple way to convert a four-byte vector to a one-bit vector is to assign a value of 1 if the original value is positive, and 0 if it is negative. Note that you might need to perform some scaling to achieve best results. After packing these bits into bytes, a 512-dimension vector can be represented in just 512 / 8 = 64 bytes, instead of 512 × 4 = 2,048 bytes.

Another advantage with using binary embeddings is that computing similarity only needs simple bitwise operations, thus vastly speeding up retrieval. However, quantization negatively affects performance.

You can use the `Sentence Transformers` library to quantize embeddings:

```
from sentence_transformers.quantization import quantize_embeddings

model = SentenceTransformer("all-mpnet-base-v2")
embeddings = model.encode(["I heard the horses are excited for Halloween.",
"Dalmatians are the most patriotic of dogs.", "This restaurant is making me
nostalgic."])
binary_embeddings = quantize_embeddings(embeddings, precision="binary")
```

`quantize_embeddings` also supports int8 quantization. In this scheme, the four bytes representing each dimension are converted into an integer value, represented in one byte. The integer can be either signed or unsigned, thus representing values between –127 and 127 or between 0 and 255, respectively. The conversion process is guided using a calibration dataset of embeddings, from which we calculate the minimum and maximum value of each dimension. These values are then used in the normalization formula to convert the numbers from one range to another.

It has been shown that for some embedding models (*https://oreil.ly/Mp3pu*), binary embeddings perform better than int8 embeddings despite the reduced precision! This is largely because of the calibration dataset used and the challenge involved in mapping float values to buckets of int8 values.

Product Quantization

Another promising quantization method is called *product quantization* (*https://oreil.ly/aJq2C*). In this technique, a vector is divided into chunks of equal size. The chunks are then clustered. The number of clusters is set to the number of values that can be represented by the quantized embedding. For example, if we aim to quantize to int8, then the number of values that can be represented is 256, and thus the number of clusters is 256. Each cluster is associated with an identifier, which is a unique value between 0 and 255. Each chunk belongs to the cluster whose centroid the chunk is closest to.

Thus, the original float32 vector can now be represented by a list of cluster identifiers corresponding to the clusters the chunks belong to. The larger the chunk size, the more the compression. Thus if the vector is divided into five chunks, the resulting embedding will have only five dimensions. Unlike int8 and binary quantization, product quantization also reduces the number of dimensions needed to represent a vector. However, the performance drop is higher.

Choose your quantization technique by determining your relative product priorities for criteria like cost, performance, and speed.

Optimizing embeddings for storage come with a performance hit. However, if there is plenty of redundancy in the document corpus, answers to typical user queries might be found in several documents, and hence the user may not feel this performance drop.

Exercise

Download the Wikipedia embeddings (*https://oreil.ly/OUq5M*) encoded with Cohere's embedding model and implement product quantization by setting the number of clusters to 256. You can also use a vector database, like Qdrant, that supports product quantization. Experiment with different chunk sizes. Where do you see the highest performance drop-off?

Additionally, implement the similarity scoring function for product quantization.

Now that we have seen various techniques to practically implement embedding-based retrieval, let's next figure out the textual units we need to embed into distinct vectors.

Chunking

As noted in "Introduction to Embeddings" on page 260, embedding models support very limited context lengths, and the effectiveness of embedding similarity matching decreases as the text length increases. Therefore, it is natural to split documents into manageable units called chunks and embed each chunk into one or more vectors.

A chunk can be defined as a semantically coherent and not necessarily contiguous part of a document. The average chunk length depends on the context length supported by the language model, and the number of chunks returned to the model (the top-k) in response to a user query. As models become increasingly affordable to operate and support ever-larger context lengths, the permissible chunk size grows.

Each chunk can either be represented by a single vector or can be further broken down into units, with each unit being represented by a separate vector. A unit could be a sentence, a paragraph, or even a section. Typically, the smaller the unit, the better. For your application, test your expected user queries against different granularities and see what works best.

Document Parsing

Unstructured data first needs to be processed to make it amenable to retrieval. This usually involves parsing text from the document, splitting it into manageable units, associating metadata with these units, generating embeddings, storing, and indexing them for easy access.

If it makes sense for your use case to have sentences as the basic unit of text, NLTK's Punkt tokenizer (*https://oreil.ly/bgxrp*) is a tried and tested tool for tokenizing text into sentences. Note that sentence tokenization is not a trivial task, especially if you have domain-specific text. Naive splitting on end marks (periods, question marks, and abbreviations) can only get you so far; abbreviations play spoilsport. You can train the Punkt tokenizer unsupervised over a large body of your target text to ensure it learns your domain-specific rules, as well as provide explicit rules and exceptions yourself. Other tools for sentence tokenization include spaCy (*https://oreil.ly/R7mFQ*), Stanza (*https://oreil.ly/xKo43*), and ClarityNLP (*https://oreil.ly/fxvBi*).

Overall, effective document parsing (extracting section and subsection boundaries; detecting and extracting tables, images, etc.; dealing with heterogeneous document formats) is the bane of NLP projects. A large proportion of failure modes in RAG can be attributed to poor document parsing. Of all the steps in a typical NLP application pipeline, I have spent the most effort on document parsing. Yes, it might not be the most glamorous task in the world, but it is the foundation on which high-quality products are built. Ignore this at your own peril!

Consider a scenario where a document corpus has been broken down into units represented by embeddings. For a given user query, we can calculate the cosine similarity between the user query vector and each of the document vectors. The chunks corresponding to the most similar vectors are then retrieved. This ensures that the embedding matching happens at a lower granularity, like a sentence, but the model receives the entirety of the chunk the sentence belongs to, thus providing sufficient background context to the model.

> **Exercise**
>
> Construct a sentence tokenizer for the Canadian parliamentary proceedings dataset provided in the book's GitHub repository (*https://oreil.ly/llm-playbooks*). What are the failure modes? Can you use rules to resolve these issues? Try unsupervised training of the Punkt tokenizer using this data. Is it effective in resolving the issues found?

A question I am frequently asked by ML practitioners is, "What is the ideal chunk size and what are some effective chunking strategies?" Determining the right chunk size and boundaries are key challenges practitioners face when using embedding-based retrieval. In this section, we will discuss a few chunking strategies, introduced in order of increasing complexity.

In the basic implementation of embedding-based retrieval, each vector is a distinct island, disconnected from all other islands. The text represented by Vector A is not able to influence text represented by Vector B in any way. Therefore, we need to connect these islands in some way or make these islands as self-contained as possible. With these objectives in mind, let's look at some chunking strategies that go beyond naive paragraph or section splitting.

Sliding Window Chunking

Consider a situation where the embedding similarity function returns a unit in Chunk 45 as the most similar vector to your query vector. However, text in Chunk 44, which immediately precedes Chunk 45 in the document, contains relevant information contextualizing Chunk 45. The vectors in Chunk 44 have a very low similarity score with the query, and as a result, Chunk 44 is not selected for retrieval. One way to fix this is by using sliding window chunking, where each text can be present in multiple chunks, thus allowing neighboring context to be effectively represented in a coherent block.

Metadata-Aware Chunking

Any metadata that you have about the document can be leveraged to determine chunking boundaries. Useful metadata information includes paragraph boundaries, section and subsection boundaries, etc. If the metadata isn't already available, you might need to use document parsing techniques to extract this information. Several libraries can facilitate this, including Unstructured (*https://oreil.ly/CoX46*).

Layout-Aware Chunking

A more involved form of metadata-aware chunking is layout-aware chunking. In this approach we use computer vision techniques to extract layout information about the document, including the placement and scope of textual elements, the titles, subtitles, font size of text, etc.; use this metadata to inform the chunking process. Both open source and proprietary tools can facilitate layout extraction. They include tools like Amazon Textractor (*https://oreil.ly/fvkiT*), Unstructured (*https://oreil.ly/CoX46*), and layout-aware language models like LayoutLMv3 (*https://oreil.ly/Od5fA*).

For example, using this approach we can know the scope of a subsection, and thus insert the subsection title at the beginning of each chunk comprising text from that subsection.

You can also use techniques like ColPali that employ vision models to directly embed a page or section of the document and perform retrieval over it. This may remove the need for chunking entirely but might be more expensive overall.

Semantic Chunking

The principle behind semantic chunking is that similar information should be grouped into coherent chunks. Paragraph boundaries provide a weak signal for semantic chunking, but more advanced methods can be employed. One approach is to cluster the document based on topics, with each chunk containing information pertaining to the same topic. The chunks need not necessarily be built from contiguous text if it makes sense for the application. A more advanced approach is to use Bollinger bands-based chunking (*https://oreil.ly/1MwK1*). The book's GitHub repository (*https://oreil.ly/llm-playbooks*) contains an experimental implementation of this form of chunking.

Semantic chunking can also be employed to connect different chunks with each other. Once the chunks have been assigned, similar chunks can be grouped based on embedding similarity, allowing them to be retrieved along with the chunk having the highest similarity score. Each chunk does not necessarily need to consist of content from the same document, as long as the metadata associated with each sub-chunk is retained.

A basic implementation of semantic chunking is available in LangChain (*https://oreil.ly/tm8tk*).

Highly performant semantic chunking can be performed through LLMs. But it will be a huge cost overhead if the size of your data corpus is very large. Sometimes good old regex can be enough. Jina AI created a complex 50-line regex-based chunker (*https://oreil.ly/x5UO8*) that you can try as an initial option.

Despite using all these techniques, effective chunking still remains a problem. Consider the following real-world example from a financial document:

> Page 5: *All numbers in the document are in millions*
>
> Page 84: *The related party transaction amounts to $213.45*

In this case the related party transaction actually amounts to $213M dollars but the LLM would never know this because the text from page 5 is not likely to be part of the same chunk.

A related problem is the difficulty in understanding scope boundaries. When does a subsection end and a new subsection begins? What is the scope of the rule in page 5 in the given example? What if it is overridden in the middle of a document? Not all documents have perfect visual cues or structure. Not all documents are well structured into sections, subsections, and paragraphs. These are unsolved problems and are the cause of a sizable proportion of RAG failure modes.

Late Chunking

One way of supporting long-range dependencies in text is to use late chunking (*https://oreil.ly/IxTQx*), a method introduced by Jina AI. Recall from earlier in the chapter that embeddings are generated by typically pooling the vectors from the last layer of the underlying language model.

Given that we have access to long-context language models that can accept an entire long document in a single input, we can use such a long-context model as our underlying model for generating embeddings. We feed an entire document (or as large a part as the model can handle) to the long-context model, so that vectors are generated for each of the input tokens. As explained in Chapter 4, each token vector encapsulates its meaning based on its relationship with all other tokens in the sequence. This enables long-context dependencies to be captured.

The pooling operation to extract the embeddings is performed on smaller segments of the input, where the segment boundaries can be determined by any of the chunking algorithms. Thus, we can have several embeddings representing the same document but each of them representing distinct parts of the input.

Exercise

Take Apple's annual report (*https://oreil.ly/Vfizz*), called a 10-K. This is a perfect document for experimenting with chunking strategies, as it is long, contains a large number of sections, sub-sections, and sub-sub-sections; contains tables; and its content has long-range dependencies. Split this document into chunks using all the different strategies presented in this chapter and generate vectors for them. Try asking questions about the annual report and evaluate the results. What chunking strategies are the most effective? What is the ideal granularity for generating the vectors?

Vector Databases

Depending on your application, you may have to deal with millions or billions of vectors, with the need to generate and store new vectors and their associated metadata tags every day. Vector databases facilitate this. Both self-hosted and cloud-based, open source, and proprietary options are available. Weviate, Milvus, Pinecone, Chroma, Qdrant, and LanceDB are some of the popular vector databases. More established players like ElasticSearch, Redis, and Postgres also provide vector database support.

These days, the features provided by vector databases are converging, given the prevalence of a small set of very popular retrieval use cases.

Let's now look at how vector databases work. Probably the simplest one to get started with is Chroma, which is open source and can run locally on your machine or can be deployed on AWS:

```
!pip install chromadb

import chromadb
chroma_client = chromadb.Client()

collection = chroma_client.create_collection(name="mango_science")
chunks = ['353 varieties of mangoes are now extinct',
'Mangoes are grown in the tropics']
metadata = [{"topic": "extinction", "chapter": "2"}, {"topic": "regions",
  "chapter": "5"}]
unique_ids = [str(i) for i in range(len(chunks))]

collection.add(
   documents=chunks,
   metadatas=metadata,
   ids=unique_ids
  )
results = collection.query(
   query_texts=["Where are mangoes grown?"],
   n_results=2,
```

```
        where={"chapter": { "$ne": "2"}},
        where_document={"$contains":"grown"}
    )
```

Most vector databases offer:

- Approximate nearest neighbor search in addition to exact search, to reduce latency
- Ability to filter using metadata, like the *where* clause in SQL
- Ability to integrate keyword search or algorithms like BM25
- Support Boolean search operations, so that multiple search clauses can be combined with AND or OR operations
- Ability to update or delete entries in the database in real time

Multi-Level Embeddings

If your retrieval performance requirements are stringent, a good strategy is to use multiple levels of embeddings if the cost justifies it. As an example, you can have sentence embeddings, paragraph or dialog-turn embeddings, section/subsection embeddings, or even document embeddings. The higher-level embeddings can represent the summary of the text and not necessarily the verbatim text itself.

You can use different embedding models at each level. As you go up in granularity, you can use more expensive and high-quality embedding models.

Depending on your specific use case, you can start from the top level and then propagate to the bottom like a tree or directly target a particular level.

Interpreting Embeddings

What features of text do embeddings learn? Why are two sentences sometimes closer to/farther from each other in the embedding space than we expect? Can we know what each dimension of an embedding vector represents?

A key limitation in embedding-based retrieval compared to traditional techniques is the lack of interpretability in ranking decisions. There is a whole body of research dedicated to improving interpretability of neural networks, LLMs, and embeddings. In Chapter 5, we introduced some interpretability techniques for understanding LLMs. In this section, we will focus on embedding interpretability in particular. One benefit of understanding the features represented in embedding space is that we could leverage that knowledge to steer embeddings for our own purposes.

One promising technique for imparting interpretability is to use SAEs. Let's understand what they mean and how they are trained and used to enhance interpretability.

A language model may learn millions of features, but for any given input, only a few of those features are relevant or activated. This is what we mean by sparsity. Even as they learn lots of features, there are only a limited number of dimensions in an embedding vector. Therefore, each dimension contributes to many features that can interfere with each other. If you train a sparse autoencoder (*https://oreil.ly/oiXb7*) over these embeddings, you can derive independent interpretable features.

In his Prism project (*https://oreil.ly/efzz1*), Linus Lee uses SAEs to explore the features of a T5-based embedding model.

Some of the identified features include:

- Presence of negation
- Expression of possibility or speculation
- Employment and labor concepts
- Possessive syntax at sentence start

For a longer list of identified features, refer to Linus Lee's blog post (*https://oreil.ly/efzz1*).

Summary

In this chapter, we introduced the concept of embeddings, examined their internals, and showed various techniques for generating them. We also discussed techniques for fine-tuning embeddings on our own data. We learned how to determine the data granularities at which we construct embeddings, discussing several chunking techniques in the process. Finally, we explored techniques to visualize and interpret embeddings.

In the next chapter, we will explore RAG, an application paradigm that is by far the most popular use case for embeddings today. We will present the steps involved in a typical RAG workflow and review each of these steps in detail. We will also discuss the technical decisions involved in building a RAG application and provide pointers on how to think through various tradeoffs.

CHAPTER 12

Retrieval-Augmented Generation

In Chapter 10, we demonstrated how to vastly expand the capabilities of LLMs by interfacing them with external data and software. In Chapter 11, we introduced the concept of embedding-based retrieval, a foundational technique for retrieving relevant data from data stores in response to queries. Armed with this knowledge, let's explore the application paradigm of augmenting LLMs with external data, called retrieval-augmented generation (RAG), in a holistic fashion.

In this chapter, we will take a comprehensive view of the RAG pipeline, diving deep into each of the steps that make up a typical workflow of a RAG application. We will explore the various decisions involved in operationalizing RAG, including what kind of data we can retrieve, how to retrieve it, and when to retrieve it. We will highlight how RAG can help not only during model inference but also during model training and fine-tuning. We will also compare RAG with other paradigms and discuss scenarios where RAG shines in comparison to alternatives or vice versa.

The Need for RAG

As introduced in Chapter 10, RAG is an umbrella term used to describe a variety of techniques for using external data sources to augment the capabilities of an LLM. Here are some reasons we might want to use RAG:

- We need the LLMs to access our private/proprietary data, or data that was not part of the LLM's pre-training datasets. Using RAG is a much more lightweight option than pre-training an LLM on our private data.
- To reduce the risk of hallucinations, we would like the LLM to refer to data provided through a retrieval mechanism rather than rely on its own internal knowledge. RAG facilitates this. RAG also enables more accurate data citations, connecting LLM outputs to their ground-truth sources.

- We would like the LLM to answer questions about recent events and concepts that have emerged after the LLM was pre-trained. While there are memory editing techniques for updating LLM parameters with new knowledge like MEMIT (*https://oreil.ly/kxI3j*), they are not yet reliable or scalable. As discussed in Chapter 7, continually training an LLM to keep its knowledge up-to-date is expensive and risky.
- We would like the LLM to answer queries involving long-tail entities, which occur only rarely in the pre-training datasets.

LLMs Struggle with the Long-Tail

LLMs typically need a lot of samples to memorize a fact. The memorization ability is probabilistic, so we cannot predict the exact number of samples the LLM needs to see during training for it to memorize. This sample-inefficiency means that the LLM will struggle to answer questions about entities and concepts that rarely occur in the training data. As an example, Kandpal et al. (*https://oreil.ly/dqXV4*) show that the accuracy of BLOOM-176B on question-answering is only 25% when the relevant documents occur only 10 times in the pre-training dataset, versus 55% when the relevant documents occur 10,000 times.

Kandpal et al. also show that larger LLMs need relatively fewer examples to memorize a fact. Even then, this leaves a large number of long-tail concepts that the LLM is unable to memorize. The relationship between LLM size and memorization capability is log-linear, meaning that the LLM needs to be in the order of quadrillions of parameters to be competitive on long-tail data-related tasks.

One way to improve the chances of LLM memorization is by training it for more epochs or upsampling data in the training set corresponding to concepts and facts we want memorized. We could also modify the learning objective to upweight the training loss for tokens representing facts.

Curriculum learning, discussed in Chapter 2, is another way to help improve memorization. Jagielski et al. (*https://oreil.ly/5BP_V*) show that samples seen earlier in the training phase tend to be forgotten. Thus we can modify the order in which we show the samples during training to ensure a higher likelihood of memorization for the data we want memorized.

Yet another way to improve performance on long-tail concepts is to use RAG, as we will discuss throughout the chapter.

Exercise

Just about every LLM has been trained on Wikipedia, which is considered a high-quality dataset. Wikipedia contains pages for lesser-known individuals, football (soccer) players of lower leagues, for instance. For any such relatively unknown individual with a Wikipedia page, try asking questions about them to LLMs, where the answers to those questions are on the Wikipedia page. Try this with LLMs of various sizes. Repeat this with relatively more well-known individuals (the size of their pages could be a pseudo-indicator of their popularity). Do you notice the size of the LLM impacting its ability to answer these questions?

Typical RAG Scenarios

Now that we have seen *why* we need RAG, let's explore *where* we can utilize it. The four most popular scenarios are:

Retrieving external knowledge
: This is the predominant use case that has seen a lot of success with productionization. As discussed earlier in the chapter, we can use RAG to plug LLM knowledge gaps or to reduce hallucination risk.

Retrieving context history
: LLMs have a limited context window, but often we need access to more context in order to answer a query than what fits in the context window. We would also like to have longer conversations with the LLM than what fits in the context window. In these cases, we could retrieve parts of the conversation history or session context when needed.

Retrieving in-context training examples
: Few-shot learning is an effective approach to help LLMs get acquainted with the input-output mapping of a task. You can make few-shot learning more effective by dynamically selecting few-shot examples based on the current input. The few-shot examples can be retrieved from a training example data store at inference time.

Retrieving tool-related information
: As described in Chapter 10, LLMs can invoke software tools as part of their workflow. The list of tools available and their description is stored in a tool store. The LLM can then use retrieval for tool selection, selecting the tool best suited to the task. Tool-related information can also include API documentation, for instance.

Deciding When to Retrieve

For each step in an agentic workflow, the LLM can advance its task using one of the following steps:

- Use its internal capabilities
- Choose from among several data stores
- Choose from among several software tools

There can be tasks that the LLM can fully solve using its parametric memory, but one or more data stores may also contain the requisite data needed to solve them. In these cases, should we just default to using RAG, given all its benefits that we presented earlier?

We have seen earlier in the chapter that LLMs struggle with long-tail information, and that RAG can be an effective means to answer questions about long-tail entities. However, Mallen et al. (*https://oreil.ly/MF7Y1*) show that for queries about more popular entities, the LLM might sometimes be better at answering queries than RAG. This is because of the inevitable limitations of the retrieval model, which might retrieve irrelevant or incorrect information that could mislead the LLM.

For a given query, you can dynamically determine whether to use retrieval or to rely on the LLM's parametric memory. The rules determining the right approach to take include:

- Whether the query is about a more frequently occurring entity. For example, the LLM is more likely to memorize the birthday of Taylor Swift than of a substitute drummer of a local band whose Wikipedia page is a stub.
- Whether the query has timeliness constraints, i.e., if the data needed to address the query may not have existed before the LLM's knowledge cutoff date.
- Whether the model has been continually pre-trained or memory tuned as described in Chapter 7, and the given query relates to concepts over which the training was performed.

If you are using LLMs for general-purpose question answering, Mallen et al. show that you can use sources like Wikipedia as a pseudo-popularity metric for entities. If the entities present in your inputs have an entity count in Wikipedia greater than a threshold, then the LLM can choose to answer the question on its own without using RAG. Note that the threshold can change across LLMs. This strategy works only if you have a good understanding about the datasets the LLM has been pre-trained on.

Dynamically deciding when to retrieve data can also help optimize the model's latency and responsiveness, as the RAG pipeline will introduce additional overhead.

Dynamic retrieval is mostly useful when you are using very large LLMs. For smaller models (7B or below), it is almost always beneficial to prefer using RAG rather than relying on the LLM's internal memory.

The RAG Pipeline

A typical RAG application follows the *retrieve-read* framework, as discussed in Chapter 11. In response to a query, a retrieval model identifies documents that are relevant to answering the query. These documents are then passed along to the LLM as context, which the LLM can rely on in addition to its internal capabilities to generate a response. In practice, we typically need to add a lot of bells and whistles to get RAG working in a production context. This involves adding several more optional stages to the retrieve-read framework. In practice, your pipeline stages might consist of a *rewrite-retrieve-read-refine-insert-generate* workflow, with some of these steps potentially comprising multiple stages. Later in the chapter, we will go through each of the steps in more detail.

Figure 12-1 shows the various stages of the RAG pipeline and the components involved.

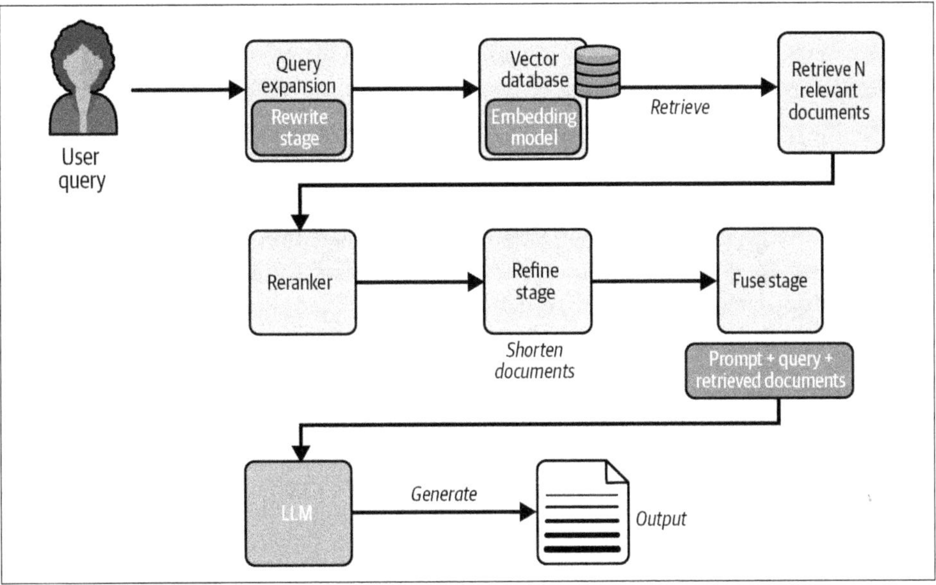

Figure 12-1. RAG pipeline

As in the rest of the book, we refer to user or LLM requests to retrieve data as queries, and units of text retrieved from the data store as documents.

Let's illustrate with an example. Consider a RAG application that answers questions about Canadian politics and parliamentary activity. The application has access to a knowledge base containing transcripts of parliamentary proceedings. We will assume that the data is represented using the representation techniques described in Chapter 11.

When a user issues a query, we might want to rephrase it before sending it to the retriever. Traditionally in the field of information retrieval (IR), this is referred to as query expansion. Query expansion is especially useful because of the vocabulary mismatch between the query space and the document space. The user might use different terminology in the query than that used in the documents. Rephrasing a query can help bridge the vocabulary gap. In general, we would like to rephrase the query in such a way that it improves the chances of the retriever fetching the most relevant documents. This stage is called the *rewrite* stage.

Next, in the *retrieve* stage, a retrieval model is used to retrieve the documents relevant to the query. In Chapter 11, we discussed embedding-based retrieval, a popular retrieval paradigm in the LLM era. The retrieval stage can be an extensive multi-stage pipeline.

The retrieval can happen over a very large document space. In this case, it is computationally infeasible to use more advanced retrieval models. Therefore, retrieval is usually carried out in a two-step process, with the first step using faster methods (these days, typically embedding-based) to retrieve a list of potentially relevant documents (optimizing recall), and a second step that reranks the retrieved list based on relevance (optimizing precision) so that the top-k ranked documents are then taken as the context to be passed along to the LLM. This stage is called the *rerank* stage.

After identifying the top-k documents relevant to the query, they need to be passed along to the LLM. However, the documents may not fit into the context window and thus need to be shortened. They also could potentially be rephrased in a way that makes it more likely for the LLM to use the context to generate the answer. This is done during the *refine* stage.

Next, we provide the output of the refine step to the LLM. The default approach is to concatenate all the documents in the prompt. However, you could also pass them one at a time, and then ensemble the results. How the documents are ordered in the prompt can also make a difference. Several such techniques determine the way the context is fed to the LLM. This is called the *insert* stage.

Finally, in the *generate* stage, the LLM reads the prompt containing the query and the context and generates the response. The generation can happen all at once or the retrieval process can be interleaved with the generation, i.e., the model can generate a few tokens, then call the retrieval model again to retrieve additional content, generate a few more tokens, and then call the retrieval model again, and so on.

The output of each stage can be run through a *verify* stage to assess the quality of the outputs and even take corrective measures. The verify stage can employ either heuristics or AI-based methods.

In this example, the query was generated by a human user. But if we consider RAG in the context of agentic workflows, the query might be generated by an LLM. In an agentic workflow, the agent can determine at any given point that it needs to retrieve data to progress with its task, which sets the aforementioned pipeline into motion.

Apart from the retrieve and generate steps, the rest of the pipeline is optional, and including other steps depends on your performance and latency tradeoffs.

Our example pertains to RAG when used at inference time. RAG can also be applied when pre-training or fine-tuning the model, which we will describe later in the chapter.

Let's examine each step in the pipeline in detail.

Rewrite

After a query is issued, it might need to be rewritten to make it more amenable to retrieval. The rewriting process depends on the retrieval models used. As mentioned before, there is usually a mismatch between the query space and the document space, as the vocabulary, phrasing, and semantics used by the query might vary drastically from how the relevant concepts are conveyed in the document.

As an example, consider the query: "Which politicians have complained about the budget not being balanced?"

and the data store contains the text "Senator Paxton: 'I just can't stand the sight of our enormous deficit.'"

If you are using traditional retrieval approaches that rely more on keywords, this text may not be selected as relevant during retrieval. Using embedding-based methods bridges the gap as embeddings of similar sentences are closer to each other in embedding space, but it does not entirely solve the problem.

If the query is coming from the user, the user might add instructions along with the query, like, "Which politicians have complained about the budget not being balanced? Provide the results in the form of a table." In this case you will have to separate the query from the instructions before feeding the query into the retrieval pipeline. This can be done by an LLM using prompting techniques like CoT, ReAct, etc., which we discussed in Chapters 5 and 10, respectively.

For systems using traditional retrieval techniques, query rewriting is typically performed using query expansion techniques, in which the query is augmented with similar keywords. Basic query expansion techniques include adding synonyms of keywords and other topic information in your query.

A well-tested method for query expansion is pseudo-relevance feedback (PRF). In PRF, the original query is used to retrieve documents, and salient terms from these documents are extracted and added to the original query.

Let's see how PRF would help with our query, "Which politicians have complained about the budget not being balanced?" We use a retrieval technique like BM25 (explained later in the chapter) to return a candidate set of k documents. We then use a technique like term frequency or, more effectively, Tf-IDf (*https://oreil.ly/5be9z*) to extract the salient terms occurring in these returned documents. For this example the salient phrases turn out to be "fiscal policy," "deficit," "financial mismanagement," and "budgetary reforms." Adding these phrases to the original query will lead to the text:

> "Senator Paxton: 'I just can't stand the sight of our enormous deficit!'" being retrieved successfully.

In recent years, LLM-driven query expansion methods are gaining more prominence. Two such examples are Query2doc (*https://oreil.ly/BDJAN*) and Hypothetical Document Embeddings (HyDE) (*https://oreil.ly/tZyUV*).

Let's explore how LLM-based query expansion works. We pass a given query to an LLM and ask it to generate a hypothetical document that contains the answer to the query.

> *Prompt:* For the provided query, generate a hypothetical document in 2 sentences or less that answers the query. Assume the documents are transcripts of Canadian parliamentary proceedings, containing verbatim statements of representatives in the House and Senate.
>
> *Query:* Which politicians have complained about the budget not being balanced?

The prompt contains:

- Instructions to generate a hypothetical document

- Desired length limit of the generated document
- Description of the document corpus containing relevant documents
- The original query

The hypothetical document generated by the LLM is as follows:

> *LLM:* "Honorable Senator Mark Wellington stated, *This government's failure to balance the budget is unacceptable and jeopardizes our economic future.* Similarly, MP Emily Fraser remarked, *We cannot continue on this path of reckless spending without addressing the deficit—it's time for real fiscal responsibility.*"

Using this hypothetical document as the query will return the sentence "Senator Paxton: 'I just can't stand the sight of our enormous deficit!'" with a higher similarity score.

While this hypothetical document is not factually accurate, and laughably so (there are no senators or MPs in Canada named Mark Wellington and Emily Fraser), it does contain verbiage and semantics very similar to what an actual politician would say. If we use this document as the query (optionally combining with the original query), then the chances of it being semantically similar to actual instances of politicians talking about the topic is higher than if matched with the query alone.

The length of the hypothetical document could be similar to the typical length of the retrieval unit. You can use a smaller LLM to generate the hypothetical document, as we do not care for factuality guarantees in this setting. However, smaller models are also not as adept as generating quality hypothetical documents, so you will have to manage the tradeoff. Both LangChain and LlamaIndex provide implementations of hypothetical document-based query rewriting.

If the model has been pre-trained or fine-tuned on the data corpus containing the relevant data, then adding descriptions of the corpus in the prompt as shown in the example will make it more likely that the generated document follows the structure, format, and linguistics of that data corpus.

One pitfall of query rewriting techniques is the risk of topic drift. In the case of hypothetical documents, the document may drift into irrelevant topics after the first few tokens. Upweighting the logits bias for tokens in the query can partially address this problem. PRF techniques are also susceptible to topic drift.

You can also combine PRF style techniques with hypothetical documents. Instead of generating hypothetical documents to replace or augment the query, you can use them to extract keywords that you can add to the original query. Li et al. (*https://oreil.ly/cOnMs*) propose a technique called *query2document2keyword*. In this technique, the LLM generates a hypothetical document using the query, similar to HyDE. The LLM is then prompted to extract salient keywords from this document.

We can then further improve the quality of the extracted keywords by taking them through a filtering step. The authors propose using the *self-consistency* method, which we discussed in Chapter 5. To recap, in the self-consistency method, we repeat the keyword generation multiple times, and then select the top keywords based on the number of generations they are present in.

Another way to combine traditional retrieval with LLM-driven query rewriting is to first return the top-k documents from the initial retrieval step, then use LLMs to generate salient keywords from the returned documents and add them to the query.

Exercise

For the Canadian parliament proceedings example in the book's GitHub repo (*https://oreil.ly/llm-playbooks*), using smaller models like Gemma 2B, Llama 2B, etc., are the hypothetical documents effective? Similarly, try increasing the size of the models and see if the performance increases. What effect does integrating hypothetical documents have on system latency overall?

So far we have discussed techniques that bridge the query document mismatch problem by modifying the query and bringing it closer to the document space. An alternative approach to solve the mismatch problem is to represent the documents in a way that brings them closer to the query space. Examples of this approach include doc2query (*https://oreil.ly/CGUtP*) and contextual retrieval (*https://oreil.ly/ZJuIu*). While document rewriting techniques initially have a large cost if the data stores are very large, they can reduce latency during inference time as no or little query rewriting needs to be performed. On the other hand, query rewriting techniques are simple to implement and integrate into a RAG workflow.

Yet another form of query rewriting is called query decomposition. For complex queries in an agentic workflow, we can have the LLM divide the task into multiple queries that can be executed sequentially or in parallel, depending on how the query was decomposed. We discussed query decomposition techniques in Chapter 10.

If your external data is in a structured form like databases, then the query needs to be rewritten into a SQL query or equivalent, as discussed in Chapter 10.

Now that we have discussed the query rewriting step of the pipeline, let's move on to the retrieve step.

Retrieve

The retrieve step is the most crucial stage of the RAG pipeline. It is easy to see why: all RAG applications are bottlenecked by the quality of retrieval. Even if you are working with the world's best language model, you won't be able to get the correct results if the retrieval step didn't retrieve the correct documents needed to answer the query. Therefore, this step of the pipeline should focus on increasing recall.

Embedding-based retrieval, which we discussed in detail in Chapter 11, is highly popular. However, traditional information-retrieval techniques should not be dismissed. The right technique to use depends on the expected nature of queries (can a significant proportion of them be answered by just keyword or regex match?), the expected degree of query-document vocabulary mismatch, latency and compute limitations, and performance requirements.

The information retrieval (IR) research field has been studying these problems for a long time. Now that retrieval is more relevant than ever in NLP, I am noticing a lot of efforts to reinvent the wheel rather than reusing IR insights. For insights in retrieval research, check out papers from leading IR research conferences like SIGIR, ECIR, TREC, etc.

The Unreasonable Effectiveness of BM25

Despite the existence of advanced deep learning techniques for retrieval, keyword matching/probabilistic retrieval techniques like BM25 (*https://oreil.ly/JqrhO*) can be a very strong baseline and, when paired with query or document rewriting, can potentially even be *good enough* for your application.

Other traditional techniques supported by Apache Lucene/ElasticSearch include term frequency-inverse document frequency (Tf-IDf), divergence from independence (DFI), divergence from randomness (DFR), information based (IB), Dirichlet similarity, and Jelinek Mercer similarity. Each of these measures has several tunable parameters. For more insight on these techniques and how to select the parameter values, check out "Tweaking the Base Score" (*https://oreil.ly/zyke4*).

Embedding-based retrieval methods are not always suitable when you would like all documents containing a specific word or phrase to be retrieved. Therefore it is customary to combine keyword-based methods with embedding methods, called hybrid search. The results from the two methods are combined and fed to the next step of the retrieval pipeline. Most vector databases support hybrid search in some shape or form.

Figure 12-2 shows the retrieval stage in action, using hybrid search.

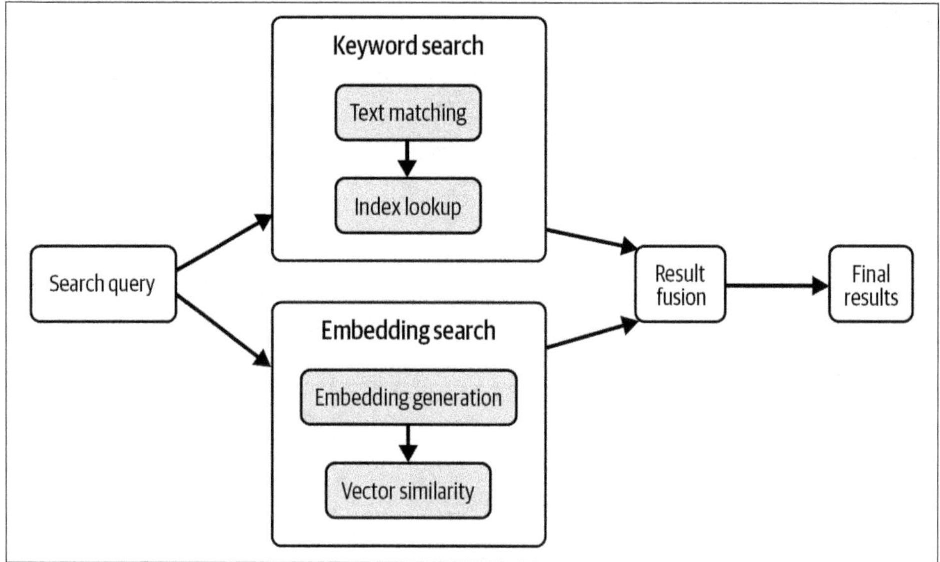

Figure 12-2. Hybrid search

I also highly recommend metadata filters for improving retrieval. The more metadata you gather during the data representation and storage phase, the better the retrieval results. For example, if you have performed topic modeling of your data store in advance, you can restrict your search results to a subset of topics, with the filters being applied either using a hardcoded set of rules or determined by an LLM.

Next, let's discuss promising recent advances in retrieval.

Generative retrieval

What if the LLM could identify the right documents(s) that need to be retrieved in response to a query, thus removing the need for retrieval techniques? This is called generative retrieval.

Generative retrieval is implemented by assigning identifiers to documents called docIDs, and teaching the LLM the association between documents and docIDs. A document can be associated with one or more docIDs. Typical docIDs can be:

Single tokens
: Each document can be represented by a new token in the vocabulary. This means that, during inference, the model needs to output only a single token for each document it wants to retrieve. Pradeep et al. (*https://oreil.ly/7JYOM*) use a T5 model where the encoder vocabulary is the standard T5 vocabulary but the decoder vocabulary contains the docIDs. This approach is feasible only with a small document corpus.

Prefix/subset tokens
: Tay et al. (*https://oreil.ly/1p1C8*) use the first 64 tokens of a document as the docID, while Wang et al. (*https://oreil.ly/lg3g3*) use 64 randomly selected contiguous tokens from the document.

Cluster tokens
: You can also perform hierarchical clustering of your document corpus based on its semantics (using embeddings, for example), and the docID can be a concatenation of the cluster IDs at each level of the hierarchy.

Salient keyword tokens
: The docIDs can also contain salient keywords representing the topics and themes contained in the document. For example, a document about the Transformer architecture can be represented by the docID "transformer_self-attention_architecture."

One way to teach the LLM the association between documents and docIDs is by fine-tuning the model. This is referred to as training-based indexing. However, fine-tuning needs a lot of resources and is not suitable in scenarios in which new documents are frequently added to the corpus.

Askari et al. (*https://oreil.ly/K5TAB*) show that we can use few-shot learning to build a generative retrieval system without needing to train the model. First, for each document in the corpus, pseudo queries are generated using a language model. The pseudo queries are the queries whose answers are present in the document. These pseudo queries are then fed to a language model in a few-shot setting and asked to generate docIDs. Figure 12-3 shows training-free generative retrieval in action.

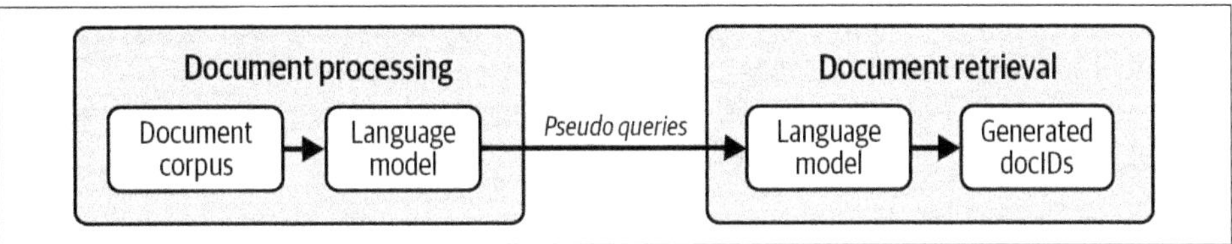

Figure 12-3. Generative retrieval

During inference, the model is provided with a query similar to the setup in Figure 12-3 and asked to generate the correct docID(s) that are relevant to the query. Constrained beam search is used to ensure that the docID generated by the model corresponds to a valid docID in the corpus.

You can also use generative retrieval to retrieve documents based on their metadata. For example, the model could ask to retrieve Apple's 2024 annual report. The model can be made to generate the right identifier by either fine-tuning the model or using few-shot learning, as shown in this section.

Ultimately, generative retrieval is suitable only if your document corpus is relatively small, there is limited redundancy within the corpus, or the documents belong to a set of well-defined categories (annual reports of all public companies in the US, for instance).

Next, let's discuss tightly-coupled retrievers, another new topic in the retrieval space.

Tightly-coupled retrievers

As seen in Chapter 11, in embedding-based retrieval, the embedding model is typically independent of the language model to which the retrieval results are fed. We will refer to them as *loosely-coupled* retrievers.

In contrast, a *tightly-coupled* retriever is trained such that it learns from LLM feedback; the model learns to retrieve text that best positions the LLM to generate the correct output for a given query. Tightly-coupled retrievers can be trained together with the generator LLM as part of a single architecture, or they can be trained separately using feedback from the trained LLM.

An example of the latter is Zhang et al.'s LLM-Embedder (*https://oreil.ly/Q__8M*), a unified embedding model that can support a variety of retrieval needs in a single model, ranging from knowledge retrieval to retrieving optimal few-shot examples. The model is trained from two types of signals: a contrastive learning setup typically used to train embedding models (presented in Chapter 11) and LLM feedback. A retrieval candidate receives a larger reward from LLM feedback if it improves the performance of the LLM in answering the query.

Exercise

Use the LLM-Embedder (*https://oreil.ly/aBwoX*) as the embedding model for the RAG case study provided in the GitHub repo (*https://oreil.ly/llm-playbooks*). How does the LLM-Embedder compare to other embedding models we have worked with so far?

Tightly-coupled retrievers are another tool in your toolkit for improving retrieval. They are by no means a necessary step in the RAG pipeline. As always, experimentation will show how much of a lift (if any) they provide for your application.

Finally, let's discuss GraphRAG, an up-and-coming retrieval paradigm that leverages knowledge graphs for better retrieval.

GraphRAG

A key limitation of the retrieval approaches we have discussed so far is their inability to facilitate answering questions that require drawing connections between different parts of the document corpus, as well as questions that involve summarizing high-level themes across the dataset. For example, all the retrieval techniques we discussed so far would do poorly on a query like, "What are the key topics discussed in this dataset?"

One way to address these limitations is by employing knowledge graphs. Microsoft released GraphRAG (*https://oreil.ly/V4n_S*), a graph-based RAG system. GraphRAG works by creating a knowledge graph from the underlying data corpus by extraction entities and relationships. The graph is then used to perform hierarchical semantic clustering, with summaries generated for each cluster. These summaries enable answering of thematic questions like, "What are the key topics discussed in this dataset?"

GraphRAG requires a lot of initial compute to prepare the knowledge graph. This can be prohibitive for larger datasets. While it is easy to extract entities, extracting relevant relationships is harder.

> **Exercise**
>
> Run GraphRAG indexing over a small subset of the Canadian parliamentary dataset. Examine the entities and relationships extracted. Is the quality satisfactory? Are there missing or spurious relationships?

Now that we have explored the retrieval stage of the RAG pipeline, let's move on to the rerank stage.

Rerank

The retrieval process can be broken into a two-stage or multi-stage process, where the initial stage retrieves a list of documents relevant to the query, followed by one or more *reranking* stages that take the documents and sort them by relevance. The reranker is generally a more complex model than the retriever and thus is run only on the retrieved results (or else we would have just used the reranker as the retriever).

The reranker is usually a language model fine-tuned on the specific use case. You can use BERT-like models for building a relevance classifier, where given a query and a document, the model outputs the probability of the document being relevant to answering the query. These models are called *cross-encoders*, as in these models the query and document are encoded together, as opposed to embedding-based retrieval models we have discussed, called bi-encoders, where the query and document are encoded as separate vectors.

The input for a BERT model acting as a cross-encoder is of the format:

```
[CLS] query_text [SEP] document_text [SEP]
```

The Sentence Transformers library provides access to cross-encoders, which can be used as rerankers in the RAG pipeline:

```
from sentence_transformers import CrossEncoder
model = CrossEncoder("cross-encoder/ms-marco-MiniLM-L-12-v2", num_labels=1)

query = 'When was the Apple iPhone 15 launched?'
documents = ['Apple iPhone 15 launched with great fanfare in New York',
'He was foolish enough to believe that gifting an iPhone would
  save the relationship',
'On September 22, 2023, I lined up at the Central Park store for the launch of
  the iPhone 15']

ranks = model.rank(query, documents)
for rank in ranks:
   print(rank['score'], documents[rank['corpus_id']])
```

Because we have set `num_labels = 1`, the model will treat it as a regression task, using the sigmoid activation function to output a score between 0 and 1.

These days, more advanced models like Contextualized Late Interaction over BERT (ColBERT) (*https://oreil.ly/N3fOv*) are used for reranking. As opposed to the cross-encoder setup we just discussed, ColBERT-style models allow for pre-computation of document representations, leading to faster inference.

In ColBERT, the query and documents are encoded separately using BERT, generating token-level embedding vectors for each token in the query and documents. For each token in the query, the corresponding embedding is compared to the embeddings of each of the token embeddings of the document, generating similarity scores. The maximum similarity scores for each query token are summed, resulting in the final relevance score. This type of architecture is called *late interaction*, since the query and document are not encoded together but interact together only later in the process. Late interaction saves time compared to traditional cross-encoders, as document embeddings can be created and stored in advance.

Figure 12-4 depicts a ColBERT model in action, illustrating the late interaction between query and documents.

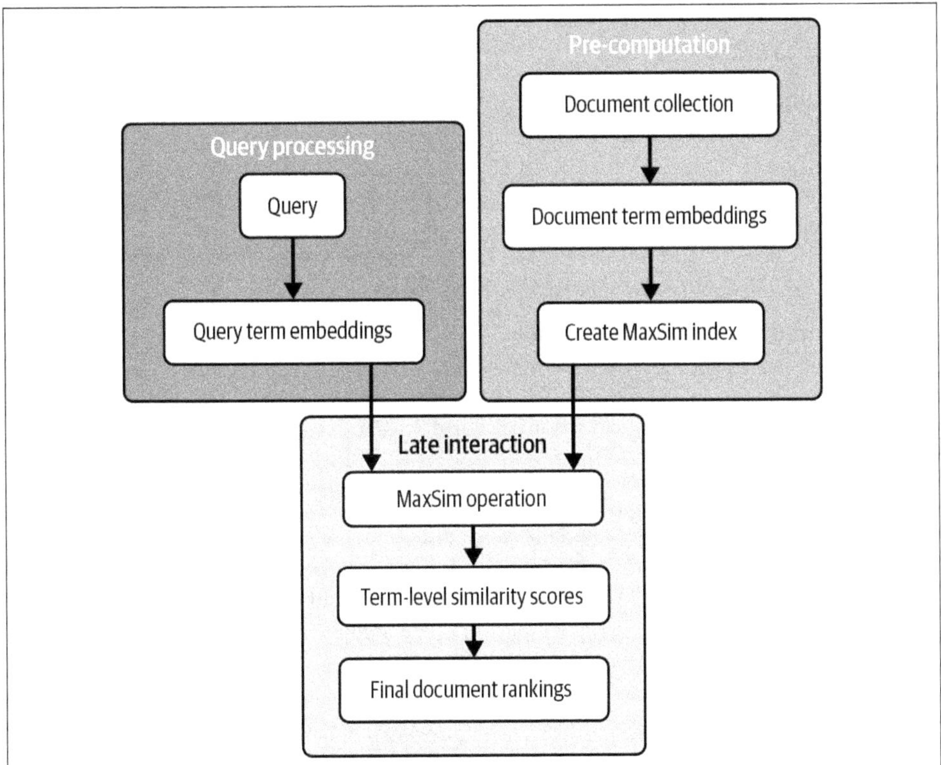

Figure 12-4. ColBERT

> **Exercise**
>
> Compare the performance of bi-encoders like the all-mpnet-base-v2 model and cross encoders like jina-colbert-v2 (*https://oreil.ly/we84L*) by generating embeddings for the iPhone Wikipedia page (*https://oreil.ly/ur7vc*). Try asking a variety of queries. On which type of queries do you see a marked improvement with cross-encoders?

Next, let's explore a few advanced reranking techniques.

Query likelihood model (QLM)

A QLM estimates the probability of generating the query given a candidate document as input. You can treat an LLM as a QLM, utilizing its zero-shot capabilities to rank candidate documents based on the query token probabilities. Alternatively, you can fine-tune an LLM on query generation tasks to improve its suitability as a QLM.

A typical prompt for a QLM would look like: "Generate a question that is most relevant to the given document <document content>".

After getting the top-k documents relevant to a query from the retrieval stage, each document is fed to the LLM with this prompt. The likelihood of the query tokens is then calculated using the model logits. The documents are then sorted by likelihood, providing a relevance ranking.

Zhuang et al. (*https://oreil.ly/QnWWh*) show that an instruction-tuned model that doesn't contain query generation tasks in its instruction-tuning training set loses its capability to be an effective zero-shot QLM. This is yet another case of instruction-tuned models exhibiting degraded performance compared to base models, on tasks they have not been trained on.

Note that to calculate the probability of the query tokens, we need access to the model logits. Most proprietary model providers including OpenAI do not yet provide full access to the model logits as of this book's writing. Thus, the LLM-as-a-QLM approach can be implemented only using open source models.

Exercise

Pick any relatively smaller open source LLM (~3B parameters) and test its suitability as a QLM. For the Canadian parliamentary dataset provided in the book's GitHub repo (*https://oreil.ly/llm-playbooks*), rank candidate retrieval documents using QLM. How effective is it?

In the interest of reducing latency, you would ideally like the QLM to be as small a model as possible. However, smaller models are less effective QLMs. Effectively fine-tuning a smaller LLM for query generation might be the sweet spot.

LLM distillation for ranking

Earlier in the chapter, we saw how encoder-only models like BERT could serve as rerankers. More recently, decoder LLMs are also being trained to directly rank candidate documents in three ways:

Pointwise ranking
: Each candidate document is fed separately to the LLM. The LLM provides a Boolean judgment on its relevance. Alternatively, it can also provide a numerical score, although this is much less reliable.

Pairwise ranking
: For each candidate document pair, the LLM indicates which document is more relevant. To get a complete ranking, N^2 such comparisons need to be made.

Listwise ranking
: All the candidate documents are tagged with identifiers and fed to the LLM, and the LLM is asked to generate a ranked list of identifiers according to decreasing order of relevance of corresponding documents.

In general, pointwise ranking is the easiest to use but may not be the most effective (*https://oreil.ly/DvmtC*). Listwise ranking might need a large context window, while pairwise ranking needs lots of comparisons. Pairwise ranking is the most effective of these techniques, since it involves direct comparison. Figure 12-5 shows how pointwise, pairwise, and listwise rankings work.

Examples of ranking LLMs include RankGPT (*https://oreil.ly/6XoOG*), RankVicuna (*https://oreil.ly/00Dan*), and RankZephyr (*https://oreil.ly/AAbUE*).

These models are trained by distilling from larger LLMs, a technique we first learned in Chapter 9. For example, the process for training RankVicuna is:

- Queries in the training set are fed through a first-level retriever like BM25 to generate a list of candidate documents.
- This list is passed to a larger LLM, which generates a rank-ordered list of candidates.
- The query and the rank-ordered list are used to fine-tune the smaller LLM.

The creators of RankVicuna (*https://oreil.ly/cFLSc*) show that as the effectiveness of the first-level retrieval increases, the possible performance gains from RankVicuna decreases due to diminished returns. They also reported that augmenting the dataset by shuffling the input order of the candidate documents improved model performance.

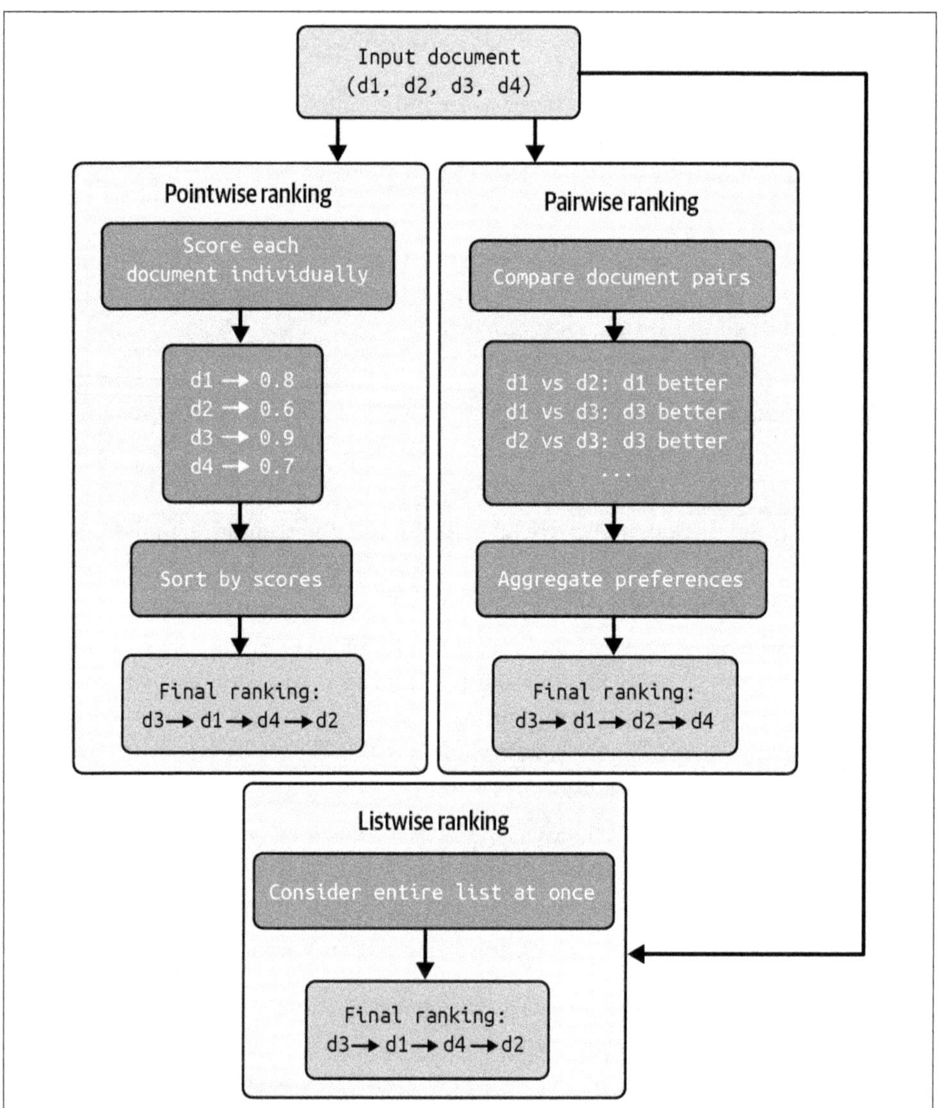

Figure 12-5. Decoder LLM rerankers

Exercise

For the Canadian parliamentary question-answering assistant example available on the book's GitHub repo (*https://oreil.ly/llm-playbooks*), use RankVicuna at the reranking step. Modify the default prompt template and see if it affects the performance.

You can combine the results of the retrieve and the rerank stages to get the final relevance ranking of candidate documents. This is needed to enforce keyword weighting, for example. You can also weight your relevance ranking by metadata like published date (more recent documents are weighted more).

Now that we have discussed the rerank stage, let's move on to the refine step of the RAG pipeline.

Refine

Once the candidate texts relevant to the given query are retrieved and selected, they can be fed to the LLM. However, the LLM context window is limited, so we might want to reduce the length of the retrieved texts. We might also want to rephrase it so that it is more amenable to being processed by the LLM. Another possible operation could be to filter out some of the retrieved texts based on certain rules. All of these are conducted during the *refine* stage. In this section, we will discuss two such techniques, summarization and chain-of-note. Let's start with discussing how we can summarize the retrieved texts.

The refine stage can be a standalone stage, or it can be paired with the final generate stage, where the final response is provided immediately after refining the retrieved documents, as part of the same prompt or prompt chain.

Summarization

Summarization is useful if the retrieval chunks are relatively large. It can be either extractive or abstractive. Extractive summaries extract key sentences from the original text without modifying it. Abstractive summaries are generated from scratch, drawing on content from the original text. The summarizer can also act as a quality filter; it can output an empty summary if the document is irrelevant to the query. Summaries should be relevant, concise, and faithful to the original text.

These summaries are not meant for human consumption but instead meant to be consumed by the LLM. Therefore, they do not always share the same objectives as traditional summarizers. The primary objective here is to generate a summary that helps the LLM output the correct answer.

Should you choose extractive or abstractive summarization? Extractive summaries are almost always faithful as they preserve the meaning of the original text. Abstractive summaries come with the risk of hallucinations. On the other hand, abstractive summaries can potentially be more relevant because of their ability to combine information from different locations within a document and across documents.

While you can leverage the LLM's zero-shot capabilities for both extractive and abstractive summarization, it is more effective (albeit expensive) to fine-tune them so that the summaries generated are specifically optimized to enable the LLM to generate the correct answer. We will call these tightly-coupled summarizers.

Xu et al. (*https://oreil.ly/XCpyr*) introduce techniques for training both extractive and abstractive summarizers. Let's go through them in detail.

For extractive summarization, we would like to extract a subset of sentences from the retrieved document as its summary. This is done by generating embeddings for the input query and for each sentence in the retrieved document. The top-k sentences that are most similar to the input query in the embedding space are selected as the summary. The embedding distance is a measure of how effective the document sentence is in enabling the LLM to generate the correct output.

The extractive summarizer is trained with contrastive learning, which we discussed in Chapter 11. Each training example in contrastive learning is a triplet: the anchor sentence, positive example similar to the anchor sentence, and negative examples dissimilar to the anchor sentence. To generate the training examples, for each sentence in the retrieved document, we prefix it to the input query and calculate the likelihood of gold truth output tokens being generated. The sentence with the highest likelihood is taken as the positive example. For negative examples, we choose up to five sentences whose likelihood is below a threshold. This dataset is then used to train the model.

For abstractive summarization, we can distill a larger LLM, i.e., use the outputs from it to fine-tune a smaller LLM.

To generate the training dataset, we can construct some prompt templates and use them with a larger LLM to generate zero-shot summaries of our retrieved documents. Note that we are generating a single summary of all the retrieved documents. Similar to the extractive summarization technique, for each generated summary, we prefix it to the input text and calculate the likelihood of the correct output tokens. We choose the summary with the highest likelihood to be part of our training set.

During inference, if prefixing any given summary has a lower likelihood of generating the correct output than not prefixing any summary at all, then we deem the text represented by the summary to be irrelevant, and an empty summary is generated. This allows us to filter out irrelevant documents.

Figure 12-6 depicts the workflow of a tightly-coupled abstractive summarizer during training.

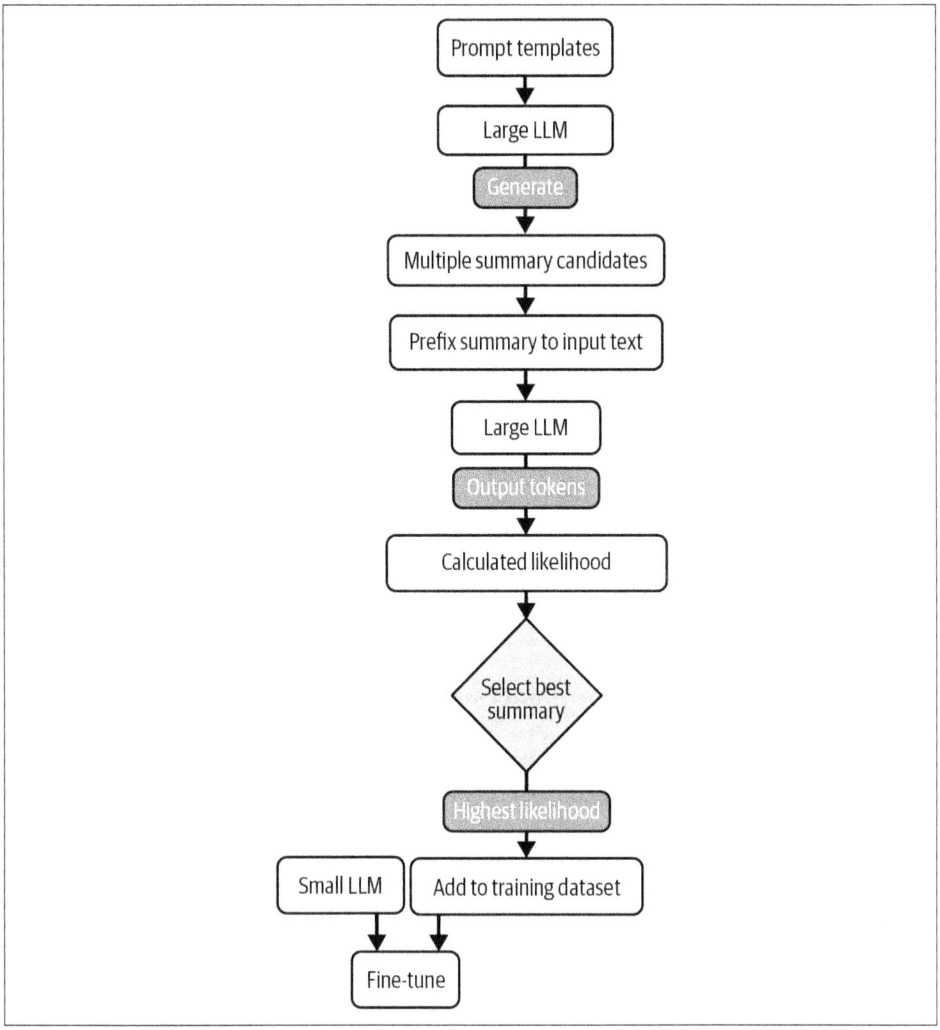

Prompt templates
Large LLM
Generate
Multiple summary candidates
Prefix summary to input text
Large LLM
Output tokens
Calculated likelihood
Select best summary
Highest likelihood
Small LLM
Add to training dataset
Fine-tune

Figure 12-6. Abstractive summarization

If you are planning to change your target LLM, you might want to retrain the summary models. While the summarizers can transfer across models, there is still a slight performance degradation.

Tightly-coupled summarizers, while expensive to train initially, can be an effective means of removing irrelevant information from the retrieved text while rephrasing it in a form that reduces ambiguity for the LLM.

> ### Exercise
>
> Use the examples provided in the book's GitHub repo (*https://oreil.ly/llm-playbooks*) to generate extractive and abstractive summaries of the retrieved documents in the Canadian parliamentary question-answering assistant task. Do the summaries succeed in removing noise? Compare this to a generic summarizer like ChatGPT. How does ChatGPT summarization compare?

Chain-of-note

Another way to rephrase the retrieved text is to generate *notes*.

It would be detrimental if the retrieved text contains irrelevant content that might mislead the model. In essence, the LLM has to contend with three types of scenarios:

- The retrieved documents contain the answer to the user query, and the LLM can use it to generate the correct output.
- The retrieved documents do not contain the answer to the user query, but they provide valuable context that the LLM can then combine with its internal knowledge to come up with the answer.
- The retrieved documents are irrelevant to the user query and should be ignored.

LLMs are not very good at distinguishing between relevant and irrelevant context. One way to address this is by generating notes for each retrieved document that contains a summary of the retrieved document along with indicating whether it contains the answer to the user query or only contains relevant context but not the answer outright, or is irrelevant. This technique is called chain-of-note (CoN), introduced by Yu et al. (*https://oreil.ly/hPkKm*)

Here is an example of how these notes look:

> *Prompt:* Who succeeded Brian Mulroney as the prime minister of Canada in 1993?
>
> Doc 1: Kim Campbell took over the reins of leadership in Canada in 1993, marking her entry into history as the country's first female Prime Minister in 1993. Her tenure, however, was short-lived, as she led the Progressive Conservative Party into a challenging federal election later that year.
>
> Doc 2: Following Brian Mulroney's tenure, Canada witnessed the historic appointment of its first female Prime Minister, marking a groundbreaking shift in the nation's political landscape.

While the first text says Kim Campbell became the prime minister in 1993, it is not apparent whether she immediately succeeded Brian Mulroney or if there was an intervening prime minister. However, the second text makes it clear that it is indeed

Kim Campbell, as the text mentions that Brian Mulroney was succeeded by a female prime minister.

The corresponding note generated by the model is the following:

> *LLM:* The first statement mentions that Kim Campbell took over the leadership in Canada in 1993, and the second statement refers to the period following Brian Mulroney's tenure, leading to the appointment of Canada's first female prime minister. This sequence implies that Kim Campbell's assumption of the prime minister role directly followed Brian Mulroney's tenure, making her his successor.

Using the note as context, the LLM can then generate the correct answer.

The true value of chain-of-note becomes apparent when the context contains irrelevant or insufficient information. The generated note can help the LLM output "I don't know."

Consider this query:

> *Prompt:* Did the Green Party of Canada support the proposed 2023 Public Transit bill?

and the retrieved documents are:

> Doc 1: The Green Party of Canada has historically emphasized the importance of sustainable transportation as a key component of their environmental platform, advocating for policies that promote green infrastructure.
>
> Doc 2: The proposed 2023 Public Transit bill garnered widespread attention and popularity, reflecting a growing public consensus on the importance of sustainable transportation solutions.

The retrieved documents do not contain the answer to the query. The corresponding note generated is:

> *LLM:* While the first passage indicates the party's historical emphasis on sustainable transportation, and the second passage mentions the bill's popularity, neither confirms the party's support or opposition to the 2023 bill.

Using this note, the LLM can generate "unknown" when the retrieved documents do not contain the answer to the query.

An example of a CoN prompt can be:

> *Prompt:* You are provided a query along with {K} passages that potentially contain information that can be used to answer the query. Write notes summarizing the key points from these passages. Discuss the relevance of each of these passages to the given question and state whether the answer to the query can be deduced from the content in these passages.

Again, we can train tightly-coupled CoN models to make it more effective. This can be done by fine-tuning an LLM to elicit CoN behavior.

To generate the fine-tuning dataset, you can prompt an LLM to generate candidate notes for example queries. Human evaluation can then filter out incorrect or poor-quality notes. The final dataset consists of the CoN prompt, the input query, and the retrieved documents as the input, and the corresponding note and the query answer as the output. An LLM can then be fine-tuned on this dataset.

The authors (Yu et al.) introduce a weighted loss scheme during training. The note can be much longer than the answer, and thus equally weighting the loss across all tokens will lead to the note getting significantly more importance during training. This harms model convergence. The weighted loss scheme involves calculating loss across answer tokens 50% of the time.

Using a CoN step is very useful, especially if the retrieval results are known to contain a lot of noise or there is a higher possibility of no relevant documents available to service the query. CoN behavior is harder for smaller models, thus a sufficiently larger model should be used.

Exercise

For the Canadian parliamentary RAG example in the GitHub repo, pose questions to the RAG system where the answers are known not to exist within the Wikipedia corpus. Use CoN prompting on ChatGPT or a similarly larger LLM to generate notes. Do the notes convey the absence of relevant information? Does the LLM acknowledge it cannot answer the question?

Now that we have discussed the refine step of the RAG pipeline, let's move to the insert step.

Insert

Once we have determined the content to be fed to the LLM that is going to generate the final response to a query, whether the original retrieved documents or their summaries or notes, we need to decide how we are going to arrange it inside the prompt.

The standard approach is to stuff all the content, or at least as much as can fit, into the context window. An alternative is to feed each retrieved document/summary/note prefixed to the input separately to the LLM, and then combine the outputs.

Liu et al. (*https://oreil.ly/LFR8r*) show that language models are more adept at recalling information present at the beginning and the end of the context window as compared to the middle. We can exploit this knowledge to reorder the retrieved documents in the prompt.

Let's say we retrieved 10 documents for the given query. The documents are ordered according to their relevance: Doc1, Doc2,...Doc10. These documents can now be arranged in the prompt in the following order:

> Doc1, Doc3, Doc5, Doc7, Doc9, Doc10, Doc8, Doc6, Doc4, Doc2

Thus the least relevant documents exist in the middle of the context window, where they are more likely to be ignored by the model due to current long context recall limitations.

Alternative approaches include arranging the documents in order of relevance, for example:

> Doc1, Doc2, Doc3, Doc4, Doc5, Doc6, Doc7, Doc8, Doc9, Doc10

Or in reverse order of relevance, like:

> Doc10, Doc9, Doc8, Doc7, Doc6, Doc5, Doc4, Doc3, Doc2, Doc1

These ordering schemes are useful only if the input context is very long (upwards of 5,000 tokens).

Finally, let's discuss the generate step in the RAG pipeline.

Generate

The LLM generates the final response to the given query during this step. The standard approach is to generate the output all at once. However, you could also interleave the generation and the retrieval process, by generating some output and retrieving more context, and generating some more output, and retrieving more context, and so on.

This approach can be useful in maintaining coherence in long-form text generation. The generated text determines what needs to be retrieved next. This process is called active retrieval.

How do we decide when to stop generating and start a new retrieval step? We could:

- Retrieve after every N tokens are generated.
- Retrieve after each textual unit is generated. (A textual unit can be a sentence, paragraph, section, etc.)
- Retrieve when currently available context is deemed insufficient for generation.

There are several ways to implement the latter. One of them is Forward-Looking Active REtrieval-augmented generation (FLARE). The authors of FLARE (*https://oreil.ly/eZRdy*) introduce two methods for active retrieval: FLARE-Instruct and FLARE-Direct.

In FLARE-Instruct, the LLM is prompted to generate queries in a specific syntax whenever it needs additional information to continue coherent generation.

In FLARE-Direct, the LLM generates a candidate-next sentence. If any of the tokens in the generated sentence have probability lower than a threshold, then the retrieval process is activated. If not, then the candidate sentence is accepted as a valid continuation and the generation process continues. If retrieval is to take place, the generated sentence can be used as the query, by masking the low-probability tokens (since they might confuse the retriever if they are irrelevant/incorrect). You can also rephrase the sentence as a question about the low-probability token(s).

Let's look at an example using FLARE-Instruct:

> *Prompt:* Write an article about Peruth Chemutai, the Ugandan Olympics medal winner.
>
> *FLARE-Instruct:* Peruth Chemutai [Search(birthdate of Peruth Chemutai)] is a Ugandan long-distance runner who specializes in the 3000 meters steeplechase. She gained international recognition after [Search(what medals did Peruth Chemutai win)] winning the gold medal in the women's 3000 meters steeplechase at the 2020 Summer Olympics, becoming the first Ugandan woman to win an Olympic gold medal.
>
> Early Life
>
> Chemutai was born in the [Search(birthplace of Peruth Chemutai)], a region known for [Search(what is the birthplace of Peruth Chemutai known for?)].'

This is a contrived example, as the true benefits of FLARE can be better appreciated on lengthier outputs. As seen in the output, the model generates search queries that can be used to retrieve factually correct information from data sources.

For the same query, using FLARE-Direct, the model generates the candidate article:

> *FLARE-Direct:* Peruth Chemutai (<u>born July 10, 1999</u>) is a Ugandan long-distance runner who specializes in the <u>3000 meters steeplechase</u>. She gained international recognition after winning the gold medal in the women's 3000 meters steeplechase at the 2020 Summer Olympics, becoming the first Ugandan woman to win an Olympic gold medal.
>
> Early Life
>
> Chemutai was born in the <u>Bukwo District</u>, Uganda, a region known for its challenging terrain and passionate long-distance runners.

The underlined tokens are low-probability tokens, which can be refilled by retrieving relevant text. We can either mask the low-probability tokens and use them as the retrieval query or generate standalone queries like, "When was Peruth Chemutai born?" based on the masked tokens.

Exercise

Use FLARE-Direct to generate Wikipedia documents! Let's see if we can create Wikipedia documents by interleaving generation and on-demand retrieval. Ask any open source LLM to generate a Wikipedia page of the Bollywood movie *Kabhie Kabhie* using FLARE-Direct. Does it effectively use retrieval?

A crucial aspect of generation includes adding appropriate citations to ground-truth sources. The LLM can be fine-tuned to make it provide citations along with the answer in response to user queries. One such model is Cohere's Command-R (*https://oreil.ly/v0KUs*) model.

As we can see, the RAG pipeline for knowledge retrieval can be rather lengthy. However, for a lot of RAG applications, latency is a key consideration. This increases the importance of smaller language models or faster, non-LLM-based approaches.

Let's put it all together by revisiting the RAG pipeline diagram first introduced at the beginning of the chapter. Figure 12-7 depicts the workflow of a comprehensive RAG pipeline.

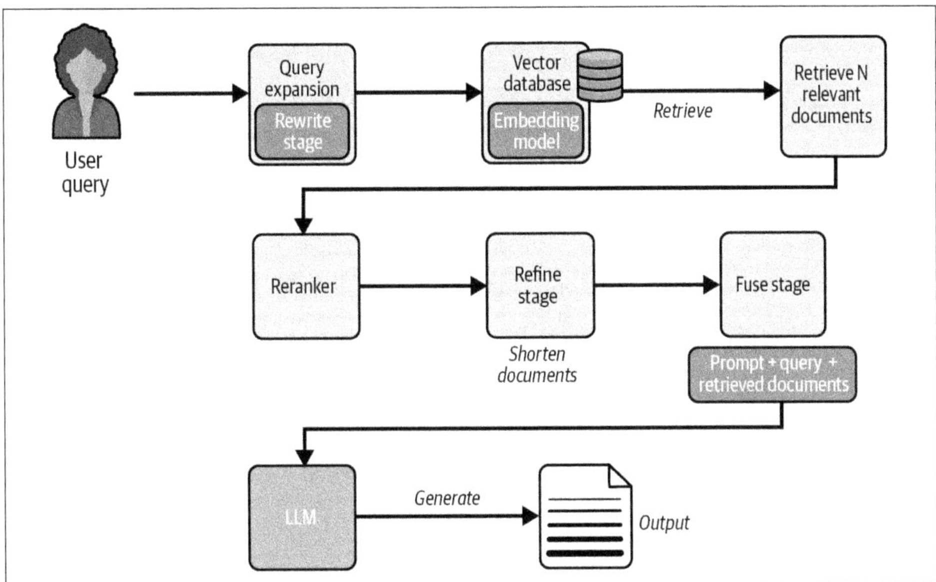

Figure 12-7. Comprehensive RAG pipeline

So far, we have focused on using RAG for knowledge retrieval. Let's now discuss a few other use cases.

RAG for Memory Management

An underrated application of RAG is expanding the context window of an LLM. To recap, an LLM prompt typically contains the following types of (optional) content:

The pre-prompt or system prompt
: These are the overarching instructions provided to the LLM included at the beginning of every query. Depending on your customization needs, the system prompt could occupy a significant part of the context window.

The input prompt
: This includes the current input and the instruction, optional few-shot training examples, and additional context, possibly fetched using retrieval.

Conversational history
: This includes the history of conversations/interaction between the user and the LLM. Including this in the context window enables the user to have a long, coherent conversation with the LLM.

Scratchpad
: This includes intermediate output generated by the LLM (discussed in Chapter 8), which can be referred to by the LLM when generating future output. Scratchpad content is an artifact of certain prompting techniques like CoT.

In many cases, the LLM's limited context window is simply insufficient to incorporate all this data. Moreover, we might like to make the conversational history available to the model through perpetuity, which means it keeps growing across time. Making all the conversational history available to the LLM is a key aspect in enabling personalization.

It's RAG to the rescue! RAG can be employed in facilitating LLM memory management by swapping in and out relevant content in the prompt as suitable. This is reminiscent of how memory management occurs in operating systems. Let's explore this abstraction further.

In an OS, memory is organized in a hierarchy, with fast (and expensive) memory being directly accessible to a processor, and higher levels of the hierarchy containing larger and slower (but relatively inexpensive) memory. When the processor needs to access some data, it tries to access it from the lowest level in the memory hierarchy. If the data is not present there, it searches the next level in the hierarchy. If present, it swaps the required data into the lower level and swaps out data that is not currently needed. This way, the OS can support a fast main memory that is directly accessible by the processor and a much larger virtual memory that can be swapped in whenever needed.

This is a very simplified explanation of OS memory management. For a more detailed explanation, check out Tony's "Operating System — Hierarchy of Memory" (*https://oreil.ly/vcciM*).

Figure 12-8 shows the memory hierarchy of a typical OS.

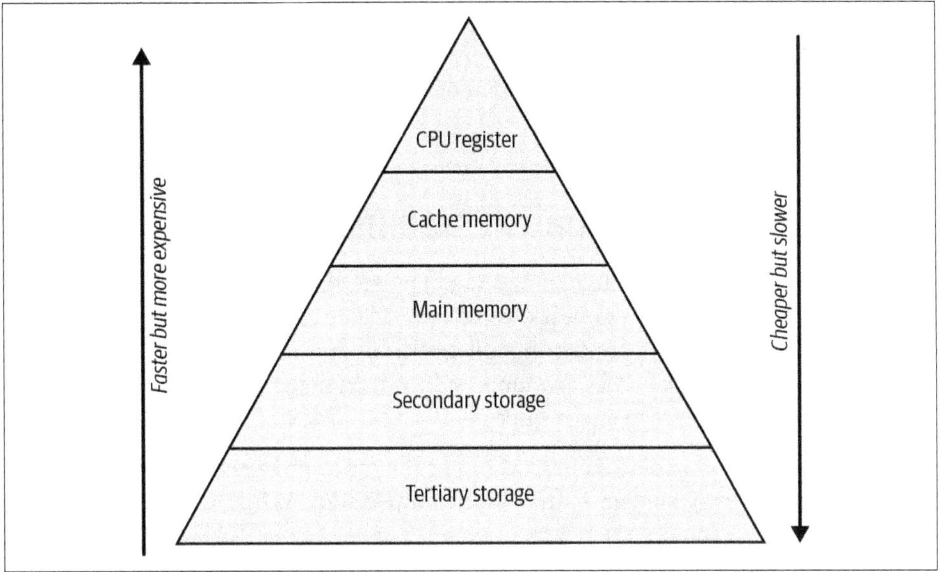

Figure 12-8. Typical OS memory hierarchy

Similarly in LLMs, the context window is analogous to the main memory as it is directly accessible to the LLM. However, we can expand the context window indefinitely by implementing a memory system analogous to the OS virtual memory. This helps in personalizing LLMs, providing them with the full access to a user's conversational history and their implicit and explicit preferences.

Examples of libraries supporting memory management for LLMs include Letta (formerly MemGPT) (*https://oreil.ly/1p8Vu*) and Mem0 (*https://oreil.ly/dgJaZ*).

An alternative or complement to swapping memory in and out is to recursively summarize the conversational history. However, summarization is a lossy process and may not be able to preserve the semantics of the text. Valuable nuances like the tone of the writer can be lost during summarization.

> **Exercise**
>
> Use the Mem0 (*https://oreil.ly/dgJaZ*) playground to carry out a very long conversation with an LLM that overshoots the context window. At various points of the conversation, refer to things or topics that one of your (hypothetical) friends likes. Ask the LLM to help choose a birthday gift for your friend that is related to their interests. Is the LLM able to recall information from the conversation pertaining to your friend? Can you generate a refined version of the conversation that makes it easier to retrieve this information?

RAG for Selecting In-Context Training Examples

As mentioned at the beginning of the chapter, another application of RAG is to dynamically select training examples for few-shot learning by retrieving the optimal examples from a data store containing a list of training examples. For a given input, the retrieved few-shot examples are supposed to maximize the LLM's chance of generating the correct answer to a user query.

A simple method is to generate embeddings of the input and retrieve examples whose embeddings are most similar to the input embedding. While this technique is a promising start, we can do much better.

Wang et al. (*https://oreil.ly/r8735*) introduce a method called LLM Retriever (LLM-R) that trains a model using LLM feedback to retrieve few-shot training examples whose inclusion will increase the probability of the LLM generating the correct answer. Figure 12-9 illustrates the LLM-R technique.

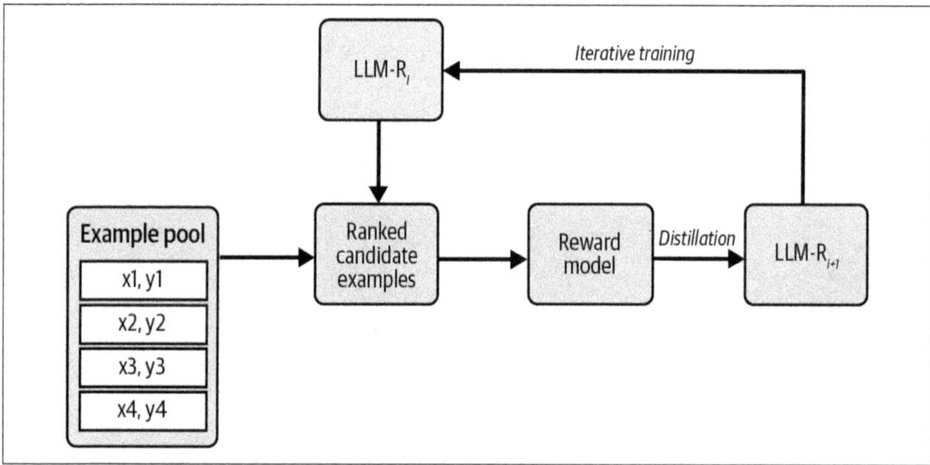

Figure 12-9. LLM-R workflow

For each input query in the training set, we retrieve the top-k few-shot examples by using a retrieval model like BM25. We then rerank the examples by using LLM feedback. Each example is prefixed to the input and the probability of the ground-truth output tokens is calculated. The examples are then ranked by decreasing order of their log-probabilities. The ranked examples are then used to train a reward model, which is distilled to train the final retrieval model.

RAG for Model Training

So far, all the RAG applications we have explored are applied during LLM inference. Can we use RAG during model pre-training and fine-tuning as well? Yes, we can! This is an underrated area of study, and I expect to see more LLMs leveraging this in the coming years. Let's look at an example in detail.

Retrieval-Augmented Language Model (REALM) is one of the pioneering works in the RAG space. REALM integrates the retrieval and generation tasks into a single model. Figure 12-10 shows the REALM framework for pre-training and fine-tuning.

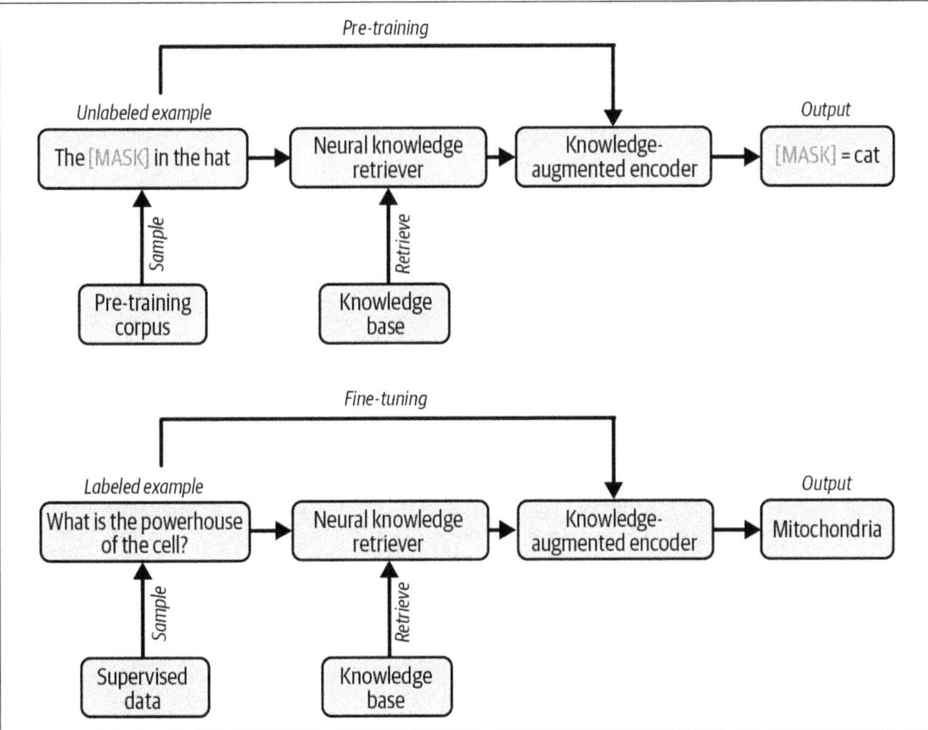

Figure 12-10. REALM architecture

The REALM architecture is composed of two components: a knowledge retriever and a knowledge-augmented encoder, which is a BERT-like encoder-only model. Both components are differentiable and thus trained together.

The knowledge retriever is used to generate embeddings for all documents in the external knowledge base. Retrieval is performed by finding documents with maximum embedding similarity to the input. During the masked-language modeling pre-training phase, the retriever loss function encourages it to fetch text that helps predict the masked tokens. The masked tokens are then predicted by attending to both the input text and the retrieved text. The retrieved text is supposed to contain relevant context that makes predicting the masked tokens much easier.

REALM also employs these strategies to optimize training:

- Named entities or dates are masked so that the model can learn to predict them using retrieved context.
- Not all masked tokens need external knowledge for their prediction. To accommodate this, an empty document is always added to the retrieved documents.
- The retrieved documents ideally contain the context required to predict the masked token, and not the token itself. Therefore, trivial retrievals that contain the masked token in the retrieved text are not included.

Limitations of RAG

While RAG is a powerful paradigm that expands the usefulness of LLMs and reduces hallucinations, it doesn't resolve all the limitations of LLMs. Some pitfalls of using RAG include:

- Relying on retrieval of text snippets can cause the LLM to depend on surface-level information to answer queries, rather than a deeper understanding of the problem space.
- Retrieval becomes the limiting factor of the pipeline. If the retrieval process fails to extract suitable candidate text, the LLM's powerful capabilities will all be for nothing.
- Sometimes the retrieval process can extract documents that are contradictory to the knowledge contained in the LLM's parametric memory. Without access to the ground truth, it is difficult for the LLM to resolve these contradictions.

How Do LLMs Deal with Contradictory Information?

Sometimes the knowledge captured in the LLM's internal representations can be contradictory to the content retrieved during the RAG. This can happen due to a multitude of reasons: outdated or incorrect content in the LLM's training datasets, errors in the user-provided context, or retrieval of incorrect or irrelevant documents during RAG. In these cases, we want the LLM to be able to ignore the incorrect content. This is extremely challenging because of the LLM's lack of access to the ground truth.

Liu et al. (*https://oreil.ly/7AOZl*) introduced a benchmark called Robustness against External CounterfactuAL knowLedge (RECALL). This benchmark tests the robustness of LLMs in the presence of counterfactual information in the prompt. Liu et al. note there is some evidence that when LLMs are fed information that is logically inconsistent, they tend to rely on their internal representations more. However, if the inconsistency is more factual, then the models tend to prefer the information in the prompts.

A significant finding in their paper is that the models' confidence in its outputs sees a notable drop when dealing with contradictory information. Thus, we can use the LLM output probabilities to guide further specialized processing.

RAG Versus Long Context

As discussed in Chapter 5, one of the limitations of LLMs is the limited effective context window available to them. However, this is one of the areas where rapid advances have been made recently. Context windows of at most a few thousand tokens were standard until early 2023, after which companies like Anthropic (*https://oreil.ly/ucbD-*) announced support for context windows spanning over 100,000 tokens. In early 2024, Google announced Gemini 1.5 Pro (*https://oreil.ly/rp7pi*), with support for one million tokens of context.

To assess the impact on LLM performance as the context size increases, several needle-in-a-haystack tests have been devised. One such implementation by Greg Kamradt (*https://oreil.ly/M8Jc9*) facilitates adding a random fact or statement (the needle) to the middle of the context (the haystack) and then asking the LLM questions for which the needle is the answer.

However, it is wise to take these tests with a grain of salt as they often evaluate only the information recall capabilities of an LLM. Moreover, very few problems in the real world are needle-in-the-haystack problems; LLMs are probably not the right tool to solve them anyway. Cheaper and faster retrieval models could adequately perform most needle retrieval tasks.

In many needle-in-a-haystack tests, random sentences or paragraphs are added to the context window as needles, with the rest of the content in the context window being orthogonal to the needle. But this does not mirror the situation in the real world, where most co-occurring text is related in some way. Related text can often act as distractors, preventing the LLM from drawing the right conclusions. In fact, it is one of the reasons for developing rigorous rerank and refine steps in the RAG pipeline!

Long-context models can be useful for analyzing very long documents and also can reduce the complexity of the rerank and refine steps. I recommend empirically calculating the trade-offs where feasible.

Exercise

Implement your own test for evaluating long-context efficacy. Extract text from all the Wikipedia pages on various rail systems (*https://oreil.ly/Q9IRP*) operating in Greater Tokyo. Devise a few questions that inquire about route information. The text containing the answer to the question will be the needle. Insert the needle into the context, and from the extracted text, insert 200 tokens of text (approximated to the closest sentence boundary) before and after the needle. Check if the LLM can answer the question by generating them 10 separate times. Insert 200 more tokens from the extracted text to the beginning and end of the prompt and iterate until the maximum context length is reached. How is performance on the task impacted as the context size increases? Try this for multiple models.

Additionally, remove the rerank and refine steps from the RAG pipeline code in the book's GitHub repo (*https://oreil.ly/llm-playbooks*) and directly feed the results of the retrieval step to an LLM supporting long context (100K tokens or more). Do you see the performance increasing or decreasing?

Finally, cost is also an important consideration for the long context versus retrieval debate. No doubt, the cost for long-context models will drop significantly in the future, but retrieval will still be relatively cheaper. Forgoing retrieval completely in favor of using long-context models is akin to buying a laptop and storing all your files in RAM instead of disk.

RAG Versus Fine-Tuning

The debate around using RAG versus fine-tuning boils down to the more fundamental question: what aspects of the task can I perform using the LLM versus relying on external sources?

In cases where external knowledge is required to solve a task, both retrieval and fine-tuning can be used. Retrieval can be used to integrate the knowledge on demand, with the drawback being that the LLM is only exposed to surface-level information and is not provided the chance to learn from connections between the data. On the other end, continued pre-training or fine-tuning can also be used to integrate external knowledge, albeit with an expensive training step.

Ovadia et al. (*https://oreil.ly/Agodo*) compared RAG and fine-tuning on tasks requiring external knowledge. They showed that RAG consistently outperformed fine-tuning for knowledge-intensive tasks. As shown earlier in this chapter, LLMs need a lot of samples to memorize a concept or fact. Thus, fine-tuning effectiveness can be improved by repetition or augmentation of the fine-tuning dataset.

Even for knowledge-intensive tasks, RAG versus fine-tuning need not be an either-or decision. If you are working on a specialized domain or need your outputs in a certain style or format, you can fine-tune your LLM on domain- and task-specific data, and use RAG with this fine-tuned model for your downstream applications. In a large proportion of use cases, RAG should be sufficient, and fine-tuning shouldn't be the first choice of solution.

Exercise

Take the Canadian parliamentary discussions dataset and fine-tune any open source LLM for multiple epochs. Check if the LLM is able to answer questions about the fine-tuning dataset. If not, continue fine-tuning (with more repetition or data augmentation) until it does so. Also analyze the impact of catastrophic forgetting as a result of this fine-tuning. In what ways does the LLM become worse? How is generalization performance affected due to the excessive memorization?

Performing this exercise will underscore the advantages of RAG over fine-tuning for knowledge-intensive tasks.

RAG and fine-tuning can be complementary. Earlier in this chapter, we saw how each step of the RAG pipeline can be optimized using fine-tuning. Similarly, we also saw how RAG can be used to optimize the fine-tuning process. Thus, both retrieval and fine-tuning are powerful parts of your LLM toolkit, and I hope that these chapters have sufficiently prepared you to implement and deploy them in the wild.

Summary

In this chapter, we conducted a deep dive into the RAG pipeline, exploring in detail the *rewrite-retrieve-rerank-refine-insert-generate* pipeline. We highlighted the effectiveness of RAG in various scenarios, including integration of external knowledge, retrieval of past conversational history, dynamic selection of few-shot learning examples, and tool selection. We also explored the limitations of RAG and scenarios where RAG may not be effective.

In the final chapter, we will explore how we can utilize all the concepts we learned so far to architect and package LLM-driven products that bring value to end users. Effective product design has become all the more important in the age of LLMs, given that a successful LLM product leverages the LLM the best it can for the capabilities it excels at, while at the same time limiting end-user exposure to LLM limitations by means of clever product design. We will also look at several LLM design patterns that put together all the concepts we learned in reusable, debuggable abstractions.

CHAPTER 13

Design Patterns and System Architecture

Throughout this book, we have explored a variety of techniques to adapt LLMs to solve our tasks, including in-context learning, fine-tuning, RAG, and tool use. While these techniques can potentially be successful in satisfying the performance requirements of your use case, deploying an LLM-based application in production requires adherence to a variety of other criteria like cost, latency, and reliability. To achieve these goals, an LLM application needs a lot of software scaffolding and specialized components.

To this end, in this chapter we will discuss various techniques to compose a production-level LLM system that can power useful applications. We will explore how to leverage multi-LLM architectures to balance cost and performance. Finally, we will look into software frameworks like DSPy that integrate LLM application development into the conventional software programming paradigm.

Treating an LLM-based application as just a standalone LLM component is inadequate if we intend to deploy it as a production-grade system. We need to treat it as a system, made up of several software and model components that support the LLM and make it reliable, fast, and cost-effective. The way these components are composed and connected is referred to as the *system architecture*.

Let's begin by discussing a specific type: multi-LLM architectures that leverage multiple LLMs to solve your task.

Multi-LLM Architectures

Throughout this book, we have discussed the tradeoffs involved in choosing the right LLM for a task. Often, it can be beneficial to leverage multiple LLMs to achieve the desired outcome. Multi-LLM architectures can exist in the following two modes (or a combination):

Each LLM is specialized for a different subtask
: Different problem subtasks may require different levels of capabilities. To minimize cost and latency, for each task we would like to use the smallest possible LLM that can solve the subtask at the performance threshold we set.

All LLMs solve the same task
: In this case, all the LLMs are solving the same task, but for each input, only one or a subset of LLMs may be chosen to solve it.

A given task can be solved by an ensemble of LLMs, and the final outputs can be chosen based on some rules (majority voting, interpolation, etc.). Refer to Jiang et al.'s ensembling framework (*https://oreil.ly/FEikT*) called LLM-Blender for an example of thoughtful ensembling.

Exercise

In the book's GitHub repo (*https://oreil.ly/llm-playbooks*), you will find a skeleton implementation of a legal agent. The agent is designed to retrieve information from the web and provide answers to user questions about court cases. This agent utilizes a multi-LLM architecture, comprising several LLMs of different sizes.

Break down the agent implementation into its constituent tasks and enumerate the set of capabilities (described in Chapter 5) required for each task. Assign the smallest possible LLMs for each task that demonstrate these capabilities beyond a satisfactory threshold. Use content from Chapters 5 and 8 to guide you in your exercise. What are the cost savings compared to solving the entire task with the largest of the given models?

Let's walk through some commonly used multi-LLM architectures.

LLM Cascades

While using the state-of-the-art LLM for processing all our inputs is an option, realistically this might be cost-prohibitive or latency sensitive. To optimize costs while keeping performance standards high, we could leverage multiple LLMs, organized in a cascade architecture.

Let's illustrate LLM cascades. Consider you have an application using three LLMs: one small, one medium, and one large, as illustrated in Figure 13-1.

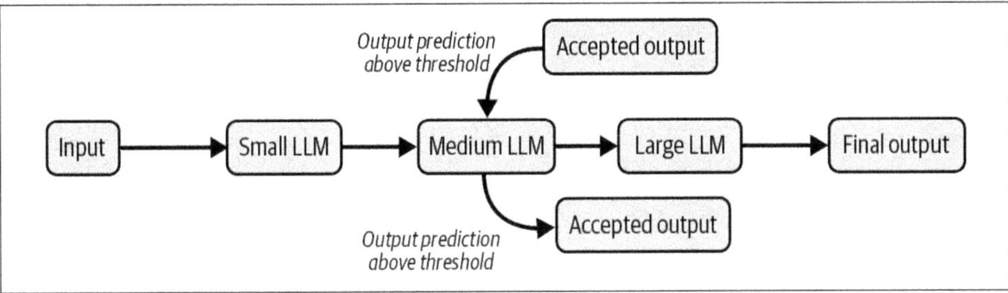

Figure 13-1. LLM cascades

The following process is observed during inference:

1. Each input is fed to the small LLM.
2. If the small LLM makes an output prediction with a confidence level greater than a threshold, then we accept the output as the final output.
3. If the small LLM makes an output prediction with a confidence level that doesn't surpass the threshold, then we pass the input to the medium model.
4. Similarly, if the medium LLM makes an output prediction with a confidence level greater than a threshold, then we stop and accept this output as the final output.
5. However, if the medium LLM makes an output prediction with a confidence level that doesn't surpass the threshold, then we pass the input to the large model.
6. The large model generates the final output.

This architecture is most beneficial when most user inputs can be processed by the small model.

If you are using encoder-only models like BERT, the output probability scores can be used as the measure of confidence. Thus, a group of well-calibrated models will enable us to efficiently route the input to the most suitable model. (Recall our discussion on model calibration in Chapter 5.)

For decoder models, a popular method is to use self-consistency as a measure of confidence. (Recall our discussion on self-consistency in Chapter 1.) If we generate multiple times from the model and the outputs are mostly consistent with each other, then we can say that the model is being confident in its predictions. If they are not consistent, then we can move down the cascade and apply the inputs to the next LLM in the cascade.

Some works propose asking the LLM to explicitly state the confidence level of its output. This has not been proven to be effective yet. Beware of asking the LLM to verify its own work in any form!

Another method for assessing confidence is to use margin sampling, as proposed by Ramirez et al. (*https://oreil.ly/5s1rJ*) In the margin sampling method, we generate the first token and use the difference in the probability of the most probable token and the second most probable token as the margin. The assumption is that the higher the margin, the more confident the model. If the margin is below a certain threshold, then the input is sent to the next model in the cascade.

> **Exercise**
>
> Compare the different confidence assessment strategies for decoder models. Test the Llama 2-3B model with facts from Wikipedia pages. Try the margin sampling method, the self-consistency method, and just asking the LLM how confident it is about the answer. Which method do you observe is a better representation of LLM confidence?

An alternative to using cascades is using a router scheme.

Routers

A router is a program or a model that processes input queries and dispatches them to the appropriate model. The advantage of using the router architecture is that, unlike cascades, the same input need not be run on potentially multiple models. However, the effectiveness of this strategy relies on the router effectively dispatching inputs to the optimal model, which may not always be fulfilled.

A router can perform intent classification, i.e., understand the intention of the user and dispatch the input to a suitable LLM that can solve the task being requested. If all the LLMs in the architecture are intended to solve the same task, then the router assesses the difficulty of the input query and dispatches the input to the smallest model that can adequately solve the task.

Figure 13-2 illustrates the role of the router in picking the right model to solve a task.

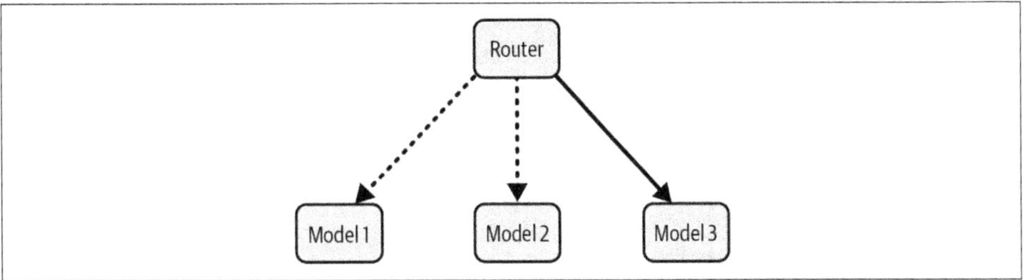

Figure 13-2. Router

Routers can also be used in RAG pipelines. The router can assess the input and dispatch it to one of several different types of retrievers.

Assessing the complexity of an input query can be done using either heuristics or a fine-tuned model. Heuristics can be based on certain keywords that appear in the input (with RAG, *When* queries are more easily answered than *How* queries) or the identity of the tasks (for instance, sentiment analysis is an easier task that can be accomplished by a smaller model).

Next, let's discuss task-specialized LLMs.

Task-Specialized LLMs

Yet another way of organizing multi-LLM architectures is to deploy a variety of task-specific LLMs, each of them specialized in solving a particular type of task or subtask.

Given a complex user query, a relatively powerful LLM can be used to decompose the query into its constituent subtasks. A router can then assign each of these subtasks to the specialized model most equipped to handle at the subtask. (Recall our discussion on task decomposition in Chapter 8.)

Specialized LLMs can be constructed by fine-tuning them on task- and domain-specific datasets.

Figure 13-3 illustrates how a complex query can be divided into several subtasks, with each subtask being dispatched to the model most likely to solve it in a cost-optimal way.

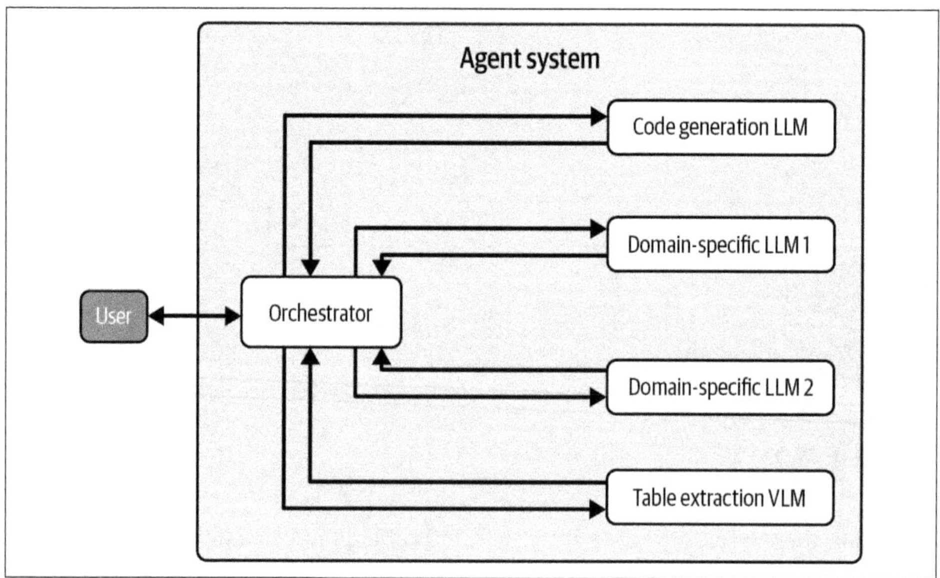

Figure 13-3. Task-specific LLMs

Let's now explore some programming paradigms that facilitate more effective LLM application development.

Programming Paradigms

As we have seen in this chapter, production-grade LLM systems can be composed of a lot of software components that help make the system robust and reliable. Naturally, we would like to use software design patterns to help us build these systems to be productive and maintainable. The developer community is still maturing in this regard, and it will take more time for tried and tested design patterns to emerge.

At this juncture, there are several proposals for LLM programming paradigms. While many are not yet well-tested, some of these paradigms are mature enough to support production-grade applications. Let's explore a couple of major ones.

DSPy

LLM application development is a highly iterative process. You might want to experiment with a few candidate LLMs before selecting the right one. You might start with zero-shot prompting, which involves a lot of iterative prompt manipulation, also called prompt engineering. If zero-shot isn't sufficient, you might venture into few-shot prompting, which involves iterating over various candidate examples. If few-shot prompting isn't sufficient, you might want to fine-tune the model, which involves iteratively preparing a dataset and trying various hyperparameters for the model.

*D*eclarative *S*elf-improving Language *P*rograms, p*y*thonically (DSPy) is an open source programming framework that seeks to abstract a large part of the iterative process. Programming, not prompting, as their motto goes.

DSPy presents a framework where the application's control flow is separated from variables that need to be iterated. The variables can be prompts, parameters of LLMs, etc. The programming blocks that manage the control flow of the application are called *modules*, and the blocks that perform the iterative updates of variables are called *optimizers*.

Modules

A module is a building block of an LLM application. Each module corresponds to an underlying prompt in the prompt chain. Each module type is an abstraction of a different prompting technique, like CoT. A module can be declared using a *signature* that declaratively provides the input-output specification.

Declaring a CoT prompting module with a signature is as simple as:

```
import dspy
summarizer = dspy.ChainOfThought('document -> summary')
```

`ChainOfThought` is a module that provides an abstraction for the CoT prompting technique. The module is declared with a signature `document → summary` that specifies the input and output types in a declarative form. For instance, if you are building a question-answering application, then the signature could be `question → answer`.

For some applications, you would like to provide more details on the input-output mapping than just a short string. For those instances, signatures can be declared using Python classes. Here's an example:

```
class RAGQA(dspy.Signature):
    """Using only information in the provided context,
       answer the question in the text"""

    context = dspy.InputField(desc="context might be irrelevant")
    text = dspy.InputField()
    answer = dspy.OutputField(desc="Answer in at most two sentences.")

context = "Tempura was invented in New Zealand by a retired rugby player. The
word 'tempura' comes from the German opera by Neubig."
text = "Which year was tempura invented in?"
answer = dspy.ChainOfThought(RAGQA)
answer(context=context, text=text)
```

In this example, instructions can be provided in three places:

- The docstring, with a more detailed description of the task
- The input field, with details on any input constraints

- The output field, with details on any output constraints

Refer to the DSPy documentation (*https://oreil.ly/4Vy5c*) for a full list of available modules. We can use these modules as building blocks for constructing complex LLM applications. Next let's look at optimizers that work under the hood to *compile* our modules into an executable program.

Optimizers

Optimizers are components that update prompts or model parameters. Several optimizers are natively supported by DSPy. An optimizer can be used to update one of the following:

- The instruction prompt
- Few-shot training examples
- Model parameters (fine-tuning)

An optimizer takes as input the modules it needs to be applied to, the metric to evaluate the output of the modules, and fine-tuning or few-shot training data consisting of input-output pairs or just inputs. Optimizers use algorithms to update the prompts or parameters to optimize the desired metric. DSPy supports metrics like *accuracy* or *precision* or *exact match*.

You can implement your own modules and optimizers if the ones provided by default are inadequate to your needs. Thus, DSPy is a powerful framework that separates the control flow of the LLM application from iterative aspects like LLM prompting and fine-tuning, and potentially automates the latter. The downsides of DSPy are that the optimizers might not be effective enough to work in an automated fashion and might need manual intervention to tune them correctly. More often than not, you will find yourself writing your own optimizers.

Exercise

Implement a question-answering assistant over the Canadian parliamentary dataset provided in the book's Github repo (*https://oreil.ly/llm-playbooks*) using the DSPy framework. How does this implementation compare to the non-DSPy version?

Let's now explore another framework called Language Model Query Language (LMQL). We have already been introduced to this framework in Chapter 5 in the context of structured generation, but here we will look at how the same framework can be used as a programming paradigm for developing LLM applications.

LMQL

LMQL is a superset of Python that enables specifying prompts, output constraints, and program control flow using declarative Python code. Here is an example:

```
import lmql

@lmql.query(model="gpt-4")
def jeopardy():
    '''lmql
    """Generate a Jeopardy! question and answer.
    A:[ANSWER]
    Q:[QUESTION]""" where STOPS_AT(ANSWER, "?") and \
                          STOPS_AT(QUESTION, "\n")
    '''

jeopardy(model=lmql.model("gpt-4"))
```

In this example we are asking the model to generate a Jeopardy! question. Jeopardy! is a TV show that executes a modified version of a trivia quiz; the host supplies the answers and the contestants provide the question for the given answer.

In LMQL, we achieve this by defining a function called `jeopardy` and supplying the prompt instructions in the doc string. The doc string contains the instruction `Generate a Jeopardy! question and answer`. The `[ANSWER]` and `[QUESTION]` markers refer to templates that the LLM will fill in based on the constraints specified in the `WHERE` clause.

For the answer (which in Jeopardy is the question), we stop generation after generating the ? symbol. Similarly, for the question (which in Jeopardy is the answer), we stop generation after the newline symbol. The `WHERE` clause can be used to provide complex constraints for generation.

LMQL syntax might take a while to get used to, but overall it provides a robust programmatic foundation for developing LLM programs. Both LMQL and DSPy have a learning curve, so I recommend being patient during your first few iterations.

As LLMs and LLM-driven applications mature, I expect more programming paradigms to emerge and for existing paradigms to vastly evolve. Current paradigms might be too brittle in many cases, so be cautious and verify they are effective before you adopt them in production.

Summary

In this chapter, we explored the construction of LLM systems and various system architectures. We showcased how we can leverage multi-LLM architectures to optimize for cost and latency. Finally, we introduced LLM programming frameworks for streamlining LLM application development.

Index

A

B

C

D

E

F

G

H

I

J

K

L

M

R

S

W

X

Z

About the Author

Suhas Pai is an experienced machine learning researcher, having worked in the tech industry for over a decade. He is the cofounder, CTO, and ML Research Lead at Hudson Labs, a Y-Combinator-backed AI & Fintech startup, since 2020. At Hudson Labs, Suhas invented several novel techniques in the areas of domain-adapted LLMs, text ranking, and representation learning that fully power the core features of Hudson Labs' products. He has contributed to the development of several open source LLMs, including being the colead of the privacy working group at Big Science, as part of the BLOOM LLM project.

Suhas is active in the ML community, serving as Chair of the Toronto Machine Learning Summit (TMLS) conference since 2021. He is also a frequent speaker at AI conferences worldwide, and hosts regular seminars discussing the latest research in the field of NLP.

Colophon

The animal on the cover of *Designing Large Language Model Applications* is the sei whale (*Balaenoptera borealis*), one of the largest species of baleen whales. Weighing as much as 28 tons and growing up to 64 feet in length, they are the third-largest species of baleen whale after the blue and fin whales. Even with its large size, it is a relatively fast swimmer, reaching speeds of up to 34 miles per hour.

Sei whales can be found all over the world in both subpolar and subtropical waters. They are dark blue/gray in color with a white underside and a hook-shaped dorsal fin about two-thirds down their back. Their skin is often covered in circular scars caused by cookiecutter sharks, which are known to feed on larger animals and leave these types of marks.

Instead of teeth, sei whales have between 200 and 400 baleen plates they use to eat about 2,000 pounds of food per day. Baleen plates are hair-thin, fringe-looking sheets of keratin (the same material as fingernails) that hang from the roof of the mouth and trap prey. Sei whales are filter feeders, which means they swim with their mouths open in areas with lots of prey (typically small fish, plankton, and squid) trapping food and water in their mouths. They then push out the excess water, leaving only their food.

The cover image is based on an antique line engraving from Wood's *British Quadrapeds*. The series design is by Edie Freedman, Ellie Volckhausen, and Karen Montgomery. The cover fonts are Gilroy Semibold and Guardian Sans. The text font is Adobe Minion Pro; the heading font is Adobe Myriad Condensed; and the code font is Dalton Maag's Ubuntu Mono.